BLOUNT COUNTY, TENNESSEE

MARRIAGES

1795-1865

by

Will E. Parham

Please direct all correspondence and orders to:

www.southernhistoricalpress.com
or
SOUTHERN HISTORICAL PRESS, Inc.
PO BOX 1267
375 West Broad Street
Greenville, SC   29601
southernhistoricalpress@gmail.com

ISBN #0-89308-240-6

Printed in the United States of America

TABLE OF CONTENTS

	Names	Date Issue Or Celebrated	By Whom/ Security on Bond
1	ABERNATHEY, BERRY et ux Miry Cobb	12/18 1819	By Samuel Douthett
2	ABOTT, B. F. et ux Jane Brickey	4/18 1861	By S. Wear, J.P. (or L. Wear)
3	ABBOTT, JAMES D. et ux Mary J. Rudd	12/10 1856	By S. L. Yearout, J.P.
4	ABBOT, JOHN et ux Winaford Bruer	2/3 1848	By Jno. Chambers, M.G.
5	ABOT, SAMUEL et ux Emley E. Tallent	1/14 1858	By H. Foster, J.P.
*	See 101		
6	ADAMS, JEFFERSON et ux Rebecca Dailey	6/17 1824	By Joe Duncan, J.P.
7	ADAMS, JESSE et ux Aggie S. Crisp	7/31 1851	By Jesse Kerr, Jr., J.P.
8	ADAMS, JOEL et ux Sarah A. Young	11/21 1843	By Edmond Wayman, J.P.
9	ADAMS, JOHNSON et ux Emaline Hill	11/18 1846	By Carran Lemons, J.P.
10	ADAMS, WILLIAM R. et ux Nancy Burchfield	12/14 1837	By Johnson Adams
11	ADAMS, PRESTON et ux Jane Hatcher	11/18 1842	By Johnson Adams, M.G.
12	ADKINS, JOHN T. et ux Nancy Luckett	6/24 1819	By Wm. Fagg
13	AIKIN, ALEXANDER et ux Tempy Crew	12/24 1816	By John Waugh, J.P.
14	AIKEN, JAMES et ux Nancy McClure	1/16 1853	By S. J. McReynolds, J.P.
15	AIKMAN, JOHN L. et ux Nancy Paul	12/7 1826	By Eleven Hitch, J.P.
*	See 99, 100		
16	AKRIGE, JOHN et ux Sally Akrige	10/22 1823	By E. Hitch, Esq.
17	AKRIDGE, ROBISON et ux Lucinda Floyd	8/6 1824	By John Dever
18	ALEXANDER, ALYHEW et ux Nancy Smith	1/12 1832	By B. Abernathey, J.P.
19	ALEXANDER, BENJAMIN et ux Ruth Wallace	9/16 1799 issued	Bond: Robert Hooke Wit: Gid Blackburn

Names	Date Issue Or Celebrated	By Whom/ Security on Bond
20 ALEXANDER, DAVID et ux Elizabeth Conn	11/28 1815	Bond: James Houston, Clk. By Dept. Jesse Beene
21 ALEXANDER, EZEKIEL et ux Elizabeth G. Ewing	10/12 1824	By Geo. Ewing, Esq.
22 ALEXANDER, FRANCIS et ux Margaret Vickers	10/14 1836	By Eli Richey, J.P.
23 ALEXANDER, HUGH E. et ux Sarah Caldwell	1/20 1824	By Isaac Anderson, Pastor of New Prov. Church
24 ALEXANDER, JAMES et ux Nancy Ford	2/4 1823	By John Norwood, J.P.
25 ALEXANDER, JAMES H. et ux Teressa Davis	5/20 1828	By Isaac Anderson, Pastor of New Prov. Church
26 ALEXANDER, JOHN J. et ux Matilda Bustle	12/15 1836	By Rev. J. Dyke
27 ALEXANDER, JOSEPH et ux Lucinda McGill	7/19 1849	By J. Dyke, Pastor of Unitia Church
28 ALEXANDER, MAT M. et ux Eliz. H. Thompson	2/12 1833	By Isaac Anderson, Pastor of New Prov. Church
29 ALEXANDER, SAMUEL et ux Ann Moreloock	12/8 1837	By Eli Richy, J.P.
30 ALEXANDER, THOMAS et ux Mary Greer	12/4 1834	By A. Vance, M.G.
31 ALEXANDER, WILLIAM et ux Margaret Duncan	1/13 1820	By Isaac Anderson,V.D.M.
32 ALEXANDER, WM. et ux Ann Bingham	9/5 1800 issued	Bond: Joseph Alexander
33 ALEXANDER, WILLIAM et ux Phebe Ish	1/6 1825	By J. Gillespie, J.P.
34 ALFORD, WILLIAM et ux Susan Rambo	11/3 1846	By Isaac Anderson, Pastor of New Provd. Church
35 ALLIN, EDWIN et ux Sarah Allin	12/23 1801 issued	Bond: Wm. Gault
36 ALLEN, ELIJAH W. et ux Margaret A. Scott	4/20 1858	By R. E. Tedofrd, M.G.
37 ALLEN, ISAACK et ux Anna Reed	11/13 1821	By Jas. Love, J.P.
38 ALLEN, JAMES P. et ux Nancy Jones	4/29 1838	By Eli Richey, J.P.
39 ALLEN, JOB et ux Margareta McClain	9/10 1818	By Samuel Douthitt

	Names	Date Issue Or Celebrated	By Whom/ Security on Bond
40	ALLEN, ROBERT J. et ux Eleanor Harmon	12/23 1834	By John Ferguson, J.P.
41	ALLEN, RUSSELL et ux Luisa Rose	8/25 1830	By John Ferguson, J.P.
42	ALLEN, THOMAS J. et ux Ann Brown	4/24 1828	By Samuel Hamill, J.P.
43	ALLEN, WILLIAM et ux Janet S. Duncan	1/10 1838	By Thomas S. Kendall
44	ALLISON, BENJAMIN et ux Susannah Keily	1/8 1851	By Spencer Henry, M.G.
45	ALISSON, ROBT. et ux Jenney Thompson	3/22 1802 issued	Bond: William Armstrong
46	ALLISON, THOMAS J. et ux E. J. Bailey	1/23 1850	By Wm. M. Brickell, J.P.
47	ALLOWAY, NELSON et ux Jane Cannon	2/18 1836	By Edmund Wayman, J.P.
48	ARMBRISTER, JOSEPH et ux Margaret Ann McCullock	12/16 1847	By Robert Porter, J.P.
49	AMBURN, ALEXANDER et ux Mary Ann Snider	9/4 1840	By William Hendrickson, M.G.
50	AMERINE, RICHARD et ux Serena J. Wells	1/30 1851	By J. G. Swishorn, M.G.
51	ANDERSON, ARCHILLAS et ux Margaret E. Hanna	12/8 1858	By James Hamil, M.G.
52	ANDERSON, ELIJAH et ux Mary R. Maxwell	4/21 1853	By Wm. M. Brickell, J.P.
53	ANDERSON, GREEN P. et ux Nancy Farr	8/1 1850	By James M. Tulloch, J.P.
54	ANDERSON, ISAAC et ux Isabella McMillin	3/10 1818	By I. Anderson
55	ANDERSON, JONATHAN et ux Julia Farmer	6/17 1819	By R. Wear
56	ANDERSON, JAMES M. C. et ux Rebecca George	1/10 1828	By William Engleton, M.G.
57	ANDERSON, JAMES M. et ux Mary Isabella Dobson	1/21 1841	By James W. Ramsey, M.G.
58	ANDERSON, JAMES R. C. et ux Rebecca E. Wright	1/20 1846	By Isaac Anderson, Pastor of New Provd. Church
59	ANDERSON, Isaac G. et ux Mary E. M. Ross	2/7 1854	By J. S. Craig, M.G.
60	ANDERSON, JAMES W. et ux Mary Ann McKaskle	2/24 1829	By D. Carson, M.G.

Names	Date Issue Or Celebrated	By Whom/ Security on Bond
61 ANDERSON, JOHN et ux Polly Coker	1/28 1819	By Wm. Williamson, J.P.
62 ANDERSON, JOHN et ux Mary Dunn	8/24 1834	By Federic Emmett, J.P.
63 ANDERSON, JOHN et ux Mary White	12/4 1838	By Wm. Rich, J.P.
64 ANDERSON, JOHN et ux Eleanor J. Pester- field	2/9 1858	By A. R. James, J.P.
65 ANDERSON, JONATHAN et ux Sarah Dunn	2/10 1848	By Wm. Henderson, J.P.
66 ANDERSON, LARKIN et ux Kesiah Hix	3/31 1836	By R. B. Billue, M.G.
67 ANDERSON, ROBERT et ux Sally Hix	3/12 1838	By Robert Delzell, J.P.
68 ANDERSON, ROBERT et ux Nancy B. Harris	11/15 1838	By Fielding Pope, M.G.
69 ANDERSON, SAMUEL et ux May R. Thompson	9/10 1835	By G. S. White, M.G.
70 ANDERSON, SAMUEL et ux Margaret McBath	8/19 1856	By James M. Tulloch, J.P.
71 ANDERSON, STEPHEN et ux Matilda Carver	1/18 1841	By Wm. Rich, J.P.
72 ANDERSON, THOMAS et ux Elizabeth Greer	8/19 1852	By Harvey H. C. Ca- ruthers, J.P.
73 ANDERSON, THOMAS et ux Mahala C. Crye	10/9 1857	By James M. Tulloch, J.P.
74 ANDERSON, WILLIAM et ux Jane Houston	10/11 1836	By Isaac Anderson, Pas- tor of New Provd. Church
75 ANDERSON, WM. et ux Rachel D. Bane	3/29 1854	By Wm. M. Brickell, J.P.

--- ANDERSON, WM. E. m. in Ky. 6/5 1817 Flora McCampbell--formerly of Blount, Newspaper Register, McGhee Library.

Names	Date Issue Or Celebrated	By Whom/ Security on Bond
76 ANDERSON, M. M. et ux Sarah A. Hix	2/27 1851	By Spencer Henry, M.G.
77 ANDERSON, WILLIAM S. et ux Nancyann Taylor	10/14 1841	By W. B. Gordon, M.G.
78 ANDERSON, WILLIAM W. et ux Elizabeth A. McCheaney	9/1 1825	By Isaac Anderson, Pas- tor of New Provd. Church
79 ANDES, JOHN et ux Selain B. Bailess	5/27 1799 issued	Bond: Washw. Snider
80 ANTHONY, JOHN et ux Betsy Oliver	3/14 1852	By John Chambers, M.G.

	Names	Date Issue Or Celebrated	By Whom/ Security on Bond
81	ANTHONY, WM. et ux Mary K. Pierce	9/26 1854	By Curran Lemons, J.P.
82	ARMSTRON, ALEXANDER S. et ux Mary Jane Henry	11/2 1837	By J. Nicholson, M.G.
83	ARMSTRONG, JAMES G. et ux Nancy W. Johnson	4/7 1857	By Tulloch, James M., J.P.
84	ARMSTRONG, JOHN et ux Nancy A. Miller	8/31 1852	By John S. Craig, M.G.
85	ARMSTRONG, JOSEPH V. et ux Nancy Cunningham	3/25 1834	By A. Vance, M.G.
86	ARMSTRONG, JOSEPH V. et ux Hulda L. Write	5/13 1847	By Samuel Tulloch, J.P.
87	ARMSTRONG, L. M. et ux C. J. Tulloch	1/24 1856	By James M. Tulloch, J.P.
88	ARMSTRONG, ROBERT G. et ux Hannah Ann Moore	6/10 1847	By Samuel Tulloch, J.P.
89	ARMSTRONG, ROBERT G. et ux Mantha Greer	3/21 1854	By James M. Tulloch, J.P.
90	ARWOOD, JOHN M. et ux Sinthy Carver	6/12 1844	By David Spradlin, J.P.
91	ARWOOD, MADISON et ux Louiza Rudd	11/13 1838	By Robert Delzell, J.P.
92	ASHLEY, JOSEPH et ux Polly Garner	12/27 1827	By Samuel Hamill, J.P.
93	AUSTIN, NATHANIEL et ux Polly Gains	8/24 1823	By Samu'l Davidson, J.P.
94	AVERETT, LEWIS et ux Martha Kinnamon	10/15 1853	By C. Long, J.P.
*	See 1128		
95	AVERETT, NOAH et ux Anna Ball	9/9 1841	By A. C. Montgomery, J.P.
96	AVERETT, SOLOMON et ux Catherine Houser	9/11 1842	By Christian Long, J.P.
97	AVERETT, WM. et ux Curkina Cavin	9/1 1853	By C. Long, J.P.
98	AYERS, ALEXANDER O. et ux Esther D. Johnston	3/9 1826	By S. B. Hamell, M.G.
---	AXLEY, R. W. JAS. m. in Green Co., Tenn. 5/9 1821 Cinthia Earnest, dghtr. of Lawrence Earnest--McGhee Library papers.		
99	ACKRIDGE, GEORGE W. et ux Elizabeth French	10/4 1831	By J. Gillespie, J.P.
100	AKRIDGE, LEVI et ux Elizabeth French	11/25 1840 issued	Bond: Samuel Ballard

101 ACKLIN, SAMUEL
et ux Rebecca Hickey — 1/23/1816 — By Hugh Bogle, J.P.

* See 5-6

102 BABB, JOSHUA
et ux Nancy Headrick — 2/5 1840 — By Johnson Adams, M.G.

103 BADGETT, B. F.
et ux N. C. Gillespy — 10/9 1856 — By Fielding Pope, M.G.

104 BADGETT, CAMBELL
et ux Cintha A. Farmer — 7/20 1847 — By James H. Donaldson, J.P.

105 BADGET, ROBERT
et ux Eliza J. Reder — 3/7 1855 issued — No returns

106 BADGETT, WILLIAM
et ux Phebe Braze — 8/14 1809 issued — No returns

107 BADGETT, WM.
et ux Polly Farmer — 11/23 1837 Thursday — By James Henry, J.P.

108 BAILEY, JOHN
et ux Neona Cannon — 12/7 1824 — By Thos. E. F. McMurry

109 BAILEY, JOHN W.
et ux Elizabeth E. James — 11/25 1852 — By Samuel L. Yearout, J.P.

110 BAILEY, MILES H.
et ux Nancy Ewing — 2/25 1834 — By Isaac Anderson, Pastor New Prov. Church

111 BAKER, ANDREW
et ux Lydia Davis — 2/21 1824 — By George Snider, M.B. of the Baptist Church

112 BAKER, CHARLES
et ux Sally Caball — 11/25 1811 issued — No returns; endorsed "The bride join the groom, lifted this bond _____ The hums."

113 BAKER, HENRY
et ux Polly Barnes — 6/6 1826 — "I joined in matremony, these." Alexander Stewart, J.P.

114 BAKER, JAMES
et ux Elizabeth Russell — 12/1 1853 — By C. Long, J.P.

115 BAKER, THOMAS
et ux Margaret Riddle — 5/25 1858 — By Wm. W. Nuchols, J.P.

116 BALES, SETH
et ux Juley Heakney — 8/7 1843 — By John Griffetts, J.P.

117 BELL, ADRON
et ux Polly Harres — 10/7 1820 — By Wm. Williamson, J.P.

118 BELL, JAMES
et ux Rebekah Shot — 3/24 1822 — By Wm. Williamson, J.P.

119 BELL, JOHN
et ux Delila Huffman — 1/4 1826 — By Archb' Maxwell, J.P.

120 BALL, THOMAS A.
et ux Elizabeth McLure or McClure? — 12/17 1856 — "Celebrated in due time" A. Bance, M.G.

	Names	Date Issue Or Celebrated	By Whom/ Security on Bond
121	BALLENGER, DEMPSY et ux Sarah Patty	7/7 1818	By James Turk, J.P.
122	BALLENGER, JAMES et ux Rebaka Bailess	6/19 1817	By Alex B. Gamble, J.P.
123	BALANGER, JAMES et ux Ruthey Bayless	8/12 1819	By Hugh Bogle, J.P.
124	BALANGER, JOSEPH et ux Anne Farmer	9/11 1817	By Hugh Bogle, J.P.
125	BALINGER, JOSIAH et ux Rebeca M. George	9/19 1854	By Wm. M.Brickell, J.P.
126	BANE, WILLIAM et ux Polly Stephenson	9/11 1819	No returns
127	BANDY, BRYANT et ux Nelly Hix	2/23 1826	By A. Ish, J.P.
128	BANTA, HENRY et ux Francis Carless	12/28 1826	No returns
129	BOURDEN, ADAM et ux Betsey Huchison	12/4 1800 issued	Bond: John Kee
*	See 304-305		
130	BARNES, JASON et ux Cerina M. Young	1/11 1849	By Samu'l Pride, J.P.
131	BARNES, JECHELAND et ux Betsey Walker	3/2 1802 issued	Bond: John Leike
132	BARNES, JOEL et ux Elizabeth Gamble	7/16 1837	By John Key, J.P.
133	BARNES, JOHN M. et ux Myra Bryant	7/28 1835	By J.H.R.G. Garner, M.G.
134	BARNES, NATHAN et ux Sally Palmer	1/11 1841	By Lorenzo Donaldson, J.P.
135	BARNES, WILLIAM et ux Jenny Walker	10/21 1800 issued	Bond: Wm. Walker
136	BARNES, WM. et ux Christian Bowerman	12/26 1801 issued	Bond: Peter Bowerman
137	BARNES, WILLIAM et ux Caselender Shay	6/26 1836	By Wm. E. Pope
138	BARNES, WM. et ux May Wright	9/23 1858	By Wm. W. Nuchols, J.P.
139	BARNHILL, JOHN et ux Hanah Alaway	8/20 1840	By Eli Richey, J.P.
140	BARNHILL, M. M. et ux Nancy L. Cummings	8/27 1849	By W. H. Rogers, M.G.
141	BARNETT. DAVIS et ux Nelly Smith	2/27 1842	By John Chambers, M.F.
142	BARNETT, JAMES et ux Polly C. Dodd	4/24 1825	By Alexr. McCollum, J.P.

	Names	Date Issue Or Celebrated	By Whom/ Security on Bond
143	BARNETT, JAMES C. et ux Tamer Bell	1/21 1819	By Wm. Gault, J.P.
144	BARNET, ROBERT et ux Betey Cannon	9/29 1807 issued	"Celebrated by me." S. George, J.P.
145	BARNETT, THOMAS et ux Nancy McKeigg	9/9 1812 issued	"Married by me." Joseph Walker, J.P.
146	BARNETT, WHOMPSON M. et ux Rachel Woddy	5/4 1843	By J. Dyke, Pastor Unitia Church
147	BARNHILL, MATHEW W. et ux Nancy J. Wayman	3/6 1845	By J. Dyke, Pastor Unitia Church
148	BANCOM, THOMAS et ux Betsey Noble	8/1 1826 issued	No returns
149	BATY, JAMES et ux Ann Spradling	4/21 1833	By Samuel Thompson, J.P.
*	See 159		
150	BATY, WM. B. et ux Amanda L. Brient	9/5 1850	By James M. Tullo ch, J.P.
151	BAYLESS, WM. W. et ux Sarah Black	5/28 1833	By A. Patton, --
152	BAYLESS, W. W. et ux Mary Caulson	4/10 1850	By A. J. McGee, M.G.
153	BAYLESS, W. W. et ux Sarah H. Lane	1/14 1859	By M. Jones, J.P.
154	BAZEL, JONATHAN et ux Nancy Mills	8/19 1796 issued	Bond: Samuel Huchison
155	BEAL, JOHN et ux Paulina A. Porter	8/15 1850	By B. F. Duncan, J.P.
156	BEARD, JAMES et ux Jane Ewing	10/14 1823	By Thomas Beverage, --
157	BEARDEN, WILLIAM et ux Joicy Rudder	8/20 1830	By I. J. Roberts, M.G.
158	BEATTY, JOHN et ux Sally Rider	2/15 1800 issued	Bond: John Bradley
159	BAITY, ROBERT et ux Rebecah Cammil	3/30 1816 issued	No returns
*	See 150		
160	BEATY, SAMUEL et ux Sarah Pate	1/27 1817 issued	"Executed by Joseph Walker, J.P."
161	BEATY, WILLIAM et ux Polly Brickey	2/10 1823	By Sam'l Davidson, J.P.
162	BECKNELL, WILLIAM et ux Nancy E. Alexander	5/5 1858	By Joseph Beeler, M.G.
163	BEDFORD, JAMES et ux Betsy Hunt	12/9 1828	By Robert B. Billue, M.G.

	Names	Date Issue Or Celebrated	By Whom/ Security on Bond
164	BEESLEY, CORNELIUS et ux Sarah Jackson	5/14 1828 issued	No returns
165	BELL, BURRELL et ux Sophia Yancey	1/17 1797 issued	Bond: Austin Yancey
166	BELL, JOHN et ux Jane Craig	4/19 1796 issued	Bond: James Bell
167	BELL, JOHN et ux Nancy Weir	3/11 1801 issued	Bond: John Carson
168	BELL, JOHN B. et ux Isabella Love	5/18 1841	By Eli Richey, J.P.
169	BELL, JOSIAH et ux Sarah Kendrick	8/12 1804 issued	No returns
170	BELL, SILAS et ux Eleanor Wallace	1/22 1826	By Sam'l Davidson, J.P.
171	BELL, SAM'L F. et ux Martha F. James	12/24 1851	By Isaac Anderson, Pastor New Provd. Church
172	BELT, JOHN et ux M. A. Hennley	10/5 1854	David Spradlin, J.P.
173	BELT, JNO. W. et ux Sally W. Spradlin	12/29 1859	By Samuel Tulloch, J.P.
174	BELT, ROBERT C. et ux Elizabeth J. Craig	9/17 1857	By Andrew Ferguson, J.P.
175	BELT, RUFUS F. et ux Elizabeth Vaught	2/5 1843	By William Hendrickson, M.G.
176	BENNETT, HAYWOOD G. et ux Esther L. Houston	11/13 1815	"EXECUTED"--No signature
177	BENEINI, L. D. et ux Isabella B. Madison	12/31 1853	By S. J. McReynolds, J.P.
178	BERRY, JAMES et ux Rebeca Regan	8/20 1798 issued	Bond: Hugh S. Cochran
179	BERRY, JAMES et ux Rebecca C. McChesney	8/13 1818	By Isaac Anderson
180	BERRY R. M. et ux M. Ellen Toole	6/5 1854	By Isaac Anderson, Pastor New Prov. Church
181	BERRY, THOMAS et ux Cyntha Russell	8/28 1821	By I. Anderson, Pastor New Provd. Church
182	BEST, ANDREW J. et ux Sarah A. Scott	11/12 1857	By Spencer Henry, M.G.
183	BEST, EMANUEL et ux Susan Taylor	12/15 1831	By Wm. Williamson, J.P.
184	BEST, FREDERICK et ux Susannah Williamson	12/23 1834	By David McKamey, J.P.
185	BEST, F. D. et ux Sarah McCoyan	11/16 1854	By James M. Tulloch, J.P.

Names	Date Issue Or Celebrated	By Whom/ Security on Bond
186 BEST, GEORGE et ux Jane Roach	3/7 1836	By Samuel Tulloch, J.P.
187 BEST, JACOB et ux Nancy Taylor	2/13 1840	By John Maxwell, J.P.
188 BEST, JAMES M. et ux Susan Ridge	5/19 1856 issued	No returns
189 BEST, JOHN et ux Esther McGanby	12/12 1818	By Wm. Williamson, J.P.
190 BEST, JOHN et ux Betsy Anderson	11/25 1830	By Wm. Williamson, J.P.
191 BEST, JOHN et ux Katherine Best	4/5 1836	By Samuel Tulloch, J.P.
192 BEST, JOHN M. et ux Martha J. Sloan	10/3 1850	By John Morton, J.P.
193 BEST, SAMUEL D. et ux Sarah A. Best	7/3 1851	By Robert Sloan, J.P.
194 BEST, MARTIN et ux Polly Martin	10/4 1832	By John Maxwell, J.P.
195 BEST, SAMUEL P. et ux Elizabeth A. Clines	12/26 1850	By James M. Tulloch, J.P.
196 BIBY, LARKIN et ux Elvira Sanders	6/14 1835	By Spencer Henry, J.P.
197 BICKNELL, SAMUEL T. et ux Mary B. Wallace	10/22 1840	By Isaac Anderson, Pastor New Provd. Church
198 BIDDY, ABEDNEGO et ux Patsy Carrol	12/14 1820	By Wm. Williamson, J.P.
199 BIGS, JOHN H. et ux Elizabeth Dixon	2/19 1841	By Eli Rich, J.P.
200 BIGGS, WM. M. G. et ux Nancy Carson	9/29 1839	By Rev. J. Dyke
201 BILLUE, WILLIAM et ux Jane James	6/14 1813 issued	No returns
202 BILLUE, WILLIAM et ux Susan Hiclh	8/26 1846	By Wm. Rogers, M.G.
203 BIRCHFIELD, WM. A. et ux Elizabeth Ragan	7/14 1851	By Curran Lemans, J.P.
204 BIRCHFIELD, ROBERT et ux Eliza Jane Swinney	1/6 1841	By Jas. Watson, J.P.
205 BIRCHFIELD, SAMUEL et ux Rosannah Hyatt	9/6 1838	By William Henry, J.P.
* See 442		
206 BILLINGS, AMOS et ux Safronia Love	5/9 1859	By I. D. Wright, J.P.
207 BINGHAM, ELKANAH et ux Harrit S. Cook	10/19 1853	By Spencer Henry, M.G.

	Names	Date Issue Or Celebrated	By Whom/ Security on Bond
208	BINGHAM, WILLIAM et ux Glatha Pugh	3/18 1829 issued	"Celebrated by Sam'l Montgomery, J.P."
209	BINGLY, CHARLES W. et ux Sarah Keller	7/4 1829	By Thomas Billue, J.P.
210	BIRD, CHRISTIAN et ux Catherine Milton	3/9 1820	By Wm. Fagg, M.G.--ok
*	See 461		
211	BIRD, EZEKEAL et ux Nancy Smith	9/20 1849	By Daniel H. Emmett, J.P.
212	BIRD, GEORGE W. et ux Sarah A. Everett	9/17 1844	By Isaac Anderson, Pas- tor New Provd. Church
213	BIRD, JACOB et ux Lucinda A. McMahan	5/18 1856	By N. Brewer, J.P.
214	BIRD, JACOB, JR. et ux Nancy Brickey	3/29 1835	By Frederick Emmett, J.P.
215	BIRD, JOHN et ux Elizabeth Shields	9/19 1839	By John Chambers, M.G.
216	BIRD, LAVENDER et ux Milly Ann Headrick	8/21 1851	By A. B. Gamble, J.P.
217	BIRD, LEVI et ux Rachel Brickey	7/19 1838	By W. W. Porter, J.P.
218	BIRD, PHILIP et ux Mary Dunn	11/11 1828	By James Cameron, J.P.
219	BIRD, PRESTON et ux Rebecca Smith	2/5 1850	By Frederic Emmett, M.G.
220	BIRD, T. W. et ux Margaret Fortner	7/23 1855	By Wm. M. Brickell, J.P.P.
221	BIRD, WILLIAM B. et ux Susan Campbell	1/27 1833	By Johnson Adams, Preacher
222	BIRDWELL, SELLERS et ux L. A. Jackson	2/28 1854	By Green B. Saffell, J.P.
223	BIRELY, ISSAAC et ux Malinda French	10/18 1840	By William Celeburn, J.P.
224	BISHOP, GEORGE et ux Susanna Fortner	5/29 1849	By Hendrickson, M.G.
225	BISHOP, ELISHA et ux Mary Gibson	2/3 1857	By H. Thompson, J.P.
226	BIVENS, BENJAMIN L. et ux Sally McKinley	1/12 1845	By John Morton, J.P.
227	BIVENS, JOSEPH W. et ux Elizabeth Settle- mire	12/26 1845	By Curran Lemons, J.P.
228	BLACK, HAMBRIGHT et ux Mary W. Barry	12/18 1817	By Isaac Anderson, --

Names	Date Issue Or Celebrated	By Whom/ Security on Bond
229 BLACK, JAMES A. et ux Rachel S. Thompson	9/30 1852	By A. Vance, M.G.
230 BLACK, JAMES et ux Nancy Bogle	2/10 1837	By Fielding Pope, M.G. (Outside is James H. Black)
231 BLACK, JAMES H. et ux Elizabeth Bogle	5/28 1854	By Fielding Pope, M.G.
232 BLACK, JOSEPH et ux Mary Hammontree of Philly	10/24 1830	By John Wood, S.Q.
233 BLACK, URIAH et ux Elizabeth Thompson	3/19 1816	By J. Anderson, --
234 BLACKBURN, ANDREW et ux Ann E. Gillespy	9/23 1847	By Isaac Anderson, Pastor New Provd. Church
235 BLACKBURN, JOHN N. et ux Eliza J. Ambrister	4/23 1850	By T. K. Munsey, M.G.
236 BLAIR, E. S. et ux Jane Henry	7/28 1831	By Wm. McTeer, J.P.
237 BLAIR, GEORGE et ux Anna Lane	3/25 1839	By Robert Shields, J.P.
238 BLAIR, JOHN et ux Isabella Hix	3/25 1832	By John Hendrixson, J.P.
239 BLAIR, SAMUEL et ux Rosanna Hall	11/9 1828	By Thomas Billue, J.P.
240 BLAIR, SAMUEL et ux Elizabeth Greenaway	3/8 1843	By Joseph A. Hutton, J.P.
241 BLAIR, SAMUEL et ux Mary C. Morgan	4/26 1857	By Jesse Kerr, Jr., J.P.
242 BLAIR, WILLIAM et ux Betsey McDowell	12/2 1799 issued	Bond: Henry Beard
243 BLAIR, WILLIAM et ux E. J. Lain	5/12 1856	By N. Brewer, J.P.
244 BLAIR, WILLIAM ASTON et ux Sarah Ann Russell	8/2 1858	By Rev. S. B. West
245 BLAIR, WILLIAM S. et ux Paty Mahala M. Hall	4/4 1820	By Andrew S. Morrison, V.D.M.
246 BLANKENBECKLER, JAMES F. et ux Martha J. Jones	11/8 1858	By Andrew Ferguson, J.P.
247 BLANKINSHIP, B. H. et ux Sarah J. Carpenter	12/7 1851	By F. K. Munsey, M.G.
248 GILBERT BLANKINSHIP et ux Edy Lane	8/9 1820	By Jas. Love, J.P.
249 BLANKINSHIP, GILBERT et ux Elizabeth Hughes	4/10 1828 issued	No returns
250 BLANTON, HORACE T. et ux Eliza J. Thompson	10/8 1847	By Isaac Anderson, Pastor New Provd. Church

	Names	Date Issue Or Celebrated	By Whom/ Security on Bond
251	BLEDSOE, MOSES et ux Rebecca Bird	12/16 1849	By Christian Long, J.P.
252	BLEDSOE, GEORGE et ux Famy Bledsoe	12/31 1839	By J. H. Duncan, J.P.
253	BLEVENS, DILLARD et ux Francis E. Ross	12/24 1858	By A. J. Wilson, J.P.
254	BLEVINS, CLARK et ux Margaret Taylor	8/30 1857	By A. J. Wilson, J.P.
255	BLEVENS, JAMES et ux Mary Stout	3/11 1856 issued	By J. M. Lain, J.P. "Solomized March 1856"
256	BLEVINS, RICHARD et ux Elizabeth Arintos	11/5 1800 issued	Bond: Michel Holder
257	BLOUNT, JAMES F. et ux Caroline E. Curtis	11/4 1831 10/27 says Knox Paper in McGhee Library.	By William Toole, --
258	BLOUNT, JAMES, JR. et ux Elizabeth Barnes	10/5 1852	By Fielding Pope, M.G.
259	BLY, JNO. et ux Rebecca Howard	10/19 1852	By John McClain, J.P.
260	BLYTHE, SAMUEL M. et ux Polly Montgomery	9/8 1825	By Joseph Duncan
261	BOGLE, HUGH et ux Hannah Caldwell	4/2 1801 issued	Bond: Andrew Bogle, Sr.
262	BOGLE, HUGH et ux Caroline M. Haddon	2/26 1852	By Jno. Russom, M.G.
263	BOGLE, HUGH et ux Jane Black	2/19 1856	By Fielding, Pope, M.G.
264	BOGLE, HUGH M. et ux Mary T. Black	2/8 1854	By F. Pope, M.G.
265	BOGLE, J.C.M. et ux Elizabeth C. Saffell	9/17 1857	By J. C. Craig, M.G.
266	BOGLE, JAMES et ux Susan Raulston	8/1 1852	By Wm. H. Anderson, J.P.
267	BOGLE, JOSEPH C. et ux Minerve Green	2/25 1834	By John Rusam, M.G.
268	BOGLE, JOHN et ux Nancy Henderson	8/29 1839	By Fielding Pope, M.G.
269	BOGLE, MATHEW H. et ux Mary L. Bogle	1/7 1845	By Fielding Pope, M.G.
270	BOGLE, ROBERT et ux Ann Boyd	5/17 1832	By A. Vance, M.G.
271	BOGLE, SAM'L et ux Holly Williams	9/14 1797 issued	Bond: James Upton

Names	Date Issue Or Celebrated	By Whom/ Security on Bond
272 BOHANAN, ROBERT et ux Elizabeth Janes	10/17 1822 issued	No returns
273 BOHANAN, THOMAS et ux Nancy Morgan	2/24 1830 issued	"Celebrated by me in Feb. 25, 1830." John Russom, M.G.
274 BOLER, HENRY C. et ux Tony Sims	8/7 1843	By John Tipton, J.P.
275 BOLING, J.S. et ux Mary Keeble	6/12 1853	By John Clark, J.P.
276 BOLING, PLEASENT M. et ux Esther Davis	4/27 1838	By Wm. McTeer, J.P.
277 BOLIN, ROBERT et ux Sally Clampet	4/12 1828	By Wm. McTeer, J.P.
278 BOLING, SHADRICK et ux Patsy Rogers	2/2 1830 issued	By William McTeer, J.P. "Celebrated by me."
279 BOLING, SHADRICK et ux Leeah Cageley	7/13 1851	By John Tipton, J.P.
280 BOND, AARON et ux Sarah Carter	12/10 1818	By Samuel Douthet, M.G.
281 BOND, BENJAMIN et ux Rosanna Martin	12/25 1817	By Samuel Douthet, M.G.
282 BOND, BENJAMIN et ux Martha McClure	7/14 1835	By Marvel Duncan, J.P.
283 BOND, GEORGE et ux Nancy Singleton	1/3 1832	By S. Douthet, E. M. Church
284 BOND, PETER et ux Joannah Martin	9/26 1819	By S. Douthet, M.G.
285 BOND, HENRY, JR. et ux Susannah Stanfield	7/10 1827	By Wm. Griffits, J.P.
286 BOND, STEPHEN F. et ux Ann E. Hamby	9/30 1856	By Fielding Pope, M.G.
287 BONHAM, JAMES S. et ux Elizabeth Henry	5/22 1846	By James Henry, J.P.
288 BONHAM, JOHN M. et ux Lucinda Vanpelt	2/19 1833	By A. Patton, --
289 BONHAM, JOHN P. et ux Sally Jones	2/21 1826	By Ethbert F. Sevier, M.G.
290 BONINE, ISAAC et ux Sarah Talbert	8/8 1814 issued	"Celebrated by me." J. Gillespie, J.P.
291 BONINE, ISAAC et ux Sally Merrett	1/26 1826	By Wm. Griffetts, J.P.
292 BONINE, JACOB et ux Christena Pester- field	3/10 1825	By Charles H. Warren, --

Names	Date Issue Or Celebrated	By Whom/ Security on Bond
293 BOOTH, ARON et ux Elizabeth Harvey	11/25 1824	By Henry Soward, M.G.
294 BOOTH, JAMES M. et ux Margaret McReynolds	1/9 1834	By Wm. Anderson, J.P.
295 BOARING, ISAAC et ux Rebecca McDaniel	11/24 1846	By W. R. Flinn, J.P.
296 BOREN, AMOS et ux Anny Hiles	3/30 1814 issued	No returns
297 BOREN, ISSAC et ux Sarah A. Headrick	8/31 1844	By Will Cumming, J.P.
298 BOREN, JAMES et ux Margaret A. Porter	3/13 1851	By Samuel Ghormly, J.P.
299 BORING, ISAAC et ux Betsy May	8/15 1818 issued	No returns
300 BORING JOHN et ux Rachel Murry	1/12/25 1826	By Billy Holloway, M.G. of Baptist Church
301 BORING, JOHN D. et ux Maryann Russell	9/24 1818	By John Black, J.P.
302 BORING, HEARTSELL et ux Emaline Parke	2/9 1843	By H. Burum, J.P.
303 BORING, NOCOLAS et ux Rody Russell	7/6 1824	By Wm. Billue, M.G.
304 BOSTICK, FLOYD et ux Rosannah Murray	6/12 1817	By Bowerman, H. H., Esq.
* See 129		
305 BOWMAN, JAMES B. et ux Hannah E. J. Griffitts	9/27 1864	By J.W.W. Neal, M.G. M.E.C. South
306 BOWMAN, JOHN et ux Catherine Bowerman	6/29 1812 issued	No returns
307 BOWMAN, JAMES A. et ux Susan Taylor	1/23 1843	By John Chandler, M.G.
308 BOWEN, ROBERT H. et ux Anna Henry	3/26 1839	By James Henry, J.P.
309 BOWERMAN, G. W. et ux Hester A. Griffetts	1/17 1859	By Wm. M. Brickell, J.P.
310 BOWERMAN, MICHAEL et ux Caity Bowers	2/25 1800 issued	Bond: ?Bartlow Cerindman?--or--Peter Bowerman?
311 BOWERMAN, MICHAEL et ux Nancy Coulbourn	7/22 1816	By Robert Parke?
312 BOWERMAN, MICHAEL et ux Sarah Blackwell	9/18 1824	By John Norwood, J.P.
313 BOWERMAN, JOHN et ux Sally McAlroy	1/20 1818	By Alex B. Gamble, J.P.

Names	Date Issue Or Celebrated	By Whom/ Security on Bond
314 BOWMAN, ROBERT et ux Nancy Ann Sloan	12/8 1837	By B.L.A. Mays, M.G.
315 BOWERS, WILLIAM et ux Lucretia Harris	4/12 1821	By Wm. Fagg, J.P.
316 BOYD, ANDERSON et ux Elizabeth C. Vinyard	4/8 1846 issued	No returns
317 BOYD, CAMPBELL et ux Mary E. Spillman	10/14 1846	By F. Pope, M.G.
318 BOYD, E. et ux M. J. Campbell	9/12 1847	By Joseph A. Button, J.P.
319 BOON, W. R. et ux Martha Hunter	2/5 1854	By William Colburn, J.P.
320 BOYD, JAMES et ux Ann Miller	7/26 1797 issued	Bond: James Sloan
321 BOYD, JAMES et ux Hannah McMurry	9/3 1799 issued	Ret. finished--no bonds- men--no signature
322 BOYD, JAMES et ux Elizabeth Murry	11/22 1826	By Billy Holloway, M.G.
323 BOYD, JAMES A. et ux Abigail Hart	3/5 1844	By J. S. Craig, M.G.
324 BOYD, JOHN et ux Caty Holloway	9/30 1799 issued	Bond: Joseph Holloway
325 BOYD, JOHN et ux Matilda Loftise	10/31 1816	By John Harris, J.P.
326 BOYD, JOHN et ux Caty Shell	4/2 1833	By John Maxwell, J.P.
327 BOYD, JOHN et ux Matilda Anderson	4/21 1848	By William Colburn, J.P.
328 BOYD, JOHN L. et ux Nancy Longbottom	2/10 1854	By T. M. Rooker, J.P.
329 BOYD, WILLIAM et ux Jane (Newcum) Newsom	12/28 1853	By S. J. McReynolds, J.P.
330 BOYD, WILLIAM C. et ux Sydney A. McReynolds	5/4 1865	By R. E. Tedford, M.G.
331 BOYD, WILLIAM et ux Eliza J. Anderson	11/12 1833	By Isaac Anderson, Pas- tor New Provd. Church
332 BRABSON, BENJAMIN B. et ux Elizabeth B. Toole of Wm.	9/5 1839	By Isaac Anderson, Pas- tor New Providence Church
333 BRABSON, THOMAS C. et ux Margaret R. Porter of Robert	12/21 1843	By Thomas K. Harman, M.G.
334 BRACKET, JACKSON et ux Rachel Ferguson	6/28 1843	By H. Buram, J.P.

	Names	Date Issue Or Celebrated	By Whom/ Security on Bond
335	BRACKITT, RICHARD et ux Sarah Tucker	8/29 1843	By John Griffetts, J.P.
336	BRADBURN, JAMES et ux Catherine Russell	7/25 1850	By Christian Long, J.P.
337	BRADBURN, JOHN et ux Rachel Heron	1/14 1849	By John Morton, J.P.
338	BRADBURY, JAMES et ux Mahala Hunt	11/21 1843	By Lemuell Adams, J.P.
339	BRADBURY, MILTON et ux Susannah Blackwell	2/13 1821	By Jas. Love, J.P.
340	BRADY, JAMES B. et ux Lucinda Haynes	4/15 1829	By Samuel Hammil, J.P.
341	BRADBERRY, WILLIAM et ux Jenny Brewer	12/21 1818 issued	No returns
342	BRADLEY, WASHINGTON et ux Margaret Hitch	8/15 1839	By Wm. Billue, M.G.
343	BRADLEY, WILLIAM et ux Mary Murphy	6/24 1799 issued	Bond: Thomas Murphy
344	BRADLEY, WM. et ux Polly Clampet	10/20 1802	No returns--both L. & B. Bond: Elijah Clampet
345	BRADLEY, ISOM et ux Susana Matkocks	5/13 1798 issued	Bond: David Haiston
346	BRADLEY, WILLIAM et ux Betsy Hudgeons	1/22 1828	By Wm. Williamson, J.P.
347	BRAIDWELL, WILLIAM et ux Ainey Fifer	5/12 1817	By George Snider, --
348	BRAKEBILL, HENRY et ux Anna Davis	10/30 1838 issued	No returns
349	BREAKBILL, JOHN et ux Anna Thomas	2/17 1817 issued	No returns
350	BREAKBILL, PETER et ux Leah L. Reagan	1/6 1835	By Spencer Henry, J.P.
351	BREAKBILL, WILLIAM et ux Mary Keller	10/4 1819 issued	No returns
352	BRANDON, DANIEL et ux Elizabeth Perry	4/22 1842	By Henry Burum, J.P.
353	BRANUM, JOHN et ux Francis M. Farr	10/4 1855	By William Kerr, J.P.
354	BRANNON, ALLEN R. et ux Eliza F. Smith	9/17 1851	By W. H. Rogers, M.G.
355	BRAWNER, JESSE et ux Maryann Fultner	12/26 1843	By W. Toole, J.P.
356	BRASSMEL, G. W. et ux Talitha Breedan	2/12 1853	By Samuel L. Yearout, J.P.

Names	Date Issue Or Celebrated	By Whom/ Security on Bond
357 BRAZELTON, ALEXANDER et ux Polly Frew	11/1 1827	By I. Anderson, Pastor New Provd. Church
358 BRAZELTON, SAMUEL et ux Jane Frew	10/26 1820	By I. Anderson, Pastor New Providence Church
359 BREAZEAL, WILLIAM et ux Margaret Phillips	5/30 1837	By W. M. Rorex, J.P.
360 BREWER, ASA et ux Leah Brickey	2/28 1828	By James Cameron, J.P.
361 BREWER, CALLOWAY et ux Barbara Shields	10/13 1832	By Johnson Adams, M.G.
362 BREWER, DANIEL et ux Elizabeth Hubbard	10/23 1825	By James Cameron, J.P.
363 BREWER, JAMES C. et ux Hetty Hatcher	10/10 1850	By John Chambers, M.G.
364 BREWER, JOHN P. et ux Judah Poindexter	10/17 1838	By W. W. Porter, J.P.
365 BREWER, LEVI D. et ux Elizabeth Hix	1/30 1850	By John Chambers, --
366 BREWER, NATANIEL et ux Isabella Davis	7/28 1831	By Samuel Henry, J.P.
367 BREWER, NICHOLAS et ux Elizabeth Dunn	12/26 1828	By James Cameron, J.P.
368 BREWER, WILLIAM et ux Mary Parker	8/24 1857	By Nicholas Brewer, J.P.
369 BRIANT, ELISHA et ux Susan Jones	4/12 1832	By Leroy Noble, J.P.
370 BRIANT, THOMAS A. et ux Betsey Singleton	4/2 1830	By John Ferguson, J.P.
371 BRIANT, LEVI et ux Elizabeth Rines	3/24 1842	By Samuel Tulloch, J.P.
372 BRIANT, JACKSON et ux Nancy Phillips	6/1 1845	By David Spradlin, J.P.
373 BRIANT, JAMES et ux Elizabeth Tucker	3/17 1825	By J. Gillispie, J.P.
374 BRIANT, JAMES et ux Maryann Roach	3/31 1839	By Wm. Riche, J.P.
375 BRIANT, JESSE et ux Polly Haskelt	12/12 1818	By Wm. Williamson, J.P.
376 BRIANT, WM. A. et ux M. E. Harper	2/2 1854	By Madison Love, M.G.
377 BRICKELL, GEO. W. et ux Lucretia Miser	9/16 1852	By A. J. McGee, M.G.
378 BRICKELL, GEO. W. et ux Sarah J. Jones	7/8 1856	By A. R. James, J.P.

Names	Date Issue Or Celebrated	By Whom/ Security on Bond
379 BRICKELL, WM. M. et ux Sarah Nix	7/19 1836	By Mathew Whittenbarger, J.P.
380 BRICKEY, WILLIAM et ux Abigail Waters	5/27 1823	By Samuel C. Davidson, J.P.
381 BRICKEY, WILLIAM et ux Susanna Calor	5/26 1859	By Nicholas Brewer, J.P.
382 BRIGHT, BARTLEY et ux Nancy Wisacarver	3/26 1848	By William Colburn, J.P.
383 BRIGHT, DAVID et ux Jane Key	7/26 1837	By Mathew Whittenbarger, J.P.
384 BRIGHT, DAVID et ux M. J. Marrow	6/1 1859	By James Mathews, J.P.
385 BRIGHT, HARVEY S. et ux Elizabeth J. Chormley	10/15 1848	By Rev. A. Glenn
386 BRIGHT, JAMES E. et ux Nancy D. King	9/10 1839	By James Henry, J.P.
387 BRIGHT, JASPER et ux Polly Key	4/16 1816 issued	By Wm. Gillespie, J.P. "Married by me."
388 BRIGHT, MICHAEL et ux Isabella Bonham	2/14 1833	By A. Patton, --
* See 3083 or 4046		
389 BRILLS, MICHEL et ux Elizabeth T. Emmett	12/11 1843	By Johnston, Adams, M.G.
390 BROILS, JACOB et ux Mary Vaught	4/19 19802 issued	Bond: George Broiles
391 BROYLES, GEORGE et ux Cathern Vaut	6/16 1796 issued	Bond: Andrew Vent
392 BROILS, DAVID et ux Elly Rooker	10/24 1805 issued	No returns
393 BROYLES, DAVID et ux Martha Pitts	3/25 1847	By Samuel Tulloch, J.P.
394 BROYLES, DANIEL N. et ux M. A. Hair	12/22 1853	By J. S. Craig, M.G.
395 BROADDY, THOMAS B. et ux Martha N. Clements	3/20 1851	By Isaac Anderson, M.G.
396 BROOKS, ALEXANDER F. et ux Margaret Wolf	8/26 1858	By B. F. Duncan, J.P.
397 BROOKE, A. K. et ux Sarah Brakebill	12/7 1854	By J. C. Martin, J.P.
398 BROOK, BOLING et ux Jane Jackson	1/22 1827	By Samuel Douthett, E.M.C.
399 BROOK, HARRISON et ux Patience Tuck	3/5 1840	By William Colburn, J.P.

Names	Date Issue Or Celebrated	By Whom/ Security on Bond
400 BROOK, JAMES et ux Pheby Hankins	1/27 1854	By John J. Hoover, J.P.
401 BROOKS, JAMES W. et ux Nancy Greenway	1/24 1850	By Wesley Earnest, J.P.
402 BROOKS, JOAB et ux Sally Barton	8/15 1822	By Wm. Gault, J.P.
403 BROOKS, JOHN et ux Betsey Hair	2/29 1827	By Wm. Griffetts, J.P.
404 BROOKS, JOHN et ux Harrit Hayden	6/14 1837 issued	No returns
405 BROOK, SAMUEL et ux Mandy Purkey	11/30 1853	By J. H. Donaldson, J.P.
406 BROOK, SAMUEL et ux Prudence Tuck	1/18 1842	By Lemuel Adams, J.P.
407 BROOKS, SAMUEL H. et ux Martha E. Jackson	10/14 1858	By James Mathews, J.P.
408 BROOKS, WASHINGTON et ux Mary Garner	7/9 1854	By Wm. M. Burnett, --
409 BROOKS, WILLIAM et ux Polly Wade	5/30 1817 issued	No returns
410 BROOKS, WILLIAM G. et ux Margaret Wheeler	5/26 1832	By Wm. McTeer, J.P.
411 BROOK, JOEL et ux Patsey Saxton	11/15 1821	By Samuel George, J.P.
412 BROWN, ARTHUR et ux Mary A. Lamons	9/6 1855	By S. L. Yearout, J.P.
413 BROWN, BENJAMIN et ux Jane White	9/1 1818 issued	No returns
414 BROWN, BENJAMIN et ux Elizabeth Halcomb	5/5 1855	By M. Kountz, J.P.
415 BROWN, BAZEL C. et ux Elizabeth C. Stephenson	2/10 1829	By S. M. Astorr, V.D.M.
416 BROWN, DAVID et ux Betsey Sloan	6/16 1800 issued	Bond: John McAlroy
417 BROWN, DAVID et ux Mary Ann France	6/24 1840	By Robert B. Billue, M.G.
418 BROWN, ELIJAH et ux Mary A. R. Billue	5/18 1843 issued	Bond: Elias Hitch
419 BROWN, ENOCH et ux Nancy Vinyard	12/14 1837	By John Russom, M.G.
420 BROWN, ISAAC W. et ux Eliza A. Key	11/11 1849	By Wm. M. Brickell, J.P.
421 BROWN, JACOB J. et ux Margaret McAfee	3/30 1842	By Wm. McTeer, J.P.

Names	Date Issue Or Celebrated	By Whom/ Security on Bond
422 BROWN, JEFFERSON P. et ux Hester Ann Cox	3/4 1835	By George Russell, --
423 BROWN, JONATHAN et ux Rebekah Bowers	2/28 1835	By Hugh Bogle, J.P.
424 BROWN, JOSEPH et ux Catherine Breakbill	10/9 1815 issued	No returns
425 BROWN, JOSEPH et ux Nancy Kirkpatrick	12/13 1832	By John Russom, M.G.
426 BROWN, JOSEPH B. et ux Seneth Farmer	10/20 1843	By William Colburn, J.P.
427 BROWN, JOHN et ux Nancy Allen	7/30 1801 issued	Bond: John Bradley
428 BROWN, JOHN et ux Nancy Diamons	8/17 1826	By Charles H. Warren, J.P.
429 BROWN, JOHN et ux Mary Ann Bright	10/12 1830	By Joseph Sanpitt, --
430 BROWN, JOHN H. et ux Mary A. Davis	1/10 1856	By M. Love, M.G.
431 BROWN, MARTIN C. et ux Nancy Cruse	8/5 1828 issued	"Celebrated by me." Alexander Stewart, J.P.
432 BROWN, RUFUS M. et ux Margaret Gardner	12/11 1856	By W. A. Lawson, M.G.
433 BROWN, SOLOMAN et ux Mary Duncan	6/6 1854	By Andrew Ferguson, J.P.
434 BROWN, WM. et ux Polly Ann Moffett	4/12 1800	Bond: Cornelius Bogart
435 BROWN, WILLIAM et ux Peggy Strain	3/10 1819 issued	"By me celebrated." David McKamy, J.P.
436 BROWN WM. L. (W. T.?) et ux M. C. Brown (N. C.?)	10/17 1855	By J. M. Thornberry, M.G. (Slansbury, M.G.?)
437 BRUNER, JOSEPH et ux Thursday Hughs	7/14 1859	By John F. Gilbreath, M.G.
438 BRYANT, JOHN et ux Margaret Avarett	1/17 1844	By Christian Long, J.P.
439 BRYANT, LNOIR et ux Nancy Blair	11/20 1832	By John Hendrix, J.P.
440 BRYANT, ROBERT et ux Barbra J. Hays	6/10 1858	By A. J. Wilson, J.P.
441 BRYANT, W. R. et ux Nancy Howard	12/5 1850	By James M. Tulloch, J.P.
442 BURCHFIELD, JESSE Y. et ux Margaret Gregorry	11/31 1845	By Curren Lemons, J.P.
443 BURCHFIELD, J. P. et ux Mary Gardiner	2/20 1853	Sam'l Ghormley, J.P.

	Names	Date Issue Or Celebrated	By Whom/ Security on Bond
444	BURCHFIELD, NATHAN et ux Elizabeth Blair	1/1 1852	By Curran Lemons, J.P.
445	BURCHFIELD, ROBERT et ux Mary Gregory	1/1 1843	By Johnson Adams, M.G.
*	See 203		
446	BIRNUM, JAMES et ux Charity Gibson	4/27 1854	By Andrew Ferguson, J.P.
447	BURKE, DAVID H. et ux Dorcas M. Lowery	7/15 1819	By I. Anderson, Pastor New Provd. Church
448	BURNETT, JOHN S. et ux Lydia S. Danforth	11/12 1818	By I. Anderson, --
449	BURNETT, WILLIAM M. et ux Laticia Sharp	3/15 1839 issued	No returns
450	BURNET, H. T. et ux Margaret Wayman	9/29 1850	By John J. Hoover, J.P.
451	BURNETT, EDWARD et ux Rachell Cheetwood	7/20 1801 issued	Bond: James Roddy
452	BURNE, GEORGE et ux Elizabeth Raper	2/14 1818 issued	No returns
453	BURNS, LEWIS et ux Nancy Vaught	8/26 1830 issued	"Solomonised by me." C. W. Parks
454	BURNS, TILGHMAN A. et ux Susannah Walker	12/16 1846	By Jas. Cumming, E.ME.C. South
455	BURNS, WILLIAM et ux Patty James	3/12 1817 issued	No returns
456	BURTON, JOHN et ux Margaret Simons	7/8 1824	By Samuel Hamel, J.P.
457	BUTLER, THOMAS H. et ux Nancy A. Kizer	2/19 1857	By J. H. Donaldson, J.P.
458	BUTLER, SAMUEL et ux Elizabeth Medlock	1/7 1819	By John Gillespie, J.P.
459	BYERLEY, MICHAEL et ux Sarah Smith	8/22 1828	By J. Gillespie, J.P.
460	BYRD, BENJAMIN et ux Hannah Hammontree	11/8 1868	By W. C. Conner, J.P. Bond: R. C. Hawkins
461	BYRD, ABRAHAM et ux Betsey Gillespie	3/20 1799 issued	Bond: Joseph Young
*	See 210		
462	BYRD, WM. J. of Jerado-- Ter. of Mo.--et ux Malinda H. Gillespy of Capt. James G.	3/24 1818	By R. H. King, M.G. Also Knox Register, "of 4/14 1818."
463	BARTON, WILLIAM et ux Nancy Bradberry	1/10 1820	By Jos. Love, J.P.

Names	Date Issue Or Celebrated	By Whom/ Security on Bond
464 CABE, JOHN et ux Margaret Cooper	2/22 1798 issued	Bond: John Jackson
465 CADDELL, MARTIN et ux Mary Davis	12/17 1818 issued	No returns
466 CAGLE, CHRISTIAN et ux Patience Cardwell	12/28 1822	By A. B. Gamble, J.P.
467 CAGLE, GEORGE et ux Polly Latham	8/2 1829	By Wm. McTeer, J.P.
468 CAGLE, HENRY et ux Betsey Hill	4/3 1828	By William McTeer, J.P.
469 CAGLE, JOHN et ux Feruby Rogers	2/22 1827	By Samuel Henry, J.P.
470 CAGLEY, JOHN et ux Martha M. Branam	7/7 1859	By Christian Long, J.P.
* See also KAGLEY		
471 CAGELEY, JOSEPH et ux Eliza Dunaway	1/25 1850	By W. M. Brickell, J.P.
472 CAIN, RUFUS et ux Mary S. Ball	12/3 1848	By Robert Sloan, J.P.
473 CALDWELL, ADAM W. et ux Nancy Waters	10/18 1838	By Jeremiah Duncan, J.P.
474 CALDWELL, ALEXANDER et ux Jane Logan	11/9 1824	By Samuel Hamill, J.P.
475 CALDWELL, A. L. et ux A.E.M. Bogle	11/6 1856	By F. Pope, M.G.
476 CALDWELL, CARSON et ux Sally Akridge	1/17 1826	By William Hagleton, M.G.
477 CALDWELL, CARSON et ux Polly E. Barrett	12/13 1836	By Fielding Pope, M.G.
478 CALDWELL, DAVID et ux Molly Russell	1/29 1799	By independence; Hance Russell 1791
479 CALDWELL, DAVID et ux Elizabeth Giffin	10/25 1800 issued	Bond: John Ewing
480 CALDWELL, DAVID et ux Sarah Yearout	4/22 1833	By Isaac Anderson, Pastor New Provd. Church
481 CALDWELL, DAVID et ux Elizabeth Russell	2/19 1835	By Fielding Pope, M.G.
482 CALDWELL, GEORGE et ux Mary Sharp	8/14 1845	By Wm. M. Burnett, --
483 CALDWELL, JAMES et ux Nancy Kelly	10/2 1817 issued	No returns
484 CALDWELL, JOSEPH et ux Anny Maize	5/16 1833	Noahbat?(Noah Abot?), M.G.
485 CALDWELL, JOSEPH et ux Mary Millsaps	11/19 1856	By W. W. Nuchols, J.P.

Names	Date Issue Or Celebrated	By Whom/ Security on Bond
486 CALDWELL, JOHN et ux Cinthia Shadden	2/22 1822	By John McCampbell, V.D.M.
* See 2276		
487 CALDWELL, JOHN C. et ux Dorcas M. G. Lowery	8/31 1847	By Will Cumming, J.P.
488 CALDWELL, ROBERT et ux Lavenia McGhee	4/14 1837	By Isaac Anderson, Pastor New Provd. Church
489 CALDWELL, ROBERT R. et ux Eliza L. Martin	10/14 1841	By William Hendrickson, M.G.
490 CALDWELL, ROBERT W. et ux Sibby Russell	1/1 1829	By William Engleton, M.G.
491 CALDWELL, SAMUEL et ux Sarah D. Bean	12/30 1856	By Andrew Ferguson, J.P.
492 CALDWELL, ST. CLAIR F. et ux Margaret Montgomery of John	1/16 1823	By Isaac Anderson, Pastor New Provd. Church
493 CALDWELL, THOMAS et ux Mary Jane Moore	5/22 1856	By James M. Tulloch, J.P.
494 CAMERON, MARION et ux Jane Myers	6/10 1855	By Nicholas Brewer, J.P.
495 CAMERON, SAM'L R. et ux Elizabeth Burnes	1/27 1849	By W. H. Bates, T.D. M.E.C. South
496 CANNON, GUILFORD et ux Jane McGhee	9/21 1843	By Isaac Anderson, M.G.
497 CANNON, JAMES et ux Emily Cummings	6/25 1840	By Isaac Anderson, M.G. Moses Willix
498 CANNON, JOHN R. et ux Patience L. Smith	10/11 1825	By Thos' J. Brown, T.D.
499 CANNON, ROBERT W. et ux Sarah A. Williams	5/19 1849	By Wm. Billue, M.G.
500 CAMPBELL, ALFRED et ux Eliza Hill	7/16 1848	By Curran Lamons, J.P.
501 CAMPBELL, ANDREW et ux Sarah Duncan	8/31 1820	By Andrew J. Morrison, V.D.M.
502 CAMPBELL, BAXTER B. et ux A. E. Sherrell	11/2 1843	By Lewis Jones, J.P.
503 CAMPBELL, CHARLES G. et ux Lucinda M. Wear	2/14 1843	By Isaac Anderson, M.G.
504 CAMPBELL, ISAAC et ux Betsey George	5/14 1818	By J. Gillespie, J.P.
505 CAMPBELL, ISAAC N. et ux Isabella I. (or J.) Gillespy	9/15 1842	By Isaac Anderson, M.G.
506 CAMPBELL, JESSE et ux Martha Porter	1/22 1823	By S. Hamill, J.P.

	Names	Date Issue Or Celebrated	By Whom/ Security on Bond
507	CAMPBELL, JOEL et ux Agnes Sloan	2/20 1818 issued	No returns
508	CAMPBELL, JOHN et ux Sally McClure	8/20 1818	By I. Anderson, --
509	CAMPBELL, JOHN et ux Ruth Thompson	11/13 1828	By Isaac Anderson, Pastor New Provd. Church
510	CAMPBELL, JOHN et ux Margaret Thompson	7/26 1831	By Isaac Anderson, M.G.
511	CAMPBELL, JOHN C. et ux Sibby Ewing	5/12 1831	By Isaac Anderson, M.G.
512	CAMPBELL, JOHNSTON H. et ux Patsey Andrews	10/7 1834	By Robert Houston, J.P.
513	CAMPBELL, SILAS et ux Matilda Todd	12/25 1826 issued	No returns
514	CAMPBELL, SMITH et ux Rebecca Pearce	5/3 1850 issued 1/16	By Curran Lamons, J.P.
515	CAMPBELL, WILLIAM et ux Margaret Sloan	10/3 1816	By John Tedford, J.P.
516	CAMPBELL, WM. H. et ux Sarah Johnson	5/28 1854	By Dan'l D. Fouts, J.P.
517	CARDEN, JAMES et ux Sarah McConnell	2/28 1821 issued	"Solomonised by me." James Turk, --
518	CARDWELL, PERRIN H. et ux Amanda M. Cates, of Reuben L.	8/17 1843	By J. Nutty, L.D. of M. E. Church "She daughter of Reuben L. Cates."
519	CARNES, JAMES et ux Caroline Barnes	8/18 1853	By Isaac Anderson, M.G.
520	CARNES, JOHN B. et ux Mary A. Clemens	9/29 1858	By J. S. Craig, M.G.
521	CARNE, SAMUEL J. et ux Dorthy Caroline Hoyle	8/6 1859	By W. W. Bayless, J.P.
522	CARPENTER, ABRAHAM et ux Susannah Hutsell	2/8 1842	By Henry Hamil, J.P.
523	CARPENTER, ADAM et ux Isabella Nelson	11/12 1839	By Samuel Tulloch, J.P.
524	CARPENTER, ANDREW et ux Arety J. Thompson	8/16 1850 issued	"Celebrated Thursday after date." B. Abernathy, M.G.
525	CARPENTER, ARMSTEAD et ux Nancy McClain	8/17 1827	By Samuel Douthit, E.M.E.Ch.
526	CARPENTER, ARMSTEAD et ux Mary McClain	10/17 1846	By B. Abernathy, M.E.P.C.
527	CARPENTER, DANIEL et ux Tilda Goff	8/1 1849	By Harvey H. C. Caruthers, J.P.

Names	Date Issue Or Celebrated	By Whom/ Security on Bond
528 CARPENTER, LAWSON et ux Sarah Costner	1/25 1838	By Henry Hamil, J.P.
529 CARPENTER, ELISHA et ux Elizabeth Cry	1/13 1841	By Samuel Tulloch, J.P.
530 CARPENTER, SAMUEL T. et ux Nancy Cry	11/20 1851	By Robert Sloan, J.P.
531 CARPENTER, THOMAS D. et ux Martha J. Tedford	3/7 1850	By Jesse Kerr, Jr., J.P.
532 CARE, ROBERT et ux Mary J. Tedford	4/26 1848	By James Law, V.D.M.
* See 2038		
533 CARROLL, ELIJAH et ux Susannah Grisham	8/23 1820	By George Ewing, J.P.
534 CARROLL, WILLIAM et ux Sally Tindel	7/20 1818 issued	By B. W. McCully, J.P.
535 CARSON, ALEXANDER et ux Jane Weir	2/3 1820	By Andrew S. Morrison, V.D.M.
536 CARSON, AMOS et ux Caroline B. Greer	2/21 1832	By Allen H. Mayhies, M.G.
537 CARSON, ANDREW et ux Esther Stone	8/15 1808 issued	No returns
538 CARSON, DAVID et ux Jane Gillespy	10/9 1827	By James Adams, --
539 CARSON, E. M. et ux Martha J. Cochran	11/25 1856	By J. Mathews, J.P.
540 CARSON, HUGH et ux V. A. Burnum	8/20 1853	By Andrew Ferguson, J.P.
541 CARSON, JOHN C. et ux Margaret St. Clair Cates	4/29 1840	By I. Anderson, Pastor of New Providence Church
542 CARSON, JOSEPH et ux Elizabeth Sumples	3/23 1826	By Samuel Hamil, J.P.
543 CARSON, ROBERT et ux Patsey Brease	10/31 1816	"By me." Wm. Gillespie, J.P.
544 CARSON, ROBERT et ux Mary J. Seaton	7/16 1822	By Wm. Griffitts, J.P.
545 CARSON, WILLIAM et ux Rosannah McCully	9/5 1816	By Jos. Alexander, J.P.
546 CARSON, WILLIAM et ux Nancy Hood	8/25 1818 issued	"By me." H. H. Bower- man, J.P.
547 CARTER, AMOS et ux Betsy Rush	2/26 1820 issued	No returns
548 CARTER, BAZEL et ux Elen McCurdy	8/3 1820	By Joseph Vaneett or Vanpelt, --

Names	Date Issue Or Celebrated	By Whom/ Security on Bond
549 CARTER, CHARLES et ux Sarah Lowe	8/3 1819	By Joe Duncan, J.P.
550 CARTER, CHESLEY P. et ux Caroline Grigsby	2/22 1838	Isaac McHean, J.P.
551 CARTER, JOHN A. D. et ux Nancy Irick	8/15 1833 issued	No returns
552 CARTER, JOSIAH et ux Jane Trent	12/13 1832	By William Toole, --
553 CARTER, L. D. et ux Mary E. Saffell	9/17 1856	By A. M. Goodakounts, J.P.
554 CARTER, SAMUEL et ux Sally Campbell	1/16 1819	By J. Cameron, J.P.
555 CARTWRIGHT, PRESTON et ux Susan Jane Brotherton	9/25 1837	"By me." Isaac M. Hair, J.P.
556 CARUTHERS, ARTHUR H. et ux Leva Jane Parsons	7/16 1846	By Joseph A. Hutton, J.P.
557 CARUTHERS, HARVEY H. C. et ux Nancy M. C. Sterling	7/19 1832	By D. Carson, M.G.
558 CARVER, CAMPBELL et ux Polly Davis	7/30 1822	By Samuel Hamill, J.P.
559 CARVER, CORNELIUS et ux Margaret J. Malcom	10/28 1845	By Harvey H. C. Caru- thers, J.P.
560 CARVER, THOMAS et ux Dicy Duncan	5/25 1840	By Wm. Toole, J.P.
561 CARVER, THOMAS et ux Rhoda James	1/20 1842	By William Hendrickson, M.G.
562 CASEY, DAN'L S. et ux Sally Boyd	4/7 1834	By John Maxwell, J.P.
563 CASHEN, OCTAVUS et ux Nancy Wimberly	6/30 1845	By Samuel Pride, J.P.
564 CASHON, RICHARD J. et ux Isabella J. McCully	8/23 1848	By S. J. McReynolds, J.P.
565 CASION, RICHARD et ux Amanda M. Young	2/7 1844	By W. Toole, J.P.
566 CASTON, THOMAS et ux C. M. Hammers	3/14 1852	By John J. Hoover, J.P.
567 CASTEEL, ABRAM et ux Mary Whittenberger	8/2 1818 issued	No returns
568 CASTEEL, JAMES et ux Mary Ann Williams	12/22 1825	By Wm. Griffitts, J.P.
569 CASTEEL, PHILIP et ux Charlotte Franks	9/29 1818	By Samuel Douthit, --
570 CATEN, JESSE et ux Lovis Edmunds	4/9 1840	By Lemuel Adams, J.P.

	Names	Date Issue Or Celebrated	By Whom/ Security on Bond
571	CATON, THOMAS et ux Francis Yount	1/23 1834	
572	CATES, ROUBAN L. et ux Amanda Wilkinson	6/3 1819	
573	CATHCART, JAMES A. et ux Cyntha Hammontree	1/15 1838 issued	No returns
574	CATLETT, JAMES et ux Dolly A. Hatcher	1/12 1854	By Nicholas Brewer, J.P.
575	CAULSON, JOHN et ux Silvany Wood	10/20 1844	By Samuel Wood, J.P.
576	CAVIN, JAMES et ux Elizabeth Toopos	4/29 1823 issued	No returns
577	CAVEN, JAMES W. et ux Elizabeth C. Murphy	2/27 1834	By Wm. McTeer, J.P.
578	CAVETT, JOHN et ux Sally Wiggins	10/6 1819 issued	No returns
579	CAWHORN, ALEXANDER et ux Elizabeth Guy	2/12 1817	By Joe Alexander, J.P.
*	See Cochron (Cochran?)		
580	CAWOOD, E. A. et ux H. B. Vance	9/29 1851	By A. Vance, M.G.
*	See 2046--Keywood		
581	CAYWOOD, MADISON et ux Catherine T. Sterling	8/27 1820	By Jas' Law, J.P. (Outside is Andrew Caywood)
582	CAWOOD, WILLIAM B. et ux Susannah M. McConnell	7/28 1842	By A. Vance, M.G.
583	CAYLOR, ELI et ux Susan Thomas	12/23 1828	By James Cameron, J.P.
584	CAILOR, GEORGE et ux Ann Dunn	11/29 1834 issued	"By me." Johnson Adans, M.G.
585	CAYLOR, GEORGE et ux Nancy Briant	11/5 1837	By Robert Shields, J.P.
586	KAYLOR, JAMES et ux Nancy Walker	3/20 1845 issued 3/13	By John Chambers, M.G.
*	See 1962		
587	CAYLOR, JOHN et ux Martha Briant	7/28 1839	By Roberts Shields, J.P.
588	CAYLOR, WILLIAM et ux Rhoda Dunn	3/3 1825 issued 2/28	By Sam'l C. Davidson, J.P.
*	See 3277, 3278		
589	CHAFFIN, GEORGE H. et ux Eliza T. Cox	1/26 1842	By J. S. Craig, M.G.

Names	Date Issue Or Celebrated	By Whom/ Security on Bond
590 CHAMBERS, MOSES et ux Dorothy Partin	5/10 1826	By Alex'r McColhum, J.P.
591 CHAMBERS, THOMAS et ux Rebecca Frazier	9/21 1839	By Robert Shields, J.P.
592 CHAMBERS, THOMAS D. A. et ux Malinda H. Cumming	4/8 1847 issued	By John Russon, Lic. Dec. M.E. Ch. So. "On same day"
593 CHAMBERS, WILLIAM et ux Rhody Dunn	6/7 1838	By Robert Shields, J.P.
594 CHAMBERS, W. B. et ux Louisa Davis	2/11 1856	By N. Brewer, J.P.
595 CHANDLER, DAVID et ux Mary Jane Porter	8/8 1843	By Leander Wilson, M.G.
596 CHANDLER, JOHN et ux Cynthia A. Clark	4/17 1845	By J. S. Craig, M.G.
597 CHAPMAN, JOHN P. et ux Sally Maclin (We know the family were McLin)	5/1 1821	By Isaac Anderson, M.G.
598 CHAPMAN, WILLIAM et ux Susan Allen	1/29 1845	By Wm. Griffitts, J.P.
599 CHARLES, SAMUEL et ux Pricilla Jones	11/12 1848	By David Spradlin, J.P.
600 CHILDS, JOHN C. et ux Jane Henry	11/30 1850	By F. Pope, M.G.
601 CHILDERS, JOHN et ux Mary Curtuy	11/8 1796	By Rovert Rhea.
602 CHEAT, CHARLES et ux Leties Camron	6/19 1812 issued	"By me." Joseph Walker J.P.
603 CHRISTIFER, WILLIAM et ux Mary A. Privett	8/12 1858	By Wm. W. Nuchols, Esq/
604 CITCHENS, CHAPMAN et ux Sarah Bird	1/16 1810 issued	No returns See Kitchens 2090
605 CLABOUGH, CHARLES et ux Lucretia Moloch	10/2 1840	By Eli Richy, J.P.
606 CLAYBO, WILLIAM et ux Elizabeth Hanley	9/23 1838	By Robert Shields, J.P.
607 CLAMPET, HENRY et ux Patsy Bolen	3/23 1829 issued	"By me." Sam'l Henry J.P.
608 CLAMPITT, JAMES et ux Elizabeth Boling	2/14 1843	By W. P. Cumming, J.P.
609 CLARK, DELIZON W. et ux Ann J. Conger	8/9 1823	By Isaac Amderson, M.G.
610 CLARK, HARVEY P. et ux Mary A. Dearmond	5/6 1857	By Wm. Billue, M.G.

	Name	Date issue Or Celebrated	By Whom/ Security on Bond
611	CLARK, JAMES et ux Esther Ann Bell	9/8 1823 issued	"By me." James Turk, J.P.
612	CLARK, JOHN et ux Letitia Sharp (on one-other Litty) (no signature)	1/29 1800 issued Feb 3 1980	By Jas. Gllespie
613	CLARK, JOHN et us Matilda Thompson	11/1 1838	By Isaac Amderson, P.N. P.Ch.
614	CLARK, JOHN et ux Priscilla B. Thompson	12/5 1859 issued	No returns
615	CLARK, THOMAS C. et ux Mary E. McCrosky	9/18 1850 issued	"By me in Sept 1850" Isaac Amderson, M.G.
616	CLARK, ROBERT et ux Ellender Parker	10/3 1826 issued	"By me" A. Ish, J.P.
617	CLARK, SEVIER et ux Elizabeth Ingram	7/7 1825 issued	No returns
618	CLARK, WM. B et ux E. E. Davis	6/5 1850	By John Russom, L.D.M. E.Ch. South
619	CLARK, WILLIAM C. et ux Nancy Davis	1/26 1842	By W. Toole, J.P.
620	Clemens, Henry et ux Elizabeth Everett	8/18 1836	By Fielding Pope, M.G.
621	CLEMENS, HENRY et ux Margaret McDaniel	5/18 1858	By Christian Long, J.P.
622	CLEMENS, JOHN A. et ux Elizabeth Cavin	10/4 1855	By J. F. Bunker, M.G.
623	CLEMENS, JOS' et ux Jane Cavin	2/17 1852	By C. Long, J.P.
624	CLEMENS, SAMUEL et ux Martha L. Teafateler	5/18 1836	By Wm. Toole, J.P.
625	CLEMENS, SAMUEL et ux Mary Headrick	8/12 1852	By S. J. McReynolds, J.P.
626	CLEMINS, WILLIAM H. et ux Mary W. Broady	12/8 1859	By John J. Robinson, M.G.
627	CLIFTON, JAMES et ux Sally Lee	12/1 1818	By J. Waugh, J.P.
628	CLINE, JOEL P. et ux Sarah J. Martin	7/24 1855	By John J. Robinson, M.G.
629	COACH, JAMES et ux Defeny Hendrixson	11/13 1833	By John Ferguson, J.P.
630	CLOATFELTER, D. H. et ux C. Y. McDonald	12/11 1851	By William A. Lawson, M.G.

	Names	Date Issue Or Celebrated	By Whom/ Security on Bond
631	COATS, JOHN et ux Sarah Rogers	1/12 1796 issued	Bond: Jas. Houston
632	COBB, SAMUEL et ux Mildred Howard	11/10 1846 issued	"By me." B. Abernathey M.E.P.Ch.
633	COCHRAN, BARNABAS et ux Sarah J. Kerr	12/21 1848	By James M. Tulloch, J.P.
634	COCHRAN, CYRUS et ux D. Caroline Henry	11/19 1855	By J. S. Craig, M.G.
635	COCHRAN, DANIEL et ux Eleanor Moore	3/1 1796 issued	Bond: John Singleton
636	COCHRAN, HUGH L. et ux Margaret Reagan	9/4 1797 issued	Bond: George Blackburn
637	COCHRAN, ISAAC et ux Polly Kelly	4/10 1799 issued	Bond: John Cochran
638	COCHRAN, ISAAC W. et ux Nancy Henry	1/9 1849	By Harvey J. G. Caruthers, J.P.
639	COCHRAN, JAMES et ux Polly Reid	10/8 1812 issued	No returns
640	COCHRAN, JAMES et ux Ruhana Irwin	7/22 1834	By A. Vance, M.G.
641	COCHRAN, JAMES B. et ux Hester A. Henry	1/1 1851	By Andrew Ferguson, J.P.
642	COCHRAN, JOHN et ux Jane Orr	1/8 1822	By Wm. Gault, J.P.
643	COCHRAN, JOHN et us Betsey Huffman	3/13 1828	By Samuel Hanill, J.P.
644	CAUGHORN, JOHN W. et us Hanna Johnston (Groom signed as above; Clerk "Mlaughen")	3/18 1802	Bond: Robert Pearoe
645	COCHRAN, ROBERT et ux Polly Rhea,	2/10 1825	By Wm. Gault, J.P.
646	COCHRAN, SAMUEL et ux Eliza Adams	8/10 1843	By Leonard Wood, J.P.
647	COCHRAN, SAMUEL D. et ux Amelia M. Dunn	10/18 1842	By Robert Shields, J.P.
648	COCHRAN, WILLIAM et ux Lucy Hammontree	11/12 1829	By Sam'l Hamill, J.P.
649	COCHRAN, W. A. et ux Mary A. Carpenter	10/30 1851	By T. K. Munsey, M.G. of M.E. Ch. So.
*	See 677		
650	COLE, ANDREW et ux Mary Ann Robertson	12/24 1827 issued	No returns
651	COLE, ISAAC et ux Rebecca Keltner	9/25 1830	By J. P. Montgomery, J.P.

Names	Date Issue Or Celebrated	By Whom/ Security on Bond
652 COLBERT, ISREAL P. et ux Ruth A. Sherrell	8/27 1842	By Jonson Adams, M.G.
653 COLBOURN, THOMAS et ux Issibella Chamberland	12/15 1808 issued	No returns
654 COLLINS, B. B. et ux I. J. Vance	7/17 1850	By A. Vance, M.G.
655 COLLINS, JAMES C. et ux Mary V. Hughes	4/4 1858	By William Kerr, J.P.
656 COLLINS, JOSEPH et ux Isabella Haines	12/14 1820	By Jos Duncan, J.P.
657 COLLINS, MATTHEW et ux Rachel Hendriexson	10/18 1836	By Lemuel Adams, J.P.
658 COLLINS, MATHEW et ux Louis Colliher	2/27 1840	By John Staley, J.P.
659 COLLINS, WILLIAM et ux Mary Sparks	2/13 1855	By David Spradlin, J.P.
660 COLLINS, ZACHARIAH et ux Rebecca J. Davis	8/12 1852	By David Spradlin, J.P.
661 COULTER, A. A. et ux Margaret A. Morton	1/2 1853	By Fielding Pope, M.G.
662 COLTER, ALEXANDER S et ux Betsy Cumming	2/23 1819	By J. Cameron, J.P.
663 COULTER, ANDREW et ux Nancy A. W. James	3/27 1828	By W. Hend _____ Esq.
664 COULTER, CHARLES et ux Isabella Tipton	10/20 1830 issued	No returns
665 COLTER, ELISON et ux Mary C. Lambert	8/18 1859	By James D. Lawson, M.G.
666 COALTER, JAMES et ux Polly Rhea	12/31 1829	By Sam'l Henry, J.P.
667 COULTER, JAMES et ux Catherine Everett	9/17 1857	By W. W. Nuchols, J.P.
668 COULTER, JAMES R. et ux Margaret Keeble	1/22 1852	By Wm. Bilhue. M.G.
669 COALTER, JOHN et ux Katherine Kitchens	5/17 1828	By Thomas Billue, J.P.
670 COLTER, JOHN et ux Elizabeth McBrient	8/13 1835	By Frederic Emmett, J.P.
671 COULTER, JOHN et us Ann W. Sharp	9/23 1852	By Wm. M. Burnett
672 COULTER, RICHARD et ux Meina Ketchens	5/19 1799	Bond: John Snider
673 COLTER, ROBERT et ux Jane Perkins	3/4 1855	By Wm. W. Nuchols, J.P.

Names	Date Issue Or Celebrated	By Whom/ Security on Bond
674 COLTER, STEPHEN et ux Hannah Caylor	7/26 1832	By Frederic Emmett, J.P.
675 COLTER, WILLIAM et ux Jane Murphy	7/19 1846	By Frederic Emmett, J.P.
676 COLVILLE, JOSEPH et ux Martha Smartt	12/21 1802 issued	Bond: Gid'n Blackburn
677 COFFIN, JOHN M. et ux Mary K. Wilson	3/1 1838	By Isaac Amderson, M.G.
* See 649, 691		
678 CONDRON, JOHN Rachel Vaught	6/27 1805 issued	No returns
679 CONGER, DAVID et ux Elizabeth Young	3/22 1831	By David McKemy, J.P.
680 CONNER, FRANKLIN, D. et ux Jane Greer	7/25 1839	By A. Vance, M.G.
681 CONNER, JAMES et ux Lucinda McCool	2/6 1817	By H. H. Bowerman, J.P.
682 CONNER, JAMES et ux Harriett A. Kuing (Ruing?)	11/5 1835	By A. Vance, M.G.
683 CONNER, JAMES et ux Margaret Fitzegeral	2/7 1858 issued	No returns
684 CONNER, JOHN et ux Leah Henson	2/22 1846	By B. F. Duncan, J.P.
685 CONNER, LEONARD et ux Margaret M. Collins (McCallen?)	2/19 1859	By A. Vance, M.G.
686 CONNER, TARRENCE et ux Evelience McWil- liams	10/8 1833	By Andrew Vance, M.G.
687 CONNER, TARRENCE et ux Polly Yount	7/18 1822	By Jos' Duncan, J.P.
688 CONNER, THOMAS et ux Dorcas Wimberly	9/18 1849	By L. L. McFarling, J.P.
689 CONNER, WILLIAM et ux Rachel Sterling	2/6 1849	By James Law, M.G.
690 CONNER, W. C. et ux Nancy M McAnderson	12/28 1857	By W. W. Bayless, J.P.
691 COMPTON, JAMES C. et ux Sarah A. Best	5/17 1855	By J. M. Stansberry, M.G.
* See 677		
692 COOK, ALESANDER et ux Louisa Ball	1/22 1818	By Wm. Williamson, J.P.
693 COOK CHRISTOPHER et ux Margaret Crawley	9/28 1845	By Robert Porter, J.P.

Names	Date Issue Or Celebrated	By Whom/ Security on Bond
694 COOK, C. W. et ux Haseltine Smith	4/2 1859 issued	"By me." James M. Lane, J.P.
695 COOK, GEORGE et ux Nancy Craw	5/8 1826	By S. Douthit, E.M.E.Ch.
696 COOKE, JAMES et ux Margaret Gould	1/22 1802 issued	Bond: James Sloan
697 COOK, JAMES et ux Mary Rolston	8/19 1846 issued	"By me." John Morton, J.P.
698 COOK, JOHN M. et ux Mancy Morton	12/24 1829	By Arch'd Maxwell, J.P.
699 COOK, PETER et ux Caroline Roddy	9/14 1838	By Robt Porter, J.P.
700 COOK, SAM'L et ux Jane C. Robbins	9/3 1857	By Spenseer Henry, M.G.
701 COOLEY, EDWARD et ux Nancy Woody	11/28 1844	By Daniel Taylor, J.P.
702 COOLEY, MICAJAH et ux Caroline Redmond	5/27 1858	By Wm. M. Brickell, J.P.
703 COUP, BENJAMIN et ux Amey Pitman	4/3 1819	By Wm. Willamson, J.P.
704 COOPE, DAVID et ux Kity Nisman See also Cupp	3/13 1802 issued	Bond: Abraham Phelips
705 COPE, JACB et ux REbecca Hawkngs	3/4 1858	By James M. Tulloch, J.P.
706 COPE, JAMES et ux Polly Hutton	1/20 1825	By Arch'd Maxwell, J.P.
707 COPE MARTIN L. et ux Martha Love	2/10 1842	By Joseph A. Hutton, J.P.
708 COOPE, SAMUEL et ux Clara Williams	9/8 1826	By Elbt F. Sevier, M.G.
709 COOPER, A. A. et ux Aleyzana Chambers	3/3 1858	By N. Brewer, J.P.
710 COOPER, JOHN R. et ux Margaret Reuen (Rouen)	12/28 1848	By Curran Lemons, J.P.
711 COOPER, WILLIAM et ux Catherine Davis	2/10 1821	Bond: David McKamy
712 COOPER, WM. et ux Margaret C. Davis	10/2 1853	By Daniel A. Emert
713 COOPER, WILLIAM et ux Barbra Campbell	12/17 1856	By Curran Lemons, J.P.
714 COPLAND, ALFRED et ux Nicy Bledsoe Thomas	9/17 1834	By J.H.R.G. Gardner,

Names	Date Issue Or Celebrated	By Whom/ Security on Bond
715 COPELAND, JAMES et ux Ann Cameron	9/11 1800 issued	Bond: James Craig
716 COPELNAD, JOEL et ux Rebecka Huchison	9/14 1798 issued	Bond: John Huchison
717 COPELAND, LEWIS et ux Wilmoth Ann Tuck	8/18 1846	By James H. Donaldson, J.P.
718 COPELAND, ALEXANDER et ux Ann Eliza Low	8/6 1832	By Wm. Bilhue, M.G.
719 COPLAND, DAVID et ux Susannah Craig	6/25 1800 issued	Bond: Jas Craig
720 COPPENBARGER, JOHN et ux Matilda Shugart	3/11 1818 issued	No return
721 COPPOCK, JOHN et ux Patsy Williams	3/24 1818 issued	By "R. B. McCully, J.P."
722 COPPOCK, JOHN M. et ux Elizabeth Hammontree	3/10 1847	By Wesley Earnest, J.P.
723 COPPOCK, JOSIAH et ux Diannah Hamerk	9/10 1828	By S. Douthit, E.M.E.Ch.
724 CORLEY, JOHN E. et ux Margaret A. Foute	7/22 1852	By Issac Anderson, Pas- tor New Providence Ch. Maryville, Tenn. Blt. Co.
725 COSLON, JOHN et ux Sally Woblet	9/26 1832	By Leeroy Noble, J.P.
726 COSTNER, PHILIP et ux Polly Hays	11/9 1837	By Henry Hamil, J.P.
727 COSTON, THOMAS et ux Eliza Haire	1/22 1828 issued	No returns
728 COTTRELL, ANDREW J. et ux Sarah White	2/2 1843	By Samuel Tullock, J.P.
729 COTTRELL, JOHN W. et ux Malinda J. Samples	9/21 1852	By James M. Tulloch, J.P.
730 COTTRELL, RICHARD et ux Matilda Vaught	12/29 1821	By Wm. Williamson, J.P.
731 COTTRELL, WILLIAM T. et ux Sarah Matilda Rich	12/25 1842	By Samuel Tulloch, J.P.
732 COULBOURN, WILLIAM et ux Caty Kee	9/28 1830	By Alexander Stewart, J.P.
733 COULSON, JABEZ et ux Jane Jones	7/20 1837	By Rev. J. Dyke
734 COVINGTON, JAMES et ux Rebecca Johnson	11/11 1841	By James Ray
735 COVINGTON, JAMES et ux Martha Donaldson	10/7 1852	By B. F. Duncan, J.P.

Names	Date Issue Or Celebrated	By Whom/ Security on Bond
736 COVENTON, RICHARD et ux Rebecka Cain	7/23 1808 issued	No returns
737 COWAN, ALFRED et ux Jane Cook	3/2 1826 issued	"By me." Samuel Montgomery, Esq.
738 COWAN, ANDREW et ux Esther F. Houston	9/25 1816	By I. Anderson,--
739 COWAN, ANDREW et ux Margaret Allen	3/29 1853	By Joseph Peeler, M.G.
740 COWAN, COLUMBUS et ux Mary J. Sharp	8/22 1850	By Ralph E. Tedford, M.G.
741 COWAN, GEORGE W. et ux Mary L. Clark	12/2 1839	By Isaac Anderson, P.N. P.Ch.
742 COWAN, GEORGE W. et ux Margaret A. Eagleton	10/6 1846	By Isaac Anderson, P.N. P.Ch.
743 COWAN, JAMES et ux Mary Montgomery	4/23 1800 issued	Bond: Samuel Cowan
744 COWAN, JOHN et ux Rosannah Gillespy	8/23 1797 issued	Bond: James Gillespy
745 COWAN, ROBERT et ux Nancy Martin	8/20 1797 issued	Bond: James Houston
746 COWAN, SAMUEL et ux Jane Houston	7/18 1810 issued	No Returns
747 COWAN, SAMUEL F. et ux Elizabeth J. McCulloch	12/6 1841	By John S. Craig, M.G.
748 COWAN, WILLIAM B. et ux Malinda E. Cobb	1/1 1850 issued	By Berry Abernathey,-- "On Thursday after date"
749 CONDEN, JOHN et ux Mary J. Hynds	9/22 1859	By W. M. Burnett,--
750 COWDEN, SAMUEL et ux Nancy Keller	3/4 1832	By James Hedrixson, J.P.
751 COX, BENJAMIN et ux Sarah Coppock	2/20 1847	By Alexander McClain, J.P.
752 COX, C. L. et ux Nancy E. Myers	7/4 1852	By William Colburn, J.P.
753 COX HENRY M. et ux Eliza Russell	4/1 1858	By Rev. Sam'l B. West
754 COX, JAMES K. et ux Sarah E. Miers	12/11 1857	By Wm. M. Brickell, J.P.
755 COX JESSE et ux Delila Dourghity	9/7 1841 issued	Bond: J. W. Haire
756 COX, J. S. et ux Ellen Rhoddy	1/10 1849	By Alex O. George, J.P.
757 COX NATHAN et ux Frances Tuck	11/13 1835 issued	"By me." A. Ish, J.P.

Names	Date Issue Or Celebrated	By Whom/ Security on Bond
758 COX, WILLIAM et ux Nancy Nicholson	9/27 1818	By I. Anderson,--
759 COXION, WILLIAM J et ux Cynthia Gardner	11/5 1840	By Wm McTeer, J.P.
760 CRAFT, ELIAS et ux Polly Kilbourne	3/6 1818 issued 2/28	By Is. Amderson
761 CRAIG, ALEX'R et ux Susanna Logan	5/23 1800 issued	Bond: Hugh Ferguson
762 CRAIG, HUGH et ux Rena Parker	10/22 1844	By Harvey H. C. Carru- thers, J.P.
763 CRAIG, HUGH H. et ux Mary E. Gardner	4/11 1855	By Andrew Ferguson, J.P.
764 CRAIG, JAMES W. et ux Jane Torbet	3/27 1837	By A. Vance, M.G.
765 CRAIG, JOHN S. et ux Sidney N. Houston	5/13 1841	By Isaac Anderson, P.N. P.Ch.
766 CRAIG, THES' et ux Jane Ferguson	10/31 1855	By H. Thompson, J.P.
767 CRAIG, WILLAIM et ux Esther Montgomery	7/5 1802 issued	Bond: Alexander Mont- gomery
768 CRAIG, WILLIAM et ux Eliza Wimberly	1/7 1841	By Alex' McCollom, Esq.
769 CRAIG, WM. B. et ux Mary C. McTeer	8/6 1854	By James M. Tulloch, J.P.
770 CRAWFORD, HARVERY H. et ux Nancy Jeffers	2/9 1844	By JOhn Tipton, J.P.
771 CRAWFORD, LINNUS et ux Susan Camp	1/1 1829	By William Toole, G.P.
772 CRAWLEY, WM. et ux Margaret Anderson	8/14 1856	By W. A. Lawson, M.G.
773 CRESAP, ROGER E. et ux Amgeline Thompson	7/20 1830	By Issac Anderson, P.N. P.Ch.
774 CRESWELL, ANDREW et ux Ann Gamble	10/11 1842	By Fielding Pope, M.G.
775 CRESWELL, SAMUEL M. et ux Catherine S. William	4/5 1833	By William McTeer, J.P.
776 CRESWELL, SAMUEL M. et ux Nancy C. Begle	11/8 1846	By F. Pope, M.G.
777 CRESWELL, WILLIAM E. et ux Elizabeth McAfee	2/8 1847	By Fielding Pope, M.G.
778 CREWS, JAMES M. et ux Katherine 3rakebill See Cruse-Cruze-Cruise	1/16 1838	By Ben Cunningham, J.P.
779 CRIGER, RUFUS M. et ux Martha P. Cummings	12/16 1852	By Sam'l L. Yearout,

Names	Date Issue Or Celebrated	By Whom Security on Bond
780 CRISP, ABLE et ux Polly Ann Porter	2/22 1821	By Wm. Williamson, J.P.
781 CRISP, GEORGE et ux Sally Anderson	2/23 1845	By David Spradlin, J.P.
782 CRISP, JAMES et ux Martha O'Donnell	5/19 1859	By Harvey Thompson, J.P.
783 CRISP, JOEL et ux Adaline Lundy	3/26 1857	By James Mathews, J.P.
784 CRISP, RICE T. et ux Sarah J. Tuch	4/8 1852	By JOhn B. Hale, J.P.
785 CRITTINGTON, HENRY et ux Polly Bowerman	7/4 1815	No returns
786 CROLEY, WILLIAM et ux Jane Chamberlain See Corly 724	12/4 1813	No returns
787 CROMWELL, ANDREW et ux Margaret Bain	1/15 1829	By John Ferguson, J.P.
788 CROMWELL, THOS' S. et ux Sally Hash	11/16 1830	By David McKamy, J.P.
789 CROSS, GEORGE W. et ux Hester Ann Curtis	12/22 1846	By James Henry, J.P.
790 CROWDER, A. M. et ux Susan Birchfield	6/4 1855	By David Spradlin, J.P.
791 CROWDER, HOBBS et ux Ann Kounse	12/24 1834 issued	By John Russom, D.M.E. "Same day by me"
792 CRUMBY, ASA G. et ux Mary J. Kackney	10/14 1847	By William Colburn, J.P.
793 CRUMLY, ISAAC H. et ux Rebecca L. Hackney	7/12 1844	By William Colburn, J.P.
794 CRUSE, GIDEON et ux Nancy Johnston	11/3 1825	By George Ewing, J.P.
795 CRUSE, JOHN W. et ux Margaret Sherrill	3/25 1849	By Lewis J. Newman,--
796 CRUISE, JOSEPH et ux Mary Johnson	1/7 1824	By James Cumming, Trav- eling Deacon M.E.Ch.
797 CRUSE, PRYOR et ux Caroline Murphy	8/10 1853	By J. C. Martin, J.P.
798 CRUSE, ROBERT et ux Patsy Palmer	9/2 1849	By Adam Haun, J.P.
799 CRUSH, WILLIAM et ux Jenny Gibbs	3/9 1819	No returns, Bond: Wm. Early
800 CRYS, DAVID et ux Elizabeth Tuck	1/2 1833	By A. Ish, J.P.
801 CRYE, ELIAS et ux Nancy J. Williamson	8/21 1851	By James M. Tulloch, J. P.

Names	Date Issue Or Celebrated	By Whom Security on Bond
802 JOHN CRYE et ux Sarah C. Bast?	9/30 1857	By James M. Tulloch, J.P.
803 CULBERSON, JASON et ux Mary Rowan	2/10 1840	By Wm. Henry, J.P.
804 CULTON JAMES et ux Peggy Heir	1/28 1801	Bond: Joseph Walker
805 Culton, JAMES A. et ux Mary Jane Runions	8/4 1842	By A. Vance, M.G.
806 CULTON, ROBERT H. et ux Lucinda Jane Henderson	11/12 1840	By Andrew Vance, M.G.
807 CULTON, ROBERT H. et ux Mary A. McConnell	9/22 1846	By A. Vance, M.G.
808 CUMMINGS, ALEXANDER M. et ux Mary C. Walker	9/4 1848	By Spencer Henry, M.G.
809 CUMMING, FRANKLIN et ux Elizabeth Peery	12/16 1846	By John Russum, M.G.
810 CUMMINGS, HUGH et ux Jane Campbell	12/23 1815 issued	"By me" (No signature)
811 CUMMING, JOSEPH V. et ux Malinda H. Hafley	7/6 1837	By F. Pope, M.G.
812 CUMMIONS, JOSEPH et ux Elizabeth Hutsell	11/8 1845	By S. J. McReynolds, J.P.
813 CUMMING, ROBERT S. et ux Ann C. McMahan	11/30 1835	No returns
814 CUMMINS, URIAH et ux Telitha Gray	12/10 1847 issued	No returns
815 COMMING, URIAH et ux Eliza Tallent	12/25 1847	By James Henry, J.P.
816 CUMMINS, WILLIAM et ux Jane Night	7/1 1824	By Hugh Bogle, J.P.
817 CUMMINGS, WILLIAM et ux Isabella Tallent	2/2 1848	By William Colburn, J.P.
818 CUMMIMGS, WM. P. L. et ux Mary Bogle	3/20 1838	By Fielding Pope, M.G.
819 CUNNINGHAM, ALFRED C. et ux Isabel Hutton	8/31 1836	By A. Vance, M.G.
820 CUNNINGHAM, ALFRED et ux Polly Hatcher	3/17 1843	By Johnson Adams, M.G.
821 CUNNINGHAM, ALLEN P. et ux Mary Cowden	11/23 1849	By M. Kounts, J.P.
822 CUNNINGHAM, BENJAMIN et ux Sarah M. Hille (Hise?)	10/9 1845	By John Clark, J.P.

	Names	Date Issue Or Celebrated	By Whom Security on Bond
823	CUNNINGHAM, DAVID et ux Pressey Lenney	1/13 1798	Bond: Miles Cunningham
824	CUNNINGHAM, HARDEN et ux Rachel Harper	4/9 1823	By A. B. Gamble, J.P.
825	CUNNINGHAM, HUGH et ux Mary Morrice	3/11 1824	By Joseph Duncan, J.P.
826	CUNNINGHAM, HUGH et ux Julian Davis	2/4 1841	By Samuel Tulloch, J.P.
827	CUNNINGHAM, JONATHAN et ux Betsy Chitty	3/2 1816	By Hugh Bogle, J.P.
828	CUNNINGHAM, JOHN et ux Nancy Orr	7/28 1824	By Samu'l Montgomery, Esq.
829	CUNNINGHAM, J. C. et ux F. A. Best	5/24 1854	By Green B. Saffell, J.P.
830	CUNNINGHAM, MILES et ux Mary Denney	5/22 1797 issued	Bond: David Cunningham
831	CUNNINGHAM, MILES et ux Betsey Chermley	8/23 1821	By Wm. Williamson, J.P.
832	CUNNINGHAM, HU et ux Lucinda McGhee	6/11 1818	By Andrew S. Morrison, V.D.M.
833	CUNNINGHAM, WILEY H. et ux Sarah Brakebill	6/17 1849	By Lewis J. Newman, J.P.
834	CUNNINGHAM, WM. et ux Hannah Torbit	1/3 1820	By Samuel Douthit, M.G.
835	CUPP, ADAM et ux Peggy Capshaw	10/18 1815 issued	No returns
*	See 704 Coope		
836	CUPP, DAVID G. et ux Nancy McDaniel	4/4 1841	By Wm. Rorex, J.P.
837	CUPP, DAVID G. et ux Susan B. Yearout	10/11 1846	By John P. Keny, J.P.
838	CUPP, FREDERICH et ux Nancy Capshaw	7/27 1815 issued	No returns
839	CUPP, GEORGE et ux Ruth Emeline Hill	11/27 1823	No returns
840	CUPP, GEORGE et ux Rebecca Murphy	9/7 1824	By David Logan, Minister
841	CUPP, GEORGE et ux Lucindy Ridle	8/19 1854 issued	No returns
842	CUPP, JACOB et ux Susan Lingumphelter	4/20 1819 issued	No returns
843	CUPP, JACOB et ux Clarenda Rogers	1/3 1860	By A. Boyd, J.P.

	Names	Date Issue Or Celebrated	By Whom/ Security on Bond
844	CUPP, JOHN et ux Sally BAker	9/26 1809 issued	No returns
845	CURLER, JOSEPH et ux Nance M. Cannon	9/27 1832	By B. Abernathy, L.E.
846	CURTES, SIRUS et ux Polly Shook	1/19 1817 issued	"Executed" by me John Waugh, J.P.
847	CUSICK, DAVID et ux Elinor Williams	3/4 1835	By Wm. McTeer, J.P.
848	CUSICK, JOHN B. et ux Hulda Durham	10/9 1799 issued	Bond: William Durham
849	DAILEY, DOUTHATE et ux Epha M. Downey	2/8 1847	By Harvey H. C. Car- ruthers, J.P.
850	DAILEY, JACOB et ux Matilda Tucker	12/15 1825	By Charles H. Warren, G.P.
851	DAILEY, WILEY B. et ux Lucy Ann Jeffreys	10/1 1857	By A. R. James, J.P.
852	DAVIS, ALFRED et ux Susan Spradling	3/11 1847	By Samuel Tulloch, J.P.
853	DAVIS, ALLEN W. et ux Mary Houston	3/7 1820	By Wm. Lowery, J.P.
854	DAVIS, ASA et ux Rody Read	3/10 1818	By Alex B. Gamble, J.P.
855	DAVIS, B. W. et ux D. J. Law?	8/26 1855	By N. Brewer, J.P.

(Found had duplicated several names and so had to cut out and go over and in that way FIVE Numbers are omitted, and this page not full. I also, afterwards, found Bond where had entered License, and Licenses here has entered bond, so one olidated into one entry)

W. E. Parham, October 25, 1832

	Names	Date Issue Or Celebrated	By Whom/ Security on Bond
861	DAVIS, CALEB F. et ux Susan J. Gamble	4/20 1854	By A. Boyd, Esq.
862	DAVIS, ELIJAH et ux Hannah Whitehead	9/25 1834	By Spencer Henry, J.P.
863	DAVIS, GEORGE et ux Alsy Rhea?	5/13 1819	By Hugh Bogle, J.P.
864	DAVIS, GEORGE et ux Catherine Garner	6/16 1849	By John Tipton, J.P.
865	DAVIS, G. C. et ux Barbra Thomas	10/13 1856	By W. T. Dowell, M.G.

Names	Date Issue Or Celebrated	By Whom/ Security on Bond
866 DAVIS, G. T. et ux Martha J. Hecks	1/27 1859	By A. R. James, J.P.
867 DAVIS, GEE. W. et ux Sarah Davis	12/21 1856	By Michael Kounts, J.P.
868 DAVIS, H. J. et ux Susannah Best	8/10 1854	By James M. Tulloch, J.P.
869 DAVIS, JAMES et ux Catherine Brewer	11/14 1826	By James Cameron, J.P.
870 DAVIS, JAMES et ux Cherry Phillips	1/1 1827 issued 1/3 1827	By John Rusam, M.G.
871 DAVIS, JAMES et ux Betty Ann Macafee	3/2 1830	By Wm. McTeer, J.P.
872 DAVIS, JAMES T. et ux Margaret Davis	4/5 1846	By W. R. Flynn, J.P.
873 DAVIS, JESSE et ux Elizabeth Garner	3/27 1828	By Samuel Hamill, J.P.
874 DAVIS, JOHN et ux Polly Low	1/3 1822	By A. B. Gamble, J.P.
875 DAVIS, JOHN et ux Elizabeth Kieer	8/2 1831	By Wm. Williamson, J.P.
876 DAVIS, JOHN et ux Martha Jane Maxwell	9/11 1834	By Isaac Anderson, M.G.
877 DAVIS, JOHN et ux Sally Hix	4/8 1838	By Rev. William Cooper
878 DAVIS, JOHN et ux Dolly Strickland (colrd)	3/4 1858	By JOhn Clark, J.P.
879 DAVIS, JOHN V. et ux Becky Tipton	4/18 1833	By William McTeer, J.P.
880 DAVIS, JOHN W. et ux Nancy Jane Cunningham	8/20 1839	By William McTeer, J.P.
881 DAVIS, JOHN M. et ux Malinda James	5/16 1851	By Isaac Anderson, M.G.
882 DAVIS, JOSEPH et ux Elizabeth Gillespie	4/1 1806 issued	No returns
883 DAVIS, MARTIN et ux Caroline Bowling	1/6 1858	By John Clark, J.P.
884 DAVIS, MARTIN et ux Eliza Bowling	6/2 1858	By Wm. W. Nuchols, J.P.
885 DAVIS, MORGAN et ux Elizabeth Hammon- tree	2/22 1827	By Billy Holloway, M.G. of Babtist Order
886 DAVIS, MOSES et ux Polly Smith	1/29 1816 issued	No retunrs

Names	Date Issue Or Celebrated	By Whom/ Security on Bond
887 DAVIS, MCLIN et ux Elizabeth McCullah	4/13 1857	By James M. Tulloch, J.P.
888 DAVIS, PETER et ux Hannah Harris	7/29 1818 issued	No returns
889 DAVIS, PHILIP et ux Mary Law	12/14 1834 issued May 17 1834	By Fedrick Emett, J.P.
890 DAVIS, PHILIP et ux Jane McClenihan	8/7 1846	By John Chambers, M.G.
891 DAVIS, REPS J. et ux Malinda Singleton	12/24 1839	By Rev. L. S. Marshall
891 DAVIS, RICHARD et ux Betsey Murray	6/28 1830 issued	"Celebrated by me" C. W. Parker
892 DAVIS, ROBERT C. et ux Elizabeth White	12/26 1843	By Samuel Tulloch, J.P.
893 DAVIS, SAMUEL et ux Ann McClannahan	3/10 1843	By Robert Shields, J.P.
894 DAVIS, STEPHEN et ux Mary Keeble	4/5 1838	By James Henry, J.P.
895 DAVIS, THOMAS et ux Elizabeth Hix	11/7 1840	By Robert Shields, J.P.
896 DAVIS, THOMAS et ux Lovenia Ogle	5/2 1857	By John Clark, J.P.
897 DAVIS, T. O. C. et ux S. E. M. Bright	10/27 1853	By W. M. Brickell, J.P.
898 DAVIS, TORENCE O. et ux Rebecca Jane Beteman	10/4 1855	By W. M. Brickell, J. P.
899 DAVIS, WILLAIM et ux Sally Bowers	5/3 1821	By Hugh Bogle, J.P.
900 DAVIS, WILLIAM et ux Anna Conners	6/5 1822	By Hugh Tarbet, J.P.
901 DAVIS, WILLIAM et ux Sarah Stewart	11/18 1827	By James Cameron, J.P.
902 DAVIS, WILLIAM et ux Susan Taylor	2/22 1827	By Wm. Williamson, J.P.
903 DAVIS, WILLOUGHBY et ux Polly Ormond (Armond or Dearmond)	11/1 1832	By Wm. McTeer, J.P.
904 DAVIS, WILLIAM et ux Mahala Goodman	2/8 1838	By William Colburn, J.P.
905 DAVIS, WILLIAM et ux Mary C. McElray	12/9 1854	By Daniel W. Emmet, J.P.
906 DAVIS, WILLIE C. et ux Nancy C. McMurray	10/3 1848	By Wm. C. Lee, J.G.

Names	Date Issue Or Celebrated	By Whom/ Security on Bond
907 DAVIS, WM. M. et ux Sarah Davis	12/21 1848	By John Russom, M.G.
908 DAVIS, WM. P. et ux Mary Edmonds	11/17 1853	By William Colburn, J.P.
909 DAWSON, JOSEPH F. et ux Mary M. Wiley	5/15 1856	By James M. Tulloch, J.P.
910 DEEN, SILAS et ux Rebeka Rogers	10/2 1821	By A. B. Gamble, J.P.
911 DEEN, SILAS et ux Lucind Foreter	5/1 1825	By Hugh Bogle, J.P.
912 Deen, Silas et ux Kitsy Davis	2/18 1827	By John Rusam, M.G.
913 DEARMOND, JAMES et ux Charlotte Wrinkle	2/13 1855	By William Lawson, M.G.
914 EARMOND, JNO. et ux Jane Chandler	12/21 1854	By Wm. Billue, M.G.
915 DEARMOND, JOHN F. et ux Margaret Hitch	9/14 1826	By William Eagleton, M.G.
916 DEARMOND, RICHARD et ux Cynthia Hix (is Hitch?)	2/10 1831	By Wm. Billue, M.G. (Richard Dearmond)
917 DEARMOND, ROBERT et ux Monarky Lucket	11/8 1825	By William Eagleton, M.G.
918 DARMOND, ST CLAIR et ux Clark, E. F.	5/3 1852	By Isaac Anderson, M.G.
919 DEARMOND, THOS et ux Elizabeth Hair	1/23 1805 issued	No returns
920 DEARMOND, THOMAS G. et ux Elizabeth Coldwell	11/6 1817	By I. Anderson
921 DEARMOND, WILLIAM H. et ux Mary Childres	12/30 1834	By Wm. Billue, M.B.
922 DEAVER, WILLIAM et ux Elizabeth Mackey	3/1 1821	By A. B. Gamble, J.P.
923 DEVER, JOHN REV. et ux Eliza Freeman	5/22 1822	By David Adams, M.G.
924 DEBUSK, ROBERT et ux Margaret Prow	12/23 1841	By Isaac Anderson, M.G.
925 DELOZIER, ANDREW et ux Clarinda Davis	3/10 1842	By Ben Cummingham, J.P.
926 DELOZIER, ASA et ux Caroline Hamil	6/17 1849	By B. B. Billue, M.G. (R. B. Bilhue) M.G.
927 DELOZIER, C et ux Vaney E. Lebow	1/9 1856	By W. A. Lawson, M.G. Bond: J. Donalson
928 DELOZIER, EDWARD et ux Sarah Davis	4/22 1324	By Hugh Bogle, J.P.

	Names	Date Issue Or Celebrated	By Whom/ Security on Bond
929	DELOZIER, JAMES et ux Mary Elezier	8/46 1848 issued 8/22 1846	By John Russum,--
930	DELOZIER, JESSE et ux Susan Newman	3/4 1851	By John Russom, M.G.
931	DELOZIER, JOHN et ux Minerva Davis	8/14 1850	By John Tipton, J.P. (outside is Joseph Delozier)
932	DELOZIER, MALDEN et ux Catherind Davis	12/15 1842	By Ben Cunningham, J.P.
933	DELZELL, ANDREW D. et ux Elizabeth M. Wilson	11/20 1845	By J. S. Craig, M.G.
934	DELSELL, DAVID et ux S. M. Duncan	9/11 1841	By Ralph E. Tedford, M.G.
935	DELSELL, DAVID S. et ux Ann Morton Ollzell, James	9/24 1835 - - - -	By John D. Wilson, M.G. Elizabeth McCully (Deeds wills? letter?)
936	DELZELL, JOHN et ux Elizabeth Blair	10/24 1823	By Arch'b Maxwell, J.P.
937	DELZELL, JOHN et ux Louisa B. Anderson	2/12 1828	By Isaac Anderson, M.G.
938	DELZELL, JOHN et ux Philena A. Parker	12/24 1833	By Isaac Anderson, M.G.
939	DELZELL, ROBERT et ux Jane McQuague	12/24 1846	By Fielding Pope, M.G.
940	DELZELL, ROBT. A. et ux Mary A. Wilson	5/15 1851	By Ralph E. Tedford, M.G.
941	DELZELL, WILLIAM et ux Mary Jane McTeer	9/22 1842	By Isaac Anderson, M.G.
942	DENWOODY, WILLIAM er ux Betsy McGinley	2/29 1820	By Isaac Anderson, V.D. M.
943	DENTON, JOHN et ux Lavenia Tipton	10/13 1825	By Eleven Hitch, Esq.
944	DEROSSET, BEN'J et ux Matila Henderson	7/5 1829	By A. Ish, J.P.
945	DEROSSETT, HENRY et ux Eliza Beid	1/26 1826 issued	No returns
946	DEBTOR, JOHN et ux Amy Saunders	1/21 1845	By Leonard Wood, J.P. (outside John Detter)
947	DEVRNEAR, JAMES MATHEW et ux Martha Blount (or Kivinney)	3/2 1859	By F. Pope, M.G. (outside is James M. Devaney or Divine?
948	DEUBERRY, JOSEPH S. et ux Marha J. Irwin	6/2 1859	By Allen Anderson, J.P.

Names	Date Issue Or Celebrated	By Whom/ Security on Bond
949 DINES, WILLIAM et ux Polly Bowers	12/1 1825	By Charles H. Warren,--
950 DINES, QUINTIN et ux Jane Branum?	11/7 1817 issued	No returns
951 DIXEN, EDOM et ux Polly Law	2/10 1821 issued	"Then was executed Samuel Douthit,--"
952 DIXON, ELIX et ux Charity James	6/2 1830	By Samuel Douthit, E.M. E. Church
953 DIXON, JAMES A. et ux Eliza Jane Tedford	3/5 1846	By Green B. Saffell, J.P.
954 DICSON, JOHN F. et ux Mary Kennedy	4/1 1828	By Samuel Hamill, J.P.
955 DICKSON, SAMUEL et ux Jane Hammill	7/20 1826	By D. Carson,--
956 DICKSON, WILLIAM et ux Eliza Cook	1/27 1831	By A. Vance, M.G.
957 DICKSON, JOHN et ux Maryan Edmondson	10/30 1802 issued	Bond: Sam'l Handly (inside is John Dixon)
958 DOROSSETT, WILLIS et ux Doshea Grimmett	3/9 1824	By S. Douthit,Elder in M.E. Church
959 DEVEPORT, WILLIAM et ux Polly Huckland	12/16 1802 issued	Bond: Terrance Conner
960 DOBSON, ROBERT C. et ux Margaret J. Wallace	5/10 1843 issued	Bond: Alvan R. James
961 DOCKERY, BENJAMIN et ux Sarah Ann Plemens	7/18 1853	By J. S. Craig, M.G. (outside is Clemens)
962 DOCKERY, WILSON et ux Margaret Roach	2/22 1859	By Harvey Thompson, J.P.
963 DOLTINEY, JAMES P. et ux Amanda J. Carteel	10/28 1850	By J. C. Roberts,--
964 DONAHOO, CHARLES et ux Margret Weir	1/8 1802 issued	Bond: Joseph Weir
965 DONOLD, MATTHEW et ux Agnus Walker?	12/9 1802 issued	Bond: John Cochran
966 DONALSON, JAMES	11/17 1858	By M. Kounts, J.P.
967 DONALDSON, JAMES H. et ux Lucinda Mathews	1/23 1838	By J. Dyke, M.G.
968 DONALSON, JESSE D. et ux Rebecca A. Henry	10/12 1855	By Rev. J. L. Bunker,--
969 DONALSON, LORENZO et ux Peggy Reyman	9/30 1828	By Wm. McTeer, J.P.
970 DONALDSON, PHILIP et ux Sally Laythan	11/7 1845	By Ben Cunningham, J.P.

Names	Date Issue Or Celebrated	By Whom/ Security on Bond
971 DONALDSON, ROBERT et ux Polly D. Kirkpaterick	3/15 1827	By A. B. Gamble, J.P.
972 DONALDSON, ROBERT et ux Barbara Hagan	4/7 1846	By B. F. Duncan, J.P.
973 DONALDSON, SAMUEL et ux Rachell Griffitts	9/5 1844	By J. Dyke, Pastor Ulitia Church
974 DOOPS, HENRY et ux Malvian Cruse	11/17 1845 issued	"Executed by me Ban Cunningham, J.P."
975 DOTSON, ISAIAH et ux Isabel Moans	3/31 1839	By Joseph Wilson, J.P.
976 DOHERTY, GEORGE et ux Nancy McDowell	4/1 1799 issued	Bond: John McDowell
977 DOUGHERTY, HARVEY et ux Christena Moor	12/8 1842	By J. Dyke, Pastor Unitia Church
978 DOUGHTY, JAMES A. et ux Sarah A. Martin	4/25 1849	By I. Anderson, M.G.
979 DOUGLAS, ISSOM et ux Nancy Martin	8/6 1812 issued	No returns
980 DOUGLAS, JAMES et ux Polly Brown	12/27 1816	No signature "Celebrated"
981 DOUGLAS, MADISON et ux Sarah Bonham	12/29 1831	By Abner W. Lansden, U. D. M.
982 DOWNEY, ANDERSON et ux Lucinda Jane Anderson	6/22 1837	By Wm. Rich, J.P.
983 DOWNEY, THOMAS et ux Matilda Caroline Briant	10/13 1836	By John Strutton, J.P.
984 DRYMOND, WILLIAM et ux Margaret E. Smith	4/18 1854	By Wm. M. Brickell, J.P.
985 DUGGAN, JOHN et ux Mary Pus	9/7 1818 issued	No returns
986 DUGAN, SAMUEL et ux Frances Childres	9/1 1815 issued	No returns
987 DUNCAN, ALEXANDER R. et ux Ferdilla	1/1 1846	By Isaac Anderson, M.G.
988 DUNCAN, BARTLEY M. et ux Rachel Thompson	9/27 1827	By Samuel Hamill, J.P.
989 DUNCAN, BERRY et ux Winney Brickey	12/22 1831	By James Taylor, M.G.
990 DUNCAN, GEO K. et ux Margaret A. Mclland	11/15 1855	By W. A. Lawson, M.G.
991 DUNCAN, JAMES et ux Jane Hankin	3/30 1820	By Isaac Anderson, M.G.

	Names	Date Issue Or Celebrated	By Whom/ Security on Bond
992	DUNCAN, JAMES et ux Caroline Wright	4/14 1825	By Isaac Anderson, M.G.
993	DUNCAN, JOSEPH W. et ux Sarah Hudson	3/4 1834	By David McKamy, J.P.
994	DUNCAN, JAMES K. et ux Sarah S. Dunlap	1/15 1835	By David McKamy, J.P.
995	DUNCAN, JEREMIAH et ux Elizabeth Chandler	8/8 1822	By R. H. King, M.G.
996	DUNCAN, JEREMIAH H. et ux Mary Stephens	1/27 1846	By J. S. Craig, M.G.
997	DUNCAN, JOHN et ux Mary Delzell	12/12 1839	By I. Anderson, M.G.
998	DUNCAN, JOHN C. et ux Sarah J. Martin	10/8 1837	By S. L. Yearout, J.P.
999	DUNCAN, JOSEPH et ux Susanna Nerwood	10/14 1828	By E. N. Sawtell,--
1000	DUNCAN, LEANDER et ux Rebecca Wimberley	8/7 1833	By Jeremiah K. Mosier, M.G. ME. C.
1001	DUNCAN, LEANDER et ux Margarette Hamnontree	1/21 1847	By Samuel Tulloch, J.P.
1002	DUNCAN, MARVEL et ux Mary Kirkpatrick	4/29 1830	By B. Abernathey, J.P.
1003	DUNCAN, PETER F. et ux Margaret E. McCamey	1/15 1857	By Fielding, Pope, M.G.
1004	DUNLAP, ADAM et ux Margary Porter	1/31 1797 issued	Bond: Samuel Porter
1005	DUNLAP, DAVID C. et ux Vira (Visa) Hunt	2/14 1849 issued	No returns
1006	DUNLAP, E. N. et ux N. J. Graston	1/3 1856	By M. Love, J.P.
1007	DUNLAP, ELIJAH T. et ux Matilda Owing	7/31 1845	By W. M. Cumin , J.P.
1008	DUNLAP, HENRY et ux Fanney Hose	12/8 1859	By John J. Hudgeons, J.P.
1009	DUNLAP, JAMES et ux Margaret Palmer	12/26 1798 issued	Bond: Stephen Graves
1010	DUNLAP, JAMES et ux Mary Harris	12/3 1835	By J. K. Mosier, M.G.E. Ch.
1011	DUNLAP, JAMES et ux Isabella T. Cumming	2/20 1844	By Fielding Pope, M.G.
1012	DUNLAP, JAMES et ux Marium Jones	5/22 1849 issued	No returns

Names	Date Issue Or Celebrated	By Whom/ Security on Bond
1013 DUNLAP, JAMES et ux Synthia Mills	7/29 1849	By Wm. M. Brickell, J.P.
1014 DUNLAP, JAMES C. et ux Rutha Beling	9/5 1850	By David R. Lamb, J.P.
1015 DUNLAP, JAMES et ux Ritty Crumley	1/29 1852 1/29 1852	By W. M. Brickell, J.P.
1016 DUNLAP, JOHN et ux Ann Mcallen (McGallon, McAllen?)	3/22 1809	No returns
1017 DUNLAP, JOHN B. et ux Nancy Hinshaw	10/16 1845	By William Colburn, J.P.
1018 DUNLAP, JOSEPH et ux Hannah Keeble	10/14 1824 issued	No return
1019 DUNLAP, ROBERT W. et ux Cynthia C. Hunt	10/26 1856	By Andrew Ferguson, J.P.
1020 DUNLAP, WILLIAM et ux Ellenor Kwing	9/24 1816	By David McKamy, J.P.
1021 DUNLAP, WILLIAM et ux Jean Coldwell	1/12 1820	By George Ewig, J.P.
1022 DUNLAP, WILLIAM et ux Rachel Clampet	3/12 1829	By Wm. Hendrix, J.P.
1023 DUNLAP, WILLIAM et ux Elizabeth A. Covett	2/10 1835	By A. Ish, J.P.
1024 DUNLAP, WILLIAM et ux Susananh Moffett	11/7 1859	By J. H. Donaldson, J.P.
1025 DUNLAP, JAMES et ux Tempy Brickell	11/15 1838	By Matthew Whittenbgr, J.P.
1026 DUNAWAY, LEROY et ux Mary A. Kagley	5/17 1849	By Wm. Brickell, J.P.
1027 DUNN, ABRAM G. et ux Rachel Henry	12/23 1846 issued	No return
1028 DUNN, ANDREW J. et ux Sarah Hipper	1/9 1850	By T. M. Rooker, J.P.
1029 DUNN, DANIEL et ux Amanda Cameron	2/14 1839	By W. W. Porter, J.P. Bond: Wm. B. Bird
1030 DUNN, DAN'L et ux Milly Lawson	3/21 1846	By Johnson Adams, M.G.
1031 DUNN, DENNIS et ux Mary Janes	12/13 1849	By John Chambers, M.G.
1032 DUNN, GILES et ux Sydney Walker	10/10 1840	By Johnson Adams, DD
1033 DUNN, JAMES et ux Anna Briant	7/26 1836	By Spencer Henry, J.P.

Names	Date Issue Or Celebrated	By Whom/ Security on Bond
1034 DUNN, JAMES W. et ux Norcisa Hill	11/18 1841	By Johnson Adams, D.D.
1035 DUNN, JOHN C. et ux Nancy Henry	9/18 1845	By Will Cuming, J.P.
1036 DUNN, LEVI et ux Betsy Walker	1/26 1832	By John Hendrix, J.P.
1037 DUNN, L. P. et ux Sarah Freshour	12/15 1850	By Curran Lemons, J.P.
1038 DUNN, WM. et ux Catherine Pope	10/12 1816 issued	"Executed by me Joseph Walker, J.P."
1039 DUNN, WILLIAM et ux Mary Shields	1/27 1833	By JOhns Adams, M.G.
1040 DUNN, WILLIAM et ux Ann Eliza Boyd	3/8 1838	By A. Vance, M.G.
1041 DUNN, WM. C. et ux Sally Lea	12/25 1848	By Willima Henderson, J.P.
1042 DUPES, BENJAMIN et ux Susan Cook	6/16 1844	By Robert Porter, J.P.
1043 DUPES, JACOB et ux Eliza Harper	3/21 1847	By Stephen J. McReyn- olds, J.P.
1044 DUPES, JAMES et ux Marha Bennett	9/20 1849	By Leroy J. Newman, J.P.
1045 DURNOLDS, JAMES et ux Elizabeth Hendricks	9/9 1796	Bond: Arch' Lacky,
1046 DYRE, ALLEN R. et ux Martha A. Mizer	5/18 1848	By William Colburn, J.P.
1047 DYER, ELISHA et ux Polly Townesley	3/25 1824	By Samuel Hamill, J.P.
* See 4080		
1048 DYRE, SARAH F. et ux Sarah F. Miser	12/24 1850	By A. J. McGee, M.G.
1049 DYRE, JOHN et ux Margaret McCurdy	2/14 1821 issued	No returns
1050 DYRE, JNO A. et ux Maragerett Yearout	11/7 1850	By John S. Craig, M.G.
1051 DYER, JOSIAH et ux Mahala King	5/31 1825 issued	"Celebrated by me Samuel Henry, J.P."
1052 DYER, S. B. et ux Lutitia Staley	9/25 1856	By A. M. Goodykoutz, G.P.
1053 EAGLETON, ALEXANDER et ux Leona Humpherys	9/25 1855	By A. Vance, M.G. (she a wedow-was a McCrosky)
1054 EAGLETON, ELIJAH M. et ux Eleanor Gault	9/7 1826	By William Eagleton, M.G/

Names	Date Issue Or Celebrated	By Whom/ Security on Bond
1055 EAGLETON, GEO. E. et ux M. E. Foute	1/23 1856	By Fielding Pope, M.G.
1056 EAKIN, JOHN W. et ux Hetty Ann Heart	12/19 1858	By John M. Caldwell, M.G.
1057 EAGLETON, DAVID et ux Elizabeth Hook	12/2 1797	Bond: Alex Logan
1058 EAGLETON, ROBERT H. et ux Elizabeth G. McCulloch	9/19 1825	By Robert Hardin, M.G.
1059 EAGLETON, WILLIZM et ux Peggy Ewing	4/2 1816	By Isaac Anderson,--
1060 EAKIN, JOHN et ux Margaret Houston	3/11 1823	By Isaac Anderson, Pas- tor, New Provd. Church
1061 EAKIN, JOHN et ux Sarah Greer	11/10 1832	By A. Vance, M.G.
1062 EAKIN, SAMUEL et ux Polly Walker	4/30 1801 issued	No returns, Bond: Hum- phrey Montgomery
1063 EAKIN, SOLOMON et ux Fanny Jenkins	9/22 1817	By David McKamy, J.P.
1064 EAKIN, THOMAS et ux Nancy Crew	6/7 1816 issued	"Executed in 1816" Joseph Duncan, J.P.
1065 EAKIN, WILLIAM et ux Jane Hooks	12/3 1820 issued	No returns
1066 EANOS, ALEX et ux Elizabeth Win- chester	10/14 1830	By Charles H. Warren, J.P.
1067 EARLY, A. H. et ux Mary J. Yearout	6/6 1854	By J. S. Craig, M.G.
1068 EARLY, ALBERT P. et ux Eliza J. Miller	8/16 1838	By Isaac Anderson, M.G.
1069 EARLY, JAMES F. et ux Sarah Divine	1/22 1839	By John D. Wilson, M.G.
1070 EARLY, WILLIAM et ux Rebecca Young	12/2 1823	By Isaac Anderson, M.G.
1071 EDMONDSON, DAVID et ux Egny Scott	10/21 1823	By Isaac Anderson, M.G.
1072 EDMONDSON, FREDERIC et ux Celia Hickland	4/23 1816 issued	"Married by me Wm. Gil- lespie, J.P.
1073 EDMONDSON, JAMES et ux Sarah Folkner	10/7 1797	Bond: Jos. Ewing
1074 EDMONDSON, JOHN B. et ux Eliza Fuller	10/27 1854 issued	No returns, Bond: J. K. Duncan
1075 EDMONDSON, JOHN H. et ux Margaret C. Dunlap	2/19 1835	By David McKamy, J.P.

Names	Date Issue Or Celebrated	By Whom/ Security on Bond
1076 EDMONSON, JOHN H. et ux Margaret C. Dunlap	2/19 1835	By David McKamy, J.P.
1077 EDMONDSON, MATTHEW W. et ux Martha A. Duncan	11/4 1838	By Ele Richey, J.P.
1078 EDMONDSON, PARKER et ux Jane Long	2/10 1827 issued	No returns
1079 EDMONSON, RICHARD C. et ux Leah Hickland	4/6 1814 issued	No returns
1080 EDMONSON, SAMUEL K. et ux Eliza Jane Duncan	8/17 1837	By Thomas S. Kendall, M.G.
1081 EDMONSON, THOMAS et ux Jane E. Keys	2/9 1832	By Isaac Anderson, M.G.
1082 EDMISON, WALLACE W. et ux Mary Early	8/21 1845	By I. Anderson, Pastor New Provd. Ch.
1083 EDWARDS, JOHN et ux Penlopy (Penelopy) Farr	12/23 1817	By George Snider, Minister of the Baptist Order
1084 EDMUNDS, MATTHEW et ux Matilda Daily	2/9 1840	By William Colburn, J.P.
1085 EDMONS, WILLIAM et ux Jane Lane	10/21 1826	By Wm. Williamson, J.P.
1086 EDMUNDS, WILLIAM et ux Charlotte Reach	11/21 1835	By Samuel Tulloch, J.P.
1087 EDMOND, WILLIAM et ux Ailse Crisp	8/24 1841	By Wm. Rich, J.P.
1088 ELDERS, JOHN et ux Nancy Cates	1/21 1846	By John Rhea, J.P.
1089 ELEGEE, JACOB et ux Emily Sarten	1/21 1857	By William Kerr, J.P.
1090 ELLIGE, JOSEPH P. et ux Betsy Garner	4/4 1824	By Sam Henry, J.P.
1091 ELLEDGE, WM. et ux Lucy Summy	3/23 1849	By Adam Haun, J.P.
1092 ELIOTT, JASON et ux Rebecca Harris	10/7 1820 issued	"Executed by me. Sam'l George, J.P."
1093 ELLIOTT, JOHN B. et ux Elizabeth J. Bell	12/29 1822	By Jas. Cumming, M.G.
1094 ELLIOTT, MOSES et ux Mary Ann Divine	2/19 1821	By Wm. Gault, J.P.
1095 ELLIOTT, THOMAS et ux Margaret Snider	1/3 1839	By William M. Roroec, J.P.
1096 ELLIOTT, WIOTT et ux Elizabeth Simerly	11/26 1828	By Thomas Budd or Roddy, J.P.

Names	Date Issue Or Celebrated	By Whom/ Security on Bond
1097 ELLIOTT, WILLIAM et ux Martha Davis	9/23 1849	By Christian Long, J.P.
1098 ELLIS, AHAZ et ux Abetha Trundle (or Aletha)	10/31 1843	By Sam'l Pride, J.P.
1099 ELLIS, AVERY et ux Elizabeth Divine	5/5 1831	By Berry Abernathy, L.D. of M.E.C.
1100 ELLIS EANOS et ux Sarah Jones	3/19 1829	By Wm. Griffetts, J.P.
1101 ELLIS, JAMES C. et ux Phebe K. Key	10/14 1853	By William Colburn, J.P.
1102 ELLIS, JOHN et ux Mary Ann McCroy	2/23 1835	By A. Ish, J.P.
1103 ELLIS, JNO. S. et ux Perlina Amorine	12/16 1855	By John Clark, J.P.
1104 ELLIS, SAMUEL et ux Abigail Kee (Returns say "Abbigal Key")	2/24 1831	By Alexander Stewart, J.P.
1105 ELLIS, WILLIAM et ux Rachel Tucker	9/11 1838	By James Henry, J.P.
1106 EMMITT, ABIJAH W. et ux Betsy Ann Cameron	4/14 1836 (issued on 8th)	By Spencer Henry, J.P.
1107 EMMERT, PETER et ux Levina Reddy	2/10 1828 issued	"Solomnised by me in Feb. W. Hendrix, Esq."
1108 ELMORE, ASA et ux Elizabeth Bidix	5/29 1851	By Andrew Ferguson, J.P.
1109 EADSLEY, ALEXANDER et ux Mary A. Lee	10/19 1848	By William Colburn, J.P.
1110 EADSLEY, ALEXANDER et ux Derenda Jones (or is it Lucinda?)	2/10 1859	By Wm. M. Brickell, J.P.
1111 EADSLEY, JAMES et ux Jane Jones	9/25 1839	By William H. Hodges, M.G.
1112 EADSLEY, JOHN et ux Hetty Allen	3/4 1852	By Jesse Kerr, Jr., J.P.
1113 ENIS, JOHN et ux Dorcas Jacobs	12/20 1821	By Charles H. Warren, J.P. (C.H.W.)
1114 ENIS, THOMAS et ux Barbara Jacobs	4/17 1823	By Charles H. Warren, J.P.
1115 ERALS(?), JOHN et ux Mary Bumgardner	12/24 1855	By A. M. Goodykoontz, J.P.
1116 ERWIN, WILLIAM et ux Elizabeth Staunton	1/11 8121 issued	No returns

Names	Date Issue Or Celebrated	By Whom/ Security on Bond
1117 ESKRIDGE, SAMUEL et ux Myruah M. Leeper (or Myrriah)	10/10 1859	By Wm. M. Brickell, J.P.
1118 EVANS, ANDREW et ux Dorothy McMurry	8/16 1827	By Isaac Anderson, M.G.
1119 EVANS, JAMES M. et ux Susannah Tipton	2/12 1835	By John Russom, M.G.
1120 EVENS, JOHN et ux Elesabeth Kelpain	12/26 1831	By Wm. Williamson, J.P.
1121 EVANS, WILLIAM D. et ux Elizabeth	11/29 1827	By Jesse A. Lockhert, M.G.
1122 EVANS, WILL H. et ux Nancy Logan	12/29 1845	By Will Cumming, J.P.
1123 EVERETT, DANIEL et ux Sally Ann McTeer	10/9 1847	By B. Abernaty, L.E.M.E. Ch.
1124 EVERETT, EPPY et ux Mary E. Karr	9/2 1852	By James M. Tulloch, J.P.
1125 EVERETT, JAMES et ux Abby Waller (returns say James Averett & Happy W.)	12/28 1828 issued	By Wm. Billue, M.G. "celebrated"
1126 EVERETT, JAMES et ux Eliza Jane Bucolds	12/16 1845	By S. J. McReynolds, J.P.
1127 EVERETT, JOHN et ux Susan Shook	10/10 1832 issued	"celebrated by me Wm. Billue, M.G."
1128 EVERETT, JOHN et ux Malinda More	3/18 1841	Bond: John Hammontree
* See 94		
1129 EVERET, LORENZO D. et ux Lucinda Houser	6/15 1848	By Christian Long, J.P.
1130 EVERETTE, ROBERT et ux Mary Ann Clemens	9/7 1837	By N. A. Penland
1131 EVERETT, ROBERT E. et ux Eliza J. Baker	12/13 1852	By C. Long, J.P.
1132 EVERETT, WILLIAM et ux Polly Gay	7/18 1818	By Alex B. Gamble, J.P.
1133 EVERET, VINCENT et ux Sarah Buchols	1/16 1851	By Christian Long, J.P.
1134 EVERETT, WM. L. et ux Mary Kinnaman	4/26 1853	By A. B. Gamble, J.P.
1135 EWING, ALEXANDER et ux Jane Warren	12/8 1817 issued	No returns
1136 EWING, ALEXANDER et ux Margaret L. McCulloch	9/14 1824	By I. Anderson, Pastor N.P.C.

Names	Date Issue Or Celebrated	By Whom/ Security on Bond
1137 EWING, ALEXANDER et ux Isabella McClure	2/24 1835	By Isaac Anderson P.N.P.C.
1138 EWING, GEORGE JR. et ux Elenor Parker	9/13 1827	By William Eagleton, Pastor of Bakers Creek & Grassy Valley Ch's.
1139 EWING, JAMES et ux Mary Thompson	4/30 1798 issued	Bond: James Edminston
1140 EWING, JOHN et ux Susanna Minnis	8/16 1812 issued	No returns
1141 EWING, JOHN et ux Sally McGauhy	12/12 1816	David McKamy, J.P.
1142 EWING, JOHN et ux Margaret Conner	1/17 1839	By John D. Wilson, M.G.
1143 EWING, NATHANIEL et ux Betcy McColloch (or Becky)	10/16 1805 issued	No returns
1144 EWING, NATHANIEL et ux Margaret Caldwell	3/16 1837	By Isaac Anderson, P.N.P. Ch.
1145 EWING, SAMUEL et ux Mary McCulloch	9/4 1824	By I. Anderson, P.N.P. Ch.
1146 EWING, WILLIAM et ux Elizabeth McNutt	11/9 1796 issued	Bond: Alex' McCulloch
1147 EWING, WILLIAM et ux Jane Tucker	4/22 1834	By Isaac Anderson, P.N.P. Ch.
1148 EWING, WM. D. et ux M.E.M. Pope	2/12 1857	By J. S. Craig, M.G.
1149 EWING, WILL N. et ux Martha Steele, M.E.	5/26 1829	By Andrew Vance, M.G.
1150 FAIN, JESSE et ux Jenny Canway	10/13 1801 issued	Bond: Jesse Canway
1151 FAGG, JOHN JR. et ux Jane White	12/31 1833	By Wm. Anderson, J.P.
1152 FAGG, JULIUS C. et ux Elizabeth Smith	9/10 1829	By Darius Hoyt, M.G.
1153 FALKNER, HENRY et ux Julia	3/1 1844	By W. Toole, J.P. (Henry Falkner ck)
* See 1199		
1154 FOLKNER, JOHN et ux Mary Roberts	12/21 1845	By Robert Porter, J.P.
1155 FANSHAW, DAVID et ux Koler (or Kaler) Ann	8/26 1858	By Richard Evans, M.G.
1156 FANCHIER, CALEB et ux Milly Myers	12/26 1850	By Johnson Adams, M.G.

Names	Date Issue Or Celebrated	By Whom/ Security on Bond
1157 FANCHER, LEVI et ux Mary Walker	12/15 1859	By James D. Lawson, M.G. M.E. Ch. South
1158 FANN, GEORGE et ux Nancy M. Bird	7/21 1851	By Frederic Emmett, M.G.
1159 FANN, WILLIAM et ux Polly Bolin	2/21 1828	By James Cameron, J.P.
1160 FANN, WILLIAM et ux Eleanor McAfee	1/22 1850	By John Tipton, J.P.
1161 FANN, WILLIAM et ux Amanda Fry	2/13 1859	By Daniel H. Emmet, J.P.
1162 FARMER, ELIJAH et ux Polly Blakinship	8/12 1812 issued	No returns
1163 FARMER, GREEN et ux Jane Waters	1/28 1826 issued	"performed by me James Taylor, M.G."
1164 FARMER, JAMES W. et ux Sally Waters	11/1 1829	By Wm. Hendrix, J.P.
1165 FARMER, JNO. et ux Emeline Summey	7/14 1859	By H. J. Henry, J.P.
1166 FARMER, JOSEPH et ux Betsy Garner	9/28 1837 issued	No returns
1167 FARMER, LEWIS et ux Lydia Snider	12/19 1820	By Alex B. Gamble, J.P.
1168 FARMER, NATHAN et ux Sussanna Dever	12/9 1822 issued	"married by me. James Cameron, J.P."
1169 FARMER, SOLOMON et ux Rebecca Keeble	7/4 1829 issued	By Wm. McTer, J.P. "on 7/2 1829"
1170 FARMER, WILL et ux Rebecca Wilson	1/8 1818 issued	"executed by me. Jos. Duncan, J.P."
1171 FARR, ABSOLOM T. et ux Lucinda McPherson	10/18 1849	By Harvey H. C. Caruthers, J.P.
1172 FAR, BAZEL et ux E. Shaver	11/18 1847	By S. J. McReynolds, J.P.
1173 FARR, DAVID et ux Hariet Mackey	8/31 1820	By Alex B. Gamble, J.P.
1174 FARR, JAMES W. et ux Elizabeth Best	9/14 1843	By John Morton, J.P.
1175 FARR, JOHN et ux Sarah C. Crisp	6/18 1848	By David Spradlin, J.P.
1176 FARR, JOHN W. et ux Margury Maxwell	12/28 1847	By Henry Hamill, J.P.
1177 FARR, LEWIS et ux Mary J. Anderson	12/23 1852	By James M. Tullock, J.P.
1178 FARR, P.G. et ux Nancy Blue	11/6 1850	By T. M. Rooker, J.P. (Might be Billue)

Names	Date Issue Or Celebrated	By Whom/ Security on Bond
1179 FARR, P.G. et ux Martha J. Nichelson	4/9 1857	By J. H. Donaldson, J.P.
1180 FARR, SAMUEL et ux Elizabeth Boren	4/15 1817	By George Snider
1181 FARR, WILLIAM et ux Rebecca M. Davis	1/24 1846 issued	By Wm. Dever, J.P. says "on 3/13 mar. the within 1/22 1846"
1182 FATHY, JOHN et ux Patsy Wear	5/2 1827	By Wm. Turk, J.P.
1183 FELTS, AARON et ux Matilda Smith	5/28 1828	By J. Gillespie, J.P.
1184 FURGESON, FRANCIS D. et ux Louisa G. Noblet	9/24 1832	By Leroy Noble, J.P.
1185 FERGUSON, JAMES et ux Isabella C. Jeffries	7/17 1845	By James Blair, M.G.
1186 FERGUSON, JAMES A. et ux Araminta J. Hamil	12/5 1855	By Andrew Ferguson, J.P.
1187 FERGUSON, JOHN et ux Matilda H. Sexton	7/24 1821	By Jas' Love, J.P.
1188 FEGUSON, SAMUEL et ux Betsy Patterick	4/12 1833	By Leroy Noble, J.P.
1189 FERGUSON, W. C. et ux Ann Frow	10/16 1852	By James Law, M.G.
1190 FERGUSON, W. W. et ux Mabla L. Alex- ander (outside says "Matilda L. A.")	2/7 1856	By Andrew Ferguson, J.P.
1191 FORGUSON, ADAM et ux Mary Henry	10/26 1847	By Lowry McBath, J.P.
1192 FURGUSON, ANDREW et ux Susan Carson	12/4 1822	By Jos' Duncan, J.P.
* See 1475		
1193 FURGUSON, JAMES et ux Elizabeth Moore- lock	12/23 1826 issued	"celebrated by Sam'l Montgomery, Esq."
1194 FURGUSON, JAMES et ux Sarah Maxwell	9/14 1826	By Isaac Anderson, P.N.P. Ch.
1195 FURGUSON, JOHN et ux Jane Tallent	8/17 1846	By James Henry, Sr., J.P.
1196 FURGUSON, JOSIAH K. et ux Katherine Noblet	10/4 1831	By Leroy Noble, J.P.
1197 FURGUSON, MOSES C. et ux Jane Hannah	1/24 1828	By William Eagleton, M.G.

Names	Date Issue Or Celebrated	By Whom/ Security on Bond
1198 FURGUSON, ROBERT et ux Ruth Duff	4/13 1820 issued	No returns (inside is Forgson)
* See 1153		
1199 FULKNER, JAMES et ux Elizabeth Keller	6/17 1845	By S. J. McReynolds, J.P.
1200 FULKERSON, WM. R. et ux Martha E.	3/30 1858	By Joseph Peeler, Minister
1201 FIGINWINTER, HENRY et ux Sally Renfro	7/3 1827	By Sam'l C. Davidson, J.P.
1202 FILPOT, BARTON et ux Polly C. Perky	3/16 1848	By Wesley Earnest, J.P.
1203 FINGER, HENRY et ux Catherine Hoat- sell (Hursell?)	9/16 1833	"celebrated by me. Robert Houston"
1204 FINGER, HENRY et ux Nancy E. Crof- fered	9/14 1854	By H. Foster, Esq. (was it Crawford?)
1205 FINGER, JAMES et ux Isabella Tallent	6/9 1859	By H. Foster, J.P.
1206 FINGER, JONATHAN et ux Ann E. Tolla (or Talley)	7/29 1858	By H. D. Hodge, M.G.
1207 FINGER, JONAS et ux Delila Sliger	7/30 1827 issued	No returns
1208 FINLEY, ALBERT et ux Betsy Kennedy	9/27 1832	By Isaac Anderson, P.N.P. Ch.
1209 FINDLEY, JAMES et ux Margaret Pickens	2/15 1816	By Hugh Bogle, J.P.
1210 FINLEY, JAMES K. et ux Temperance Kenney	8/14 1828	By William Eagleton, M.G.
1211 FINLEY, JAMES K. et ux Margaret Palmer	10/1 1849	By Thos. M. Rooker, J.P.
1212 FINLEY, JOHN et ux Edy Saffell	2/15 1825	By J. Turk, J.P.
1213 FINLEY, JOHN et ux Mary McMurry	9/10 1846	By John Russom, M.G.
1214 FINLEY, JOHN M. et ux Eliza J. Delany	2/18 1840	By Samuel Tulloch, J.P.
1215 FINLEY, JOSEPH W. et ux Polly Nicholson	1/1 1833	By Jeremiah K. Moser, M. E. Church
1216 FINLEY, SAMUEL S. et ux Betseyann Delaney	10/27 1836	By Samuel Tulloch, J.P.
1217 FIPLEY, ROBERT et ux Agnes Edmiston	2/8 1822 issued	No returns

Names	Date Issue Or Celebrated	By Whom/ Security on Bond
1218 FISHER, CHARLES et ux Elizabeth Hamilton	9/17 1835	By Spencer Henry, J.P.
1219 FISHER, CHARLES et ux Amanda Sparks	8/8 1845 (issued July 21)	By Wm. Dever, J.P.
1220 FISHER, JOHN et ux Jean Palmer	7/25 1800 issued	Bond: James Crai
1221 FITTSIMMONS, JAMES et ux Nelly Hubbard	1/1 1844	By Robert Shields, J.P.
1222 FLANAGAN, ROBERT A. et ux Sarah C. Pattey	3/31 1859	By A. Boyd, J.P.
1223 FLINN, JOSEPH B. et ux Rebecca Hatcher	8/27 1851	By Wm. P. Flinn, Esq.
1224 FLINN, JOSEPH et ux Leah Rush	4/10 1825	By James Cameron, J.P.
1225 FLINN, WILLIAM et ux Caty Headrick	12/25 1829	By James Cameron, J.P.
1226 FLINN, WM. P. et ux Anna Christopher	12/19 1852	By C. Long, J.P.
1227 FELKNER, JOSEPH et ux Martha Franks	7/21 1800 issued	Bond: James Folkner
1228 FORRESTER, LEWIS et ux Ann Vinyard	7/24 1834	By Edward Mitchell, J.P.
1229 FORRESTER, MILES et ux Amanda Collins	3/19 1829	By William McTeer, J.P.
1230 FOSHA, JESSE et ux Sally Fosha	4/7 1819 issued	No returns
1231 FOSTER, JEREMIAH et ux Polly Rhea	3/8 1825	By Hugh Bogle, J.P.
1232 FOSTER, JOHN et ux Sarah Cunningham	10/1 1857	By A. Boyd, Esq.
1233 FOUTE, JACOB F. et ux Martha E. Berry	9/29 1818	By Isaac Anderson, M.G.
1234 FOX, DAVIS et ux Mary Greene	7/13 1855	By Frederic Emmett, M.G.
1235 FOX, JAMES N. et ux Prudence Felkner	12/1 1802	Bond: James Felkner
1236 FRANCE, JOHN et ux Abby Ellis	5/6 1845	By John Rhea, J.P.
1237 FRANCIS, WM. et ux Rebecca Miller	10/19 1801 issued	Bond: James Danforth
1238 FRANKLIN, ESOM et ux Rebecca Majors	7/17 1797 issued	Bond: Samuel Majors

Names	Date Issue Or Celebrated	By Whom/ Security on Bond
1239 FRANKLIN, ESOM et ux Lucy Forester	2/3 1802 issued	Bond: John McDowel
1240 FRANKLIN, GEORGE et ux Jenny (Jenney) Shaw	9/1 1802 issued	Bond: Josiah Payne
1241 FRANKLIN, JOHN et ux Polly Irwin	8/2 1799 issued	Bond: Wm. Irwin
FRANKLIN, JOHN et ux Lida Hart	6/14 1796	Bond: Joseph Hart
1242 FRANKS, BENJ'M et ux Elizabeth Vaut	2/27 1807 issued	No returns
1243 FRASIER, HAMELTON et ux Ann Hauter (outside is Hunter)	4/1 1828	By William Eagleton, M.G.
1244 FREEMAN, DREAD J. et ux Betsy Thompson	5/2 1820	By Isaac Anderson, P.N.P. Ch.
1245 FRENCH, FREDERICK et ux Polly Hensley	4/15 1822	By James Gillespy, J.P.
1246 FRENCH, HUGH et ux Martha Young	9/7 1842	By William Colburn, J.P.
1247 FRENCH, JOHN et ux Rebecca Finger	10/16 1856	By A. J. McGee, M.G.
1248 FRENCH, JOSEPH et ux Sarah Casteel	12/3 1833 issued	"by me celebrated A. Ish, J.P."
1249 FRENCH, JOSEPH et ux Sarah Hobbs	1/2 1844	By James Henry, J.P.
1250 FRENCH, LEONIDES et ux Rachel E. McTeer	10/22 1858 issued 10/20 1857	By W.T. Dowell, M.G.
1251 FRENCH, PETER et ux Malinda C. Kidd	11/21 1855	By W. T. Dowell, M.G.
1252 FRENCH, SAMUEL et ux Salina Parks	9/2 1847	By James H. Donaldson, J.P.
1253 FRENCH, THOMAS et ux Elizabeth Rhea	7/19 1840 (issued 4/30 1840)	By James Henry, J.P.
1254 FREW, JAMES et ux Jane Scott	11/10 1825	By Isaac Anderson, P.N.P. Ch.
1255 FREW, JOHN R. et ux Jane Hammil	1/3 1826	By D. Carson, M.G.
1256 FREEHOUR, JACOB et ux Elizabeth Dunn	11/29 1855	By Nicholas Brewer, J.P.
FRIAR, JOHN et ux Tabitha Ewing (Avery?)	11/11 1799	By Henry Beard

*   See Trias, 3704

Names	Date Issue Or Celebrated	By Whom/ Security on Bond
1257 FRONABARGER, JONAS et ux Missouri Davis	12/26 1831	By Wm. Williamson, J.P.
1258 FROST, JONAS B. et ux Ursula Cox	10/19 1834	By Russell Reneau, M.G.
1259 FROST, PAUL C. et ux Nancy O. Vinyard	9/22 1852	By Wm. Billue, M.G.
1261 FULTNER, DANIEL et ux Elizabeth Fultner	4/25 1848	By C. Cowan, J.P.
1262 FULKNER, DAVID et ux Sarah Cruise (at res. of G. Faulkner)	5/6 1843	By B. F.Duncan, J.P.
1263 FULTNER, DANIEL et ux Elizabeth Fultner	5/31 1848	By Columbus Cowan, J.P.
1264 FULTNER, ELIJAH et ux Nancy Cruze	1/4 1847	By James Ray
1265 FULTNER, JOHN et ux Rhody Ross	3/3 1831	"married by me on date" No signature
1266 FULTNER, JOHN et ux Martha J. Roberts	9/16 1848	By C. Cowan, J.P.
1267 FULTNER, WILLIAM et ux Jane Wheeler	12/6 1845	By Robt. Porter, J.P.
1268 FULTON, CREED REV. et ux Elizabeth T. Wear of Capt. Robert (Outside says Rev. Creede Fulton.)	8/14 1827	By John Henninger, M.G.
1260 FUQUAY, ASBURY et ux Sydney S. Gamble	1/7 1835 (issued 1/6 1836)	By James Axley, M.G.
1269 GALLAHER, JOHN C. et ux Mary A. Ambrester	10/23 1851	By J. Atkins, M.G.
1307 GALAHOR, JOSEPH et ux Mrgaret Gillespie	4/16 1799	Bond: John Cochran
1270 GALLYDAN, ANDERSON et ux Lucinda Vinyard	11/5 1848	By Ben Cunningham, J.P.
1271 GALLEAN, WILLIAM Y. et ux Mary J. Lunday	4/2 1857	By James Mathews, J.P.
1272 GAMBLE, ANDREW D. et ux Mary Dean	12/29 1846	By John Tipton, J.P.
1308 GAMBLE, JOHN et ux Sarah Williams	11/21 1798	Bond: Richard Williams
1309 GAMBLE, ANDREW et ux Elizabeth Davidson	4/23 1799 issued	Bond: William Armstrong
1310 GAMBLE, HUGH et ux Betsey Whiten- barger	12/21 1799 issued	Bond: John Edmonds

Names	Date Issue Or Celebrated	By Whom/ Security on Bond
<u>1311</u> GAMBLE, WM. et ux Sarah Gillespie	12/10 1799 issued	No returns Bond: Jonathan Trippet
<u>1312</u> GEMMELL, WM. et ux Ann McGaughy	10/12 1797 issued	Bond: Wm. Hanna
1273 GAMBLE, HUGH H. et ux Evaline Davis	10/4 1848	By John Tipton, J.P.
1274 FAMBLE, JOHN et ux Elizabeth C. Reagan	4/14 1829	By A. B.Gamble, J.P.
1275 GAMBLE, JOHN et ux Malvina Williams	11/18 1847	By Wm. Billue, M.G.
1276 GAMBLE, JOHN et ux Elizabeth Thompson	5/27 1852	By Fieldin Pope, M.G.
1277 GAMBLE, JOHN et ux Isabella Davis	4/20 1859	By W. W. Buchols, Esq.
1278 GAMBLE, JOSIAH et ux Polly Farmer	2/3 1820	By Alex B. Gamble, J.P.
1279 GAMBLE, JOSIAS et ux Polly Henry	10/31 1826	By A. B. Gamble, J.P.
1280 GAMBLE, JOSIAH et ux Rebecca McCamy	11/14 1850	By J. G. Swisher, M.G.
1281 GAMBLE, JOSIAS et ux Mary Ann Henry	9/15 1853	By John Clark, J.P.
1282 GAMBLE, A. LEONIDAS et ux Eliza E. Steele	12/21 1853	By W. W. Neal, M.G. M.E.C. South
1283 GAMBLE, MOSES et ux Jane McCallie	11/28 1822	By A. B. Gamble, J.P.
1284 GAMBLE, MOSES et ux Mary Henry	1/28 1849	By F. Pope, M.G.
1285 GAMBLE, MOSES et ux Ann G. Henry	10/1850	By A. B. Gamble, J.P.
1286 GAMBLE, MOSES et ux Sarah J. Goddard	1/29 1852	By J. C. Martin, J.P.
1287 GAMBLE, MOSES et ux Angeline F. Thompson	5/28 1852	By John J. Robinson, M.G.
1288 GAMBLE, WILL M. et ux Dorcas L. Berry	1/19 1825	By A. B.Gamble, J.P.
* See 1308-1312		
1289 GARDNER, DAVID et ux Nancy Thompson	10/25 1840	By Wm. Rorex, J.P.
1290 GARDNER, MATTHEW et ux Elizabeth Grace	9/5 1843	By Green B. Saffell, J.P.
1291 GARDNER, JOHN et ux Jane Farr	3/23 1819 issued	No returns

Names	Date Issue Or Celebrated	By Whom/ Security on Bond
1292 GARDNER, SAMPSON et ux Martha J. Davis	4/18 1858	By Michael Kountz, J.P.
1293 GARDNER, WILLIAM et ux Mary Thompson	3/22 1838	By Henry Hamill, J.P.
1294 GARNER, ADAM et ux Teletha Rogers	5/31 1855	By M. Kountz, J.P.
1295 GARNER, ELI et ux Elizabeth Rogers	1/12 1837	By Wm. McTeer, J.P.
1296 GARNER, ELISHA et ux Mary Furgison	7/8 1844	By B. F.Duncan, J.P.
1297 GARNER, ELISHA et ux Matilda W. Wear	8/13 1846	By S. J. McReynolds, J.P.
1298 GARNER, JACKSON et ux Elizabeth Palmer	6/5 1836	By Lorenze Donaldson, J.P.
1299 GARNER, JOHN et ux Rachel Henry	10/17 1798 issued	Bond: James Garner
1300 GARNER, JOHN F. et ux Martha J. Dewberry	1/4 1855	By James M. Tulloch, J.P.
* See 1374		
1301 GARNER, SAMUEL H. et ux R. J. Huckaby	2/20 1854	By James M. Tulloch, J.P.
1302 GARNER, WILLIAM et ux Elthey Garner	2/19 1835	By James Langford, M.G.
1303 GARNER, WM. H. et ux Mary Dewberry	8/5 1849	By James M. Tulloch, J.P.
1304 GARRARD, BRITTAIN et ux Hazy Smith	10/30 1827	By Creed Fulton, M.G. of Methodist Ch.
1305 GARREN, LEANDER et ux Savillar Hobbs	4/21 1836	By Edmund Wayman, J.P.
1306 GARSUCH, WM. et ux Rachael Bovenn	12/3 1828	By Leroy Noble, J.P.
* See 1268-1272		
1313 GAY, ALEXANDER et ux Jane Aiken	9/17 1822	By Wm. Griffetts, J.P.
1314 GAY, JOHN W. et ux ----- Branham	12/27 1838	By William M. Rorex, J.P.
1315 GAY, RICHARD et ux Catherine Ransberger	1/5 1819	By Alex B. Gamble, J.P.
1316 GAY, SAMUEL et ux Elizabeth Milligan	11/14 1820	By John Lambert, J.P.
1317 GAY, WILLIAM et ux Elizabeth Furguson	11/7 1822	By A. B.Gamble, J.P.

Names	Date Issue Or Celebrated	By Whom/ Security on Bond
1318 GAULT, JAMES W. et ux Susan J. Love	11/16 1848	By James Law, V.D.M.
1319 GAULT, JOHN et ux Jane A. Thompson	8/29 1821	By I. Anderson, P.N.P. Ch.
1320 GAULT, JOHN et ux Margaret Weir	6/5 1823	By Isaac Anderson, P.N.P. Ch.
1321 GAULT, JOHN et ux Susan H. Culton	4/11 1833	By Isaac Anderson, P.N.P. Ch.
1322 GAULT, JOHN et ux Polly Logan	6/17 1834	By Fielding Pope, M.G.
1323 GAULT, SAM'L M. et ux Sally Wallace	1/7 1819	By I. Anderson
1324 GAULT, WILLIAM et ux Peggy Orr	10/9 1826 issued	"celebrated by me Sam'l Montgomery, J.P."
1325 GEDIONS, WAYN et ux Mary J. Hitch	7/15 1833 issued	"Celebrated by me Wm. Billue, M.G."
1326 GENTRY, PHILIP et ux Sally Frazier, a black woman	12/16 1808 issued	No returns
1327 GENTRY, PLEASANT W. et ux Jane Cottrell	3/18 1836	By W. Toole, J.P.
1328 GEORGE, ALEXANDER O. et ux Elizabeth Paul	12/24 1822	By E. Hitch, Esq.
1329 GEORGE, DAVID et ux Ann Eliza Edmonston	8/28 1822	By Hugh Tarbet, J.P.
1330 GEORGE, EDWARD et ux Dorcas Chandler ("Darcus" on 5/10 say newspaper, Knox McPelve(?) Lib.)	5/3 1832	By Joseph Tarpelt
1331 GEORGE, EDWARD et ux Mary Jane Thompson	4/22 1845	By Samuel Pride, J.P.
1332 GEORGE R. et ux Catherine Hoover	1/14 1856	By Wm. M.Brickell, J.P.
1333 GHORMLEY, D. C. et ux Jane McEldry	4/11 1850	By Robert B.Billue, M.G.
1334 GHROMLEY, JAMES et ux Elizabeth Thompson	4/5 1821	By Joseph Duncan, J.P.
1335 GHORMLEY, JASPER et ux Lucretia Cobb	1/13 1841	By Henry Hamil, J.P.
1336 GHORMLEY, J. C. et ux E. E. Birchfield	5/19 1853	Samuel Ghormley, J.P.
1337 GHORMLEY, JOHN et ux Margaret J. McClure	2/25 1841	By Isaac Anderson, P.N.P. Ch.

Names	Date Issue Or Celebrated	By Whom/ Security on Bond
1338 GHORMLEY, MICH'L et ux Melinda Vaught	2/12 1814	By J. Harris, J.P.
1339 GHORMLEY, MICHAEL et ux Ethelinda Tedford	2/2 1841	By Henry Hamil, J.P.
1340 GIBBS, ARCHIBALD et ux Margaret Gallion	5/23 1820 issued	"Executed by S. George, J.P."
1341 GIBBS, ALFRED W. et ux Nancy Hicks	2/6 1845	By Joseph A. Hutton, J.P.
1342 GIBBS, LEVI et ux Milly Louiza McDonald	5/14 1840	By William Colburn, J.P.
1343 GIBBS, LEVI et ux Betsy Morgan	10/14 1849	By Wm. M. Brickell, J.P.
1344 GIBBS, WILLIAM Y. et ux Martha J. Smith	5/8 1842	By Robt. Porter, J.P.
1345 GIBSON, ATLAS et ux Orphy Pierce	9/3 1822	Sam'l Davidson, J.P.
1346 GIBSON, EDWARD et ux Martha A. Carson	7/29 1846	By J. Dykes, Pastor Unitia Church
1347 GIPSON, GRAYHAM et ux Jane Husky	1/9 1848	By Fredrick Emmett, M.G.
1348 GIBSON, JAMES P. et ux Minerva J. Folkner	6/17 1851	By S. J. McReynolds, J.P.
1349 GIBSON, SAMUEL et ux Ruthy Hall	11/6 1838	By W. M. Rorex, J.P.
1350 GIBBS, LYNNVILLE et ux Elizabeth Mahaley Speers	4/1 1838	By William Colburn, J.P.
1351 GIFFIN, DAVID et ux Malvina Roddy	8/14 1838	By Robt. Porter, J.P.
1352 GIFFIN, JOHN et ux Hannah Jordon	3/30 1820	By James Gillesphy, J.P.
1353 GILLESPIE, Alexander et ux Margaret Young	8/3 1799 issued	Bond: Robert Young
1354 GILLESPIE, ALEX et ux Sarah Rhodes	9/28 1802	Bond: Robert Bailey
1355 GILLESPIE, ALEX et ux L. E. Blackburn	8/20 1859	By R. E.Tedford, M.G.
1356 GILLESPY, CAMPBELL et ux Hannah C. Wallace	12/3 1833	By D. Carson, M.G. Ass. Pres. Ch.
1357 GILLESPY, CAMPBELL et ux Ann Holliday	10/29 1856	By J. C.Craig, M.G.
1358 GILLESPY, CAMPBELL, M. et ux N. L. Clark	10/9 1850	By Isaac Anderson, P.N.P. Ch.

Names	Date Issue Or Celebrated	By Whom/ Security on Bond
1359 GILLESPIE, JAMES et ux Patsy W.	8/12 1823	By Isaac Anderson, P.N.P. Ch.
1360 GILLESPIE, JAMES et ux Hester Ann H. Talbott	3/16 1826	By Elbert F. Sevier, M.G. (Knoxville Register says 3/15)
1361 GILLESPIE, JOHN et ux Ann Chamberlin	10/18 1802 issued	No returns Bond: William Gilles- pie
1362 GILLESPIE, JOHN et ux Patsey Houston	2/7 1799 issued	Bond: Robert Gillespie
1363 GILLESPIE, JOHN et ux Jane Kilburn	10/16 1823	By Isaac Anderson, P.N.P. Church
1474 GILLESPIE, ROBERT et ux Betsey Houston	2/7 1799 issued	Bond: John Gillespie
1364 GILLESPY, WILLIAM C. et ux Nancy Kennedy	2/5 1846	By Fielding Pope, M.G.
1365 GILLESPIE, WM. G. et ux Mary J. Blackburn	9/25 1850	Fielding Pope, M.G.
1366 GILLESPIE, ZACH et ux Elizabeth Roads	4/16 1802 issued	Bond: George Montgomery
1367 GILBERT, GEORGE S. et ux Nancy M. Saffell	12/21 1830	By Russell Birdwell, M.G.
1368 GINNINGS, JESSE et ux Nancy Pearson	2/19 1824	By Hugh Bogle, J.P.
1369 GILMORE, JAMES et ux Sarah Glass	8/30 1801 issued	Bond: Alexander Tedford
1370 GILMORE, JOHN et ux Elenor McEnney (or Kenney, or McKenny)	3/13 1797	Bond: Andrew Woods
1371 GILLMORE, MATHEW et ux Margaret Logan	2/13 1800	Bond: George Davison
1372 GIVENS, WILLIAM et ux Hannah Thomas	3/3 1824	By Wm. Williamson, J.P.
1373 GIVENS, WILLIAM et ux Narcissa Small	4/24 1845	By James Henry, J.P.
1374 GIRDNER, MICHAEL et ux Eliza Wear	10/27 1824 (issued 10/18)	By Samuel Douthit, E.M.E. Ch., A.D.
* See 1300		
1375 GLASS, ALEXANDER et ux Ann McCulloch	8/26 1812 issued	No returns
1376 GLASS, ISAAC et ux Elizabeth Noblet	4/29 1824	By S. Douthit, Elder in M.E. Ch.
1377 GLASS, JAMES et ux Peggy Noblet	10/4 1824 issued	No returns
1378 GLASS, JOHN et ux Rachel Vickers	3/31 1831	Robert B. Billue, M.G. of Babtist Order

66

Names	Date Issue Or Celebrated	By Whom/ Security on Bond
1379 GLASS, SAMUEL et ux Elizabeth M. Glass	1/21 1817	By I. Anderson, M.G.
1380 GLASS, SAMUEL T. et ux Nancy McQuaig	10/14 1841	By Isaac Anderson, P.N.P. Ch.
1381 GLASS, WM. et ux Agnus McCulloch (outside is Nancy)	4/2 1811 issued	Bond: James Frue & Leroy Rankin
1382 GLASS, WILLIAM W. et ux Malinda Miller	1/4 1838	By John D. Wilson, M.G.
1383 GODDARD, JOSEPH et ux Margaret J. McGinley	11/5 1857	By J. S. Craig, M.G.
1384 GODDARD, WILLIAM et ux Margaret Hitch	11/7 1837	By Wm. Billue, M.G.
1385 GODFREY, ROBERT et ux Surena Mays	12/23 1858	By I. D. Wright, J.P.
1386 GOENS, DANIEL et ux Jane Jenkins	1/12 1841	By Henry Hamil, J.P.
1387 GOEN, WILLIAM et ux Patsy Hix	12/31 1837	By Wm. Rich, J.P.
1388 GOEN, WILLIAM et ux Rachel Rudd	9/7 1838	By Robert Delzell, J.P.
1389 GOFORTH, JNO. et ux Jane R. Briant	11/7 1852	By John Givens, M.G.
1390 GOLIHER, JAMES et ux Lucinda C. Houston	12/4 1816	By I. Anderson
* See 1369		
1391 GOLLIHOR, KING et ux Peggy McWhinney	6/22 1816 issued	By Wm. Gillespie, J.P. "married by me"
1392 GOODIN, ISAAC et ux Susan Palmer	3/3 1841	By Brittain Garrard, L.D.
1393 GOODIN, JAMES et ux Margaret S. Burnet	8/22 1855	By J. C. Wrught, J.P.
1394 GOODMAN, AMOS et ux Sarah Conway	8/30 1801 issued	Bond: Thomas Conway
1395 GOODMAN, JOHN et ux Ruthy Roach	6/10 1819	By Wm. Gault, J.P.
1396 GOODMAN, JOEL et ux Polly Wright	4/8 1827 issued	No returns
1397 GOODMAN, THOMAS et ux Mary Hix	9/4 1838	By Matthew Whitten- barger, J.P.
1398 GOODMAN, WILLIAM et ux Betsy Samples	3/5 1824	"celebrated by me A. Ish, J.P."
1399 GOODMAN, W. H. et ux Rebecca Fortner	2/1 1856	By J. H. Donaldson, J.P.

Names	Date Issue Or Celebrated	By Whom/ Security on Bond
1400 GOODLINK, JOSEPH et ux Margaret A. Maxwell	8/32(?) 1840 (issued 8/31)	By Henry Hamil, J.P.
1401 GORMLY, WILLIAM S. et ux Mary Milsaps	3/9 1833	By John Hendrix, J.P.
1402 GOSSAGE, GEORGE W. et ux Rachel Coppack	1/29 1845	By James H. Donaldson, J.P.
1403 GOSSAGE, JOSEPH et ux Mary J. Hope	5/21 1845	By George Ekin
1404 GOSSAGE, WILLIAM et ux Mary Hendrickson	8/6 1824	By Samuel Douthit, E.M.E. Ch. (is elder)
1405 GOULD, ANDREW et ux Jane Early	10/30 1834	By Isaac Anderson, P.N.P. Ch.
1406 GOULD, JOHN et ux Jane Richey	11/10 1827	"by me Sam'l Montgomery, Esq."
1407 GOLD, SAMUEL et ux Mary Jackson	9/13 1797 issued	Bond: Samuel Rowan & Robert Wilson
1408 GOULD, SAMUEL J. et ux Jane Maxwell	10/11 1831	By Samuel Hamil, J.P.
1409 GOURLEY, JOHN et ux Sarah Beasley	2/4 1843	By W. Earnest, J.P.
1410 GOURLEY, JNO. et ux Lucinda Sparks	8/22 1854	By Curran Lemons, J.P.
1411 GOURLEY, WM. et ux Ann Shields	2/26 1848	By Frederic Emmett, M.G.
1412 GRACE, GEORGE C. et ux Isabella J. Gardner	12/27 1849	By Robert Sloan, A.J.P.
1413 GRADY, JAMES H. et ux Jane Hobbs	1/3 1848 issued	No returns
1414 GRAHAM, GEORGE et ux Luticia Cowan	9/11 1828	By William Eagleton, M.G.
1415 GRAHAM, JOHN et ux Elizabeth E. Yearout	11/17 1829	By Isaac Anderson, P.N.P. Ch.
1416 GREYHAM, C. C. et ux Martha O. (or E.) Lawrence	9/29 1858	A. Vance, M.G.
1417 GRAYHAM, ROBISON et ux Martha E. Lane	4/9 1857	H. Thompson, J.P.
1418 GRASTON, JOSIAH et ux Ann Hitch	11/25 1825 issued	"Complied with James Turk"
1419 GRASTON, WILEY et ux Margaret J. Frow	7/30 1851	By J. S. Craig, M.G.
1420 GRASTON, WILLIAM et ux Catherine Hich	10/24 1832	By William Toole

Names	Date Issue Or Celebrated	By Whom/ Security on Bond
1421 GRAVES, ADAM et ux Mehala Hubbard	4/2 1846	By John Tip on, J.P.
1422 GRAVES, SILAS et ux Nancy Wilson	5/11 1843	By Gen. Cunningham, J.P.
1423 GRAVES, STEPHEN et ux Harriett King	2/28 1829 issued	"Celebrated by me Sam'l Henry, J.P."
1424 GRAVES, RILEY et ux Elizabeth Wilson	1/1 1846	By John Tip on, J.P.
1425 GRAVES, WILLIAM et ux Mary Holloway	4/25 1833	By George Snider
1426 GRAY, JAMES M. et ux Lucy Badgett	10/16 1851	By C. D.Smith, M.G.
1427 GRAY, JOHN et ux Malinda Wallace	3/1 1836	By Fielding Pope, M.G.
1428 GRAY, JOSEPH et ux Rachael McCall	10/14 1847	By Samuel Tulloch, J.P.
1429 GRAY, THOMAS et ux Lucinda Berry	6/19 1815 issued	No returns
1430 GRAY, WILLIS et ux N. J. Hensely	5/19 1858 issued	No returns
1431 GREGORY, DRURY et ux Martha A.Brown	5/27 1851	By Curran Lemons, J.P.
1432 GRIGORY, CHARLES et ux Ceily Carver	12/3 1848	By Curran Lemons, J.P.
1433 GREGORY, WALTER et ux Rutha Oliver	7/29 1852	By Curran Lemons, J.P.
1434 GREENE, JOSEPH et ux Nancy Brewer	2/24 1828	By James Cameron, J.P.
1435 GREENE, WM. et ux Jean Lackey	9/4 1804 issued	No returns
1436 GREENE, WILLIAM et ux Mary Bonham	10/15 1818 issued	No returns
1437 GREENWAY, JOHN B. et ux Peggy Ann Hair	2/29 1846	By B. Abernathy, L.E.M.E. Ch.
1438 GREENWAY, JOHN C. et ux Rebecca McLain	9/29 1838	By Isaac M.Hair, J.P.
1439 GREER, ARTHUR et ux Jenny Hart	8/29 1799 issued	Bond: Joseph Hart
1440 GREER, ARTHUR et ux Elizabeth Jones	10/18 1827	By Wm. Griffitts, J.P.
1441 GREER, ARTHUR et ux Mary A. McConnell	2/20 1840	A. Vance, M.G.
1442 GREER, ARTHYR et ux Almyra E. Key	11/4 1852	By Wm. Brickell, J.P.

Names	Date Issue Or Celebrated	By Whom/ Security on Bond
1443 GREER, DAVID et ux Telitha Johnson	8/16 1840	By John Chambers, M.G.
1444 GREER, DAVID et ux Rachel Wilburn	2/8 1843	By Lewis, Jones, J.P.
* See 1900-1994, Gentry - Green		
1445 GRIDER, JOSEPH et ux Ann Eliza Tuck	1/8 1846	By James H. Donaldson, J.P.
1446 GRIFFIN, JOHN et ux Catherine Griffin	6/22 1858	By J. L. Biemans, Cutt Pastor
1447 GRIFFIN, MILES et ux Nancy Hammontree	7/12 8132	By John Maxwell, J.P.
1448 GRIFFIN, YOUNG H. et ux Anna Heath	2/11 1820	By Jos' Love, J.P.
1449 GRIFFITTS, ENGLE et ux Eleanor Vanderpool	10/4 1837	By Wm. Billue, M.G.
1450 GRIFFITTS, GEORGE et ux Martha Stanfield	7/14 1827 issued	"Executed by me A. Ish, J.P."
1451 GRIFFITTS, JAME et ux Mary P. Scott	2/28 1837	By Isaac Anderson, P.N.P. Ch.
1452 GRIFFITTS, JOHN et ux Mary Lee	4/25 1824	By Samuel Douthit, Elder in M.E. Ch. South
1453 GRIFFITH, JOHN JR. et ux Margaret Lea	5/21 1833	By Leroy Noble, J.P.
1454 GRIFFITTS, JOHN et ux Nancy Ann Black	5/21 1846	By A. Vance, M.G.
1455 GRIFFETTS, JOHN JR. et ux Phebe M. Houston	11/25 1856	By A. Vance, M.G.
1456 GRIFFETTS, JOHN W. et ux Mary E. Donaldson	3/8 1856	By Andrew Ferguson, J.P.
1457 GRIFFETTS, MARTIN et ux Elizabeth J. Staley	1/15 1846	By W. Earnest, J.P.
1458 GRIFFITTS, SAM'L J. et ux Rutha J. Cook	3/11 1852	By Spencer Henry, M.G.
1459 GRIFFETTS, WILLIAM et ux Mary Mathus	6/15 1799 issued	Bond: Hugh Hackney
1460 GRIFFITTS, WILLIAM et ux Saphronia Jones	11/7 1850	By John J. Hoover, J.P.
1461 GRIFFITTS, W. H. et ux Lucy S. (or A.) Burton	9/21 1848	By A. J. McGee, M.G.
1462 GRIFFITS, WILLIAM R. et ux Elizabeth J. Harris	9/16 1858	By B. F. Duncan, J.P.

Names	Date Issue Or Celebrated	By Whom/ Security on Bond
1463 GRIFFETTS, WILLIAM S. et ux Kerren H. Pugh	7/27 1858	By G. W. Alexander, M.G.
1464 GRIGSBY, AARON et ux Eliza M. Maclin	9/26 1832	By Isaac Anderson, P.N.P. Ch.
1465 GREGSBY, GEORGE et ux Margaret Means	11/24 1829	By Isaac Anderson, P.N.P. Ch.
1468 GRIGSBY, GEORGE et ux Nancy L. Whittenburger	1/5 1837	By R. Reneau, M.G.
1467 GRIGSBY, SAMUEL et ux Dorcus Wyly	7/9 1818 issued	No returns
1468 GREGSBY, WILLIAM et ux Polly Greenway	11/20 1823 issued	No returns
1469 GRIMETT, SAMUEL et ux Fanny Rankin	2/9 1824	By Samuel Douthit, Elder M.E. Ch. A.D. (or A.L.)
1470 GRISHAM, ARCHIBALD et ux Polly McRanalds	3/21 1822	By Isaac Anderson,
1471 GRUBB, FRANKLIN et ux Teressa W. Eouthit	9/12 1833	By Arnold Patton
1472 GUINN, JOHN et ux Jane Walker	4/8 1812 issued	"married by me Joseph Walker, J.P."
1473 GARNER, WM. et ux Patsy Boyd	10/8 1847	By Robt' Porter, J.P.
* See 1302		
* See after 1363		
1475 FURGESON, HUGH et ux Margaret Craig	11/10 1796 issued	Bond: William Gay
* See after 1192		
1476 HACKNEY, A. T. et ux A. E. Bright	7/31 1854	By A. R.James, J.P.
1477 HACKNEY, DAVID et ux Elizabeth Underwood	11/27 1851	By Wm. Brickell, J.P.
1478 HACKNEY, FRANCIS et ux Ann Miser	11/22 1838	By William Colburn, J.P.
1479 HACKNEY, F. R. et ux M. J. Griffitts	5/16 1856	By J. H. Donaldson, J.P.
1480 HACKNEY, GEORGE et ux Susan Hickman	12/10 1847	By William Cliburn, J.P.
1481 HACKNEY, HUGH et ux Ann Lambert	6/15 1799	Bond: Wm. Griffetts
1482 HACKNEY, HU L. W. et ux Elizabeth Bowerman	9/28 1847	By William Colburn, J.P.

Names	Date Issue Or Celebrated	By Whom/ Security on Bond
1483 HACKNEY, JOHN et ux Rachel Jones	8/9 1817	By Henry H. Bowers, J.P.
1484 HACKNEY, JOHN et ux Phebo Perkins	4/23 1829	By Wm. Griffitts, J.P.
1485 HACKNEY, JOSEPH et ux Malanda Pickering	5/26 1852	By Spencer Henry, M.G.
1486 HACKNEY, SAMUEL et ux Polly Lambert	4/28 1815 issued	No returns
1487 HACKNEY, THOOS L. et ux Marijean A. Jones	8/1 1851	By W. M. Brickell, J.P.
1488 HACKNEY, WILLIAM J. et ux Martha Dunlap	12/27 1836	By William Colburn, J.P.
1489 HADDON, GEORGE et ux Jane McWilliams	11/6 1834	By Robert H. Snoddy, M.G.
1490 HADDON, WILLIAM et ux Nancy Vinyard	3/8 1832	By Thos. White, J.P.
1491 HADDOX, ISAAC et ux Elizabeth Yonts	10/2 1845	By Robt' Porter, J.P.
1492 HADDON, JAMES et ux Rebecca Harris	1/1 1846	Robt' Porter, J.P.
1493 HADDOX, SAMUEL et ux Eleanor Ann Jones	11/30 1837	By James Ray, J.P.
1494 HAFLEY, BARCKLEY M. et ux Elizabeth Bennett	6/5 1845	By John Clark, J.P.
1495 HAFLEY, JOHN et ux Elizabeth Kirk- patrick	11/30 1837	By James Ray, J.P.
1496 HAGLER, DAVID et ux Albina Cowan	4/9 1840	By George Snider, M.G.
1497 HALE, GUY et ux Rachel Boling	11/13 1828 (issued 10/31)	By William McTeer, J.P. Bond: Benjmin Upton
1498 HALE, JOHN B. et ux Jane McClung	6/17 1817	And'w S. Morrison, V.D.M. or L.D.M.
* See 1633		
1499 HAIL, THOMAS et ux Rossana Denne	4/23 1801 issued	Bond: Joseph James & Luke Hail
1500 HALE, WILLIAM et ux Elizabeth Taylor	9/30 1830 issued	By Joseph Vanpelt (is a name on outside, no remarks)
* See 1633		
1501 HAIR, ISAAC M. et ux Lucinda Gaston	2/12 1831	By B. Abernathy, L.D.
* See Hair, 1596		
1502 HAIR, ISAAC M. et ux Mary West	8/21 1857	By J. H. Donaldson, J.P.

Names	Date Issue Or Celebrated	By Whom/ Security on Bond
1503 HAIRE, JACOB et ux Elizabeth McClain	2/14 1822	By Wm. Griffetts, J.P.
1504 HAIR, JAMES M. et ux Sarah West	1/20 1848	By Joseph A. Hutton, J.P.
1505 HAIR, JOHN H. et ux Elizabeth McClure	12/5 1822	By Samuel Douthit, Elder in M.E. Ch. A.D.
1506 HAIR, JOSEPH et ux Delila Perkins	11/17 1825	By Wm. Griffitts, J.P.
* See 1596		
1507 HALL, ADISON A. et ux Lucy A. Harris	9/2 1858	By Wm. T.Henderson, J.P.
1508 HALL, ALLEN et ux Priscilla Pippins	2/21 1853	By J. S. Craig, M.G.
1509 HALL, CASSWELL et ux Mary Ann Thompson	9/6 1832	By B. Abernathy, L.E.
1510 HALL, JAMES et ux Lucinda Caston	2/26 1854	By John J. Hoover, J.P.
1511 HALL, JOHN et ux Elizabeth Wyley	11/6 1820	By Samuel Douthit, M.G.
1512 HALL, JOSEPH C. et ux Lucy Ann Rider	4/7 1840 issued	Bond: James M. Leeper
1513 HALL, WILLIAM et ux Elizabeth Whitehead	3/5 1851	By Christian Long, J.P.
1514 HAMBY, CHRISTOPHER C. of Knox Co., Tenn. et ux Juliett E. Cox	2/7 1839	By Edward Reed, M.G.
1515 HAMIL, DAVID et ux Nancy Walker	8/28 1827	By D. Carson, M.G.
1516 HAMIL, GEORGE E. et ux Margaret A. Wilson	8/18 1842	By Andrew Vance, M.G.
1517 HAMIL, ISAAC et ux Elizabeth A. Gorley	2/5 1848	By Curran Lemaons, J.P.
1518 HAMILL, JAMES et ux Jane L. Simms	2/22 1831	By D. Carson, M. of C.P. Ch.
1519 HAMIL, JAMES et ux Margaret R. Hanah	9/7 1854	By R. E. Tedford, M.G.
1520 HAMMIL, JOHN et ux Ann Anna(?) (Hanna)	11/5 1787(?)	Bond: James Danforth
1521 HAMIL, JOHN et ux Caroline Cotterill	2/1 1844	By Joseph A. Hutton, J.P.

Names	Date Issue Or Celebrated	By Whom/ Security on Bond
1522 HAMIL, JNO. W. et ux Mary A. Hannah	10/9 1851	By Ralph E. Tedford, M.G.
1523 HAMIL, ROBERT et ux Mary Cochran	7/30 1840	By Samuel Tulloch, J.P.
1524 HAMIL, ROBT' et ux Nancy J. Tedford	2/26 1852	By James Law, M.G.
1525 HAMIL, Sam'l B. et ux Susan E. Coldwell	12/24 1850	By James M. Tulloch, J.P.
* See 2445		
1526 HAMELTON, DAVID et ux Katherine Potter	6/4 1835	By Spencer Henry, J.P.
1527 HAMILTON, JAMES et ux Terressa Berry	4/27 1830	By Isaac Anderson, P.N.P. Ch.
1528 HAMILTON, JOSHUA et ux Margaret Dearmon	12/15 1825	By William Eagleton, M.G.
1529 HAMELTON, JOHN et ux Elizabeth Baugher	7/21 1803 issued	No returns
1530 HAMELTON, WM. et ux Elizabeth Rogers	8/24 1800	On back license is "August 28" (no signature Bond: David Lovelace
1531 HAMILTON, WILLIAM et ux Elizabeth Keller	7/4 1838--On back, "She moved to Ala. no property found in Blount" signed William Hamilton"	
1532 HAMMER, JESSE S. et ux Mary A. Perkins	6/15 1854	By John J. Hoover, J.P.
1533 HAMMER, ISAAC et ux Mary B. Gossage	8/15 1850	By Wesley Earnest, J.P.
1534 HAMMOND, JONATHAN et ux Rachel G. Henry	3/2 1852	Fielding Pope, M.G.
1535 HAMMON, MICHAEL et ux Malinda McCool	7/30 1823	By Joseph Duncan, J.P.
1536 HAMMONTREE, ALEX' et ux Rebecca Robinson	12/22 1818	By George Snider, M.G. of Babtist Ch.
1537 HAMONTREE, ALEXANDER et ux Jane Thompson	1/7 1844	By J. Dyke, Pastor Unitia Church
1538 HAMMONTREE, JAMES et ux Nancy Holoway	4/30 1800 issued	Bond: John Holloway
1539 HAMMONTREE, JAMES et ux Nancy Devine	12/18 1826 issued	"celebrated by me Alex'r McCollom, J.P."
1540 HAMMONTREE, JEREMIAH et ux Alcey Wiles (or Niles) (Brother of James, ref. 1539)	7/15 1824	By Jos. Duncan, J.P.
1541 HAMMONTREE, Jeremiah et ux Hannah Murry	1/18 1844	By John Morton, J.P.

Names	Date Issue Or Celebrated	By Whom/ Security on Bond
1542 HAMINTREE, JEREMIAH et ux Malinda Thomson	7/11 1850	By Leonord L. McFarliy, J.P.
1543 HAMMONTREE, HARRIS et ux Sarah Robertson	1/12 1822	By Arch'l Maxwell, J.P.
1544 HAMMONTREE, HARVEY et ux Hetty Ann McCrockey	9/9 1834	By A. Vance, M.G.
1545 HAMMONTREE, JOHN et ux Rhody M. Griffin	7/25 1832	By Joseph Vanpelt
1546 HAMMONTREE, JOHN et ux Mary Murry	8/8 1836 issued	No returns
1547 HAMINTREE, JOHN et ux Eliza J. Woods	12/4 1849	By L. L. McFarling, J.P.
1548 HAMINTREE, JOHN et ux Elizabeth E. McTeer (of J. Campbell)	7/5 1857	By William Kerr, J.P.
1549 HAMMONTREE, WILLIAM et ux Jane Carson (outside is Peggy Carson)	4/20 1826	By Alex'r McCollum, J. P. Bond: James Hammontree
1550 HAMINTREE, WILLIAM (of John (Tubby) et ux Martha S. Craig	1/5 1849	By L. L. McFarling, J.P.
1551 HAMPTON, BENJAMIN et ux Cintha Haze	9/21 1839	By James Taylor, M.G.
1552 HANES, CLINTON et ux Jane Hood	2/22 1842	By W. Toole, J.P.
1553 HANES, JAMES et ux Mariah Henley	2/8 1830 issued	"celebrated by me A. Ish, J.P."
1554 HANNAH, ADDISON et ux Margaret Scott	8/29 1833	By Isaac Anderson, P.N.P. Ch.
1555 HANNAH, ANDREW F. et ux Cyntha Hiton	11/6 1833	By Wm. Billue, M.G.
1556 HANNAH, ANDREW et ux Mary L. Best	3/27 1851	By Robert Sloan, J.P.
1557 HANNAH, JOSEPH A. et ux Lutica Best	8/8 1857	By Spencer Henry, M.G.
1558 HANNAH, JOHN et ux Martha Miller	9/5 1796 issued	Bond: William Miller
1559 HANNA, JOHN et ux Jane Trimble	2/15 1796 issued	Bond: William Cochran
1560 HANNA, JOSEPH et ux Mary Walker	3/25 1797 issued	Bond: David Taylor
1561 HANNA, MATHEW et ux Margaret Weir	4/29 1836	By Isaac Anderson, P.N.P. Ch.
1562 HANNA, WM. et ux Mary Moor	5/1 1798 issued	Bond: John Cochran

Names	Date Issue Or Celebrated	By Whom/ Security on Bond
1563 HANNA, WILLIAM et ux Sally Endsly	7/22 1824	By Charles H. Warren, J.P.
1564 HANNUM, JAMES W. et ux Laura A. Martin	6/15 1854	By R. B.McMullen, Pastor, 1st Presb. Ch. Knoxville, Tenn.
1565 HARDEN, ALFRED S. et ux Jane R. Burchfield	9/13 1855	Iredell D. Wright, J.P.
HARDIN, JNO. H. m. in Meigs Co., Tenn. Susan E., daughter of James Patterson (Newspaper in McGhee Library)	12/10 1854	
1566 HARDIN, THOMAS et ux Candee E. Hicks	11/13 1854	By Wm. H. Anderson, J.P.
1567 HARDON, WM. G. et ux Nancy J. Hutton	4/25 1856	By Jessee Kerr, Jr., J.P. (Wm G. Hardon)
1568 HARDWICK, ACY et ux Mary Knoblete	5/18 1820	By Samuel Douthitt (Should be Noblette)
1569 HARGIS, NATHAN et ux Rebecca Tulluch	2/22 1816	By Wm. McClung, J.P.
1570 HARGUS, DAVID et ux Sarah Stout	10/20 1859	By A. J. Wilson, J.P.
1571 HARLE, BALDWIN et ux Isabella Miller	2/13 1800 issued	No signature, but himself
1572 HARLE, ELBRIDGE et ux Susan Yearcut	4/19 1859	By J. S. Craig, M.G.
HARLEY, GEORGE D. et ux Sarah A. Hale	1/5 1846	
1573 HARLES, HIRAM et ux Franky Perkins	7/11 1850	By Christian Long, J.P.
1574 HARP (or Hack or Hash) MCAJOR et ux Susana Roberts	9/5 1797 issued	Bond: John Roberts
1575 HARPER, MARTIN et ux Betsy McConnell	12/9 1831	By William Toole, J.P.
1576 HARPER, WILLIAM et ux Polly Kenniman	6/22 1820	By Alex B. Gamble, J.P.
1577 HARMON, JAMES et ux Maryann Duncan	12/24 1840	By Eli Richy, J.P.
1578 HARMON, JOHN W. et ux Margaret E. White	1/29 1845	By W. Earnest, J.P.
1579 HARMON, WILLIAM et ux Anna Jones	8/20 1818	By And's S. Morrison, V.D.M. or L.D.M.
1580 HARRIS, ADLY et ux Rebecca Gracy	4/29 1817	By J. Alexander, J.P.

Names	Date Issue Or Celebrated	By Whom/ Security on Bond
1581 HARRIS, ANDREW et ux Maria Harris	12/6 1831 issued	"celebrated by me George Ewing, J.P."
1582 HARRIS, B. B. et ux Mary Jane Wright	5/7 1847	By B. J. McReynolds, J.P. (outside Bonet Harris)
1583 HARRISON, JAMES et ux Malinda Roddy	9/14 1826	By E. Hitch, J.P. (is James Harrison)
1584 HARRIS, JOHN et ux Rebecka Paul	11/26 1812 issued	No returns
1585 HARRIS, JOHN N. et ux Nancy Garner	5/14 1829	By Samuel Hamil, J.P.
1586 HARRIS, JOSEPH et ux Martha Jane Stinnett	3/22 1838	By Wm. Billue, M.G.
1587 HARRIS, JOHN et ux Lotta Crawley	7/7 1845	By Robt' Porter, J.P.
1588 HARRIS, JNO. L. et ux Hester A. Davis	7/8 1858	By James Hamil, Elder
1589 HARRIS, NATHAN et ux Jane Lowery, daughter of Col. John	2/27 1822	By Isaac Anderson,
1590 HARRIS, SAMUEL et ux Elizabeth Harris	5/30 1840	By W. Toole, J.P.
1591 HARRIS, SHELTON et ux Lucinda Childers	1/20 1824	By E. Hitch, Esq.
1592 HARRIS, TOLIVER et ux Patsy Hope	7/30 1816 issued	No returns
1593 HARRIS, WILLIAM et ux Martha (Matha) Roddy	9/29 1826	By Eleven Hitch, Esq.
1594 HARRIS, WILLIAM RUFUS et ux Betty Ann Wright	2/18 1841	By Fielding Pope, M.G.
1595 HARRIS, ZEPHENIAH et ux Jude Kidd	2/27 1834	By Wm. Billue, M.G.
1596 HAIR, JAMES W. et ux M. J. Lain	7/15 1854	By J. H. Donaldson, J.P.
* See 1504		
1597 HARRELSON, JAMES D. et ux Martha Jane Meroney	2/28 1838	By James Henry, J.P.
1598 HARRISON, JOHN et ux Mary Dills	9/29 1839	By John Stratton, J.P.
1599 HARRISON, MICHAEL et ux Sarah Grant	10/1 1846	By R. B.Billue, M.G.
1600 HART, ALEXANDER et ux Jemimah Price	5/22 1818	By Isaac Anderson, M.G.

Names	Date Issue Or Celebrated	By Whom/ Security on Bond
* See Hart, 1631		
1601 HART, ISAAC et ux Martha Roddy	10/9 1821 issued	No returns
1602 HART, SILAS et ux Susan Straine	2/20 1823	By Isaac Anderson, P.N.P. Ch.
1603 HART, THOMAS et ux Melissa Moon	10/1 1856 issued	No returns
1604 HARTSELL, ABRAHAM et ux Louisa Rankin	9/4 1834	By F. Pope, M.G.
1605 HARTSELL, A. L. et ux M. M. Steele	11/1 1855	By A. M. Goodykountz, J.P.
1606 HARTSELL, WM. T. et ux Francis C. Hitch	4/29 1857	By H. Foster, J.P.
1607 HARVEY, JAMES N. et ux Elizabeth Birdwell	12/17 1833	By J.H.R.G. Gardner, M.G.
1608 HARVEY, JOHN et ux Elizabeth Dial	12/29 1824	By Wm. Griffitts, J.P.
1609 HARVEY, MICHAEL et ux Sally Tallent	11/10 1829	By C. H. Warren, J.P.
1610 HARVEY, ONEY et ux Mariah Huffman	5/10 1827	By Henry Soward, M.G.
1611 HARVEY, WILLIAM et ux Carsa Hunt	7/11 1839	By Clemmons Sanders
1612 HASKEW, WILLIAM et ux Telletha Gourly	6/17 1830	By K. Birdwell, M.G.
1613 HATCHER, ELIJAH et ux Rebecca Walker	8/6 1819 issued	No returns
1614 HATCHER, ELIJAH, JR. et ux Hannah J. Hix	12/21 1848	By Lowey McBath, J.P.
1615 HATCHER, JOHN R. et ux Nancy J. Rollins	3/16 1849	By Jesse Kerr, Jr., J.P.
1616 HATCHER, REUBIN et ux Martha McGill	6/1 1821 issued	No returns
1617 HATCHER, RICHARD et ux Ludicia (Leodocia) Kenneman	4/14 1859	By W. W.Nuchols, J.P.
1618 HATCHER, ROBT. et ux Elizabeth Starky	3/4 1852	By A. B. Gamble, J.P.
1619 HASKET, JOS' et ux Patsy Briant	12/10 1818	By Wm. Williamson, J.P.
1620 HAUN, ADAM et ux Maryann Eliott	10/7 1841	By Isaac Anderson, P.N.P. Ch.
1621 HAUN, ADAM et ux Jane Logan	2/25 1849	By F. Pope, M.G.

Names	Date Issue Or Celebrated	By Whom/ Security on Bond
1622 HAWKINS, ALLEN D. et ux Mary C. O'Dam	12/26 1859 issued on 12/17 1859	By Robert McTeer, J.P.
1623 HAWKINS, THOMAS et ux Sally Wimberly	8/13 1838	By Alex'er McCollum, J.P.
1624 HAYSE, GEORGE et ux Avice Greer	9/15 1825	By Joseph Vanpelt, D.D.
1625 HAYS, JAMES A. et ux Mary Stinnett	2/23 1842	By Henry Hamil, J.P.
1626 HAYS, JEREMIAH et ux Margaret Hodd	5/23 1821 issued	"Executed by me Sam'l George, J.P."
1627 HAYS, JOSHUA O. et ux Margaret R. Ewing	9/25 1855 issued	"Executed in due time A. Vance, M.G."
1628 HAYS, ROBT. M. et ux Nancy J. Hale	12/14 1848	By Spencer Henry, M.G.
1629 HAYS, WILLIAM et ux Betsey Brown	3/29 1821	By Samuel Douthit
1630 HEARD, JOH N et ux Rebeckah Martain	11/21 1824 issued	No returns
1631 HEART, EDWARD (HART) et ux Nelly White	10/18 1804 issued	(on back is October 19, 1804; no signature)
* See 1600		
1632 HART, EDWARD et ux Elizabeth Hood	2/21 1814 issued	No returns (Family Book m. 2/22 1814, "Hart")
1633 HALE, THOMAS T. et ux Sobrena Grisham	1/16 1851	By Joseph A. Hutton, J.P.
* See 1499		
1634 HEARTSELL, HIRAM et ux Amanda M. F. Wright	6/8 1837	By Isaac Anderson, P.N.P. Ch.
1635 HEDRICK, DANIEL et ux Mary Jones	5/26 1836	By Geo. Snider, J.P.
1636 HEDRICK, JACOB et ux Polly Rice	2/12 1823	By Samuel Davidson, J.P.
1637 HEDRICK, JACOB et ux Zilpha Brewer	12/26 1831	By James Taylor, M.G.
1638 HEDRICK, JACOB B. et ux Narcissa K. Watters	1/11 1849	By Lowery McBath, J.P.
1639 HEDRICK, JAMES et ux Manervia Stevenson	8/8 1829	By Thomas Billue, J.P.
1640 HEDRICK, JAMES et ux Polly Carvin	5/12 1842	By Ben Cunningham, J.P.

Names	Date Issue Or Celebrated	By Whom/ Security on Bond
1641 HEADRICK, JAMES et ux Mary Jane Rhea	10/1850	By James M. Tulloch, J.P.
1642 HEDRICK, JOHN et ux Susannah Long	10/21 1838	By D. S.Schoolfield, M.G.
1643 HEDRICK, PETER et ux Polly Stinson	6/28 1831	By Sam Henry, J.P.
1644 HEDRICK, PETER et ux Mary J. Mosely	11/27 1854	By David Spradlin, J.P.
1645 HEADRICK, THOMAS P. et ux Salethia Bryant	7/23 1835	By Frederic Emmett, J.P.
1646 HEDRICK, WILLIAM M. et ux Susana Borden	8/7 1824	By Samuel Davidson, J.P.
1647 HEADRICK, WILLIAM et ux Mary C. Emmitt	9/1 1843	By John Adams, M.G.
1648 HEADRICK, WILLIAM et ux Nancy J. Best	10/2 1851	By James M. Tulloch, J.P.
1649 HEADRICK, WM. et ux Martha Clemens	5/27 1852	By C. Long, J.P.
1650 HEADRICK, WILLIAM et ux Nancy L. Myers	9/23 1852	By Daniel H. Emmert, J.P.
1651 HENDERSON, A. L. et ux Jane Thompson	1/23 1855	By James M. Lane, J.P.
1652 HENDERSON, ALEX. T. et ux Rhoda A. Alexander	3/21 1850	By Andrew Ferguson, J.P.
1653 HENDERSON, FRANCIS J. et ux Ellen Pickens	3/11 1823	By Hugh Bogle, J.P.
1654 HENDERSON, GEORGE et ux Nancy Ann Thompson	5/24 1820	By J. Anderson, P.N.P. Ch.
1655 HENDERSON, GEORGE P. et ux Tennessee Wrinkle	10/24 1857	By W. A. Lawson, M.G.
1656 HENDERSON, JAMES et ux Rachel Debausk	4/28 1808 issued	No returns
1657 HENDERSON, JAMES et ux Mary Hunter	12/30 1817	By And'w S. Morrison, V.D.M.
1658 HENDERSON, JAMES et ux Betsey Reynolds	9/22 1818	By John Black, J.P.
1659 HENDERSON, JOHN et ux Nancy Tuck	8/13 1835	By A. Ish, J.P.
1660 HENDERSON, JOHN L. et ux Margaret Walker	9/20 1831	By James Templeton, M.G.
1661 HENDERSON, JOHN J. et ux Esther Allen	12/22 1847	By James Law, Min. of Asct. Syd. of N.A.
1662 HENDERSON, JOHN S. et ux Winneford Davis	12/30 1838	By Wm. Henry, J.P.

1663 HENDERSON, JOSEPH   4/1 1819   By Hugh Bogle, J.P.
    et ux Jennet McClung

1664 HENDERSON, JOSEPH   1/29 1824   By Isaac Anderson,
    et ux Sarah D. White   P.N.P. Ch.

1665 HENDERSON, JOSEPH   1/8 1828   By D. Carson, M.G.
    et ux Nancy Minis

1666 HENDERSON, SAMUEL   1/19 1849   By F. Pope, M.G.
    et ux Sarah A. Reeder

1667 HENDERSON, THOS.   3/24 1818   By John Black, J.P.
    et ux Cristina Currier

1668 HENDERSON, THOMAS   11/14 1848   By J. S. Craig, M.G.
    et ux Elizabeth A. Ganet   (may be Gault)

1669 HENDERSON, THOS. H.   2/9 1843   By John S. Craig, M.G.
    et ux Eliza J. Gault

1670 HENDERSON, WM.   1/12 1819   "R. B. McCully, J.P."
    et ux Elizabeth McGill   issued

1671 HENDERSON, WILLIAM   7/27 1826   By A. Ish, J.P.
    et ux Polly Young

1672 HENDERSON, WILLIAM   5/11 1842   By Isaac Anderson,
    et ux Elizabeth C.   P.N.P. Ch.
    Bogle

1673 HENDERSON, WM.   9/23 1858   By Wm. M. Brickell,
    et ux Elizabeth C. Coston   J.P.

1674 HENDERSON, WILLIAM J.   1/14 1846   By J. S. Craig, M.G.
    et ux Martha Jane Frew

1675 HENDERSON, WILLIAM M.   7/23 1822   By Wm. Griffitts, J.P.
    et ux Cynthia Walker

1676 HENDERICKSON, ABRAM   1/22 1833   By Alexander Ish, J.P.
    et ux Polly Parkins

1677 HENDRICKSON, EILLIS   2/9 1838   By Wm. Billue, M.G.
    et ux Nancy Elvina
    Maze

HENLY, ARTHUR m. Ann Evelyn Moore in Brickvill. Ch.--claim of
family; she of Alex. Spottswood Moore of Virginia; he of
Bunk Moore.

1678 HENLY, A. S.   6/19 1854   By Wm. Wiley Neal, M.G.
    et ux Elizabeth Henry   of M.E. Ch. So.

1679 HENLEY, JOHN   1/6 1835   By William Colburn,
    et ux Aloy (or Aley)   J.P.
    Privey

1680 HENLEY, JOHN W.   1/1 1857   By Daniel H. Emmett,
    et ux Mary J. Stephenson   J.P.

1681 HENRY, AKE   3/15 1836   By Spencer Henry, J.P.
    et ux Sarah B. Green

1682 HENRY, ALBERT G.   8/7 1838   By James Henry, J.P.
    et ux Maryann Henry

Names	Date Issue Or Celebrated	By Whom/ Security on Bond
1683 HENRY, ARTHUR M. et ux Mary E. Snider	10/13 1859	By James D. Lawson, M.G.M.E. Ch. So.
1684 HENRY, GEORGE W. et ux Isabella Harle	1/20 1852	By A. Vance, M.G.
1685 HENRY, HUGH et ux Nancy Henry	10/18 1825	By A. B. Gamble, J.P.
1686 HENRY, HUGH et ux Martha R. Hafley	3/8 1840	By James Ray, J.P.
1687 HENRY, HUGH J. et ux Mary M. Reagan	10/4 1847	By Will Cumming, J.P.
1688 HENRY, JAMES et ux Esther Rogers	11/25 1814 issued	"married on Nov. 25" (No signature)
1689 HENRY, JAMES et ux Sally Walker	8/22 1822	By A. B. Gamble, J.P.
1890 HENRY, JAMES et ux Catherine Keamy	1/7 1827	By A. B. Gamble, J.P.
1691 HENRY, JAMES et ux Elizabeth Gamble	1/31 1833	By Wm. McTeer, J.P.
1692 HENRY, JAMES M. et ux Ann Hutton	11/19 1839	By Joseph A. Hutton, J.P.
1693 HENRY, JOHN et ux Asther Gamble (outside is Esther)	10/8 1817	By Hugh Bogle, J.P.
1694 HENRY, JOHN et ux Sarah Smith	10/22 1831	By William McTeer, J.P.
1695 HENRY, JOHN et ux McClanahan, A.	2/22 1857	By N. Brewer, J.P.
1696 HENRY, JOSEPH B. et ux Tabitha A. Hese	2/9 1844	By William Cumming, J.P.
1697 HENRY, PLEASANT H. et ux Margaert A. Keeble	3/12 1857	By John Clark, J.P.
1698 HENRY, SAMUEL et ux Elizabeth Garner	3/26 1798 issued	Bond: George Colville
1699 HENRY, SAMUEL L. et ux Margaret T. Hammontree (of James)	12/11 1851	By A. Vance, M.G.
1700 HENRY, SAMUEL et ux Mary C. Murphy	2/21 1850	By A. B. Gamble, J.P.
1701 HENRY, SAMUEL H. et ux Julia H. Stone (not sure of surname)	3/2 1859	By H. Foster, J.P.
1702 HENRY, SAMUEL T. et ux Rebecca Clampet	1/29 1859	By H. J. Henry, J.P.
1703 HENRY, SPENCER et ux Elizabeth Maze	1/17 1828	By A. B.Gamble, J.P.

Names	Date Issue Or Celebrated	By Whom/ Security on Bond
1704 HENRY, THOMAS et ux Mary J. Mason	6/12 1847	By S. J. McReynolds, J.P. (groom may be Hervey or Kervey or Kenry)
1705 HENRY, WILLIAM et ux Polly Gamble	12/10 1800 issued	Bond: Samuel Henry
1706 HENRY, WILLIAM et ux Sarah E. Stone	9/23 1859	By Harvey Thompson, J.P.
1707 HENRY, WM. W. et ux Sarah Utter	10/7 1820	By Andrew S. Morrison, V.D.M.
1708 HENRY, WILL W. et ux Jane Tulloch	12/25 1823	By Wm. Gault, J.P.
1709 HENRY, WILLIAM et ux Catherine Henry	11/30 1853	"Executed by me Henry Rule, M.G."

* *HERD _____ of Georgia m - 10/1 1822 Regia _____ dau. of Dr. Isaac Wright "newspaper in McGee Library" by Dr. Isaac Henderson*

1710 HENSHAW, NARA et ux Nancy Hackney	9/30 1840	By William Colburn, J.P.

* See 1736

1711 HESS, JOHN et ux Polly Garner	4/26 1820	By Hugh Bogle, J.P.
1712 HERRIN, JAMES et ux Artarameren Stinett	8/19 1858	By A. R. James, J.P.
1713 HERIN, JOHN et ux Mary A. McCully	3/1 1855	By John Waler, M.G. (Wear?)
1714 HERREN, THOS. et ux Mariah Anthoney	2/14 1856	By Curran Lemons, J.P.
1715 HERROLD, GEORGE D. et ux Sarah Ann Hale	9/26 1833	By W. G.Brownlow, M.G.
1716 HETTON, LANDON C. et ux Martha J. Headston	10/1 1848	By Thos. M. Rooker, J.P.
1717 HIATT, GEORGE W. et ux Mary Jones	8/5 1838	By William Henry, J.P.
1718 HICKMAN, WM. et ux Mary E. (or C.) Johnson	1/8 1857	By Wm. M. Brickell, J.P.
1719 HICKMAN, ISAIAH et ux Margarette I. Johnston	9/14 1856	By Wm. M. Brickell, J.P.
1720 HICKS, ABRAHAM et ux Betsa Blair	11/8 1832	By John Hendrix, J.P.
1721 HICKS, ABRAHAM et ux Rachel Henry	10/6 1859	By Nichols Brewer, J.P. Esq.

Names	Date Issue Or Celebrated	By Whom/ Security on Bond
1722 HICKS, ISAAC et ux Sarah Long Walker	10/27 1812 issued	Bond: George Snider
1723 HICKS, JAMES et ux Sarah E. Wright	10/31 1854	By H. Foster, J.P.
1724 HICKS, JOHN et ux Catty Simons	12/28 1813 issued	No returns
1725 HICKS, JOHN et ux Phoebe Bayless	5/2 1816	By George Snider, J.P.
1726 HICKS, JOHN et ux Rebekah Wade	3/14 1816 issued	No returns
1727 HICKS, MATHEW et ux Telitha H. Hargis	1/31 1858	By James M. Tulloch, J.P.
1728 HICKS, ROBERT et ux Rebecca Pickens	8/4 1842	By Lemuel Adams, J.P.
1729 HICKEY, DANIEL et ux Betsey Tipton	7/5 1823	By Hugh Bogle, J.P.
1730 HICKY, DAVID et ux Fanny Bohannan	3/21 1822	By Hugh Bogle, J.P.
1731 HIESKELL, JOHN M. et ux Elizabeth A. R. Leeper	11/14 1839	By Andrew Vance, M.G.
1732 HIGHTON, WARREN et ux Martha M. Key	4/6 1853	By Wm. Henderson, J.P.
1733 HILL, PLEASANT et ux Matilda Moore	6/16 1859	By Wm. H. Anderson, ·J.P.
1734 HILL, ROBERT et ux Eliza E. Perkey	12/17 1857	By Wm. M. Brickell, J.P.
1735 HINTON, JETHRO et ux Mary A. Bailey	1/16 1851	By Will M. Brickell, J.P.
1736 HINSHAW, EVAN et ux Nancy Hackney	2/11 1836	By A. Ish, J.P.
* See 1710		
1737 HITCH, ARCHIBALD et ux Evalene Kidd	11/6 1851	Jno. S. Craig, M.G.
1738 HITCH, BENJAMIN et ux Eliza Jones	9/22 1836	By James Ray, J.P.
1739 HITCH, ELISE et ux Polly Shook	12/26 1822	By Billy Holloway, M.G. of Babtist Order
1740 HITCH, ELIAS et ux Apaliza Jane Losseon Bilhue	1/2 1840	By Sam'l Love, M.G.
1741 HICH, ELIAS et ux Letitia Sharp	10/1 1846	By Wm. Billhue, M.G.

Names	Date Issue Or Celebrated	By Whom/ Security on Bond
1742 HITCH, STEPHEN et ux C.A.L. George	9/16 1849	By Cu Cowan, J.P.
1743 HITTLE, FREDRICK et ux Polly Edmonds	10/2 1819	By James Gillespy, J.P.
1744 HIX, ANDREW et ux Sarah Brickey	6/22 1838	By Robert Shields, J.P.
1745 HIX, Elijah et ux Sarah Starkey	3/13 1834	By Spencer Henry, J.P.
1746 HIX, HANCIL et ux Lucy Fea	9/16 1809 issued	No returns
1747 HIX, LANCIN (or LAUCIN) et ux Rosa H. Pass	12/8 1853	By C. Cowan, J.P.
1748 HIX, SAML M. et ux Martha M. Phelps	12/10 1857	By H. Foster, J.P.
1749 HIZE, JACOB et ux Sally Rogers	9/22 1847	By John Tipton, J.P.
1750 HODGES, AARON et ux Jane Houk	10/15 1827	By A. B.Gamble, J.P.
1751 HODGES, WILLIAM et ux Angeline Moss	5/17 1857	By W. A. Lawson, M.G.
1752 HODGE, WILLIAM H. et ux Lucinda Jeffries	2/14 1822	By Elijah Rogers, M.G.
1753 HOFF, DANIEL et ux Betsey Chisom	1/9 1798 issued	Bond: John Chisom
1754 HOFFMEISTER, JOHN M. et ux Elizabeth C. McGhee	9/28 1848	By J. S. Craig, M.G.
1755 HOLIDAY, JOSEPH et ux Nancy Everett	9/30 1858	By R. E. Tedford, M.G.
1756 HOLLARS, DANIEL et ux Polly Goodwin	6/21 1828	By Saml Hamill, J.P.
1757 HOLLINGSWORTH, ENOCH et ux Sally Burk	7/21 1830 issued	"by me Wm. Billue, M.G., celebrated"
1758 HOLLINGSWORTH, JACOB et ux Jane Crawford	4/22 1823	By Charl H. Warren, J.P.
1759 HOLLINGSWORTH, LEVI et ux Polly Boshears	3/1 1827 issued	"joined by me Alex'er Stewart, J.P."
1760 HOLLOWAY, BARNES et ux Ruth Wallace	6/20 1816	By George Snider, J.P.
1761 HOOD, AARON et ux Sarah Kidd	2/24 1848	By Robt' Porter, J.P.
1762 HOOD, ALEXANDER et ux Sarah Frow	3/30 1830	By Darius Hoyt, M.G.
1763 HOOD, DAILY W. et ux Nancy Tipton	7/19 1832	By Wm. Toole, J.P.

Names	Date Issue Or Celebrated	By Whom/ Security on Bond
1764 HOOD, FRANCIS M. et ux Eliza A. McTeer	10/13 1843	By Wm. B. Brown, V.D.M.
1765 HOOD, ISAAC et ux Sarah Crawly	3/21 1845	By Robt' Porter, J.P.
1766 HOOD, JASPER et ux Celia A. Kidd	11/3 1853	By D. Caldwell
1767 HOOD, JOHN et ux Susan Barnett	2/7 1839	By B. H. Mayo, M.G.C.P.C.
1768 HOOD, JOHN et ux Elizabeth J. Stoops	4/20 1848	By Robt' Porter, J.P.
1769 HOOD, JOHN B. et ux Polly Dyer	2/16 1832	By Isaac Anderson, P.N.P. Ch.
1770 HOOD, ROBERT et ux Elanor Tyly (outside is Tally)	3/25 1847	By B. F.Duncan, J.P.
1771 HOOD, THOMAS et ux Rebecca Roddy	9/7 1852	By D. Caldwell
1772 HOOD, WILLIAM et ux Margaret J. Cupp	4/13 1848	By Alex O. George, J.P.
1773 HOOK, ALFRED et ux Elizabeth Howell	6/12 1836	By William Colburn, J.P.
1774 HOOK, ANDREW et ux Betsey Jinkens	1/27 1831	By Wm. Williamson, J.P.
1775 HOOKS, JAMES H. et ux Margaret E. McGraw	11/27 1828	By William Eagleton, M.G.
1776 HOOK, JOHN P. et ux Mary E.Hart	5/15 1849	By Isaac Anderson, P.N.P. Ch.
1777 HOOKS, ROBERT et ux Abbigail Alexander	11/27 1795 issued	Bond: John Alexander
1778 HOOKS, ROBERT et ux Elizabeth Kilburn	9/8 1824	By Isaac Anderson, P.N.P. Ch.
1779 HOOK, ROBERT et ux Susan Roach	10/3 1837	By William Colburn, J.P.
1780 HOCKER, JOSHUA W. et ux Nancy J. Tedford	12/12 1844	By Green B. Saffell, J.P.
1781 HOOPER, MILAS et ux M. R. McColloch	9/18 1851	By Isaac Anderson, P.N.P. Ch.
1782 HOOPER, THOMAS et ux Margaret Simms	9/4 1827	By William McTeer, J.P.
1783 HOPE, JAMES B. et ux Margaret Ritchey	2/26 1850	By J. H. Donaldson, J.P.
1784 HOPE, W. A. et ux Hannah Tedford	12/18 1851	By Ralph E. Tedford, M.G.

Names	Date Issue Or Celebrated	By Whom/ Security on Bond
1785 HOOVER, JOHN D. et ux Elizabeth Lingenfelter	2/5 1845	By James H. Donaldson, J.P.
1786 HOOVER, JOHN J. et ux Sarah Bowerman	9/4 1834 issued	"by me William Colburn, J.P."
1787 HOUSER, ALEXANDER et ux Mary Everett	10/6 1842	By Christian Long, J.P.
1788 HOUSER, HENDERSON et ux Susan Smith	2/17 1848	By Wesley Earnest, J.P.
1789 HOUSER, JOHN et ux Sarah Boyd	5/2 1854	By Wm. W. Nuchols, J.P.
1790 HOUSER, PETER et ux Sarah A. Coulter	11/29 1849	By Christian Long, J.P.
1791 HOUSER, LEWIS et ux Caroline Cruse	2/20 1858	By John Clark, J.P.
1792 HOUSTON, JAMES et ux Mary Gillespie	10/6 1798 issued	Bond: Barclay McGhee
1793 HOUSTON, JOHN C. et ux Olivia C. Duncan	12/28 1841 issued	Bond: B. F.Duncan
1794 HOUSTON, JOSEPH B. et ux Huldah D. Cusick	12/7 1837	By F. Pope, M.G.
1795 HOUSER, PETER et ux Elizabeth Waters	5/27 1856	By W. W. Nuchols, J.P.
1796 HOUSER, PHILLIP et ux Sereana Everett	12/6 1849	By Christian Long, J.P.
1797 HOUSEHOLDER, JAMES P. et ux Betsy Wiginton	9/17 1829	By Charles H. Warren, J.P.
1798 HOUSTON, JAMES et ux Ann Houston	10/17 1816	By Isaac Anderson, P.N.P. Ch.
1799 HOUSTON, JAMES et ux Mary Gillespy	10/6 1796	No returns
1800 HOUSTON, JOHN et ux Patsy Gillespie	10/16 1817	By R. H. King, M.G.
1801 HOUSTON, JOHN et ux Ann G. White	7/16 1829	By Isaac Anderson, P.N.P. Ch.
1802 HOUSTON, JOHN et ux Elinor Wilson	12/17 1835	By A. Vance, M.G.
1803 HOUSTON, MATTHEW M. et ux Mary Gillespie	11/29 1821	By R. H. King, M.G.
1804 HOUSTON, MATHEW C. et ux Esther H. Gillespie	8/1 1822	By R. H. King, M.G.
1805 HOUSTON, J. A. et ux Mary J. McReynolds	9/16 1856	By R. E. Tedford, M.G.

Names	Date Issue Or Celebrated	By Whom Security on Bond
1807 HOUSTON, ROBERT et ux Dorothy Creswell	8/9 1826	By Isaac Anderson, P.N.P. Ch.
1808 HOUSTON, ROBERT F. et ux Ann Gillespie	4/13 1826	By George Donnell, V.D.M.
1809 HOUSTON, SAMUEL et ux Nancy Stephens	5/24 1821	By Wm. Fagg, J.P.
1810 HOUSTON, SAMUEL et ux Ann Huchison	2/15 1825	By Isaac Anderson, P.N.P. Ch.
1811 HOWARD, EPHRIAM et ux Sarah Vaught	6/23 1797 issued	Bond: Isiah Stephens
1812 HUCKSBY, ARTHUR et ux Millinda Wiging- ton	7/6 1823	By Samuel Douthit, Elder in the M.E. Ch. A.D.
1813 HUDGEONS, WILLIAM B. et ux Rebecca McClure	6/20 1826	By Douthit, Samuel, E.M.E. Ch.
1814 HUFFMAN, JACOB et ux Polly Lawrence	12/4 1818	By Samuel Douthit
* See 1841		
1816 HOWARD, ALFORD B. et ux Euphemia Howard	11/24 1843	By Samuel Tulloch, J.P.
1817 HOWARD, CORNELIUS L. et ux Betsy J.	10/16 1828	By Jos' Cumming, Tra- veling Elder M.E. Ch.
1818 HOWARD, JOHN et ux Salena Brient	3/20 1851	By James M. Tulloch, J.P.
1819 HOWARD, JOHN et ux Kity Vaught	10/8 1807 issued	No returns
1820 HOWARD, WM. et ux Milly Barnhill	11/24 1852	By John McClain, J.P.
1821 HOWARD, WILLIAM W. et ux Martha Ann Harden	10/16 1846	By Joseph Pesler, M.G.
1822 HOWEL, JOSEPH et ux Amanda McCallie	2/6 1834	By William Anderson, J.P.
1823 HOYLE, ANDREW et ux Vicey Love	2/10 1842	By T. K. Harmon, M.G.
1824 HOYLE, JOHN et ux Margaret H. Cope (of Geo. and Elizabeth Cope)	10/27 1842	By Joseph A. Hutton, J.P.
1825 HOYT, DARIUS et ux Lucinda M.Bogle	5/3 1827	By Isaac Anderson, P.N.P. Ch.
1826 HUBBARD, CHARLES et ux Sarah Townsell (is Townsend)	8/28 1845	By W. R. Flinn, J.P.
1827 HUBBARD, GEORGE By Clarressa Taylor	4/1 1858	By James M. Tulloch, J.P.

Names	Date Issue Or Celebrated	By Whom Security on Bond
1828 HUBBARD, JAMES et ux Sarena Ballinger	8/5 1845	By W. R. Flinn, J.P.
1829 HUBBARD, JOSEPH et ux Elizabeth Hatcher	8/27 1846	By John Tipton, J.P.
1830 HUTCHENSON, WILLIAM et ux Nelly Brewer	8/27 1830	By thomas Bilhue, J.P.
1831 HUCKABY, JOHN et ux Amelia Adaline Rusten	10/2 1839	By John Maxwell, J.P.
* See 1812		
1832 HUDGEONS, JOHN J. et ux Eliza Parks	7/3 1837	By Eli Richy, J.P.
* See 1813		
1833 HUDSON, SAMUEL et ux Britann Bowerman	3/7 1839	By John D. Wilson, M.G.
1834 HUFFAKER, JESSE et ux Elender Rooker	1/17 1818	By Nicholas Norwood
1835 HUFFMAN, JAMES et ux Hetty J. Henry	11/30 1848	By James M. Tulloch, J.P.
1836 HUFSTUTLER, ELI et ux Mary A. Carpenter	9/15 1853	By Spencer Henry, M.G.
1837 HUFSTEETLER, HARLEY et ux Rachael Kosner (See Costner)	11/21 1831	By Wm. Williamson, J.P.
1838 HUFFSTUTER, MICHAEL et ux Elizabeth.A. Bingham	1/4 1855	By Spencer Henry, M.G.
1839 HUFSTETLER, M. A. et ux Margaret A. Hutsell	11/10 1858	By Wm. M. Brickell, J.P.
1840 HUGHS, CHARLES et ux Eliza A. Black- burn	4/19 1840 (issued 4/18 1838 is inside)	By J. Dyke, M.G.
1841 HUGHES, MOSES et ux Mariam Kelso	4/15 1801 issued	Bond: James Mayo
* See 1815		
1842 HUGHS, MOSES H. et ux Hester C. Stone	11/18 1847	By Alexander McClain, J.P.
1843 HUGHS, MOSES H. et ux Polly Duncan	10/7 1830	By B. Abernathy, L.D.
1844 HULING, JOHN et ux Sally Snider	6/20 1816	By George Snider, M.G. or J.P., either
1845 HUMPHREY, ARTHUR C. et ux Martha J. Brown	2/3 1850	By L. L. McFarling, J.P.

Names	Date Issue Or Celebrated	By Whom Security on Bond
1846 HUMPHREY, DAVID et ux David(?) Carson	12/26 1844	By Edmund Wayman, J.P.
1847 HUMPHRIES, JAMES et ux Nancy McClung	1/31 1828	By William Eagleton, M.G.
1848 HUMPHREY, JAMES A. et ux A. Dolley Talley	1/10 1850	By W. A.Lawson, M.G.
1849 HUMPHREY, J. C. et ux M. A.Ferguson	11/27 1851	By Andrew Ferguson, J.P.
1850 HUMPHREY, J. C. et ux E. J. Alexander	12/13 1853	By John J. Hoover, J.P.
1851 HUMPHREY, JOSEPH et ux Rachael H. Sparks	8/20 1851	And' Ferguson, J.P.
1852 HUMPHREY, SAMUEL et ux Mary B. McCafary	3/14 1843	By J. Dyke, Pastor Unitia Ch.
1853 HUMPHREY, WM. et ux Nancy C. M. Cochran	10/12 1848	By A. J. McGee, M.G.
1854 HUMPHREY, WM. C. et ux Leonora McCrosky	10/15 1851 issued	"by me in due time, A. Vance, M.G."
1855 HUMPHREY, WILLIAM C. et ux Mary E. Hudgeons	2/22 1865	By A. Vance, M.G.
1855 HUNT, ABRAHAM et ux Patsey McDaniel	7/7 1838	By William Cilburn, J.P.
1856 HUNTT, EDMOND By Anne Newman	7/27 1809 issued	No returns
1857 HUNT, EDMUND et ux Floria Houk	8/28 1815 issued	No returns
1858 HUNT, GEORGE W. et ux Sarah A. Alexander	2/17 1857	Andrew Ferguson, J.P.
1859 HUNT, HENRY et ux Judy Starky	1/13 1829	"by me on date, Charles H. Warren, J.P."
1860 HUNT, JAMES et ux Freshy Rose	4/2 1829	By Robert B. Billue, M.G. of Babtist Order"
1861 HUNT, JAMES et ux Eddy (Eady) Lain	3/12 1853	By A. J. McGee, M.G.
1862 HUNT, JOHN et ux Nancy Patrick	12/17 1835	By Rev. M. Pope
1863 HUNT, JOHN et ux Polly O'Dear (Adair	1/27 1837	By William Colburn, J.P.
1864 HUNT, JOHN et ux Liza Goforth	7/3 1845	By Edmund Wayman, J.P.
1865 HUNT, MADISON et ux Jean Bradberry	2/27 1847	By William Colburn, J.P.

Names	Date Issue Or Celebrated	By Whom Security on Bond
1866 HUNT, SAMUEL et ux Mira Tucker	1/2 1851	By Andrew Ferguson, J.P.
1867 HUNTER, ANDREW C. et ux Martha A. Humphreys	12/26 1850	By W. H. Rogers, M.G.
1868 HUNTER, GEORGE I. et ux Mary C. Wells	7/29 1841	By A. C. Montgomery, J.P.
1869 HUSKY, ISAAC et ux Delilah Gipson	10/4 1849	By Daniel H. Emmett, J.P.
1870 HUSSEY, ELIJAH et ux Elizabeth Baker	7/26 1801 issued	Bond: William Baker
1871 HUTCHINSON, W. P. et ux Nancy A. Roberts	4/29 1858	By Cu Cowan, J.P.

*   See 1830

1872 HUTTON, JOSIAH et ux Isabella McConnal	1/7 1796 issued	Bond: James McConnell
1873 HUTTON, JOSEPH A. et ux Elizabeth Henry	12/3 1829	By A. Vance, M.G.
1874 HUTTON, WILLIAM et ux Narcissa Moore	11/30 1824	By Isaac Anderson, P.N.P. Ch.
1875 HUTTON, WM. L. et ux Nancy C. Wells	12/23 1858	By J. S. Craig, M.G.
1876 HUTSELL, GEORGE et ux Katherine Skipper	3/27 1848	By John Morton, J.P.
1877 HUTSELL, GEORGE et ux Elizabeth Maxwell	10/1 1851	By John Morton, J.P.
1878 HUTSEL, JOHN et ux Sarah Hutsel	2/23 1843	By Christian Long, J.P.
1879 HUTSEL, JOHN K. et ux Nancy A. Willox	8/12 1844	By John Morton, J.P.
1880 HUTSELL, JOSEPH et ux Mary Ann Long	8/23 1839 issued 8/23 1838	By W. M. Rorex, J.P.
1881 HUTSELL, LEWIS et ux Nancy Hendrickson	7/26 1858	By John Gault, J.P. (Louis Hutsell)
1882 HUTSELL, WILLIAM et ux Elizabeth A. Hutsell	3/8 1842	By Robert Delzell, J.P.
1883 HYATT, BENJAMIN et ux Lucy Tipton	4/27 1844 issued	(Undecipherable, but "executed")
1884 HYCE, FELIX et ux Nancy J. Nelson	5/12 1850	By Christian Long, J.P.
1885 HYDE, JASON et ux Nancy Dever	9/5 1848	By Curran Lemons, J.P.

Names	Date Issue Or Celebrated	By Whom/ Security on Bond
1886 ILES, WILLIAM R. et ux Elizabeth A. Kenedy	1/4 1844	By Samuel Tulloch, J.P.
1887 INGE, W. M. et ux A. C. Coulson.	12/12 1859 issued	"by me in due time, A. Vance, M.G."
1888 INGRAM, JOHN et ux Martha Tharp	10/24 1810 issued	No returns
1889 INGRUM, WM. et ux Mary McClure	12/25 1851	By S. J. McReynolds, J.P.
1890 INMAN, WILLIAM et ux Mary Wear	5/26 1823	By Sam'l Hamill, J.P.
1891 IRLAND, WM. et ux Deborah Huffman	12/14 1818 issued	No returns
1892 IRVIN, ALEX M. et ux Polly A. Moor	11/6 1851	By Wm. M. Brickell, J.P.
1893 IRWIN, BARCKLY M. et ux Elizabeth M. Cumming	9/26 1839	By Henry Hamil, J.P.
1894 IRVIN, BARTLEY M. et ux Rachel N. McGinley	4/23 1857	By J. S. Craig, M.G.
1895 IRWIN, CHARLES A. et ux Margaret Hamil	4/18 1837	By Joseph A. Hutton, J.P.
1896 IRWIN, DAVID et ux Dorcas Wright	7/16 1817 issued November 22, 1817!!	By Sam'l George, J.P.
1897 IRVIN, JAMES B. et ux M. J. Thompson	6/18 1850	By Isaac Anderson, P.N.P. Ch.

IRWIN, JAMES P. m. in Campbell Co., Tenn. 3/24 1845, Nancy Young, daughter of John Kincaid.

1898 IRWIN, JOHN et ux Lovina Jane Johnston	9/18 1841	By W. Toole, J.P.
1899 IRVIN, WM. et ux Betey Jouster	1/9 1806 issued	No returns
1900 IRIAR, WM. et ux Bessy Jentry	9/19 1810 issued	No returns

*   See Wm. Greer & Bessy Gentry, 1444

1901 IVINS, SOLOMON et ux Maryann Moore	10/4 1837	By George Russell, M.G.
1902 ISH, A. J. et ux Susan Henderson	6/1 1854	By Joseph Peeler, M.G.
1903 IVEY, BAXTER et ux Susana Ellidge	10/23 1823	By A. B.Gamble, J.P.
1904 JACOBS, GUSTAVIA et ux Rachel Gibs	4/22 1858	"at 9 o'clock a.m., Samuel Pride, J.P."

Names	Date Issue Or Celebrated	Security on Bond
1905 JACK, ALLEN G. of Knox Co. et ux Betsey W. McCallie	12/14 1820	By Thomas H. Nelson, Rev.
1906 JACK, JAMES et ux Nancy McCallie	2/6 1816	By I. Anderson, M.G.
1907 JACKSON, ANDREW et ux Jean Sloan	6/8 1797 issued	Bond: Samuel Gould
1908 JACKSON, JAMES R. et ux Sarah Keene	5/27 1858	By Rob't Williams, M.G.
1909 JACKSON, JOHN et ux Eliza Brown	7/4 1822	By Samuel Hamil, J.P.
1910 JACKSON, WILLIAM et ux Mary Majors	*/10 1817	By Jos' Alexander, J.P.
1911 JAMES, A. R. et ux Salena Key	3/21 1855	By Wm. M. Brickell, J.P.
1912 JAMES, BENJAMIN et ux Elizabeth Gelbreath	10/2 1810 issued	No returns
1913 JAMES, ELIJAH et ux Malinda Tucker	1/16 1820	By Samuel Douthitt, M.G.
1914 JAMES, J. A. et ux Cynthia McMahan	2/26 1849	By Isaac Anderson, P.N.P. Ch.
1915 JAMES, JESSE et ux Polly Rocker	3/19 1818 issued	No returns
1916 JAMES, JESSE H. et ux Aryth Stone	12/25 1856	By John Gault, J.P.
1917 JAMES, JOHN H. et ux Sarah E. McCullough	3/7 1850 issued	Bond: John W. Bailey
1918 JAMES, PLEASANT et ux Catherine E. Easterly (outside is Catherine E. Coston)	7/24 1856	By A. R.James, J.P.
1919 JAMES, P. C. et ux Isabella Perkins	9/17 1853	By Wm. H. Anderson, J.P.
1920 JAMES, WILLIAM et ux Margaret Jones	10/30 1832	By John Hendrix, J.P.
1921 JEFFRIES, JAMES et ux Elizabeth Bowers	11/15 1827	By klijah Rogers, M.G.
1922 JENKINS, DAVID et ux Nancy Ware	9/10 1844	By W. Toole, J.P.
1923 JENKINS, BENJAMIN et ux Margaret Brawner	11/16 1843	By Christian Long, J.P.
1924 JENKINS, JONES et ux Eleanor Craig	12/30 1834	By Ro. Thompson, J.P.

Names	Date Issue Or Celebrated	Security on Bond
1925 JENKINS, JONES et ux Susanah Dunn	3/26 1850 issued	"executed as per law"
1926 JENKINS, JOHN et ux Elizabeth Sawyer	9/30 1847	By Frederic Emmett, M.G.
1927 JIMENSON, JOHN R. et ux Elizabeth Tharp	12/28 1819	By Samuel Douthit, M.G.
1928 JOHNSON, ALBERT F. et ux Martha Young	9/1 1853	By S. J. McReynolds, J.P.

*   See 2410

1929 JOHNSON, BENJAMIN et ux Ritter Roddy	8/12 1852	By D. Caldwell, J.P.

JOHNSON, BENJAMIN m. 12/24 1824 Judah May: found 6/13 1922 by
W. E. Pat house of a decendent of McKamey, J.P.

1930 JOHNSTON, ELI et ux Polly Winchester	2/18 1822	By William Williamson, J.P.
1931 JOHNSTON, JAMES R. et ux Hannah C. Shelly	3/25 1857	By W. A. Lawson, M.G.
1932 JOHNSON, JOSHUA et ux Ann E. Frazier	12/23 1858	By Absolom Abbot, M.G.
1933 JOHNSON, PETER et ux Nancy A. Rorex	1/10 1854	By E. F. Sevier, M.G.
1934 JOHNSON, R. M. et ux Jane Wheeler	3/24 1854	By F. Pope, M.G.
1935 JOHNSON, WILLIAM et ux Elizabeth Whittenberger	8/20 1821	By Joseph Vanpelt, M.G.
1836 JOHNSON, ELIJAH et ux Martha Mays	11/20 1855	By B. F.Duncan, J.P.
1937 JOHNSTON, FRANCES et ux Polly Johnston	11/23 1802 issued	Bond: David Oats
1938 JOHNSTON, FRANCES et ux Jane Ferguson	8/29 1815 issued	"celebrated by me in 1815, Jas. Stevean, J.P."
1939 JOHNSTON, FRACIS et ux Polly Bond	3/20 1830	By Leroy Noble, J.P.
1940 JOHNSTON, GEORGE T. et ux Elizabeth A. McMahan	12/15 1859	By Harvey Thompson, J.P.
1941 JOHNSTON, JAMES et ux Nancy Davis	1/16 1816	By Hugh Bogle, J.P.
1942 JOHNSTON, JEREMIAH et ux Polly R. Kimber- land	1/17 1816	By Hugh Bogle, J.P.
1943 JOHNSTON, JEREMIAH et ux Martha Cowan	9/9 1823	"Celebrated (No Name) (No signature)"

Names	Date Issue Or Celebrated	Security on Bond
1944 JOHNSTON, JOHN et ux Kezia Rowan	5/9 1815 issued	No returns
1945 JOHNSTON, JOSEPH et ux Esther Henderson	11/7 1815 issued	No returns
1946 JOHNSTON, ROBERT et ux Barby Ormand	1/27 1820	By Alex B. Gamble, J.P.
1947 JOHNSTON, ROBERT et ux Sarah Steele	9/8 1834	By Edward Mitchell, J.P.
1948 JOHNSTON, SAMUEL et ux Margaret Johnston	11/14 1818 issued	"on back is R. B. McCully, J.P.: no other words nor dates"
1949 JOHNSTON, WESLEY et ux Harriett Johnston	10/29 1840	By John Russom, M.G.
1950 JOURNEY, JOSEPH et ux Elizabeth Jackson	6/2 1801 issued	Bond: Joseph Doherty
1951 JONES, ABNER et ux Louisa Brown	11/8 1852	By John B. Hail, J.P.
1952 JONES, ABRAHAM et ux Rebecca Yunt	9/4 1814	By Andrew Jackson, J.P.
1953 JONES, A. H. et ux Eliza Montgomery	4/4 1857	A. Vance, M.G.
1954 JONES, EDWARD et ux Jane Brooks	1/1 1824	By Charles H. Warren, J.P.
1955 JONES, CHARLES et ux Patsey Durham	7/28 1810 issued	No returns
1956 JONES, ELISHA A. et ux Elizabeth Lane	12/2 1852	By J. H. Donaldson, J.P.
1957 JONES, EDWIN G. et ux Lucinda Alexander	7/29 1852	By John J. Hoover, J.P.
1958 JONES, HIRAM et ux Zenea Hicks	12/2 1823	By Charles H. Warren, J.P.
1959 JONES, ISAAC et ux Harriett C. Kerby	6/15 1848	By David Spradlin, J.P.
1960 JONES, ISAAC et ux Martha Oody	4/10 1854	By A. M. Goodykoontz
1961 JONES, JAMES et ux Polly Miser	2/21 1833	By Hu Tarbit, J.P.
1962 JONES, JAMES et ux Margaret Shanks	12/30 1841	By John Dyke, Pastor Unitia Ch.
1963 JONES, JOHN et ux Sally Ambrister	4/7 1825	By Thos. J. Brown, Traveling Deacon, M.E. Ch.
1964 JONES, JOHN et ux Isabella Roulston	9/8 1831	By A. C.Renfro, J.P.
1965 JONES, JOHNSON et ux Delila Mills	11/12 1846	By William Colburn, J.P.

Names	Date Issue Or Celebrated	By Whom/ Security on Bond
1966 JONES, JOSEPH et ux Tamer Bryant	10/22 1833	By Leroy Noble, J.P.
1967 JONES, LEWIS et ux Sarah Simons	5/1 1831	By Sam Henry, J.P.
1968 JONES, LEWIS et ux Hannah Parsins	5/30 1854	By Andrew Ferguson, J.P.
1969 JONES, LOUIS B. et ux Nancy H. Presley.	12/28 1854	By Fielding Pope, M.G.
1970 JONES, M. et ux Isabella J. Humphreys	10/14 1847	By A. Vance, M.G.
1971 JONES, ORIN et ux Susannah Rogers	11/24 1802 issued	Bond: John Rogers
1972 JONES, RUSSELL et ux Jane Carver	12/26 1837	By Wm. Rich, J.P.
1973 JONES, SAMUEL et ux Joana Allin	11/28 1800 issued	Bond: Thomas Jones
1974 JONES, SAMUEL SR. et ux Mary Mills	3/22 1842	By David Walker, J.P.
1975 JONES, SAMUEL N. et ux Amanda A. Alexander	8/3 1854	By J. M. Caldwell, M.G.
1976 JONES, THOMAS et ux Agnew Lambert	5/13 1819	By Wm. Griffitts, J.P.
1977 JONES, WM. et ux Mary Lambert	3/25 1817	By H. H. Bowerman, Esq.
1978 JONES, WM. R. et ux Polly Jones	11/15 1845	By William Colburn, J.P.
1979 JORDON, MOSES S. et ux Rachel White	11/9 1850	By B. F.Duncan, J.P.
1980 JULIAN, JOHN et ux Sally Murphy	8/4 1831	By Wm. McTeer, J.P.
1981 KAGLE, CHRISTIAN et ux Nancy Wheeler (See also Cagley)	8/14 1836	By Wm. McTeer, J.P.
1982 KALER, DANIEL et ux Elender Brickey	1/4 1855	By Freeric Emmet, M.G.
* See 595		
1983 KANARD, WILLIAM et ux Elizabeth McKaskel	9/17 1831	By David McKamy, J.P.
1984 KEEBLE, JAMES H. et ux Mary A. Sneed	2/25 1844	By Christian Long, J.P.
1985 KEEBLE, JOHN et ux Catty Leadbatter	9/3 1819	By Hugh Bogle, J.P.
1986 KEEBLE, LANSON W. et ux Elizabeth A. Chambers	4/18 1850	By Curran Lemons, J.P.

Names	Date Issue Or Celebrated	By Whom/ Security on Bond
1987 KEEBLE, MANLY et ux Rebecca Rhea	8/9 1829	By Thomas Billue, J.P.
1988 KEEBLE, RICHARD et ux Betsy Rhea	11/17 1831 issued	No returns
1989 KEEBLE, THOMAS et ux Betsy Smith	10/14 1823	By A. B.Gamble, J.P.
1990 KEEBLE, THOMAS et ux Nancy Ann Cannon	2/16 1847	By Will Cummin J.P.
1991 KEEBLE, WALTER H. et ux Polly White (also says Mary White)	8/15 1836	By William McTeer, J.P. Bond: Richard Keeble
1992 KOBBLE, WILLIAM et ux Polly Townsel	11/20 1845	By John Tipton, J.P.
1993 KELLER, HENRY et ux Mary Barnett	1/25 1821	By Jos' Alexander, J.P.
1994 KELLER, HENRY et ux Mary Ann Fultner	11/26 1846	By B. F. Duncan, J.P.
1995 KELLER, JACOB et ux Elizabeth A. Keller	3/15 1850	By John Morton, J.P.
1996 KELLER, JOHN et ux Jane McKaskele	10/30 1832	By Jame McKamy, J.P.
1997 KELLER, SAMUEL et ux Caty Hix	3/1 1827 issued	No returns
1998 KELLER, JOH N et ux Sarah Hutsell	9/21 1856	By John Davis, M.G.
1999 KELLY, ALEX et ux ----- (no name; placed in a blank space)	5/27 1802 issued	Bond: David Craig
2000 KELLY, JOHN et ux Nancy Mayho	4/9 1799 issued	Bond: John Cochran
2001 KELLY, JOSEPH et ux Mary James	11/22 1849	By S. J. McReynolds, J.P.
2002 KELLER, JOSEPH et ux Elizabeth Herron	11/28 1850	By Christian Long, J.P.
2003 KELLER, THOMAS et ux Mary J. Patey	7/26 1859	By A. Boyd, J.P.
2004 KELLER, WM. R. et ux Nancy J. Smith	9/23 1851	By John C. Martin, J.P.
2005 KELLY, WM. et ux Julia Ingram	4/30 1857	By S. J. McReynolds, J.P.
2006 KEELON, LEONARD et ux Elizabeth M. Hackney	12/31 1848	By J. Dyke, Pastor of Unitia Church
2007 KELSO, HUGH et ux Sarah McLamahan	2/22 1816 issued	No returns

Names	Date Issue Or Celebrated	By Whom/ Security on Bond
2008 KEEN, JAMES et ux Malinda Blanken- ship	3/5 1844	By J. Dyke, Pastor Unitia Church
* See 2105		
2009 KELSOE, JOHN et ux Martha A. Lee	9/23 1851	By Wesley Earnest, J.P.
2010 KEETH, GABRIEL P. et ux Eliza Jane Fuller	8/10 1858	By A. Vance, M.G.
2011 KEETIN, JOSEPH et ux Elizabeth Sesler	10/26 1857	By S. J. McReynolds, J.P.
2012 KEETIN, JEFFERSON et ux Emeline Sesler	2/11 1857	By Fieldin Pope, M.G.
2013 KELTNER, WILLIAM A. et ux Elizabeth Ward	5/9 1825	By J. Gillespie, J.P.
2014 KENEDY, ADAM Q. et ux Betsy McTeer	10/20 1847	By Samuel Tulloch, J.P.
2015 KENEDY, Alexander et ux Hetty Henry	7/29 1824	By Hugh Bogle, J.P.
2016 KENEDY, ALEX et ux Mary Ann Thomas	2/1 1848	By Robert Porter, J.P.
2017 KENNEDY, ARTHUR A. et ux Sarah C. Martin	12/1 1847	By Andrew Gass, M.G.
2018 KENNEDY, DAVID et ux Rebecca Montgomery	11/20 1823	By Jos' Duncan, J.P.
2019 KENNEDY, FELIX et ux Betsy Long	9/15 1800 issued	Bond: John Kenedy
2020 KENNEDY, JAMES H. et ux Sarah M. Sims	2/7 1856 issued	"Executed by me B. F. Duncan, J.P."
2021 KENNEDY, JOHN et ux Nancy Townsley	7/5 1821	By And'w S. Morrison, V.D.M.
2022 KENNEDY, JOSEPH C. et ux Ann Thompson (widow of David T. See Deeds Vol. S-97, 1841)	7/17 1823	By Samu'l Hamill, J.P.
2023 KENNEY, JOHN P. et ux Alley Plumblee	4/23 1823	By James Gillespy, J.P.
2024 KERR, DAVID et ux Polly Miller	10/27 1820 issued	No returns
2025 KERR, DAVID et ux Martha Henry	4/5 1834	By Wm. Wijliamson, J.P.
2026 KERR, DAVID MACLIN et ux Elizabeth Thompson	8/13 1833	By J. D. Wilson, M.G.
2027 KERR, G.C.C. et ux Martha E. Thompson	4/13 1847	By A. Vance, M.G.

Names	Date Issue Or Celebrated	By Whom/ Security on Bond
2028 KERR, HENDERSON et ux Mary Cook	2/22 1844	By John Morton, J.P.
2029 KERR, HENDERSON et ux Elizabeth E. J. Pugh	11/14 1850	By Joseph A. Hutton, J.P.
2030 KERR, JAMES M. et ux Betsey Best	12/26 1831 Rpt. 10/7 1831 celebrated (issued 10/7 1831)	By Wm. Williamson, J.P.
2031 KERR, JESSE JR. et ux Polly Ann Henry	4/3 1834	By A. Vance, M.G.
2032 KERR, JOHN et ux Ann Cowden	3/22 1832	By John Hendrix, J.P.
2033 KERR, JOHN et ux Juliann Townsley	8/14 1838	By Samuel Tulloch, J.P.
2034 KERR, JOHN D. et ux Nancy Jane Walker	8/12 1858	By A. Vance, M.G.
2035 KERR, JOHN P. et ux Jane B.McClure	10/8 1833	By William Toole
2036 KERR, JOS' C. et ux H. V. Wood (H.O.N.)	11/29 1855	By Phillips Wood, M.G.
2037 KERR, MACLIN et ux Lucinda Davis	3/6 1832	By Samu'l Hamill, J.P.
2038 KERR, RANSOM et ux Sally Best	10/10 1826	By Wm. Williamson, J.P.
* See Care		
2039 KERR, WILLIAM et ux Letitia Wear	3/28 1833	By C. Fulton, L.E.M.E.C.
2040 KERR, WILLIAM et ux Mildred Davis	12/15 1859	By J. C. Wright
2041 KERRICK, STEPHEN et ux Mariah Hayden (outside is Elizabeth Hayden)	8/30 1831	By John Russom, M.G.
2042 KEY, ANDREW et ux Rosannah Wright	2/21 1854	By Harvey H. C. Caruthers, J.P.
2043 KEY, DAVID et ux Nancy Bright	9/21 1815	"by me, Wm. Gillespie, J.P."
2044 KEY, DAVID HENNEGAR et ux Nancy Ward	7/21 1847	By James H. Donaldson, J.P.
2045 KEY, C. C. HAMBEY et ux Margaret Wayman	9/30 1857	By H. Thompson, J.P.
2046 KEYWOOD, EDWARD et ux Jane Duff	1/5 1808 issued	No returns

Names	Date Issue Or Celebrated	By Whom/ Security on Bond
* See 589		
2047 KEY, GEORGE W. et ux Mary Lincumpelter	11/7 1852	By William Colburn, J.P.
2048 KEY, JAMES et ux Urserla Greer	11/18 1825	By Charles H. Warren, J.P.
2049 KEY, JAMES R. et ux Mary A. Beddex	2/24 1857	By James Mathews, J.P.
2050 KEY, JAMES M. et ux Martha J. Myers	10/26 1848	By William Colburn, J.P.
2051 KEY, JOHN et ux Margaret Brown	11/25 1841	By W. W. Wallace, J.P. Bond: Joseph Brown
2052 KEY, JOSEPH et ux Telitha Haydon	3/23 1827	By Arch'd Maxwell, J.P.
2053 KEY, PETER et ux Avice Hayse	10/18 1831	By Charles H. Warren, J.P.
2054 KEY, R. M. et ux Margaret T. Mc- ghee	3/6 1856	By James M. Tulloch, J.P.
2055 KEY, WESLEY M. et ux Catherine Ward	12/27 1854	By J. H. Donaldson, J.P.
2056 KEY, WILLIAM et ux Jane Stewart	2/2 1841	By William Colburn, J.P.
2057 KEY, WILEY D. et ux A. M. Bidix	6/23 1853	By W. M. Brickell, J.P.
2058 KIDD, FRANCIS A. et ux Mary A. Wear	1/28 1849	By Alex O. George, J.P.
2059 KIDD, JAMES et ux Mary Cook	4/16 1840	By Robert Porter, J.P. Bond: Augustine Bad- gett
2060 KIDD, J. L. et ux Mary J. McCamy	4/14 1859	By George Caldwell, J.P.
2061 KIDD, JOHN et ux Mary Harris	3/27 1835	By Wm. Billue, M.G.
2062 KIDD, JOHN et ux Polly Mitchell	3/3 1842	By A. C. Montgomery, J. P.
2062 KIDD, JUDE M. et ux Zefheniah? Harris	2/27 1839	--
2063 KIDD, LEWIS et ux Lidia Tupes	3/30 1841	By James Ray, J.P.
2064 KIDD, RANDELL et ux Mary Call	10/22 1824	By Jn Gillespie, J.P. (I know this should be Paul) (W. E. P.)
2065 KIDD, ROBERT et ux Esther Neiman	10/3 1837	By Ben Cunningham, J.P.

Names	Date Issue Or Celebrated	By Whom/ Security on Bond
2066 KIDD, T. JEFFERSON et ux Mary Jane Eagleton	12/24 1855	By James Hitch, J.P.
2067 KIDD, WILLIAM et ux Tennessee Jafley	7/17 1831	By Sam Henry, J.P.
2068 KIDD, WILLIAM et ux Susan Maze	12/29 1853	By Spencer Henry, M.G.
2069 KINDRICK, ROBERY et ux Frankey Reeder (may be Rudd)	1/20 1812 issued	No returns
2070 KIKER, G. W. et ux Elizabeth H. Bonham	12/27 1849	By A. J. McGee, M.G.-C. P.
2071 KING, ANDREW H. et ux Terrissa Lorence	3/20 1833	By John Wood, L. E. M. Ep.
2072 KING, E. C. et ux M. T. Pass	2/6 1856	By David Spradlin, J.P.
2073 KING, GEORGE A. et ux Nancy J. Calor	11/24 1859	By James D. Lawson, M.G. M.E.C. South
2074 KING, JOHN et ux Becky Pride	6/11 1800	Bond: Samuel King
2075 KING, SAMUEL et ux Agness Hannah	8/26 1797 issued	Bond: Samuel Eakin
2076 KING, STEPHEN et ux Winny Peterson	7/19 1849	By Jesse Kerr, Jr, J.P.
2077 KING, WILLIAM et ux Elendor Keller	5/22 1824	By Jos' Alesander, J.P.
2078 KING, W. E. B. et ux Caroline Peeler	9/2 1858	By M. Jones, J.P.
2079 KINNAMAN, JAMES et ux Talby Dodson	8/14 1825	By A. B. Gamble, J.P.
2080 KINNAMAN, JAMES M. et ux Mary A. Mills	2/8 1859	By Wm. Nuchols, J.P.
2081 KINNAMAN, JOHN et ux Rachell Rhea	8/6 1844	By B. F. Duncan, J.P.
2082 KINNAMAN, JAMES et ux Mary A. Steele	1/18 1854	By C. Long, J.P.
2083 KENNAMAN, ROBERT B. et ux Sally Snider	2/4 1830 issued	"By Me" Wm. Billue,--
2084 KINNEMAN, SAMUEL et ux Jane Reed	3/25 1834	By William Dever, J.P.
2085 KINNEMAN, SAMUEL et ux Rachel Gamble	2/5 1857	By W. W. Nuchols, J.P.
2086 KENNEMAN, THOMAS et ux Lucretia Smith	1/13 1842	By A. C. Montgomery, J. P.

Names	Date Issue Or Celebrated	By Whom/ Security on Bond
2087 KIRBY, JOSHUA et ux Jane Singleton	1/22 1824	By John Dever,--
2088 KIRBY, RICHARD et ux Polly Trice	2/8 1823	By James Duncan,--
2089 KERBY, RICHARD et ux Narcissa P. Wright	7/26 1849 issued	Bond: T. K. Munsey
<u>2089</u> KIRBY, RICHARD et ux Sarah Tayor	6/14 1860	By Rev. L. C. Delashmit, M.G.
2090 KITE, JOHN et ux Margaret A. Ogle	2/1 1855	By Davis Spradlin, J.P.
* See 588		
2091 KIZER, A. R. et ux P. J. Hudgeons	3/6 1856	By A. Vance, M.G.
2092 KIZER, GEORGE et ux Honor Emaline Weir	12/2 1841	By John Maxwell, J.P.
2093 KIZER, HENRY et ux Salena Wynn	3/7 1944	By J. Dyke, Pastor Unitia Church
2094 KIZER, JACOB et ux Amy Waddle	7/29 1852	By John J. Hoover, J.P.
2095 KIZER, JOHN et ux Malinda Cope	9/15 1836	By A. Vance, M.G.
2096 KIZER, JOHN W. et ux Sarah A. Duncan	1/21 1858	By Andrew Ferguson, J.P.
2097 KIZER, JOSEPH et ux Mary Tucker	1/25 1839	By J. R. Mosier, M.G. (may be J. K. M.)
2098 KNIGHT, WILLIAM et ux Priscilla Underwood	1/16 1823	By A. B. Gamble, J.P.
2099 KNOX, JOHN et ux Lucinda Blackburn	1/21 1840	By Rev. J. Dyke
2100 KNOX, MATHEW et ux Elizabeth B. Bond	7/26 1824	By William Eagleton, Pastor of Bethel Church
2101 KIRKPATRICK, CHARLES B. et ux Elizabeth Ann Kirkpatrick	6/10 1847	By Wm. Billue, M. G. S.
2102 KIRKPATRICK, JAMES et ux Elizabeth Shadden	9/24 1834	By John McCampbell, V.D. M.
2103 KIRKPATRICK, THOMAS et ux Winey Brawn	3/2 1825	By Hugh Bogle, J.P.
2104 KIRKPATRICK, THOMAS et ux Nancy Kirkpatrick	9/18 1845	By Wm. Billue, M.G.S.
2105 KUNS, ADAM et ux Rachel Logan	2/25 1835 issued	No returns (may be Koons Koonts)
* See 2008		

	Names	Date Issue Or Celebrated	By Whom/ Security on Bond
2106	KYLE, MARVIN et ux Betsey Possey	12/28 1802 issued	Bond: Lsaac D. Willcox
2107	LACKEY, ANDREW et ux Esther Johnston	12/10 1800 issued	Bond: Wood Lackey.
2108	LACKEY, ARCH'D et ux Isabella Trimble	12/24 1798	Bond: John Trimble
2109	LACKEY, JAS B. et ux Nancy E. Ish	5/19 1853	By A. J. McGee, M.G.
2110	LACKEY, JOHN W. et ux Margaret J. Russell	8/14 1849	By Rev. John Nicholson
2111	LAKE, THOMAS et ux Jenney Majors	1/1 1800 issued	Bond: Samuel Majors
2112	LAKEY, MAYNER et ux Patsey King	1/29 1848	By Darby Rayan, J.P.
2113	LAMBERT, AARON et ux Eliza Jones	10/17 1837	By Robert Shields, J.P.
2114	LAMBERT, DANIEL et ux Nancy Lawson	7/10 1841	By Robert Shields, J.P.
2115	LAMBERT, HIRIAM W. et ux Catherine Mc-Quage	11/16 1825	"On day issued Thos' E. T. McMurray, J.P."
2116	LAMBERT, JOSEPH et ux Sarah A. Davis	2/10 1850	By R. Flinn, J.P.
2117	LAND, BENJAMIN B. et ux Matilda W. Rawlsten	5/16 1844	By Green B. Saffell, J. P.
2118	LAND, JEREMIAH W. et ux Martha E. Raulsten	2/19 1843	By Curran Lemons, J.P.
2119	LAND, RUFUS et ux Roody A. Emit	9/27 1846	By Lowery McBath, J.P.
2120	LANE, ABRAHAM et ux Delila Williams	5/26 1836	By Spencer Henry, J.P.
2121	LAIN, ANDREW et ux M. E. J. Maupin	4/6 2854	By John J. Hovver, J.P.
2122	LANE, DANIEL et ux Mary Robertson	12/16 1819 issued	"Executed by me S. George, J.P."
2123	LAIN, DAVID et ux Loueriza A. Elder	8/15 1858	By Harvey Thompson, J.P.
2124	LANE, JAMES et ux Malinda Hollers	2/8 1827	By Thos' E. T. McMurray, J.P.
2125	LANE, JAS B. et ux Sarah H. Greenway	12/9 1851	By John J. Hoover, J.P.
2126	LANE, JAMES M. et ux Eliza H. Henry	9/5 1850	By A. Vance, M.G.

Names	Date Issue Or Celebrated	By Whom/ Security on Bond
2127 LANE, JAMES W. et ux Sally Bird	1/23 1845	By William Colburn, J.P.
2128 LAIN, JOHN et ux Jane Carson	12/28 1824	By Wm. Gault, J.P.
2129 LANE, JOSEPH et ux Artimicia Caton	2/19 1852	By W. M. Brickell, J.P.
2130 LANE, MERIDA S. et ux Salena Conner	9/21 1848	By Wm. M. Brickell, J.P.
2131 LAIN, M. A et ux Nancy Alford	9/27 1853	By A. J. McGee, M. G.
2132 LANE, MIDDLETON et ux Nancy Forister	12/30 1819 issued	"& ok Samuel Douthit,--"
2133 LANE, MIDDLETON et ux Nancy Winters	12/22 1833	By Leroy Noble, J.P.
2134 LANE, NATHAN et ux Sussey Manson	12/27 1815 issued	"Married in December 1815" (No signature)
2135 LANE, PEYTON et ux Peggy Love	2/4 1823	By Wm. Griffitts, J.P.
2136 LANE, SAMUEL et ux Williams Elizabeth	4/27 1836	By Spencer Henry, J.P.
2137 LANE, SAMUEL D. et ux Martha S. Blankin- ship	4/12 1859	By M. Jones, J.P.
2138 LANE, SAM'l O. et ux Mary E. Keene	4/21 1853	By Jes' Matthews, J.P.
2139 LAYNE, STREET et ux Matilda Blackwell	2/12 1824	By Joseph Duncan, J.P.
2140 LANE, TANDY et us Jenny Tuck	1/2 1823 12/27 1822 issued	By Wm. Griffits, J.P.
2141 LANE, THOMAS et ux Patsey Kayton	3/8 1821	By Charles H. Warren, G.P.
2142 LAIN, THOMAS et ux Elizabeth Grayham	8/5 1858	By James Matthews, J.P.
2143 LANE, WILLIAM et ux Rebecca Hair	9/2 1847	By W. Earnest, J.P.
2144 LAIN, WILLIAM et ux Ann Mc. Richards	9/2 1850	By Harvey H. C. Carru- thers, J.P.
2145 LANEY, WILLIAM et ux Nancy Smith	9/27 1826 issued	No returns
2146 LANGFORD, JAMES et ux Ruthy Gamble	7/22 1828	By A. B. Gamble, J.P.
2147 LANGFORD, JOHN et ux Phebe Brooks	10/24 1825	"By me on day of issue" Thos E. T. McMurray, J.P.

Names	Date Issue Or Celebrated	By Whom/ Security on Bond
2148 LANTER, F. M. et ux M. J. Scott	11/21 1856	By W. A. Lawson, M.G.
2149 LARGE, WM. B. et ux Nancy Smith	10/24 1856	By H. I. Hodge, M.G.
2150 LATIMORE, DANIEL W. et ux Margaret McCall	2/28 1839	By R. B. Billue, M.G. of Babtist Persuaision
2151 LATIMORE, D. W. et ux Rebecca E. Howard	2/7 1844 issued Jan 31	By Joseph Peeler, Minis-
2152 LATHAM, GEORGE et ux Manervia Garner	1/25 1844	By William Cummings, Esq.
2153 LATHAM, JOHN et ux Beedy Rogers	11/27 1831	By Wm. McTeer, J.P.
2154 LATHAM, WILLIAM et ux Zilpha Rodgers	9/4 1849	By John Tipton, J.P.
2155 LAW, ANDERSON et ux Jennet Walker	5/6 1847	By Lowery McBath, J.P.
* See 2202,2203,2204		
2156 LAW, SILVESTER et ux Nancy Williams	1/22 1834	"Celebrated by me John- son Adams, M.G."
2157 LAWPASER, JOSEPH et ux Jemima Betsaws (may be Lampaswe to Bet- sams)	12/22 1825	By Hugh Bogle, J.P.
2158 LAWRENCE, BEVERAGE et ux Kezia A. Patton	12/22 1814 issued	No returns
2159 LAWRENCE, WM. et ux M. R. Warren	8/25 1851	By J. C. Martin, J.P.
2160 LAWSON, BARTLEY et ux Elizabeth Douherty	7/14 1819	By Jos. Duncan, J.P.
2161 LAWSON, DANIEL B. et ux Mary Cable	11/14 1850 (issued 11/4)	By Curran Lemons, J.P.
2162 LAWSON, JACOB et ux Cecil Hill	7/25 1840	By Robert Shields, J.P.
2163 LAWSON, JAMES D. et ux Sarah Jane Burns	12/24 1846	By Andrew Gass, M.G.
* See 2236		
2164 LAWSON, JAMES D. et ux Hettey E. Morton	2/23 1860	By Fielding Pope, M.G.
2165 LAWSON, JOHN W. et ux Martha C. Gibbs	5/31 1840	By William Colburn, J.P.
2166 LAWSON, PHILIP et ux Martha C. Gibbs	4/20 1843	By Robert Shields, J.P.
2167 LAWSON, THOMAS et ux Rebecca Lambert	8/11 1841	By Robert Shields, G.P.

Names	Date Issue Or Celebrated	By Whom/ Security on Bond
2168 LAWSON, WM. H. et ux Elizabeth Mc-Campbell	12/27 1855	By Curran Lemons, J.P.
2169 LAYMAN, HENRY et ux Elizabeth Elliott	12/31 1829	By Isaac Anderson, P.N. P. Ch.
2170 LEBO, HENRY et ux Sarah Jane Heart-sell	1/9 1840	By M. C. Graves, M.G. of M.E.C.
2171 LEBOW, HIRAM et ux Sarah Bledsoe	12/24 1839	By James Henry, J.P.
2172 LEBOW, RICHARD et ux Amy Eliza George	9/1 1836	By Darius Hoyt, M.G.
2173 LEBOW, W. A. et ux A. E. Bond	9/12 1855	By W. A. Lawson, M.G.
2174 LEE, CLEMUEL et ux Sally Chammels	8/23 1822	By Char'l H. Warren, J.P.
2175 LEA, EPHRIAM et ux Elizabeth Endsley	10/7 1852	By William Colburn, J.P.
2176 LEE, M. HANSON et ux Martha Cates	10/23 1839	By Henry Hannum, J.P.
2177 LEE, JAMES W. et ux Melvina Wear	7/18 1831	By C. Fulton, L.E.M.E.C.
2178 LEA, JOHN et ux Maryann Evans	8/27 1823 issued	No returns
2179 LEE, JONATHAN et ux Sarah Cry	7/27 1843	By Wm. Griffitts, J.P.
2180 LEE, SAMUEL et ux Mary Hackney	8/21 1823	By Wm. Griffitts, J.P.
2181 LEA, THOMAS J. et ux Eliza J.G. Rankin	2/14 1838	By Isaac Anderson, P.N. P.Ch.
2182 Lee. T. R. et ux Ruth B. Allen	12/29 1859	By A. R. James, J.P.
2183 LEA, WILLIAM et ux Sarah Hackney	8/15 1833	By A. Ish, J.P.
2184 LEECH, ENOCH et ux Perlina Ragan	12/28 1840 issued	No returns Bond: Thomas Turk
2185 LEGG, JONATHAN et ux Mary Hirfley	9/6 1796 issued	Bond: Ambrose Lagg
2186 LEEPER, HUGH B. et ux Esther Harden	11/6 1859	By Samuel Tulloch, J.P.
2187 LEEPER, SANDERS M. et ux Eliza D. Abernathey	11/18 1841	By T. K. Harmon, M.G.
2188 LEATHERDALE, WILLIAM et ux Elizabeth Wills	3/16 1799	Bond: James Willis & James Hail

Names	Date Issue Or Celebrated	By Whom/ Security on Bond
2189 LIKENS, JOHN et ux Isabella Sloan	8/22 1799 issued	Bond: David Brown
2190 LEINBACK, JACOB et ux Barbara Keller	8/23 1827	By Ewing, George,--
2191 LEMONS, CURRAN et ux Mary A. Hill	8/27 1843	By Lewis Jones, J.P.
2192 LEMONS, SAMUEL M. et ux Ann Weldon	12/16 1816 issued	No returns
2193 LEMINGHAM, THOMAS et ux Betsey Harris	12/15 1823	By Wm. Griffitts, J.P.
2194 LESTER, WILLIAM et ux Martha Presley	2/1 1855	By Fielding Pope, M.G.
2195 LEVERTER, SILAS et ux Katy Greenfield	2/23 1831 issued	No returns
2196 LEWIS, HENRY et ux Keziah Perkins	1/8 1824	By Wm Griffetts, J.P.
2197 LEWIS, JOHN CUMMINGS et ux Barbary Jane Tee- fateller	6/16 1840	By W. M. Rorex, J.P.
2198 LILLARD, JOHN et ux Betsey Taylor	12/26 1815 issued	No returns
2199 LINCUMPELTER, HENRY et ux Phebe Trice	12/29 1853	By Richard Kirby, J.P.
2200 LINCUMPELTNER, SAMUEL et ux E. A.Robinson	4/22 1850	By Wm. M.Brickell, J.P.
2201 LITTLE, WILLIAM et ux Susannah Johnson	3/17 1821	By David Logan, M.G.
2202 LAW, JEREMIAH et ux Sally Russell	7/8 1819	By Alex B. Gamble, J.P.
* See 2155		
2203 LAW, JOHN et ux Nancy Greene	7/24 1811 issued	No returns
2204 LAW, JOHN et ux Malyssa McGinley	10/24 1837	By William M. Rorex, J.P.
* See 2155		
2205 LOGAN, ALEX A. et ux Lucinda Brake- bill	4/3 1851	By Jno. C. Martin, J.P.
2206 LOGAN, ALEXANDER et ux Mary A. Edmonson	12/26 1816 issued	"Executed A.D. 1816" Wm. Hartt
2207 LOGAN, ALVAN et ux Mavina Jane Norwood (Malvina Jane)	10/20 1842	By Fielding Pope, M.G.
2208 LOGAN, ANDREW PRESTON et ux Maryann Martin	1/9 1840	By Joseph A. Hutton, J.P.

Names	Date Issue Or Celebrated	By Whom/ Security on Bond
2209 LOGAN, DAVID L. et ux Peggy Philips	5/1 1823	By David Logan, M.G.
2210 LOGAN, DAVID et ux Margaret Conner (Looks like Cosner)	8/27 1835	By Samuel Tulloch, J.P.
2211 LOGAN, JAMES et ux Lourinda Dyke	12/19 1837	By Rev. J. Dyke
2212 LOGAN, JAMES A. et ux Martha C. Bowerman	8/8 1844	By J. S. Craig, M.G.
2213 LOGAN, JAMES R. et ux Rachel Philips	2/8 1821	By David Logan, L.P.
2214 LOGAN, JAMES W. et ux Mary A. Henry	12/30 1830	By S. M. Aston, M.G.
2215 LOGAN, JOHN et ux Polly McFee	6/8 1828	By John Russom, M.G.
2216 LOGAN, JOSEPH B. et ux Sarah Cohem (May be Cohern)	8/21 1832	By Samu'l Hamil, J.P.
2217 LOGAN, LEOROY et ux Nancy J. McCall	1/7 1847	By Samuel Tulloch, J.P.
2218 LOGAN, SAMUEL et ux Martha Strain	10/3 1837	By John D. Wilson, M.G.

LOGAN, SAMUEL, b. 10/10 1810 in Blount Co., m. Nancy Walker Hamel--by family in Chattanooga Times, 1934.

Names	Date Issue Or Celebrated	By Whom/ Security on Bond
2219 LOGAN, William P. et ux Uterpe A.	10/27 1835	By Isaac Anderson, P.N.P. Ch.
2220 LONG, ALEXANDER et ux Elizabeth Vicars	8/24 1802 issued	Bond: John Vickers
2221 LONG, A. J. et ux Nancy Johnson	9/4 1854	By B. F. Duncan, J.P.
2222 LONG, COLUMBUS et ux Elizabeth Murr	9/17 1848	By H(W.) Toole, J.P.
2223 LONG, GEORGE T. et ux Elizabeth White	11/7 1850	By Christian Long, J.P.
2224 LONG, GEORGE T. et ux Mary A. Baker	2/11 1858	By Wm. W. Nuchols, J.P.
2225 LONG, GREEN D. et ux Easter Barker	10/4 1858	By Andrew Ferguson, J.P.
2226 LONG, HENRY et ux Easther McCallie	3/21 1841	By W. M. Rorex, J.P.
2226 LONG, HENRY et ux Christiana Myrrh	9/23 1847	By S. J. McReynolds, J.P.
2227 LONG, JAMES L. et ux Mary J. Keller	10/21 1858	By C. Long, J.P.

Names	Date Issue Or Celebrated	By Whom/ Security on Bonds
2228 LONG, JOHN et ux Agnes Finley	8/22 1833	By A. Ish, J.P.
2229 LONG, JOHN et ux Jane Low	10/6 1836	By W. Toole, J.P.
2230 LONG, JNO. et ux Elizabeth Thomas	9/6 1849	By Lewis J. Newman, J.P.
2231 LONG, JOHN et ux Samantha Everett	10/20 1853	By C. Long, J.P.
2232 LONG, THOMAS et ux Caroline Hall	6/9 1858	By J. D. Sewell
2233 LONG, WM. et ux Sofena Simerly (or Sofina)	12/6 1858	By Wm. H. Anderson, J.P.
2234 LONGBOTTOM, BENJAMIN et ux Elizabeth Tallent	8/19 1848	By T. M. Rooker, J.P.
2235 LONGBOTTOM, ELIJAH et ux Elizabeth Bonham	11/14 1826	By Charl' H. Warren, J.P.
2236 LOSSON, TURNER LANE et ux Rachel Hunt	2/2 1840	By William Colburn, J.P.
2237 LOVE, AARON et ux Cindy Hitch	1/31 1851	By Harvey H. C. Caruthers, J.P.
2238 LOVE, DANIEL et ux Frances Ann George	2/10 1842	By Joseph A. Hutton, J.P.
2239 LOVE, J. R. et ux H. E. Badgett	10/4 1853	By W. A. Lawson, M.G.
2240 LOVE, JOSIAH F. et ux Martha J. Cox (daughter of Ambrose Cox)	9/17 1847	By Sam B. Hammell, M.G.
2241 LOVE, PRESTON B. et ux M. M. Howal	12/1 1859	By George Caldwell, J.P.
2242 LOVE, ROBERT S. et ux Sarah Jane Dickson	9/2 1847	By Jas' Law, M.G.
2243 LOVE, ROBT. S. et ux Isabeella Dunlap	3/10 1857	By John McIlfatrick, M.G.
2244 LOVE, SAMUEL et ux Mary Beeler	6/30 1818	By John Waugh, J.P. (Also in Knoxville Reg. Off.)
2245 LOVE, WESTLEY et ux Caroline May	8/17 1843	By Joseph A. Hutton, J.P.
2246 LOVE, WILLIAM L. et ux Clarinda S. Hamil (or Clarinda J.) (daugh- ter of Hugh Hamil)	12/30 1840	Bond: Archibald G. Maxwell

Names	Date Issue Or Celebrated	By Whom/ Security on Bonds
2247 LOVELACE, BARTON et ux Mary Lovel	6/30 1798 issued	Bond: William McNabb
2248 LOW, ABRAHAM N. et ux Arah Bonham	9/22 1836	By Isaac J. Bonham, M.G.
2249 LOW, GEORGE et ux Nancy Whitten- barger	9/10 1816 issued	"Married by me Wm. Gillespie, J.P."
2250 LOW (LAW?), NELSON et ux Semanthe Yearout	10/22 1835	By Rev. George Bussell
2251 LOW, THOMAS et ux Jan M. Maxwell	3/1 1821 issued	"Executed--Sam'l George, --"
2252 LOWE, WILLIAM et ux Mary Russell	1/26 1844	By Christian Long, J.P.
2253 LOW, WILLIAM M. et ux Orpah H.	11/18 1841	By Jeremiah R. Fryer, M.G.

** (Cannot be sure that several are "Law" & visa versa)

2254 LOWRY, ALEX (inside is ABRAHAM) et ux Elizabeth Johnson	12/13 1821	By Samuel Hamill, J.P.
2255 LOWERY, J. M. et ux Mary Gamble	6/10 1852	By Fielding Pope, M.G.
2256 LOWERY, MITCHELL et ux Ruthy Ann Tedford	10/8 1846	By Harvey H. C. Caruthers, J.P.
2257 LOWERY, SAM'L F. et ux S. A. Houser	10/2 1851	By C. Long, J.P.
2258 LOWERY, WM. et ux Ann Wallace	3/17 1797 issued	Bond: Wm. Wallace
2259 LOWERY, WILLIAM et ux Hetty Houston	12/13 1825	By And'w S. Morrison, M.G.
2260 LOYD, JESSE et ux Fanny Greer	2/24 1826	By Sam'l Davidson, J.P.
2261 LUCKET, THOMAS L. et ux Jane Martin	4/30 1835 issued	No returns
2262 LUNDY, WILLIAM et ux Rachel Perkins	8/12 1849	By Wm. M. Brickell, J.P.
2263 LUNSFORD, ALEXANDER et ux Ann M. Brown	2/25 1858	By Wm. M. Brickell, J.P.
2264 LUSK, DAVID D. et ux Mary E. Davis	9/1 1859	By James Hamil, J.P.
2265 LUTE, STEPHEN et ux Elizabeth Dillard	6/8 1833	"Celebrated by me" A. C. Renfro, J.P.
2266 LYON, THOMAS et ux Susan Legg	7/21 1832	By William Toole, J.P.
2267 LYRY, DAVID et ux Martha Malinda Campbell	8/27 1829	By Isaac Anderson, P.N.P. Ch.

Names	Date Issue Or Celebrated	By Whom/ Security on Bonds
2268 LEE, JOHN et ux N. E. McCaslin	5/15 1850 issued	Bond: Charles Hughes
* See 2178		
2269 McAFFRY, JOHN T. et ux Margaret A. Kile	10/1 1818 issued	No returns
* See 2444		
2270 McANELLY, JOHN et ux Levina Davis	6/15 1843	By John Tipton, J.P.
2271 McADOO, WILEY et ux Martha Bell	3/19 1858	By John Gault, J.P.
2272 McBATH, ANDREW N. et ux Jane Singleton	3/7 1850	By F. Pope, M.G.
2273 McBATH, LOWERY et ux Hariet McBath	4/9 1847	By Sam'l Pride, J.P.
2274 McBRIANT, JOHN et ux Sarah Scott	11/31 1836 (issued 10/1)	By Geo. Snider, J.P.
2275 McBRIANT, WILLIAM et ux Mary Scott	10/27 1825	By Sam'l E. Daviston, J.P.
2276 McCALDWELL, JOHN et ux Mary R. Anderson (May be John M. Caldwell)	11/4 1847	By Isaac Anderson, P.N.P. Ch.
* See 486		
2277 McCALE, BENJAMIN et ux Margaret Cannon	3/9 1824 issued	By R. B. McCully, J.P. "executed"
2278 McCALL, JAS. H. et ux Mary M. Cottral	8/22 1858	By David Spradlin, J.P.
2279 McCALL, SAM'L et ux Mary Jane Armstrong	6/4 1846	By Samuel Tulloch, J.P.
2280 McCALLAN, JAMES C. et ux Peggy C. Wells	2/7 1843	By Fielding Pope, M.G.
2281 McCALLON, JOHN et ux Polly McCartney	3/24 1818	By Andrew S. Morrison, V.D.M.
2282 McCALLIE, ARCHIBALD et ux Sally Thompson	7/26 1821	By Arch'l Maxwell, J.P.
2283 McCALLIE, DAVID E. et ux Nancy Hart	9/26 1835	By Thos' White, Esq.
2284 McCALLIE, RUFUS et ux Catherine Averett	9/7 1843	By Fielding Pope, M.G.
2285 McCALLIE, THOS. (Col. of Washington, Tenn.) et ux Mary A. Hook (Daughter of Robert Hook)	12/26 1831	By Isaac Anderson, P.N.P. Ch.
2286 McCALLEY, WM. et ux Isabella J. Kinnaman	1/1 1857	By W. W.Nuchols, J.P.

Names	Date Issue Or Celebrated	By Whom/ Security on Bonds
* See 2409		
2287 McCABE, JAMES et ux Nelly Woody (May be McCalle, McCale, or McCalee)	12/30 1809	No returns
* See 2277		
2288 McCAMY, DAVID et ux Mary Simons	9/8 1812	Bond: WM. McGAUGHEY & John Means
* See 2449		
2289 McCAMY, MAJOR et ux Margaret Hafley	3/10 1839	By James Ray, J.P.
2290 McCAMY, SAM'L et ux Martha B. Martin	1/12 1854	By Andrew Gal----, M.G. (mutilated)
2291 McCAMY, WILLIAM et ux Matilda Davis	12/15 1841	By Lorenzo Donaldson, J.P.
2292 McCAMPBELL, ANDREW et ux Martha G. Steele	9/23 1819	By Isaac Anderson, P.N.P. Ch.
2293 McCAMBELL, ANDREW L. et ux Jane Caldwell	12/27 1825 issued	By Isaac Anderson, P.N.P. Ch. "same day"
2294 McCAMPELL, ISAAC et ux Martha Michell	1/10 1856	By Curran Lemons, J.P.
2295 McCAMBELL, JAMES et ux Cintha Jane Lemonds	7/22 1847	By Isaac Anderson, P.N.P. Ch.
2296 McCAMPBELL, SOLOMON et ux Nancy Duran (Mrs.)	3/3 1818	By Wm. Williamson, J.P.
2297 McCAMPBELL, THOMAS et ux Mary Ann Wrinkle	12/14 1853	By W. A. Lawson, M.G.
2298 McCAMPBELL, WILLIAM A. et ux Jane M. Wallace (Knox Register says daughter of Jesse Wallace)	10/25 1825	By Isaac Anderson, P.N.P. Ch.
2299 McCAMPBELL, WILLIAM E. et ux Mary J. Hook	2/20 1851	By Isaac Anderson, P.N.P. Ch.
2300 McCAMPBELL, WM. et ux Mary M. Singleton	2/11 1852	By F. Pope, M.G.
2301 McCAMPBELL, WILLIAM S. et ux Nancy K. Reagan	5/5 1818	By Curran Lemons, J.P.
2302 McCAMMON, JOHN et ux Elizabeth Upton	5/14 1798	Bond: James Upton
2303 McCAMMON, SAMUEL et ux Rachel Inman	11/24 1826	By Saml Hamil, J.P.
2304 McCANDLES, JAMES et ux Elizabeth Caldwell	2/10 1801 issued	Bond: John Kelly

Names	Date Issue Or Celebrated	By Whom/ Security on Bonds
* See 2596		
2305 McCARTY, CHARLES et ux Polly Means	11/12 1840	By Joseph Wilson, J.P.
2306 McCARTNEY, JAMES et ux Jane M. Russell	3/3 1818	By And'w S. Morrison, V.D.M.
2307 McCARTNEY, JOHN et ux Peggy Boyd	7/13 1815 issued 7/30 married	By Jn. Harris, J.P.
2308 McCASLAND, JOHN et ux Polly Winter	8/6 1823	By Wm. Griffitts, J.P.
* See 644, McCAUGHAM, JOHN		
2309 McCAULY, JAMES et ux Mahaley Shook	2/23 1833 issued	"celebrated the within" J. Webb, M. of G.
2310 McCLANNAHAN, JAMES et ux Polly A. Hubbard	11/27 1849	By William McTeer, J.P.
* See 2463		
2311 McCLANEHAN, JOHN et ux Polly Snider	3/22 1832	By John Hendrix, J.P.
2312 McCLANAHAN, MATT et ux Sally Bradley	5/16 1801	Bond: Robert McMurray
2313 McCLANAHAN, MATHEW et ux Catharine Russell	5/13 1849	By William R. Flinn, J.P.
2314 McCLANAHN, WM. et ux Jane McMahan	4/6 1856	By N. Brewer, J.P.
2315 McCLAIN, ANDREW et ux Susan E. Sawtell	1/15 1835	By Isaac Anderson, P.N.P. Ch.
2316 McCLAIN, JOHN et ux Ann Duncan	10/23 1832	By B. Abernathy, L.E.
2317 McCLAIN, NEAPOLIAN B. (BONAPART)("BONY") et ux Dorthula Hitch	5/16 1843	By J. S. Craig, M.G.
2318 McCLAIN, ROBT. et ux Susannah Casteel	11/30 1819 issued	"Executed same day" S. Douthit, M.G.

McCLELLAN, JOHN m. 5/14 1794 Polly Wallace of William. See Knoxville Gazette of 5/22 174?. This William on Bakers Creek d. 179?, Revolutionary soldier, burried ----ville, New Prov. Ch. Cemetery; SAA marker.

Names	Date Issue Or Celebrated	By Whom/ Security on Bonds
2319 McCLUNG, GEORGE et ux Betty Wilson	4/23 1816	By J. Harris, J.P.
2320 McCLUNG, JAMES et ux Peggy Montgomery	8/8 1816	By And'w S. Morrison, V.D.M.
2321 McCLUNG, J. H. et ux Martha J. Shedden	11/1 1853	By Andrew Ferguson, J.P.
2322 McCLUNG, JAMES H. (or P.) et ux Rachel L. Houston	11/25 1858	By A. Vance, M.G.

Names	Date Issue Or Celebrated	By Whom/ Security on Bonds
2323 McCLUNG, JOHN et ux Nancy J. Wilson	2/5 1828	By William Eagleton, M.G.
2324 McCLUNG, PATRICK et ux Margaret Cowan	5/31 1821	By Samuel Hamill, J.P.
2325 McCLURE, ELI et ux Martha D. Smith	10/12 1852	By S. J. McReynolds, J.P.
2326 McCLURE, HARVEY et ux Mary Phelps	8/28 1848	By S. J. McReynolds, J.P.
2327 McCLURE, JAMES et ux Margaret Gamble	9/12 1797 started, not finished	Bond: Samuel King
2328 McCLURE, JAMES A. et ux Sarah Ferguson	10/8 1833	By W. Toole, J.P.
2329 McCLURE, JOHN et ux Elizabeth Mitchell	1/28 1819	By Samuel Douthit, M.G.
2330 McCLURE, JOHN R. et ux Mary W. George	3/11 1825	By Isaac Anderson, P.N.P. Ch.
2331 McCLURE, JOHN R. et ux Lucitta Goff	10/28 1847	By J. S. Craig, M.G.
2332 McCLURE, JOSEPH et ux Elizabeth Greenway	10/20 1836	By Isaac W. Haire, J.P.
2333 McCLURE, SAMUEL et ux Elvira M. Douthit	7/16 1822	By David Adams, M.G.
2334 McCLURE, WILLIAM H. et ux Elizabeth Havens	11/17 1825	By Isaac Anderson, P.N.P. Ch.
2335 McCLURE, WILLIAM H. et ux Ruth P. Havens	8/15 1843	By R. B. Billue, M.G.
2336 McCLURE, WM. C. et ux Nancy Clemens	3/4 1852	By S. J. McReynolds, J.P.
2337 McCLURG, HARVY B. et ux Nancy L. Dixon	2/2 1832	By D. Carson, M.G.
2338 McCLURG, JAMES et ux Jane Henderson	6/3 1820	By Jos' Love, J.P.
2339 McCLORG, WILLIAM et ux Elizabeth Henderson	12/22 1828 issued	"Celebrated by me" A. Ish, J.P.
2340 McCERG, WILLIAM et ux Malinda Hooper	11/22 1831 issued	No returns
2341 McCLURKIN, THOMAS et ux Delina Goodwin	6/19 1820	By Jos' Duncan, J.P.
2342 McCULLOCH, ALEX (McCullough by clerk) et ux Margaret McNutt	9/22 1795 issued	Bond: Wm. Ewing
2343 McCOLLOCH, SAMUEL et ux Margaret Porter (outside is Peggy Porter)	10/22 1800 issued	Bond: James McColloch

Names	Date Issue Or Celebrated	By Whom/ Security on Bonds
2344 McCOLLOM, ALEXANDER et ux Pheby Hammontree	7/11 1833	By Jeremiah K. Mosier, M.G., M. E. Church (names corrected by Preacher)
2345 McCOLLOM, JOHN et ux Elizabeth Bolton (outside Betsy)	2/9 1801 issued	Bond: James Folkner
2346 McCOLLOM, RICHARD S. et ux Mary Ellis	4/14 1828 issued	No returns
2347 McCOMB, JOHN et ux Lethia Davis	5/13 1801 issued	Bond: Henry Long
2348 McCONNELL, ALEXANDER H. et ux Mary A. Rhea	1/9 1845	By Harvey H. C. Caruthers, J.P.
2349 McCONNELL, ALFORD et ux Susannah Matthews	1/1 1851	By Isaac Anderson, P.N.P. Ch.
2350 McCONNELL, ANDREW V. et ux Cornelia A. Reavley	2/21 1855	By A. Vance, M.G.
2351 McCONNELL, CALVIN A. et ux Elizabeth Cochran	2/4 1857	By Daniel H. Emmet, J.P.
2352 McCONNEL, FRENCH et ux Jane Everett	1/27 1824	By A. B. Gamble, J.P.
2353 McCONNELL, GEORGE et ux Mary J. Adams	11/15 1838	By John D. Wilson, M.G.
2354 McCONNELL, ISAAC W. et ux Caroline McClung	2/20 1845	By A. Vance, M.G.
2355 McCONNELL, ISAAC W. et ux Lucinda Ann Walker	1/6 1848	By James Law, M.G.
2356 McCONNELL, JAMES et ux Ann McKee	8/26 1800 issued	Bond: Andrew Gammell
2357 McCONNEL, JAMES et ux Martha D. Wear	8/24 1848	By I. Anderson, P.N.P. Ch.
2358 McCONNELL, JAMES H. et ux Phebe McClung	12/2 1830	By Saml Hamill, J.P.
2359 McCONNEL, JOHN et ux Ann Stuart	10/25 1815 issued	No returns
2360 McCONNELL, MILES et ux Martha Scroggs	2/8 1825	By Arch'd Maxwell, J.P.
2361 McCONNEL, MOSES et ux Jane Rensbarger	4/1 1839	By Fielding Pope, M.G.
2362 McCONNELL, NEWTON et ux Nancy Brody	4/12 1833	By Isaac Anderson, P.N.P. Ch.
2363 McCONNELL, TELFORD et ux Nancy Billew	12/19 1829	By Wm. Billue, M.G.

Names	Date Issue Or Celebrated	By Whom/ Security on Bonds
2364 McCOOL, NICHOLAS et ux Ellender Conner	9/17 1817 issued	"solominezd by me" J. Gillespy, J.P.
2365 McCORD, DAVID et ux Jane McNeily	3/18 1812 issued	No returns
2366 McCORD, JAMES et ux Dorcas Cowan (is outside, inside-- hard to say!)	5/30 1801 issued	Bond: Saml Handly
2367 McCOY, GEORGE et ux Jane S. Duncan	4/17 1832	By David Carson, M.G.
* See 2456		
2368 McCROSKEY, JOHN et ux Lucinda A. Grant	4/4 1820	By I. Anderson, P.N.P. Ch.
2369 McCROSKEY, SAMUEL et ux Polly McCollom	11/12 1816	By And'w S. Morrison, V.D.M.
2370 McCROY, ADAM et ux Rebecca Hendrick- son	1/31 1827 issued	"Did join them in mat- rimony" Alex'r Stewart, J.P.
2371 McCROY, LEWIS et ux Malicia Goodwin	3/6 1822	By Sameul Douthit, M.G.
2372 McCROY, WILLIAM et ux Kesiah Pass	12/4 1849	By Wm. M. Brickell, J.P.
McCULLOCH, ALEXANDER m. 9/25 1795 Margaret McNutt.		
* See 2342		
2373 McCULLOCH, GEORGE E. et ux Mary McKamy	10/19 1847	By I. Anderson, P.N.P. Ch.
2374 McCULLOUGH, JOHN et ux Hannah H. Boring	1/24 1828	By Charles H. Warren, J.P.
2375 McCULLOUCH, JNO. A. et ux Martha Hooper	1/15 1850	By F. Pope, M.G.
2376 McCULLOCH, ROBERT P. et ux Christiana Caldwell	10/8 1835	By Fielding Pope, M.G.
2377 McCULLOCH, SAMUEL et ux Eleanor Ewing	7/20 1824	By Isaac Anderson, P.N.P. Ch.
* See 2749		
2378 McCULLOCK, WILLIAM et ux Priscilla Cunning- ham	11/24 1817 issued	"Executed" Jos. Duncan, J.P.
2379 McCULLY, HENRY et ux Rebecca Caldwell	9/3 1827	By Eleven Hitch, Esq.
2380 McCULLY, HENRY F. et ux Nancy Delzell	9/5 1826	By Jos' Alexander, J.P.
2381 McCULLEY, ISAAC A. et ux Nancy Hitch	11/12 1852	By Samuel L. Yearout, J.P.

Names	Date Issue Or Celebrated	By Whom/ Security on Bonds

McCULLEY, JAMES m. 12/30 1818 Margaret Ferguson: found at home of a descendent of David McKamy, Jr. on 6/13 1922.

2382 McCULLY, JAMES
et ux Elizabeth Bond
2/4 1823 — By Wm. Griffitts, J.P.

2383 McCULLY, JAMES
et ux Margaret Dixon
12/19 1826 — By Thomas Beverage, --

2384 McCULLY, JOHN
et ux Eleanor Frew
8/12 1823 — By Isaac Anderson, P.N.P. Ch.

2385 McCOLLEY, JNO.
et ux Elizabeth Ann Hamill
(J.P. says "John McCulley.")
9/12 1844 — By Joseph A. Hutton, J.P.

2386 McCULLY, JOHN
et ux Martha F. Goodlin
1/22 1846 — By Harvey H. C. Caruthers, J.P.

2387 McCULLY, JOSEPH
et ux Elizabeth Stinnett
8/13 1850 — By William Colburn, J.P.

2388 McCULLY, SAMUEL
et ux Betsy Rhea
9/29 1825 — By Wm. Gault, J.P.

2389 McCULLY, SOLOMON
et ux Ann M. Hammill
9/1 1825 — By D. Carson, M.G.

2390 McCURDY, HENRY
et ux Hannah Stone
8/25 1818 issued — No returns

2391 McDANIEL, EDWARD
et ux Margaret Bright
1/8 1851 — By Will M. Brickell, J.P.

2392 McDANEL, DAVID
et ux Sarah Sherril
9/22 1853 — By Curran Lemons, J.P.

2393 McDANIEL, JAMES
et ux Mary Tefateler
5/22 1854 — By Wm. H. Anderson, J.P.

2394 McDANIEL, JOHN
et ux Manervia Pearce
1/3 1847 — By Wm. Henderson, J.P.

2395 McDANIEL, JOHN
et ux Nancy Jane Cupp
9/23 1847 — By Saml Pride, J.P.

2396 McDANIEL, RICHARD
et ux Nancy Steel
12/6 1840 — By James Matson, J.P.

2397 McDANIEL, STEPHEN
et ux Elizabeth Sneed
12/17 1845 — By John P. Keny, J.P.

2398 McDANIEL, THOMAS D.
et ux Salenia Snead
8/31 1847 — By S. J. McReynolds, J.P.

2399 McDANIEL, WILLIAM
et ux Matilda Kirk-
patrick
1/16 1821 — By Jno. McGhee, --

2400 McDANALD, WILEY
et ux A. A. Casteel
6/12 1853 — By Thos. M. Rooker, J.P.

2401 McDONOLD, FREDERICK
et ux Locky Davis
9/4 1817 — By George Snider, --

Names	Date Issue Or Celebrated	By Whom/ Security on Bonds
2402 McDOWELL, JAMES et ux Nancy Coner (outside is Conner)	9/30 1799 issued	Bond: James McLanahan
2403 McDOWELL, JOHN et ux Phebe Frankland	9/20 1797 issued	Bond: Francis Irwin
2494 McELDER, WILLIAM et ux Mary A. Spradlin	5/1 1859	By A. J. Wilson, J.P.
2405 McELDRY, EDMUND et ux Hetty Roddy	11/15 1821	By Saml George, J.P.
2406 McFADDIN, ANDREW et ux Martha Alford	8/15 1849	By William Colburn, J.P.
2407 McFEE, THOMAS et ux Elizabeth James	3/15 1836	By John Tate, M.G.
2408 McFEE, WILLIAM et ux Eliza R. Davis	8/2 1836	By William McTeer, J.P.
2409 McCALLY, JAMES et ux Margaret Ferguson	12/30 1818 issued	J. F. Foute, Clk (saw in hands of Robt. Hatcher, 1932, from David McKamy, J.P. home, Clover Hill, in 6th Dist.) (also below)
* See 1928		
2410 JOHNSTON, BENJ. et ux Judah May	12/14 1824 issued	No returns on it. JAC. F. FOUTE, Clk by Dept. Geo. W. Foute
* See 1928		
2411 McGAHA, AARON et ux Caroline McClinton	9/24 1819	By Wm. Williamason, J.P.
2412 McGAUGHEY, JAMES et ux Margaret McCain	4/12 1798 issued	Bond: William McGaughey
2413 MOGHEE, ALEXANDER et ux Ann B. McLin	3/26 1833 issued "executed 3/28 1833"	By Isaac Anderson, P.N.P. Ch.
2414 McGHEE, BARCKLEY et ux Eliza V. Hannaum	11/23 1848	By Isaac Anderson, P.N.P. Ch.
2415 McGHEE, JAMES et ux Elisabeth Hays (of Jno.; she d. in Oregon)	8/21 1851	By John Morton, J.P.
2416 McGHEE, JOHN et ux Mary White	5/3 1821	By Ach'd Maxwell, J.P.

JOHN McGHEE of Maryville m. 9/5 1820 Betsey J. of Charles McClung in Knox Co., Tenn. by Rev. Richard H. King. Knox Register and Newspaper.

Names	Date Issue Or Celebrated	By Whom/ Security on Bonds
2417 McGHEE, JOHN et ux Margaret Campbell	12/23 1845	By Green B. Saffell, J.P.
2418 McGHEE, JNO. et ux Ainzy Hammontree	1/26 1852	By John McClain, J.P.
2419 McGHEE, JOSEPH et ux Elizabeth Calor	3/27 1823	By Samuel C. Davidson, J.P.
2420 McGEE, JOSEPH et ux Cynthea Murphy	1/9 1826	By George Ekin, J.P.
2421 McGHEE, SILAS et ux Arminta Carroll	10/19 1824 issued	No returns
2422 McGEE, WILLIAM et ux Maryann Ross	9/28 1825	By Arch'b Maxwell, J.P.
2423 McGILL, ALEX et ux Orelenia McCasland	12/3 1847	By John Dyke, Pastor Unitia Church
2424 McGILL, CHARLES et ux Peggy Barnett	1/21 1832	By John Hendrix, J.P.
2425 McGILL, JAMES HARVEY et ux Nancy Duncan	10/29 1840	By Eli Richey, J.P.
2426 McGILL, JAMES et ux Mahala Doston	9/23 1847	By W. R. Flinn, J.P.
2427 McGILL, JOHN et ux Elizabeth Cowden	8/4 1859	By Nicholas Brewer, Esq.
2428 McGILL, JOSEPH et ux Susan Barnett	9/7 1834	By Spencer Henry, J.P.
2429 McGILL, JOSEPH et ux Polly Keller	8/12 1841	By W. R. Flinn, J.P.
2430 McGILL, ROBT. et ux Vienna Thompson	7/19 1849	By J. Dyke, Pastor Unitia Ch.
2431 McGILL, SAM et ux Sally Leventer	12/23 1831 "celebrated 12/13 1831"	By James Taylor, M.G.
2432 McGHILL, WILLIAM et ux Polly Macklin	2/22 1837	By Rev. J. Dyke
2433 McGILL, WILLIAM et ux Rachel Bird	8/25 1847	By Jno' Chambers, M.G.
2434 McGINLEY, EBENEZER et ux Polly Tefetallor	8/7 1828	By A. B. Gamble, J.P.
2435 McGINLEY, JACOB E. et ux Sibby E. Rhey	5/25 1854	By J. S. Craig, M.G.
2436 McGINLEY, JAMES et ux Margaret Previtt	1/23 1821	By Alex B. Gamble, J.P.
2437 McGINLEY, JAMES et ux Polly Kenney	4/21 1829 issued	"By me Wm. Billue, M.G."

Names	Date Issue Or Celebrated	By Whom/ Security on Bonds
2438 McGINLEY, WM. D. et ux Margaret C. Kinney	8/29 1850	By F. Pope, M.G.

m. 2nd 5/8 1860 Elizabeth C. Duncan (of family)

2439 McGLAUGHLIN, JAMES C. et ux Margaret McCannell (or McCaunell)	11/4 1852	By A. B. Gamble, J.P.
2440 McGLOTHLIN, JAMES L. et ux Sarah Ballinger	6/12 1851	By W. H. Rogers, M.G.
2441 McGREW, PLUMBLY et ux Jane Lawrence	5/10 1844	By W. Toole, J.P.
2442 McGUIRE, ISACK et ux Martha Jackson	7/14 1796 issued	Bond: John (Dinning) Dining
2443 McGUIRE, MICHAL et ux Polly Forister	2/18 1819 issued	No returns
2444 McHAFFY, ANDREW et ux Nancy Kilburn	7/7 1838	By George Russell, M.G.

*   See 2269

2445 McHAMIL, WILLIAM et ux Caroline P. Ted- ford	7/13 1837 "Thursday"	By Thomas S. Kendall, M.G.

*   See below 2457-58

2446 McILHERON, JAMES et ux Betsy Ann Bilderbea	1/5 1832	By J. Gillespie, J.P.
2447 McINTURF, ALEXANDER et ux Sarah J. Porter	6/29 1851	By Samuel L. Yearout, J.P.
2448 McINTURFF, ALFRED et ux Mary Hunt	12/16 1853	By J. H. Donaldson, J.P.
2449 McKAMY, DAVID C. et ux Ann Tedford	10/17 1849	By James Lawson, M.G.

*   See 2288

2450 McKAMY, JAMES et ux Sally Julian	2/18 1823	By George Ewin J.P.
2451 McKAMY, JAMES et ux Ann Hanna	6/8 1824	By Jos' Alexander, J.P.
2452 McKAMY, JOHN et ux Elizabeth Shaver	3/16 1834	By Edward Mitchell, J.P.
2453 McKAMY, ROBERT et ux Martha Julian	3/29 1827	By A. B.Gamble, J.P.
2454 McKAMY, WILLIAM et ux Nancy Coldwell	1/27 1820	By Wm. Gault, J.P.
2455 McKAMY, ROBERT A. et ux Louisa F. Thompson	6/14 1855	By Rev. J. F. Bunker

Names	Date Issue Or Celebrated	By Whom/ Security on Bonds
* See next as 2367		
2456 McCOY, JAMES A. et ux Margaret Maroney (outside groom is McKay)	9/27 1846	By Danl Taylor, J.P.
2457 McKENRY, SAMUEL et ux Cathorine Peery	9/5 1850 issued	"Executed same day" John Russum, L.D.M.E.Ch.So.
2458 McHENRY, THOMAS B. et ux Fanny McMurry	7/17 1817	"By me" (no signature legible)
* See 2445 above		
2459 McKENZEY, DANIEL et ux Jenny Tippet	12/20 1798 issued	Bond: Humphrey Montgomery, sec.
2460 McKINZIE, JOHN L. et ux Mary Grigsby	10/17 1821	By S. Douthit, M.G.
2461 McKINLY, JAMES et ux Sally Stewart	6/8 1836	By Spencer Henry, J.P.
2462 McKINLEY, JOHN et ux Sarah Lane	2/25 1836	By Spencer Henry, J.P.
2463 McLANAHAN, DAVID et ux Polly Ingrum	9/28 1818 issued	By Jn. Walker, a preacher "by me"
* 2310		
2464 McLENAHAN, D. et ux Milly Hubbard	1/21 1846	By John Tipton, J.P.
2465 McLENAHAN, SAMUEL et ux Sally Lane	2/12 1846	By Robert Shields, J.P.
2466 McLEMORE, JOSEPH L. et ux Mary Roper	4/19 1853	By John J. Hoover, J.P.
2467 McLIN, GEO. A. et ux Amanda J. McConnell	11/25 1857	By A. Vance, M.G.
2468 McMAHAN, MOSES W. et ux Mary Taylor	3/21 1833	By Arnold Patton, --
2469 McMAHAN, WILLIAM et ux Elizabeth Taylor	11/10 1835	By John Maxwell, J.P.
2470 McMILLAN, JAMES ALEXANDER et ux Rosannah Mowry	8/10 1858	By William Kerr, J.P.

"Knoxville Register" James McMILLAN of B. C., Tenn. on
12/30 1824 Nancy W. Kennedy of Knox Co., Tenn.

Names	Date Issue Or Celebrated	By Whom/ Security on Bonds
2471 McMALLOON, LEWIS et ux Margaret Hamontree (of James) (outside is McMillan)	7/24 1832	By A. Vance, M.G.
2472 McMURRAY, BOYD et ux E. J. Erwin	2/6 1851	By John Russom, M.G.

Names	Date Issue Or Celebrated	By Whom/ Security on Bonds
2473 McMURRAY, JAS. H. et ux Jane Henry	2/7 1849	By John Russum, --
2474 McMURRY, NEWTON et ux Elenar Bogle	12/16 1824	By Hugh Bogle, J.P.
2475 McMURRY, SAMUEL H. et ux Harriet Houston	12/4 1855	By F. Pope, M.G.
2476 McMURRY, WILLIAM et ux Peggy Malcam	9/22 1825	By Hugh Bogle, J.P.
* See 2500		
2477 McMURRY, WM. N. et ux Elizabeth H. Creswell	9/14 1848	By John Russom, Deacon M. E. Church
2478 McNABB, JOHN et ux Elizabeth McConnel	2/2 1837	By A. Vance, M.G.
2479 McNABB, MARSHAL et ux Mary Adams	11/12 1818 issued	"Executed by J. Duncan, J.P."
2480 McNAB, WILLIAM et ux Margret Mitchel	6/3 1801 issued	Bond: James Mitchell
2481 McNABB, WM. S. et ux Susan R. McNabb (outside is Susan R. Hodge)	1/7 1858 issued	No returns
2482 McNALLY CHARLES et ux Caty Shook	1/25 1820	By James Gillespy, J.P.
2483 McNELLEY, JAMES et ux Betsy Houston	7/14 1812 issued	No returns
2484 McNEELY, WILLIAM H. et ux Mary G. Luster	10/30 1834	By Fielding Pope, M.G.
2485 McNALLY, SAMUEL et ux Mary Hooper	3/12 1850	By John Russom, M.G. Bond: Calvin Johnson
2486 McNUTT, ALEXANDER et ux Polly Singleton	9/24 1816	By I. Anderson, --
2487 McNUTT, JAMES et ux Susananh McCulloch	11/29 1833	By Isaac Anderson, P.N.P. Ch.
2488 McNUTT, JOHN et ux Elizabeth McCulloch	12/9 1824	By Isaac Anderson, P.N.P. Ch.
2489 McQUAGUS, WILLIAM et ux Jane Hamilton	12/19 1826	By Thos. E. T. McMurray, J.P.
2490 McREYNOLDS, GUILFORD et ux Permelia Gamble	10/4 1838	By Fielding Pope, M.G.
2491 McRANALDS, JOSEPH et ux Sally McClure	11/21 1815 issued	No returns
2492 McRANDLE, JOHN et ux Jane McRandle	11/27 1799 issued	Bond: Jos' Alexander

Names	Date Issue Or Celebrated	By Whom/ Security on Bonds
2493 McREYNOLDS, JOSEPH et ux Eleanor Edmonson	1/21 1830	By Andrew Vance, M.G.
2494 McREYNOLDS, ROBERT et ux Sarah Wear	2/20 1833	By Isaac Anderson, P.N.P. Ch.
2495 McREYNOLDS, ROBERT H. et ux Dicy Brown	9/8 1836	By Fielding Pope, M.G.
2496 McREYNOLDS, SAMUEL et ux Jane Hale	5/10 1821	By Samuel Hamill, J.P.
2497 McREYNOLDS, STEPHEN et ux Eleanor Tedford	2/6 1834	By Isaac Anderson, P.N.P. Ch.
2498 McRANDALS, WOODS et ux Polly McClure	2/18 1819 issued	No returns
2499 McROBERTS, ANDREW et ux Susannah Bond	12/13 1831 issued	No returns
2500 McMURRY, WILLIAM et ux Peggy McKenry	3/21 1817 issued	No returns
2501 McTEER, ANDREW B. et ux Nancy Gamble	12/1 1842	By Fielding Pope, M.G.
2502 McTEER, HENRY F. et ux Sarah A. Williamson	6/4 1850	By James M. Tulloch, J.P.
2503 McTEER, JAMES et ux Martha Ferguson	9/29 1795 issued	Bond: Barclay McGhee
2504 McTEER, JAMES et ux Jenny McTeer	8/7 1798 issued	Bond: Wm. Glass
2505 McTEER, JAMES et us Martha Gardner	12/22 1836	By John Maxwell, J.P.
2506 McTEER, JAMES A. et ux Levirea C. Pitner (of John) (Knoxville paper says Lovicy C. Pitner)	11/6 1843	By Fielding Pope, M.G.
2507 McTEER, MONTGOMERY et ux Martha W. Bogle	3/12 1835	By Isaac Anderson, P.N.P. Ch.
2508 McTEER, ROBERT et ux Mary Sherrell	3/22 1798 issued	Bond: John McCain
2509 McTEER, ROBERT et ux Ellen Conner	12/18 1817	By Wm. Gault, J.P.
2510 McTEER, SAMUEL et ux Sally Cummins	7/19 1821	By Hugh Bogle, J.P.
2511 McTEER, SAMUEL et ux Isabella Cooper	9/20 1837	By John D. Wilson, M.G.
2512 McTEER, WILLIAM et ux Mary McTeer	10/20 1802 issued	Bond: Jacob Moore
2513 McTEER, WILLIAM et ux Mary Bogle	9/16 1819	By George Snider, M.G. of "Babtist Order"

Names	Date Issue Or Celebrated	By Whom/ Security on Bonds
2514 McTEER, WILLIAM et ux Margaret Jane Tedford	5/25 1837	By Fielding Pope, M.G.
2515 McWHINNEY, WM. et ux Betsey Kindrick	10/5 1810	No returns
2516 MADDEN, GEORGE et ux Delilah Hartsell	11/10 1820	By J. Norwood, J.P.
2517 MADDEN, JAMES et ux Peggy Vaught	8/24 1809 issued	No returns
2518 MADDIX, WILLIAM et ux Catherine Shields	2/10 1853	By Curran Lemons, J.P.
2519 MAJOR (or MASSON) JAMES et ux Margaret Brumley	1/13 1803 issued	"No signature (on back is January 20, 1803 in another hand)"
2520 MALCOM, ALEXANDER et ux Mary Edmunson	5/16 1848	By Harvey H. C. Caru- thers, J.P.
2521 MALCOM, JOHN et ux Jane Henry	8/17 1837	By John D. Wilson, M.G.
2522 MALCOM, SAM N. et ux Ruth C. Hale	8/21 1855 issued	"In due time by A. Vance, M.G."
2523 MALCOM, SILAS et ux Nancy Hammontree	11/12 1842	By Joseph A. Hutton, J.P.
2524 MALCOM, WILLIAM B. et ux Elizabeth Ann McConnel	8/21 1851	By A. Vance, M.G.
2525 MALONE, J. D. et ux Nancy J. Bogle	8/4 1844	By J. S. Craig, M.G.
2526 MALONE, JEREMIAH D. et ux Mary Hale	5/13 1852	By Spencer Henry, M.G.
2527 MALONE, WILLIAM et ux Nancy Hix	3/14 1820	By J. Gillespie, J.P.
2528 MANER, ELLERY et ux Sarah Bussell	9/30 1858	By Andrew Ferguson, J.P.
2529 MANSON, WILLIAM S. et ux Isabella Gibbs	6/29 1814 issued	"solemnized" J. Gillespie, J.P.
* See 2582		
2530 MARONE, JOHN et ux Rosanna Roberts	3/27 1823	By Saml Hamill, J.P.
2531 MAROON, SAMUEL et ux Elizabeth Hannah	6/28 1824	By Wm. Williamson, J.P.
2532 MERONE, BENJAMIN et ux Mary Nolen	5/24 1831	By David McKamy, J.P.
2533 MERONEY, NELSON et ux Elizabeth Reagan	1/18 1820	By John Norwood, J.P.

Names	Date Issue Or Celebrated	By Whom/ Security on Bonds
2535 MARONEY, WRIGHT et ux Mary J. Crawford	11/30 1853	By Thos. M. Rooker, J.P.
2536 MARTIN, ADRIAN et ux Sarah Kerr	4/26 1838	By J. K. Mosier, M.G.
2537 MARTIN, GEORGE et ux Lucy Saunders	8/23 1817 issued	"Executed, J. Waugh, J.P."
2538 MARTIN, GEORGE et ux Sally Davis	12/3 1818 issued	"Celebrated" John Waugh, J.P.
2539 MARTIN, GEORGE W. et ux Mariah Francis Martin	6/15 1840	By A. N. Harris, M.G.
2540 MARTIN, HUGH E. et ux Mary Griffitts	4/27 1840	By J. Dyke, M.G.
2541 MARTIN, IGNATIUS et ux Mary R. Kenney	1/15 1846	By Isaac Anderson, P.N.P. Ch.
2542 MARTIN, JAMES et ux Jane Glass	11/9 1819	By Jos' Alexander, J.P.
2543 MARTIN, JAMES et ux Rosannah Low	12/6 1838	By William M. Borex, J.P.
2544 MARTIN, JOSEPH C. et ux Mary Balling	4/8 1824	By Hugh Bogle, J.P.
2545 MARTIN, JOSEPH et us Peggy Jane White	12/25 1846	By Green B. Saffell, J.P.
2546 MARTIN, JOHN et ux Caroline Ridge	11/11 1847	By David Spradlin, J.P.
2547 MARTIN, JOHN C. et ux Isabella S. Porter	5/12 1853	By Andrew Gass, M.G.
2548 MARTIN, LEVI et ux Matilda Caldwell	11/8 1859	By C. Long, J.P.
2549 MARTIN, MARK et ux Cyntha Tucker	10/2 1828 issued 9/28	By Samuel Douthit, E.M.E. Ch.
2550 MARTIN, MOSES et ux Sally Greenway	9/20 1818 issued	No returns
2551 MARTIN, MOSES et ux Celia Kerr	4/28 1836	By John D. Wilson, M.G.
* See 2731		
2552 MARTIN, ORAN D. et ux Jane Farmer	5/5 1829	By James Cameron, J.P.
2553 MARTIN, THOS. et ux Elizabeth McCulley	9/18 1851	By C. Long, J.P.
2554 MARTIN, WILLIAM B. (Esq. Attorney-at-Law says Knox Register, McGhee Library) et ux Susan J. Montgomery	4/26 1832	By Isaac Anderson,

Names	Date Issue Or Celebrated	By Whom/ Security on Bonds
2555 MARTIN, WILLIAM A. et ux Mary C. Cunningham	10/10 1850	By Isaac Anderson, P.N.P. Ch.
2556 MARTIN, WILLIAM et ux Amanda J. Kerr	3/6 1853	By Spencer Henry, M.G.
2557 MARTIN, W. A. et ux Jane Kenney	1/12 1854	By F. Pope, M.G.
2558 MARTIN, WM. et ux Jane A. Taylor	11/22 1855	By Phillips Wood, M.G.
2559 MARLAR, HENRY H. et ux Barbara Carolina Rine (Groom may be Meslar or Merler)	5/29 1845	By John Morton, J.P.
2560 MATSON, JAMES et ux Lavenia Hart	9/13 1836	By Isaac Anderson, P.N.P. Ch.
2561 MATHES, GEORGE A. REV'D. et ux Nancy Hart	4/7 1836	By D. Hoyt, M.G.
* See 2583		
2562 MATHEWS, HARLAH et ux Nancy McCaslin	4/3 1817 issued	No returns
2563 MATHEWS, JAMES et ux Sarah L. Humphrey	7/24 1845	By A. Vance, M.G.
2564 MATHEWS, JAMES et ux Nancy Tuck	2/29 1828 issued	No returns
2565 MATTHEWS, JOHN et ux Elizabeth Lain	12/29 1830	By Wm. Griffitts, J.P.
* See 2748		
2566 MATTHEWS, S. et ux M. A. Hope	6/8 1854	By John J. Hoover, J.P.
2567 MATTHEWS, WM. A. et ux Margaret M. Hart	12/5 1837	By Fielding Pope, M.G.
2568 MAUPIN, MORGAN et ux Polly Elmyra Barnes	8/12 1834	By Leroy Noble, J.P.
2569 MAXWELL, ARCHIBALD G. et ux Margaret E. Goodlink	9/20 1848	By James Law, V.D.M.
2570 MAXWELL, GEORGE H. et ux Margaret A. McKamy	9/28 1848	By James Law, V.D.M.
2571 MAXWELL, HARVEY T. et ux Mary C. Crumwell	3/25 1852	By Wm. M. Brickell, J.P.
* See 2584		
2572 MAXWELL, JAMES et ux Elizabeth Jenkins	8/3 1824	By C. H. Warren, J.P.
2573 MAXWELL, JOHN et ux Eliza Love	10/30 1832	By D. Carson, V.D.M.

Names	Date Issue Or Celebrated	By Whom/ Security on Bonds
2574 MAXWELL, JOHN C. et ux Elizabeth Ann McCulley	5/12 1840	By Isaac Anderson, P.N.P. Ch.
2575 MAXWELL, WM. et ux Hannah Henney	5/2 1809	By S. George, J.P.
2576 MAXWELL, WILLIAM et ux Martha Utter	1/3 1828 issued	Bond: James Hoge "by me 1/3 William Eagleton, M.G."
2577 MAXWELL, WM. et ux Margaret Hutsell	8/24 1856	By John Davis, M.G.
2578 MAYFIELD, JAMES et ux Mary Hood	2/11 1847	By R. Porter, J.P.
2579 MAYO, BLACKMORE H. et ux Grizy Kelso	7/9 1818	By Samuel Douthit, M.G.
2580 MAYO, GEORGE W. et ux Polly H. Woods	7/11 1823	By Samuel Douthit, Elder M.E. Ch. A.D.
2581 MAYREEN, JAMES et ux Letisha Jeffers	6/2 1843	By John Tipton, J.P.
2582 MANUEL, FLEET et ux Polly Rossom	8/4 1801 issued	No returns Bond: John Rossom
* See 2529		
2583 MATHES, JONATHAN et ux Mary Allin	11/23 1800 issued	Bond: Thomas Jones
* See 2561		
2584 MAXWELL, JAMES et ux Mary Majors	5/22 1802 issued	Bond: John Murphy
* See 2571		
2585 MAXWELL, JAMES et ux Sarah Moore	8/18 1802 issued	Bond: John Gillespie
2586 MAXWELL, THOMAS et ux Esther Hogg	9/17 1798 issued	Bond: John Simmons
2587 MAYS, B. P. et ux Rebecca French	8/29 1843	By C. Taliaferro, M.G. of Babtist Ch.
2588 MAY, JAMES -----	2/16 1801 issued or dated	(No name, or faded)
2589 MAY, JAMES et ux Susan Pugh	8/18 1829	By David McKamy, J.P.
2590 MAYS, JAMES et ux Sarah Roddy	10/26 1859	By H. T. Linginfelter, J.P.
2591 MAYS, JOHN et ux Emeline Griffin	10/5 1859	By Green B. Saffell, J.P.
2592 MAYSON, JESSE et ux Elizabeth Martin	8/27 1846	By John Chambers, M.G.

Names	Date Issue Or Celebrated	By Whom/ Security on Bonds
2593 MAZE, DAVID et ux Luscinda Tipton	7/15 1830	By Wm. McTeer, J.P.
2594 MAZE, FLEMING et ux Jane Shirrell	8/2 1838	By Wm. Billue, M.G.
2595 MAIZE, JAMES et ux Susan Breakbill	7/31 1845	By John Clark, J.P.
2596 MEANALES, JAMES et ux Elizabeth Caldwell (Groom may be McCandles (McCanalis))	2/10 1801 issued	"On back is: February 12, 1801" (No other words, no signature)
* See 2304		
2597 MEANS, ANDREW M. et ux Elizabeth Caruthers	12/16 1841	By Isaac Anderson, P.N.P. Ch.
2598 MEANS, BEARD H. et ux Betsy Ann Houston	2/2 1843	By A. Vance, M.G.
2599 MEANS, WILLIAM et ux Lucinda Ann Frow	6/9 1840	By Isaac Anderson, P.N.P. Ch.
2600 MEANS, WM. W. et ux Mary A. Wallace	8/24 1854	By J. S. Craig, M.G.
2601 MEDLOCK, ISSAAC et ux Margaret Lea	3/30 1837	By James Henry, J.P.
2602 MEDLOCK, WILEY et ux Nancy Kirtis	8/8 1837	By W. Toole, J.P.
* See 748, CURTIS		
2603 MEDLOCK, WILLIAM C. et ux Sophina Roddy	11/11 1846	By Daniel Taylor, J.P.
2604 METLOCK, WILLIAM et ux Hesterann Curtis	7/7 1842	By James Henry, J.P.
2605 MEEKS, JEREMIAH et ux Betsey Blevins	2/8 1802 issued	Bond: John Kee
2606 MELSON, ABRAM et ux Rebecca Gipson	3/11 1849	By Andrew Ferguson, J.P.
2607 MELSON, ABSALEM et ux Dorcas Thompson	12/10 1850	By L. L. McFarling, J.P.
2608 MELSON, ABSLEM et ux Elizabeth Craig	8/9 1855	By John McClain, J.P.
2609 MELSON, WILLIAM et ux Rahamy Fortner	7/6 1851	By Samuel Hendrick- son, M.G.
2610 MELTON, JAMES et ux Hannah Stallions	10/6 1825	By Thos' E. T. McMur- ray, J.P.
2611 MENIFOLD, HENRY et ux Rebecca Scott	11/11 1830	By Darius Hoyt, M.G.
2612 MENIS, SAMUEL et ux Polly Pickins	4/7 1817 issued	No returns

Names	Date Issue Or Celebrated	By Whom/ Security on Bonds
2613 MENIS, THOMAS et ux Pemelia Warren	4/10 1817	By David McKamy, J.P.
2614 MERCER, ELBERT F. et ux Mary Ann Norwood	10/20 1840	By Andre Vance, M.G.
2615 MICKLE, JOHN et ux Rebecka Hussey	6/12 1802 issued	Bond: Elijah Brown
2616 MILLER, ABRAHAM et ux Elizabeth Cannada (outside is Kennedy)	1/8 1822	By Joseph Duncan, J.P.
2617 MILLER, BENJAMIN et ux Naoma Lewis	1/4 1827	By A. Ish, J.P.
2618 MILLER, ANDREW et ux Sally Scott	9/23 1813	By And'w Jackson, J.P.
2619 MILLER, CULLINUS et ux Polly Sloan	10/22 1800 issued	Bond: James Boyd
2620 MILLER, DOUGLASS et ux Nancy Tipton	4/2 1839	By James Ray, J.P.
2621 MILLER, HENRY et ux Z. M. Fagg	1/2 1855	By Spencer Henry, M.G.
2622 MILLER, JAMES et ux Soynthia Anderson	12/1829 (issued 11/10)	By C.H. Warren, J.P.
2623 MILLER, JAMES M. et ux Mary Glass	3/4 1841	By Isaac Anderson, P.N.P. Ch.
2624 MILLER, JOHN et ux Sally Wood	8/5 1801 issued	Bond: Thomas Taylor
2625 MILLER, JOHN A. D. et ux Darcas Hammintree	9/20 1833	By Andrew Vance, M.G.
2626 MILLER, JOHN K. et ux Rhoda Kirby	10/23 1849	By Fielding Pope, M.G.
2627 MILLS, RICHARD et ux Delbly Cross (or as outside, is Dullilly or Dillily)	7/24 1832	By W. M. Smith, M.G.
MILLER, WILLIAM et ux Jean Scott	3/8 1805	Found 1934
2628 MILLER, WILLIAM R. et ux Mary C. Jackson	5/1 1845	By J. S. Craig, M.G.
2629 MILLIGAN, BARTON et ux Margaret Bell	3/7 1841	By William Colburn, J.P.
2630 MILLICAN, HUGH et ux Mary Tallent	12/15 1844	By James Henry, J.P.
2631 MILLIGAN, MINATE et ux Charlotta Giles	8/31 1845	By William Colburn, J.P.
2632 MILLIGAN, SAMUEL H. et ux Mary J. Loftice	10/23 1849 issued	No returns

Names	Date Issue Or Celebrated	By Whom/ Security on Bonds
2633 MILLIGAN, WILLIAM R. et ux Huldah Ann James	12/18 1848	By James H. Donaldson, J.P.
2634 MILES, WILLIAM et ux Jean Scott	3/8 1805 issued	No returns
2635 MILLS, WILLIAM et ux Tirressa An Jones	8/29 1850	By W. M. Brickell, J.P.
2636 MILLSAPS, ANDREW et ux Mary Melson	12/1 1842	By W. Toole, J.P.
2637 MILSAPS, ANDREW et ux N. J. Ghormley	10/7 1853	By S. J. McReynolds, J.P.
2638 MILSAPS, CLINTON et ux Polly Tipton	3/1 1832	By John Hendrix, J.P.
2639 MILSAPS, JAMES et ux Artelissa Wright	7/17 1851	By A. B. Gamble, J.P.
2640 MILSAPS, JESSE et ux Dolly Farmer	3/2 1826 issued 2/23	By Wm. Billue, M.G. Bapt.
2641 MILSAPS, JESSE et ux Jane Kinnemon	1/22 1852	By A. B.Gamble, J.P.
2642 MILSAPS, JOHN E. et ux Elizabeth Hatcher	11/14 1844	"Perpertrated by James Taylor, M.G."
2643 MILSAPS, WILLIAM et ux Rebecca McGill	9/23 1847	By W. R. Flinn, J.P.
2644 MINGLE, GEORGE W. et ux Melvina Murr	5/9 1854	By Wm. H. Anderson, J.P.
2645 MINES, JNO. et ux Sarah A. Everett (or groom may be Menes)	10/28 1856	By W. W. Bayless, J.P.
2646 MINIS, JOHN et ux Nancy Warren	11/13 1816 issued	No returns
2647 MINNIS, JOHN et ux Elizabeth J. Debusk	10/11 1838	By John D. Wilson, M.G.
2648 MINIS, ROBERT et ux Margaret G. Steele	4/10 1827	By D. Carson, M.G.
2649 MINNIS, WILLIAM et ux Catherine Coonse	4/26 1825	By Isaac Anderson, P.N.P. Ch.
2650 MINNIS, WM. of Jefferson Co., Tenn. et ux Ellen Eagleton ("Mrs." says Knoxville paper)	4/15 1856	By J. S. Craig, M.G.
2651 MINTON, ELDRIDGE H. et ux Mary A. Richey	4/27 1849	By J. H. Donaldson, J.P. Bond: C. F.Chapman
2652 MIZER, GEORGE W. et ux Nancy J. McCulloigh	9/16 1852	By A. J. McGee, M.G.

Names	Date Issue Or Celebrated	By Whom/ Security on Bonds
2653 MIZER, GEORGE et ux Elizabeth Pickering	10/14 1836	By Eli Richey, J.P.
2654 MIZER, GEORGE et ux Sarah Brooks	11/6 1838	By William Colburn, J.P.
2655 MISER, HENRY et ux Francis Farmer	2/4 1823 issued	(in corner outside R. B. McCully)
2656 MISER, JOSEPH et ux Polly Hays	12/21 1848	By Wm. M. Brickell, J.P.
2657 MISER, MICHAEL et ux Susan Moore	1/8 1841	By William H. Hodge, M.G.
2658 MITCHELL, ALLEN et ux Eliza Kidd	3/19 1840	By Robert Porter, J.P.
2659 MITHCELL, DAVID F. et ux Fanny Long	12/31 1846	By S. J. McReynolds, J.P.
2660 MITCHELL, ELIJAH et ux Polly Campbell	9/25 1827 issued	No returns
2661 MITCHELL, HEZEKIAH et ux Mary D. Houston	3/18 1819	By I. Anderson, V.D.M.
2662 MITCHELL, JAMES et ux Rebecca Sharp	10/29 1833	By Wm. Billue, M.G.
2663 MITCHELL, JASPER N. et ux Fanny Williams	8/24 1848	By Wm. Billue, M.G.
2664 MITCHEL, JESSE et ux Providence Norwood	10/6 1818 issued	No returns
2665 MITCHELL, JOHN et ux Mary Ann Tipton	3/11 1841	By Wm. Billue, M.G.
2666 MICHEL, JOHN C. et ux Maryann Ferguson	9/23 1841	By Thomas H. Kendall, M.G.
2667 MITCHEL, SAMUEL et ux Susan Johnston	12/27 1840	By Wm. Billue, M.G. Bond: John Kidd
2668 MOFFITT, KENNEDAY et ux Zalera Witcher	8/30 1808 issued	No returns
2669 MONTGOMERY, ANDREW C. et ux Ann M. Houston	10/24 1822	By Isaac Anderson, P.N.P. Ch.
2670 MONTGOMERY, ANDREW C. et ux Evelinea C. Green	3/28 1833	By Arnold Patton, --
2671 MONTGOMERY, A. et ux Rebecca (I know was widow-- 1st Thompson)	5/2 1854	By Fielding Pope, M.G.
2672 MONTGOMERY, DAVID et ux Margate McCameron (outside is McCorete-- hard to say)	2/7 1799	Bond: Watt'w Wallace

Names	Date Issue Or Celebrated	By Whom/ Security on Bonds
2673 MONTGOMERY, Gillespy et ux Jane Burton	10/1 1846	By J. S. Craig, M.G.
2674 MONTGOMERY, JAMES et ux Dorcas Russell	12/30 1817	By And'w S. Morrison, V.D.M.
2675 MONTGOMERY, JAMES et ux Polly Ann Thompson	5/26 1826	By S. Douthit, E.M.E. Ch.
2678 MONTGOMERY, JAMES H. et ux Martha W. Frow	10/1 1835	By Fielding Pope, M.G.
2677 MONTGOMERY, JAMES S. et ux Charity Carretson	9/9 1802 issued	Bond: Andrew Agnew
2678 MONTGOMERY, JOHN et ux Peggy	11/23 1798 issued	Bond: George Wallace
2679 MONTGOMERY, JOHN et ux Patsey Macheaney (a will gives it McCheeney)	6/9 1801	Bond: Tho's Berry
2680 MONTGOMERY, JOHN M. et ux Polly Craft	4/6 1826	By Isaac Anderson, P.N.P. Ch.
2681 MONTGOMERY, JOHN et ux Sarah Ann Bussell	8/7 1845	By Fielding Pope, M.G.
2682 MONTGOMERY, JEFFERSON E. et ux Grissy Thompson	6/8 1827	By Isaac Anderson, P.N.P. Ch.
2683 MONTGOMERY, RHADAMANTHUS J. et ux Harriet N. Bogle	5/26 1838	By Isaac Anderson, P.N.P. Ch.
2684 MONTGOMERY, ROBT. M. et ux Nancy A. McGhee	12/21 1847	By Henry Hamil, J.P.
2685 MONTGOMERY, SAMUEL et ux Mary Montgomery	8/7 1832	By G. Russell, --
2686 MONTGOMERY, SAMUEL et ux Hetty A. Montgomery	9/30 1852	By Fielding Pope, M.G.
2687 MONTGOMERY, THOMAS et ux Franky Carter	1/19 1826 issued	No returns
2688 MONTGOMERY, WILLIAM et ux Phebe James	7/17 1806 issued	No returns
2689 MONROE, JAMES et ux Sarah E. Sims	9/29 1857	By W. W. Bayless, J.P.
2690 MORGAN, JIRDAN et ux Polly Bohannan	3/24 1825	By Hugh Bogle, J.P.
2691 MANCOCKEY, WILLIAM et ux Winafred McConel	10/27 1832	By William Toole, J.P.
2692 MOORE, ALEXANDER et ux Eliza M. Montgomery	1/17 1832	By A. Vance, M.G.

Names	Date Issue Or Celebrated	By Whom/ Security on Bonds
2693 MOORE, DAVID et ux Rachel Mills	9/23 1852	By William Colburn, J.P.
2694 MOORE, ELISHA et ux Harriott Creswell	5/15 1815 issued	No returns
2695 MOORE, ELISHA B. et ux Sarah R. James	10/30 1856	By Wm. M. Brickell, J.P.
2696 MOORE, ENOCH et ux Sarah S. Sketchly	12/7 1845	By E. Bowley, M.G. (or Bowlen)
2697 MOORE, HENRY D. et ux M. M. Gillespy	10/18 1849	By Rev. John Nocholson
2698 MOORE, JAMES et ux Hapy Caldwell	10/21 1831	By W. Toole, J.P.
2699 MOORE, JOSEPH M. et ux Rebecca J. A. Morton	12/24 1857	By A. J. Wilson, J.P.
2700 MORE, JAMES W. et ux Nancy E. Enis	2/10 1840	By James Henry, J.P.
2701 MOOR, JOHN et ux Elizabeth Tulloch	9/25 1823	By Saml Hamill, J.P.
2702 MOORE, JOHN et ux Mary Todd	2/14 1826	By Saml Hamill, J.P.
2703 MOORE, JOHN G. et ux Ruth A. Heartsell	12/28 1848	By Willi m Colburn, J.P.
2704 MOORE, JOHN L. et ux Sarah Mackey (outside "McKey")	4/13 1831 issued	"by me in April 1831" A. C. Renfro, J.P.
2705 MORE, JOSEPH H. et ux Cinthy Seals	10/1 1838	By Ben Cunningham, J.P.
2706 MOOR, LAUSCIN C. et ux Rachael McFee	8/12 1828	By William McTeer, J.P.
2797 MOORE, H(N?)EMIVILLE et ux Reller Perkins	1/25 1848	By Wm. Henderson, J.P.
2708 MORE, L. H. et ux Sarah Covington	11/28 1844	By James Ray, M.G.
2709 MOORE, SAMUEL et ux Jane Utter	7/13 1824	By Saml Hamill, J.P.
2710 MOORE, SAML A. et ux Eliza Ann Houston	6/21 1821	By Andrew S. Morrison, V.D.M.
2711 MOORE, THOMAS et ux Sally Kilpatrick	9/8 1823	By Jos' Duncan, J.P.
2712 MOORE, WILLIS et ux Mary Clampet	10/20 1795 issued	Bond: John Cochran
2713 MORE, WILLIAM JR. et ux Jenney Montgomery	5/5 1802 issued	Bond: Hugh Montgomery

Names	Date Issue Or Celebrated	By Whom/ Security on Bonds
2714 MOORE, WILLIAM D. et ux Sarah Hutton	11/7 1829	By Andrew Vance, M.G.
2715 MOORE, W. A. et us Sophiaha J. Byerley	2/22 1857	By Harace Foster, J.P.
2716 MOOREFIELD, MARTIN et ux Polly Weaver	9/24 1817 issued	No returns
2717 MOORELOCK, GEORGE et ux Jane C. Ritchy	11/28 1833	By Andrew Vance, M.G.
2718 MORROW, GEORGE et ux Martha J. Steele	4/15 1857	By B. F.Duncan, J.P.
2719 MORROW, JAMES R. et ux Ameviry (or Aeavery) Brook	1/27 1846	By J. Dyke, Pastor Unitia Ch.
2720 MORSE, BRIAN C. et ux Ann Cope	10/2 1823	By Arch'd Maxwell, J.P.
2721 MORRES, BLOUNT et ux Mary Browner	2/29 1832	By William Toole, --
2722 MORRIS, HAMPTON et ux Polly Louisa Smoot	8/4 1830	By B. Abernath y, L.D.
2723 MORRIS, JOHN et ux Elizabeth Kay	2/4 1823	By Charles H. Warren, --
2724 MORRIS, WILLIAM et ux Elezabeth Eanis	12/1 1822	By Charles H. Warren, --
2725 MORRISON, JOEL et ux Nancy Low	4/20 1819	By George Snider, M.G. Babtist Order
2726 MORRISON, THOS' et ux Francie Beard	6/13 1799 issued	Bond: George Beard
2727 MORTON, DAVID et ux Margaret M. Delzell	2/19 1835	By Isaac Anderson, P.N.P. Ch.
2728 MORTON, ISAAC W. et ux Eliza Murry	12/21 1843	By Green B. Saffell, J.P.
2729 MORTON, JOHN et ux Mary Wella	10/3 1820	By Billy Holloway, M.G., Baptist Order
2730 MORTON, JOSEPH M. et ux Mary A. Saffell	10/10 1850	By Jesse Kerr, Jr., J.P.
2731 MORTON (MARTIN?), MADSON, M. et ux Sarah A. Hufstet- ler	12/28 1858	By Spencer Henry, M.G.
* See 2551		
2732 MORTON, ELLAS J. et ux Sarah Poland	12/4 1849	By Robert Delzell, J.P.
2733 MORTON, WILLIAM et ux Nancy Mackey	2/23 1825	By A. B. Gamble, J.P.

Names	Date Issue Or Celebrated	By Whom/ Security on Bonds
2734 MORTON, WILLIAM et ux Mary E. Brook	2/27 1851	By W. Earnest, J.P.
2735 MORTON, WILL H. et ux Celia Herrin	11/25 1848	By Jno. Boring, M.G.
2736 MOSELY, THOMAS et ux Elizabeth Bird	8/3 1843	By David Spradlin, J.P.
2737 MOSIER, JEREMIAH K. et ux Mary Ann Wallace	6/1 1824	By Thos' Paine, M.G.
2738 MOSER, JOSEPH V. et ux Sarah Biddle	5/20 1824	By Isaac Anderson, P.N.P. Ch.
2739 MOSSES, JOSHUA et ux Sally Samples	9/16 1817 issued	No returns
2740 MUCK, JNO. et ux Theresa Curtis (later "Mook")	6/22 1853	By S. J. McReynolds, J.P.
2741 MUCCLEROY, LEWIS et ux Matilda Davis	8/29 1845	By Wm. Dever, J.P.
2742 MUCKLEHERING, JOHN et ux Elizabeth Fowler	8/4 1845	By William Colburn, J.P.
2743 MULLENS, ROBERT et ux Sarah Elliott	3/12 1847	By W. Toole, J.P.
2744 MULLENS, HENRY H. et ux Tempy Rollin	5/20 1845	By W. Earnest, J.P.
2745 MURRIN, ANDREW J. et ux Charlotta W. Kibble	8/27 1844	By Will Cummin J.P.
2746 MURREN, ROBERT JR. et ux Caty Bowers	3/7 1822	By Elijah Rogers, M.G.
2747 MURREU, ROBERT et ux Sally Davis	6/27 1830	By William McTeer, J.P.
2748 MURRIN, SAMUEL et ux Margaret Knight	10/13 1838 issued	No returns
2749 MURPHY, ISAAC A. et ux Elizabeth Delezier	10/3 1839	By John Russom, Deacon, M. E. Ch.
2750 MURPHY, JAMES et ux Mary Walker	10/2 1815 issued	"Executed September 3, 1816" George Snider, --
2751 MURPHY, JAMES et ux Mary McCarroll	9/2 1824	By Arch'd Maxwell, J.P.
2752 MURPHY, JAMES et ux Mary Smith	2/13 1831	By Jos' R. Sensabaugh, M.G.
2753 MURPHY, JOHN et ux Sally Johnson	1/27 1846 issued	No returns
2754 MURPHY, W. C. et ux Luretta McBath	9/10 1858	By Fielding Pope, M.G.

Names	Date Issue Or Celebrated	By Whom/ Security on Bonds
2755 MURR, ISAAC et ux Katherine Long	12/30 1847	By S. J. McReynolds, J.P.
2756 MURR, JACOB et ux Fanny Long	12/23 1847	By Rev. Jacob M. Shaffer
2757 MURR, JOHN et ux Ellen E. Keller	8/9 1858	By Christian Long, J.P.
2758 MURRAY, ADAM et ux Mahala Carson	10/19 1841	By W. B. Gordan, M.G.
2739 MURRAY, ELIHU et ux Mary J. Morris	10/2 1851	By S. J. McReynolds, J.P.
2740 MURRAY, JEREMIAH et ux Mary Hammontree	11/16 1824	By Billy Holloway, M.G. of Baptist Order
2741 MURRY, WILLIAM et ux Nancy A. Spradling	3/25 1850	By Ralph E. Tedford, M.G.
2742 MUSSER, HENRY F. et ux Mary A. Spillman	9/13 1857	By H. Foster, J.P.
2743 MYERS, DANIEL et ux Matilda Cable	8/19 1838 issued 8/11	By W. M. Porter, J.P.
2744 MIERS, JACB et ux Matilda Cox	3/15 1827	By Creed Fulton, D.M.E. Ch.
2745 MYERS, JOHN et ux Mary A. Tipton	12/19 1850	By Johnson Adams, --
2746 MYERS, JOSIAH L. et ux Eliza Adams	12/7 1840 issued	Bond: George A. Molin
2747 MYERS, WILLIAM et ux Mary Walker	1/21 1840	By Johnson Adams, --
2748 MATTHEWS, LEONIDAS et ux Catherine R. Moore	8/6 1849 issued	Bond: John Dyke
* See 2565		
2749 McCULLOCH, SAMUEL et ux Margaret Porter (outside is "Peggy")	10/22 1800 issued	"October 23 1800" (on outside no signature)
* See 2377		
2750 NEAL, ALEXANDER et ux Sarah Hix	12/2 1834	By Joseph Wilson, J.P.
2751 NEAL, JAMES et ux Lucinda Hammentree	4/25 1844	By John Morton, J.P.
2752 NEAL, GREENBERRY et ux Sarah D. Blevens	12/30 1857	By A. J. Wilson, J.P.
2753 NEEL, ROBERT et ux Nancy Henderson	1/30 1822	By Arch'd Maxwell, J.P.

Names	Date Issue Or Celebrated	By Whom/ Security on Bonds
2754 NEELY, JOHN et ux Seelia Rush	12/17 1826	By James Cameron, J.P.
2755 NEEL, THOMAS et ux Mary A. Safford	12/19 1858	By A. J.Wilson, J.P.
* See 2793		
2756 NEIMON, JACOB et ux Mary Dugan	8/18 1827	By Saml Hamill, J.P.
2757 NELSON, ELIJAH et ux Nancy Kinneman	9/8 1835	By James Trundle, J.P.
2758 NELSON, ELIJAH et ux Martha Nuchols	6/5 1838	By William H. Hodge, M.G.
2759 NELSON, E. R. et ux A. C. Clemens	12/8 1859	By W. W. Nuchols, J.P.
* See 2795		
2760 NEWBERRY, STEPHEN C. et ux Barbary Rose	8/6 1839	By William H. Hodge, M.G.
2761 NEWMAN, MARTIN et ux Hannah Logan	12/25 1838	By Lorenzo Donaldson, J.P.
2762 NEWBERRY, THOMAS et ux Mary Patrick	2/21 1839	By Eli Richey, J.P.
2763 NEWBERRY, ENEOCH et ux Mary E. Quiet	3/8 1849	By James M. Tulloch, J.P.
2764 NEWMAN, C. C. et ux Martha E. Wallace	12/19 1859 issued	No returns
2765 NEWMAN, JACOB T. et ux Elizabeth A. Davis	1/16 1845	By John Russom, M.G.
2766 NEWMAN, THOMAS et ux Jane H. McGhee	9/6 1859	By John J. Robinson, M.G.
2767 NEMON, G. et ux Any Thompson	1/13 1819	By George Ewing, J.P.
2768 NEYMAN, JOSEPH et ux Thirzee Ann Clark	3/20 1832	By William McTeer, J.P.
2769 NEYMEN, LEWIS et ux Rachel M. Logan	6/20 1831	By William McTeer, J.P.
2770 NICKLES, GEORGE et ux Evaline Strutton	7/1 1855	By J. C. Wright, J.P.
2771 NICHOLS, EDWARD H. et ux Hetty Houston	2/17 1831	By Darius Hoyt, M.G.
2772 NICKOLS, FRANCIS et ux Nancy Bunitt (outside is Burnitt)	5/11 1842	By Curran Lemons, J.P.
2773 NICHOLS, WILLIAM et ux Sally Norton	9/15 1829	By George Ewing, J.P.

Names	Date Issue Or Celebrated	By Whom/ Security on Bonds
* See 2794		
2744 NICHALSON, DANIEL et ux Mary Talent	1/15 1836	By James Henry, J.P.
2775 NICHEOLSON, THOS' of Cumberland Co., Tenn. et ux Catherine E. Heair (daughter of I. M. Hair of Unitia--says Knox Register of 1/19 1856)	6/5 1856	By J. H. Donaldson, J.P.
2776 NIPPER, JAMES et ux Betsy Whitten- berger	8/4 1846	By James Henry, J.P.
2777 NIPPER, SAMUEL et ux Nancy Anderson	4/5 1851	By Thos. M. Rocker, J.P.
2778 NOBLE, SANDERS et ux Mary Robenitt	10/7 1830	By B. Abern t hey, L.D. or L.O.
2779 NOBLET, JOHN et ux Bethenia Noble	2/19 1828 issued	No returns
2780 NOEL, EPHRAIM P. et ux Jane Fleshhart	3/29 1831	By Isaac Anderson, P.N.P. Ch.
2781 NORTON, GEO. W. et ux F. A. Sharp	9/10 1858	By Wm. M. Burnett, --
2782 NORTON, JAMES et ux Prudence See- bastain	5/31 1823 issued	No returns
2783 NORTON, JOHN W. et ux Nancy Gamble	8/17 1843	By Fielding Pope, M.G.
2784 NORTON, WM. et ux S. M. Householder	7/17 1856	By W. T.Dowell, M.G.
2785 NORWOOD, CALEB M. et ux Jane Manson	12/5 1818	By Jno. Bowman, M.G.
2786 NORWOOD, C. W. et ux Malinda Thompson	1/15 1850 issued	Bond: John E. Toole
2787 NORWOOD, JOHN H. et ux Margaret J. Becknell	1/29 1851	By Joseph Peeler, M.G.
2788 NORWOOD, THOMAS et ux Anna Rice	2/19 1822	By Wm. Fagg, L.D.
2789 NUCHELS, DAVID et ux Elizabeth Ingram	11/8 1855	By W. W. Nuchols, J.P.
2790 NUCKOLS, RICHARD et ux Rebecca White	10/15 1840	By Wm. Rorex, J.P.
2791 NUCKLES, THOMAS et ux Mary Waters	9/26 1852	By C. Long, J.P.
2792 NUNN, ELI et ux M. E. Thompson	7/14 1853	By Isaac Anderson, P.N.P. Ch.

Names	Date Issue Or Celebrated	By Whom/ Security on Bonds
2793 NEILY, WILLIAM et ux Jane Hogg	2/7 1800 issued	Bond: Solomon McCamp- bell
* See 2755		
2794 NICKELS, WILLIAM et ux Elizabeth Vaun	8/19 1796	Bond: Archd' Trimble
* See 2775		
2795 NETHERTON, JOHN et ux Elizabeth Hardan	8/9 1797 issued	Bond: Animaas Reagan
* See 2750		
2796 O'BRIANT, EDWARD et ux Elizabeth Jones	7/26 1836	By Isaac M. Haire, J.P.
2797 O'BRIANT, JAS. W. et ux M. E. Thompson	1/31 1856	By Andrew Ferguson, J.P.
2798 O'CONNER, GRANDISON G. et ux Mary Ann Myers	7/10 1849	By William Colburn, J.P.
2799 O'CONER, G. G. et ux Elizabeth West	12/6 1855	By A. M. Goodykoontz, --
2800 O'CONNOR, THOMAS D. et ux Mary McFaddin	4/24 1820 issued	"Executed by me Saml George, --"
2801 O'DENEAL, HENRY et ux Nancy A. Tuck	8/19 1859	By John J. Hudgsons, J.P.
2802 O'NEAL, REED or RUEL et ux Maria Denison	11/7 1836	By William Colburn, J.P.
2803 O'NEAL, WILLIAM et ux Lucinda Tuck	1/3 1847	By Wm. Henderson, J.P.
2804 OGLE, JAMES W. et ux Rutha Davis	3/17 1859	By Nicholas Brewer, J.P.
2805 OGLE, JOHN et ux Mary A. Young	8/20 1856	By S. L. Yearout, J.P.
2806 OGLE, SPENCER et ux Viney or Veney Davis	1/26 1838	By Frederic Emmett, J.P.
2807 OGLE, THOMAS et ux Elizabeth Davis	12/31 1854	By N. Brewer, J.P.
2808 OLIVER, ELIJAH et ux Mary Lawson	4/4 1852 issued 3/27	By Curran Lemons, J.P.
2809 OLIVER, JAMES et ux Polly White	11/28 1821	By Arch'd Maxwell, Esq.
2810 OLIVER, LAZARUS et ux Mary McDaniel	1/6 1852 issued	"Celebrated by D. D. Foute, J.P."
2811 ORR, ALEX'D et ux Rebecca McNabb	12/27 1825 issued	"Celebrated--Saml Montgomery, Esq."
2812 ORE, BENJAMIN et ux Eliza McCully	5/6 1850	By Wm. M. Brickell, J.P.

Names	Date Issue Or Celebrated	By Whom/ Security on Bonds
2813 ORE, CLEMENT S. et ux Elizabeth Cox	7/17 1844	By William Colburn, J.P.
2814 OAR, JACOB et ux Margaret Mackel-herin (may be Muckel-herin)	8/7 1855	By H. Foster, J.P.
2815 ORR, JAMES K. et ux Martha S. McCulley	1/27 1858	By J. S. Craig, M.G.
2816 OAR, MARAH A. et ux Nancy Johnson	10/5 1854	By H. Foster, J.P.
2817 OER (or AER, FEE, FER) SAMUEL et ux Elizabeth Roberts-son	5/4 1809 issued	No returns
2818 ORE, WILLIAM et ux Mary Cannon	3/26 1844	By William Colburn, J.P.
2819 ORMAND, DAVID et ux Zelphy Davis	1/20 1821	By Hugh Bogle, J.P.
2820 ORMAN, MARTIN et ux Sally Rogers	4/4 1827	By William McTeer, J.P.
2821 OSBURN, ENOS et ux Mary A. Bright	12/24 1849	By Wm. M. Brickell, J.P.
2822 OTT, CHARLES et ux Mary Wolf	7/6 1856	By B. F.Duncan, J.P.
2823 OWENS, THOMAS et ux Rebecky Jordon	12/22 1808 issued	No returns
2824 PACELY, HEZEKIAH	3/24 1839	By Samuel Tullock, J.P.
2825 PADGETT, NATHAN et ux Eleanor Underwood	3/13 1823 issued	No returns
2826 PAGE, JAMES et ux Jane Brooks	12/8 1818	By I. Anderson, --
2827 PAGE, WM. J. et ux Sarah E. E. Smith	11/4 1852	By S. J.McReynolds, J.P.
2828 PALMER, JESSE et ux Ellen Cowden	1/13 1853	By A. B. Gamble, J.P.
2829 PALMER, JESSE et ux Martha Rogers	12/17 1856	By A. Boyd, Esq.
2830 PALMER, JOHN et ux Sarah McFee	12/22 1836	By Lorenzo Donaldson, J.P.
2831 PALMER, JOS' et ux Caroline Brakbill	9/25 1858	By A. Boy , Esq.
2832 PALMORE, SAMUEL B. et ux Elizabeth Garner	4/10 1844	By William Cuming, J.P.
2833 PARMER, WILLIAM et ux Susan Parmer	9/12 1833	By Saml Henry, J.P.

Names	Date Issue Or Celebrated	By Whom/ Security on Bonds
2834 PANNELL, WILLIAM T. et ux Cathorine Arrowood	11/21 1850	By J. H. Donaldson, J.P.
2835 PARISH, WM. B. et ux Mary A. Peery	1/20 1859	By M. Kountz, Esq.
2836 PARHAM, JOHN et ux Elizabeth Johnson	1/28 1847	By James Henry, J.P.
2837 PARKS, AZARIAH et ux Jane Golph	7/29 1829	By Wm. Fagg, L.D.
2838 PARKS, CALVIN et ux Vina Hickman	8/3 1849 issued	Bond: Wm. M. Brickell
2839 PARKS, JAMES et ux Nancy Walden	7/20 1818 issued	"Celebrated H. H. Bowerman, J.P."
2840 PARKS, JOHN et ux Routh Brown	8/13 1816 issued	No returns
2841 PARKES, JOHN W. et ux Sarah Sharp	2/25 1834	By Thos. White, J.P.
2842 PARKS, JOSHUA et ux Elizabeth Vaught	7/13 1820 issued	No returns
2843 PARKS, SAMUEL et ux Serene Cook (or Lerene)	6/19 1832	By Jeremiah K. Mosier, M.G.
2844 PARKINS, SAML et ux Nancy J. McCurly (outside is McCully)	9/7 1854	By Wm. Brickell, J.P.
2845 PARKER, JACKSON et ux Rachel Nichols	9/21 1856	By J. C. Wright, J.P.
2846 PARKER, LEVEN et ux Elizabeth Dyer	12/5 1855	By A. R.James, J.P.
2847 PARKER, WILL S. et ux P. A. Delzell	8/15 1850	By John Morton, J.P.
2848 PARKER, WM. S. et ux Elizabeth Rowlet	1/11 1853	By C. Long, J.P.
2849 PARKHILL, DAVID et ux Martha Wassham	8/2 1799 issued	Bond: John Trimble
* See 2909		
2850 PARSONS, ALFRED et ux Hannah Tuck	11/3 1845	By James H. Donaldson, J.P.
2851 PARSONS, HOLDEN R. et ux Artemize M. Williams	7/23 1846	By Joseph A. Hutton, J.P.
2852 PARSONS, HOLDEN R. et ux Margaret A. Eakin	11/23 1852	By Andrew Ferguson, J.P.
2853 PARSONS, H. R. et ux P. J. Taylor	6/3 1854	By A. Vance, M.G.

Names	Date Issue Or Celebrated	By Whom/ Security on Bonds
2854 PARSONS, JAMES K. et ux Sarah M. Hammill	2/20 1851	By James M. Tulloch, J.P.
2855 PARSONS, JONATHAN et ux Nancy Jenkins	3/6 1838	By D. B. Carter, O. Mis. M. E. Ch.
2856 PARSONS, ROBERT S. et ux Nancy Shanks	9/25 1823	By Samuel Douthit, Elder M. E. Church A.D.
2857 PASS, ARCY. et ux Mary Hall (or Hale)	11/28 1844	By B. F. Duncan, J.P.
2858 PASS, EDMAND et ux Kesiah King	6/15 1859	By John J. Hudgeons, J.P.
2859 PASS, GREEN et ux Sarah Morgan	11/7 1844	By John Clark, J.P.
2860 PASS, RUSSELL R. et ux Margary M. Taylor	6/16 1858	By J. A. Houston, J.P.
2861 PASS, SAMUEL T. et ux Sarah Perkins	2/13 1851	By And' Ferguson, J.P.
2862 PATE, RUFUS et ux Eliza S. Brown	12/13 1838	By Matthew Whittenberger, J.P.
2863 PATE, WILLIAM C. et ux Maratha E. Pugh	2/13 1846	By William Hendrickson, M.G.
2864 PATRICK, HILLERY et ux Mary Houston	7/28 1826	By William Eagleton, M.G.
2865 PATRICK, WILLIAM et ux Polly Williams	10/29 1822	"Celebrated" (& date is all, 10/29 1822, no signature)
2866 PATTERSON, ALEXANDER et ux Betey Stuard	3/21 1814 issued	No returns
2867 PATTERSON, GEORGE et ux Susannah Garren	8/13 1831	By B. Abernathy, L.D. or L.L.
2868 PATTERSON, LEVI et ux Emeline Patty	4/27 1839	By James Henry, J.P.
2869 PATTERSON, SAMUEL et ux Peggy Taylor	4/30 1808 issued	No returns
2870 PATTON, R. S. et ux Therresa C. Pope	8/29 1849	By I. Anderson, V.D.M.
2871 PATTY, JAMES W. et ux Elizabeth Hunter	11/8 1859	By A. Boyd, J.P.
2872 PATTY, JOSHUA et ux Jane Dunn	11/27 1851	By G. G. Sims, M.G.
2873 PATTY, JOSIAH et ux Elisabeth Rooker	5/25 1809 issued	No returns
2874 PAUL, JAMES A. et ux Susan J. Parks	1/12 1854	By Wm. Billue, M.G.

Names	Date Issue Or Celebrated	By Whom/ Security on Bonds
2876 PAYNE, WILLIAM et ux Susan Hitch	3/21 1837	By Wm. Billue, M.G.
2877 PEARCE, DAVID et ux Sarah Bartlett	3/23 1808 issued	No returns
2878 PEARCE, EDGAR et ux Elizabeth Stuart	10/8 1857	By Danl D. Foute, J.P.
2879 PEARCE, HIRAM et ux Sarah Smith	3/18 1848	By Wesley Earnest, J.P.
* See 3018		
2880 PEARCE, ROBERT D. et ux Elizabeth Cook	2/8 1849	By Spencer Henry, M.G.
2881 PIERCE, WM. et ux Joannah Lewis	1/1 1839	By William Colburn, J.P.
2882 PEARSON, SILAS et ux Jane Smith	1/11 1849	By L. L. McFarling, J.P.
2883 PENDERGRAFT, TITUS et ux Elizabeth Alloway	11/15 1838	By Eli Richey, J.P.
2884 PENNEL, JOHN et ux Jane McClannahan	9/17 1818 issued	No returns
2885 PANTHER (PENTER?),JOHN et ux Sarah Waters (Groom signs "John Penter")	6/26 1802	Bond: Thos. Clerk
2886 PERKINS, LEVI et ux M. A. Ferguson	8/2 1849	By Andrew Ferguson, J.P.
2887 PERKINS, LORENZO et ux Mahala Key	11/12 1830 issued 10/12	By Alexander Ish, J.P.
2888 PERKINS, LORENZO et ux Serepta Ward	3/9 1848	By Harvey H. C. Caruthers, J.P.
2889 PERRY, WILLIAM et ux Nancy M. C. Strain	7/23 1833	By Andre Vance, M.G.
2890 PERY, WM. et ux Elizabeth Stephenson	10/20 1859	By James D. Lawson, M.G.M.E.Ch.
2891 PEERY, W. W. et ux Rachel T. Henry	2/5 1857	By W. T.Dowell, M.G.
2892 PESTERFIELD, DAVID et ux Esther Dunley	1/2 1825	By Charles H. Warren, J.P.
2893 PESTERFIELD, GEORGE et ux Tempy Caton	1/27 1835	By William Colburn, J.P.
* See 2910		
2894 PESTERFIELD, JOHN et ux Quilla Bonine	11/2 1826	By Charles H. Warren, J.P.
2895 PETERSON, TOBIAS et ux Nancy Belt	3/25 1855	By James M. Lane, J.P.

Names	Date Issue Or Celebrated	By Whom/ Security on Bonds
2896 PETERSON, WILLIAM P. et ux Elizabeth Brewer	11/28 1820	No returns
2897 PHELPS, A. J. et ux Sarah J. Miser	7/6 1854	By Wm. M. Brickell, J.P.
2898 PHELPS, WM. T. et ux Nancy Fletcher James	3/3 1853	By Thos. H. Rooker, J.P.
* See 2906		
2899 PHILLIPS, ABRAHAM et ux Nancy Wheeler	11/7 1822	By George Ewing, J.P.
2900 PHILLIPS, ISAAC et ux Margaret Plumer	12/24 1822	By Saml Hamil, J.P.
2901 PHILLIPS, JAMES et ux Eliza Hutsell	10/31 1858	By Wm. M. Brickell, J.P.
2902 PHILLIPS, JOSIAH et ux Elizabeth Dun	2/24 1820	By Samuel Hamill, J.P.
2903 PHILIPS, JOHN et ux Sally Whitten- berger	2/10 1818 issued	No returns
2904 PHILLIPS, P. H. et ux E. A.McGhee	10/7 1856	By Wm. M. Brickell, J.P.
2905 PHILLIPS, R. T. et ux C. C. Hood	7/3 1857	By J. S. Craig, M.G.
2906 PHILIPS (PHELPS?), TURNER et ux Rebecca P. Bonham	11/28 1839	By James Blair, M.G.
2907 PHILIPS, URIAH et ux Jane McMurray	6/30 1853	By John Clark, J.P.
2908 STUART, WILLIAM S. et ux Isabella James (of Knoxville at Chill- hewee in Blount County, Tenn., Knoxville paper of 3/21 says--covered with mud, not decipherable)	3/14 1857 issued 2/18 1857	By Thos. W. Humes
* See 3478; found Deeds Vol. Z-110-1858; 3509(?)		
* See 3298		
2909 PARSALL, N. G. et ux Louise C. Shearon	8/22 1854	By L. D. Tipton, M.G.
* See 2849		
2910 PESTERFIELD, HENRY et ux Eleanor Cayton	5/3 1825	By Charles H. Warren, J.P.
* See 2893		
2911 PICKENS, ROBERT et ux Elizabeth R. Houston	12/29 1846	By F. Pope, M.G.

Names	Date Issue Or Celebrated	By Whom/ Security on Bonds
2912 PICKENS, THOMAS et ux Harriet McBath (of Andrew)	2/8 1844	By Fielding Pope, M.G.
2913 PICKENS, WILLIAM C. et ux Susan McCammon	2/11 1847	By John Russom, M.G.
2914 PIGG, JOHN et ux Elizabeth Jones	3/1 1826 issued	"Executed by me Wm. Billue, M.G. on January 31, 1826"
2915 PINEXO, FNCON'co et ux Liddy Casteel (Groom a Spaniard-- Francisco or Francis Pinno)	3/5 1800	Bond: Joseph Casteel
2916 PITMAN, LEWIS et ux Pamella L. Warren	2/28 1836	By Joseph Vanpelt, M.G.
2917 PITNER, TILMAN M. of Murray Co., Ga. et ux Malinda Russell (of John R.) --says Knox Reg. of 3/22 1856	3/18 1856	By Rev. S. A. Taylor
2918 PLEMING, WILLIAM et ux Susan Smith	2/26 1833 issued	and "Celebrated" (no signature)
2919 PLUMLEE, JACKSON C. et ux Mary Ann Rogers	12/24 1839	By William McTeer, J.P.
2920 PLUMMER, JEREMIAH et ux Jane Snider	11/5 1820	By Wm. Williamson, J.P.
2921 PLUMMER, JEREMIAH et ux Rebeccah Gates	6/17 1826	By Wm. Williamson, J.P.
2922 PLUMMER, JOH(N?) et ux Rachel Davis	8/7 1828	By Samuel Hamill, J.P.
2923 POE, JAMES et ux Nancy Mayfield	3/25 1841	By James Henry, J.P.
2924 POLAND, DAVID et ux Prudence C. Ellis	11/3 1855	By A. R. James, J.P.
2925 POLLEN, JAMES et ux Christiana Taylor	9/2 1805 issued	No returns
2926 POLAND, JOHN et ux Emily McCartney	3/10 1818	By Andrew S. Morrison, V.D.M.
2927 POLLAND, JOHN et ux Nancey Davis	10/12 1821	By Wm. Williamson, J.P.
2928 POLAND, THOS. J. et ux Mary M. (outside is Mary M. Waters)	12/18 1856	By N. Brewer, Esq.
2929 POLIN, WM. H. et ux Mary Hamil	7/20 1854	By Wm. Cook, J.P.

Names	Date Issue Or Celebrated	By Whom/ Security on Bonds
2930 POOR, JESSEE et ux Martha Sartan	5/23 1857	By A. Boyd, Esq.
2931 POPE, FIELDING et ux Ann Eliza Hannaum	10/6 1859	By R. E.Tedford, M.G.
2932 POPE, THOS. A. et ux Mary A. J. Pride	1/13 1853	By Isaac Anderson, P.N.P. Ch.
2933 POPLAND, GEORGE et ux Nancy Edmons	7/18 1827	By Samuel Hamill, J.P.
2934 POPLIN, JOHN et ux Avey Poplin	20/26 1828 issued	By Thomas Billue, J.P. "on Oct. 26, 1829"
2939 PORTER, ANDREW et ux Louisa Harden	2/7 1856	By W. A. Lawson, M.G.
2935 POTTER, ANDREW et ux Betsy Holloway	9/17 1823	By Arch'd Maxwell, J.P.
2936 POST, CALVIN et ux Martha Thompson	11/3 1846	By Isaac Anderson, P.N.P. Ch.
2937 POWELL, ABRAHAM et ux Phebe Anderson	12/12 1818	By Wm. Williamson, J.P.
2938 POWERS, JOSIAH et ux Malinda C. Thompson	12/17 1856	By Harvey Thompson, J.P.
* See after 2934		
2940 PORTER, JAMES S. et ux Jeane Kirby	2/15 1805 issued	No returns
2941 PORTER, JAMES P. H. et ux Jane Owens	12/29 1842	By W. Toole, J.P.
2942 PORTER, MITCHELL W. et ux Susannah Foute	7/26 1838	By John Chambers, M.G.
2943 PORTER, ROBERT et ux Elizabeth Singleton	9/9 1824	By John Dever, --
2944 PORTER, ROBT et ux Rebecca M. Thomp- son	9/9 1845	By Fieldin Pope, M.G.
2945 PORTER, STEPHEN et ux Margaret Jane McNutt	1/23 1838	F. Pope, M.G.
2946 PORTER, S. S. et ux Mary E. Henry	3/20 1849	By F. Pope, M.G.
2947 PORTER, WILLIAM S. et ux Phebe Jane Mont- gomery	7/13 1843	By Leander Wilson, M.G.
* See 2937, POWELL, POWERS		
2948 PRATER, H. G. et ux Elizabeth J. Warren	11/25 1858	By Rev. S. J. Taylor at W. Y. Warren's

Names	Date Issue Or Celebrated	By Whom/ Security on Bonds
2949 PRATER, JAMES A. et ux Arta A. Abernetha	4/14 1859	By J. Hood, M.G.
2950 PRATER, SAMUEL et ux Mary Wright	4/29 1833 issued	"Rights of H. C." George Roossett (or Rockett)
2951 PRATER, WILLIAM et ux Mary B. Leeper	7/28 1836	By George Sevier or M.G.
2952 PRATHER, W. G. et ux Eliza Mangum	7/10 1845	By William Colburn, J.P.
2953 PRESLEY, WILLIAM et ux Margarett Johnston	10/25 1842	By A. C. Montgomery, J.P.
2954 PRESLEY, WM. et ux M. E.Shelley (2d marriage)	9/11 1856	By John Gault, Esq.
2955 PRICE, AARON et ux Betsy Wheeler	1/15 1840	By Wm. McTeer, J.P.
2956 PRICE, DENNIS et ux Rodah McMahan	1/13 1856	By J. C. Wright, J.P.
2957 PRICE, GEORGE W. et ux Maraget Davis (Margaret)	8/7 1851	By John C. Martin, J.P.
2958 PRICE, JAMES et ux Nancy Wilson	8/26 1837	By Lorenzo Donaldson, J.P.
2959 PRICE, JOSEPH et ux Sarah Bond	4/26 1821	By James Turk, J.P.
2960 PRICE, WILLIAM N. et ux Martha J. Hartsell	3/14 1858	By J. S. Craig, M.G.
2961 PRICE, WILLIAM et ux Mary Bearden	3/19 1833	By William Toole, J.P.
2962 PRITCHARD, AUSTIN et ux M. J. Anderson	2/24 1853	By William Colburn, J.P.
2963 PRITCHARD, ALFRED et ux M. E. McDaniel	7/12 1854	By J. S. Craig, M.G.
2964 PRITCHARD, BENONE et ux Fanny McNeal	1/28 1841	By Leonard Wood, J.P.
2965 PRITCHARD, JOSEPH H. et ux Poly H. Williamson	1/5 1833 issued	No returns
2966 PRICHARD, REUBEN T. et ux Anna Huckaby	3/23 1849	By James Henry, J.P.
2967 PRIVITT, HEZEKIAH et ux Elizabeth Endsley	9/10 1825 issued	"Celebrated by me" Alex'd Stewart, J.P.
2968 PRIVIT, HEZEKIAH et ux Eliza Roberts	10/30 1828	By Isaac Anderson, P.N.P. Ch.
2969 PRIVETT, MATTHEW P. et ux Elizabeth Mitchell	6/7 1857	By C. Cowan, J.P.

Names	Date Issue Or Celebrated	By Whom/ Security on Bonds
2970 PROCTER, MOSES et ux Phebe C. Henry	12/26 1858	By Daniel H. Emmet, J.P.
2971 PRYOR, SAMUEL et ux Neomi Rose	11/13 1846	By Ben Cunningham, J.P.
2972 PUGH, JONATHAN et ux Elizabeth Bingham	12/15 1825	By Saml Hamill, J.P.
2973 PUGH, WILLIAM et ux Lucreti Valentine Trice	5/26 1825	"Celebrated this day" (no signature)
2974 QUIET, JAMES et ux Mary Hubbard	12/25 1844	By Robert Shields, J.P.
* See 3129		
2975 RAGSDALE, LUTHER et ux Mary A. Scot	5/3 1855	By R. E. Tedford, M.G.
2976 RAINS, HIRAM et ux Polly Wooden	12/20 1827 issued	No returns
2977 RAYNES, JAMES K. et ux Elizabeth Payne	12/21 1825	By George Ewing, J.P.
2978 RAINES, JESSE et ux Maryann Merriet	1/26 1826	By Wm. Griffitts, J.P.
2979 RAINES, JOHN et ux Polly Huckaby	7/20 1822	By Samuel Douthitt, Elder in M. E. Ch.
2980 RAMSEY, JOHN et ux Susannah Griffitts	1/26 1822	By Samuel Douthit, --
2981 RAMSEY, R. A. (Col. of Dogwood, Ga.) et ux Anna B. McGhee (Mrs. Anna B. McLin, widow of ----- McGhee, says Knox. Reg. 3/6 in issue 2/26 1845)	2/6 1845	By A. Vance, M.G.
2982 RAMSEY, WILLIAM et ux Elizabeth Cunning- ham	3/24 1824 issued	No returns
2983 RAMSOWER, JOHN et ux Hannah Danton	12/29 1821	By Wm. Williamson, J.P.
2984 RAMBO, ANDREW L. et ux Susan Wright	10/8 1838	By W. Toole, J.P.
2985 RAMBO, ROBERT et ux Lydia Emmett	11/13 1856	By Daniel H. Emmett, J.P.
2986 RANKIN, JOHN et ux Margaret Weir	2/23 1801 issued	Bond: Alex'r Wilson
2987 RANKIN, JOHN M. et ux Polly Ann Weir	8/15 1818	By I. Anderson, M.G.
2988 RANKIN, JAMES et ux Sarah Gault	11/4 1819	By Andrew S. Morrison, V.D.M.

Names	Date Issue Or Celebrated	By Whom/ Security on Bonds
2989 RANKIN, SAMUEL M. et ux Mary A. Duncan	1/15 1824	By Isaac Anderson, P.N.P. Ch.
2990 RANKIN, SAMUEL W. et ux Isabella Ewing	1/27 1831	By Isaac Anderson, P.N.P. Ch.
2991 RANKIN, WILLIAM C. et ux Catherine Gault	11/30 1815	"Executed" (No signature)
2992 RANKIN, WILLIAM et ux Eliza Singleton	2/10 1842	By Isaac Anderson, P.N.P. Ch.
2993 RASOR, JAMES et ux Melvina Thompson	2/4 1855	By Wm. H. Anderson, J.P.
2994 RASSER, WILLIAM et ux Rutha Hix	12/30 1815 issued	No returns
2995 RATLEDGE, JOHN et ux Sarah Rudd	10/1 1859	By John McCulley, J.P.
2996 RAULSTON, JAS. et ux Matilda Howard	9/11 1855	By John Gault, J.P.
2997 RAULSTON, P. N. et ux T. C. Gray	8/13 1850	By Saml L. Yearout, J.P.
2998 RAULSTON, W. W. et ux Susan E. Hannah	4/21 1859	By James Hamil, M.G.
2999 REA, JAMES S. et ux Evaline E.	2/18 1834	By Isaac Anderson, P.N.P. Ch.
* See 3039 and 3693		
3000 RAY, JESSEE et ux Margaret Blair	12/7 1802 issued	Bond: William Blair
3001 RHEA, JOSEPH et ux Amy Allen	8/21 1817	By H. H. Bowerman, J.P.
3002 RAY, LEONARD et ux Martha Cochran	1/29 1824	By Wm. Gault, J.P.
3003 OBEDIAH, RAY et ux Susan M. Vaught	8/24 1853	By David Spradlin, J.P.
3004 REGAN, EPHRAIM et ux Hannah Harper	1/2 1821	By Alex B. Gamble, J.P.
3005 REAGAN, HENRY et ux Malinda Delosure	2/29 1816	By Alex B. Gambl , J.P.
3006 RAGAN, JAMES et ux Elizabeth H. Bates	11/26 1818	By John Walker, M. Preacher
3007 REAGAN, JEFFERSON et ux Fanny C. Johnson	10/17 1833	By William McTeer, J.P.
3008 REAGAN, JOEL B. et ux Aley Tuck	7/4 1835	By A. Ish, J.P.
3009 REAGAN, JOSIAH et ux Elizabeth Henry	2/14 1822	By A. B. Gamble, J.P.

Names	Date Issue Or Celebrated	By Whom/ Security on Bonds
3010 RAGAN, MOSES et ux Rachel Bonoin	8/25 1835	By A. Ish, J.P.
3011 RAGAN, NATHAN et ux Nancy S. Heartsell	9/5 1839	By B. H. Mayo, M.L.C. P.C.
3012 REAGAN, RICHARD et ux Barcella Stallions	7/27 1826	By Thos E. T. McMurray, J.P.
3013 RAGAN, RICHARD et ux Martha Black	6/2 1842	By A. Vance, M.G. at Bakers Creek Church
3014 REAGEN, SAMUEL et ux Esther Hargis	2/13 1817	By J. Harris, J.P. (or Samuel Harris in a monagram)
3015 REAGAN, SAMUEL et ux Elizabeth Delzell	9/3 1846	By Fielding Pope, M.G.
3016 REAGAN, WILLIAM H. et ux Margaret Carnard	12/6 1821	By A. B. Gamble, J.P.
3017 RAGANS, WILLIAM C. et ux Loisa Tuck (outside is Louisa)	7/23 1835	By A. Ish, J.P.
3018 REACE, JOHN et ux Precilla Kendrick (May be Pearce)	8/24 1803 issued	No returns
* See 2879		
3019 RECEMPECKER, WILLIAM et ux Caterine Abbott	4/1 1823	By James Gillespy, J.P.
3020 RECTER, WM. H. et ux Augusta M.	9/18 1848	By S. Patton, M.M.E.C. (Minister of M.E.Ch.)
3021 REDMON, WILLIAM et ux Rebecca Pate	5/4 1819	By John Gillespie, J.P.
3022 REED, ADISON et ux Nancy D. Henson	3/3 1853	By Wm. W. Neal, M.G. M.E.C. south
3023 REID, DAVID D. et ux Eleanor Debusk	4/14 1840	By Isaac Anderson, P.N.P. Ch. Bond: Montgomery McTeer
3024 REEID, HOBERT et ux Sarah A. Barnhill	12/14 1859	By James Matthews, J.P.
3025 REID, JAMES et ux Polly B. Thompson	8/12 1823 issued	(No returns unless the name on back is, as "R. B. McCulley, J.P.")
3026 REED, JAMES et ux Harriet Elizabeth Cashon	5/13 1834	By John Ferguson, J.P.
3027 REED, JAMES et ux Lucinda Austin	11/14 1836	By James Henry, J.P.
3028 REED, JOSEPH et ux Jane Reed	2/8 1831	By Sam Henry, J.P.

Names	Date Issue Or Celebrated	By Whom/ Security on Bonds
3029 REESE, DR. JOSEPH B. M. et ux Sophia T. Emmerson	11/1 1820	By Isaac Anderson, P.N.P. Ch.
3030 REED, JOSEPH et ux Lovenia Ingrum	3/12 1851	By J. G. Swisher, M.G.
3031 REED, MITCHEL et ux Mary Harden	6/3 1834	By Edward Mitchell, J.P.
3032 REEDER, L. R. et ux Eliza Green	1/14 1847	By Alexander F. Cox, M.G.
3035 REMERTON, JOSEPH et ux Polly Johnston	7/15 1814	By J. (or S.) Harris, --
3034 RENFRROW, JEFFERSON T. et ux Lucend R. Harris	12/27 1842	By Robert Porter, J.P.
3035 HENSHAW, GEORGE A. M. et ux Emily M. McCrosky	10/21 1841	By John S. Craig, M.G.
REYNOLDS, GILMER H. et ux Sarah Scrivner	12/31 1863	By J. W. Mann, M.G.
3036 REYNOLDS, HENRY et ux Polly Gault	8/12 1823	By Isaac Anderson, P.N.P. Ch.
3037 RENNELE, SHADRICK et ux Cynthia Garner	9/21 1824	By Joseph Duncan, J.P.
3038 REYNOLDS, THOS. L. et ux Nancy Henderson	9/23 1818	By John Black, J.P.
3039 RHEA, DAVID et ux Polly Akrige	1/23 1827	By Wm. Turke, J.P.
* See 2999, 3000, 3693		
3040 RAY, GEORGE et ux Elizabeth Hufman	3/20 1819 issued	No returns
3041 RHEA, JAMES et ux Elizabeth Wright	7/27 1851	By W. M. Brickell, J.P.
* See 3693		
3042 RHEA, JOHN et ux Rebecca Miller	3/3 1800 issued	Bond: James Ray (both on bond sign "Ray")
3043 RHEA, JOHN et ux Jane Cameron	1/5 1831	By James Taylor, M.G.
3044 RHEA, JOHN et ux Sarah A. Fingaer	2/7 1855	By Wm. G. Brooks, J.P.
3045 RHEA, JOHN P. et ux Mary M. Eakin	3/6 1856	By D. Loindsay, M.G.
3046 RHEA, LUNA et ux Peggy Brooks	5/18 1816	By H. H. Bowerman, Esq.
3047 RHEA, MARTIN et ux Polly Tipton	4/15 1819	By Hugh Bogle, J.P.
3048 RHEA, MASSINBERG et ux Martha McTeer	2/6 1849	By James M. Tulloch, J.P.

Names	Date Issue Or Celebrated	By Whom/ Security on Bonds
3049 RHEA, SILAS A. et ux Martha T. Kenney	10/22 1857	By J. S. Craig, M.G.
3050 RHEA, WILLIAM et ux Hariet Farmer	4/21 1829	By Charles H. Warren, J.P.
3051 RAY, JESY et ux Margaret Blair	2/23 1801 issued	Bond: Wm. Blair
3052 RHODEN, M. D. et ux Mary Jenkins	2/2 1854	By J. H. Donaldson, J.P.
3053 RHYNE, JAMES et ux Rebecca Belt	5/26 1858	By David Spradlin, J.P.
3054 RHYNE, LABAN J. et ux Evaline Johnson	8/7 1851	By Robert Sloan, J.P.
3055 RHYNE, THOMAS et ux Agness Wethers	6/1 1820 issued 5/20	By Samuel Hamill, J.P.
3056 RICE, ALEXANDER et ux Elizabeth B. Cusack	9/21 1824	By Isaac Anderson, P.N.P. Ch.
3057 RICE, CHARLES et ux Jane Rhea	1/16 1823	By Chas. H. Warren, J.P.
3058 RICE, JAMES et ux Sally Hedrick	10/12 1828 issued 10/11 1827	By James Cameron, J.P.
3059 RICE, LEWIS (RICE) et ux Eliza Scott	9/20 1825	By Isaac Anderson, P.N.P. Ch.
3060 RICE, THOMAS et ux Eliza Daneson	2/10 1831	By Robert B. Billue, M.G. of Baptist Denomination
3061 RICHARDS, CHARLES et ux Patsy Boren	6/29 1830	By David McKamy, J.P.
3062 RICHARDS, JOHN M. et ux Hester M. Staley	4/29 1855	By Jas' Matthews, J.P.
3063 RICHARDS, NATHAN et ux Nelly Gladden	8/23 1823 issued	(No report, but on back, in his peculiar monogram, is "R. B. McCulley"; he was J.P.)
3064 RICHARDS, NATHAN et ux Elizabeth Ann Philips	11/28 1852	By Jesse Kerr, Jr., J.P.
3065 RICHARDS, SAML LASLEY et ux Maleney Crisp	2/15 1848	By Samuel Jackson,
3066 RICHARDS, WM. D. et ux Sarah J. Jones	2/11 1858	By Harvey Thompson, J.P.
3067 RICHARDSON, GEORGE et ux Ellen McCartney	3/3 1818 issued	No returns

*   See 3130

Names	Date Issue Or Celebrated	By Whom/ Security on Bonds
3068 RICHARDSON, JOHN et ux Jane Davidson	4/4 1826 issued 4/28 (3/28)	By James Cameron, J.P.
3069 RITCHEY, DAVID et ux Margaret A. Furguson	8/1 1844	By A. Vance, M.G.
3070 RITCHEY, JAMES H. et ux Matilda Adams	1/25 1844	By A. Vance, M.G.
3071 RICHEY, JOHN C. et ux Elizabeth N. Duncan	11/12 1835	By A. Vance, M.G.
3072 IRCHEY, THOMAS et ux Jenney Greenaway	2/25 1800 issued	Bond: John Trimble
3073 RICHMAN, CHARLES et ux Rodah Franks	10/25 1819	By S. Douthit, --
3074 RICKETTS, ISAAC D. et ux Amanda A. McGhee	4/7 1840	By Isaac Anderson, P.N.P. Ch. Bond: John S. Craig
3075 RICKET, JOHN et ux Susannah Hannah	9/11 1834	By David McKamy, J.P.
3076 RIDDLE, THOMAS et ux Margaret Hamelton	2/18 1858	By J. C. Wright, J.P.
3077 RIDER, JOHN JR. et ux Dorcas Thompson	3/8 1821	By Jos' Duncan, J.P.
3078 RIDER, WM. et ux Malissa McLain	8/31 1854	By Spencer Henry, M.G.
3079 RIDGE, ABRAHAM et ux Elizabeth Johnston	3/13 1834	By Wm. Williamson, J.P.
3080 RIDG, JACOB et ux Delila Russell	2/24 1833	By Wm. Williamson, J.P.
3081 RIDGE, JOHN et ux Catherine Borden	5/21 1857	By David Spradlin, J.P.
3082 WRIGHT, R. R. et ux Mary A. Birchfield	11/20 1856	By David Spradlin, J.P.
* See 388, 4046		
3083 ROACH, ANDREW et ux Sally Adams	2/18 1827	By Wm. Gault, J.P.
3084 ROACH, ARMSTER N. et ux Sarah C. Best	11/4 1845	By Joseph A. Hutton, J.P.
3085 ROACH, HARRISON et ux Patsy Bryant	4/11 1836	By Samuel Tulloch, J.P.
3086 ROACH, JAMES et ux Catherine Clift	8/1 1819	By Wm. Griffitts, J.P.
3087 ROACH, JOHN et ux Polly Mash	8/31 1814 issued	No returns

Names	Date Issue Or Celebrated	By Whom/ Security on Bonds
3088 ROACH, MATTHEW et ux Susannah Hunt	1/11 1832	By Joseph Vanpelt, M.G.
3089 ROACH, MORGAN et ux E. J. Key	6/28 1856	By J. H. Donaldson, J.P.
3090 ROACH, THOMAS et ux Rebecca May	9/7 1826	By Joseph Vanpelt, M.G.
3091 ROACH, WILLIAM et ux Sally Hancock	12/10 1829	By W. Toole, J.P.
3092 ROADMAN, MARCUS A. et ux Martha J. Henry	2/27 1850	By Thos. K. Harman, M.G.
3093 ROBBINS, JOHN et ux Sarah D. Cook	12/27 1849	By Spencer Henry, M.G.
3094 ROBERTS, JOSIAH et ux Polly Stone	12/25 1823	By John Norwood, J.P.
3095 ROBERTS, JOHN et ux Rachel Robenett	12/9 1796 issued	Bond: Jacob Meek
3096 ROBERTS, JONATHAN et ux J. L. Kidd (outside is J. M. Kidd)	10/12 1853	By C. Cowan, J.P.
3097 ROBERTS, PETER et ux Mary Blevens	3/9 1801 issued	Bond: John Kee
3098 ROBERTS, WILLIAM et ux Sally Crisp	11/20 1823	By Saml Hamil, J.P.
3099 ROBERTSON, ISAAC et ux Polly Shell	5/28 1823	By Samuel Douthit, Elder in M.E. Ch. A.D.
3100 ROBERTSON, ISAAC et ux Jane Dickson	6/26 1845	By J. Dyke, Pastor Unitia Ch.
3101 ROBERTSON, JOHN et ux Sarah Perkins	9/30 1824	By A. Ish, J.P.
3102 ROBISON, JESSEE D. et ux Eleyath Tala (outside is Elizabeth Tolly)	2/21 1832	By B. Abernathy, L.E. (outside is Joseph D. Roberson)
3103 ROBERTSON, JULIUS et ux Peggy Reagan	5/14 1818	By Alex B. Gamble, J.P.
3104 ROBERTSON, THOMAS et ux Nancy Dayl (outside is Nancy David)	12/18 1825 issued	No return
3105 ROBISON, THOMAS J. et ux Margaret Jeffeirs	10/13 1849	By Thos. M. Rooke , J.P.
3106 ROBESON, ISAAC et ux Mary Wayman	4/18 1856	By J. H. Donaldson, J.P.
3107 ROBINSON, J. J. et ux M. A. Wallace (outside is John J. Robinson to Margt A. Wallace)	10/4 1854	By Isaac Anderson, P.N.P. Ch.

Names	Date Issue Or Celebrated	By Whom/ Security on Bonds
3108 ROBINSON, WILLIAM R. et ux Sally Witcher	9/29 1808 issued	No returns
3109 ROBENETT, BENJAMIN et ux Rebeckah Franks	12/24 1817 issued	No returns
3110 ROBINET, BENJAMIN et ux Dahlilah Cox	1/12 1848	By James H. Donaldson, J.P.
3111 ROBENITT, ENOCH et ux Talitha T. (Tellitha T.) Fosha	3/20 1820 issued	"celebrated by S. Douthit, M.G."
3112 ROBENETT, GEORGE et ux Delelah Fosha	2/16 1819	By Samuel Douthit, M.G.
3113 ROBENETT, JOHN D. et ux Lucinda Barnes	1/24 1844	By Wesley Earnest, J.P.
3114 RODDY, ALFRED et ux Elizabeth Cook	2/28 1839	By Robert Porter, J.P.
3115 RODDY, CALVIN et ux Sarah Wheeler	11/3 1845	By B. F. Duncan, J.P.
3116 RODDY, GIDEON et ux Milly Harris	3/31 1825	By E. Hitch, Esq.
3117 RODDY, HENRY et ux Peggy Harris	11/13 1828	By E. Hitch, Esq.
3118 RODDY, HAMELTON (or Holston) et ux Nancy J. Gibbs	3/30 1859	By C. Cowan, J.P.
3119 RODDY, JOSEPH et ux Margaret Duncan	1/25 1850	By S. J. McReynolds, J.P.
3120 RODDY, SAMUEL et ux Lucinda Davis	12/12 1843	By Robert Porter, J.P.
3121 RODDY, WM. et ux Mary A. Hutton	11/16 1854	By Jesse Kerr, Jr., J.P.
3122 ROE, JOHN et ux Mary Tuck	8/24 1840	By J.H.R.G. Gardner, Pastor Shady Grove Ch.
3123 ROE, ROBT. et ux Susan Phelps	1/13 1854	By W. M. Brickell, J.P.
3124 ROORK, SAMUEL et ux Tabitha Phillips	9/6 1815 issued	No returns
3125 RORAX, JOHN et ux Caroline Henry	7/28 1842	By Fielding Pope, M.G.
3126 ROAREX, JOSEPH M. et ux Rossy Ann Harris	12/5 1833	By Isaac Anderson, P.N.P. Ch.
3127 ROORK, THOMAS et ux Sudannah Huffman	12/15 1818	By Samuel Douthit, M.G.
3128 ROREX, WILLIAM M. et ux Margaret Ann Anderson	3/31 1838	By Isaac Anderson, P.N.P. Ch.

Names	Date Issue Or Celebrated	By Whom/ Security on Bonds
3129 EAGLE, WILLIAM R. et ux Elizabeth Taylor	1/29 1843	By Robert Shields, J.P.
* See 2974		
3130 RICHARDSON, HOWARD et ux Sarah Reed	3/31 1798 issued	Bond: James Blair
* See 3067		
3131 ROGERS, ASA et ux Eliza R. McFee	3/17 1844	By John Tipton, J.P.
3132 ROGERS, GEORGE et ux Sarah Devers	7/9 1843	By Lewis Jones, J.P.
3133 ROGERS, GEORGE et ux Phareby Boling	2/19 1854	By William McTeer, J.P.
3134 ROGERS, JAMES et ux Anna Blair	3/12 1800 issued	Bond: Isiah Brown
3135 ROGERS, JAMES W. et ux Peggy White	4/2 1819 issued (celb. soon after date)	By Robert Harden, Pastor West Minester Church
3136 ROGERS, JESSE et ux Celia Kagle	7/29 1820	By Hugh Bogle, J.P.
3137 ROGERS, JOHN N. et ux Sally Shahan	7/10 1821	By Hugh Bogle, J.P.
3138 ROGERS, JOHN H. et ux Hetty Rogers	4/25 1846	By John Tipton, J.P.
3139 RODGERS, JNO. et ux Mary J. McCollouh	3/30 1852	By Fielding Pope, M.G.
3140 RODGERS, JOSEPH N. et ux Mary Ann Rankin	7/10 1845	By James Blair, M.G.C. P.C.
3141 ROGERS, LOT et ux Rebecah Boling	2/24 1838	By Wm. McTeer, J.P.
3142 RODGERS, MARION W. et ux Margaret V. Tipton	3/22 1849	By John Russom, L.D. M.E. Ch. So.
3143 ROGERS, NELSON WRIGHT et ux Veny Emily Davis	10/20 1846	By John Tipton, J.P.
3144 RODGERS, P. W. et ux Elizabeth Boling	11/27 1851	By William McTeer, J.P.
3145 ROGERS, SHEDRECH et ux Sally Balling	7/6 1825	By Hugh Bogle, J.P.
3146 ROGERS, TEDFORD et ux Martha Gardner	4/2 1852	By William McTeer, J.P.
3147 ROGERS, TILFORD WARREN et ux Margaret Rogers	10/12 1846	By John Tipton, J.P.
3148 ROGERS, THOMAS et ux Mary McCarter	7/5 1796 issued	Bond: John Hickley

Names	Date Issue Or Celebrated	By Whom/ Security on Bonds
3149 ROGERS, THOMAS et ux Leoana Garner	3/28 1833	By William McTeer, J.P.
3150 ROGERS, VINCEN et ux Abby Hardin	9/5 1816	By Hugh Bogle, J.P.
3151 ROGERS, WILLIS et ux Sally Ingram	12/30 1829	By William McTeer, J.P.
3152 ROGERS, WILLIAM et ux Eliza Jane Williams	10/27 1846	By Wm. Billue, M.G.
3153 ROGERS, W. H. et ux Nancy Palmer	7/29 1854	By Boyd Anderson, Esq.
3154 RODGERS, WILLOBY et ux Martha Tipton	1/11 1849	By Wm. M. Burnett, M.G.
3155 ROLAND, WILLIAM et ux Hally (or Molly) Johnston	3/24 1859	By Wm. H. Anderson, J.P.
3156 ROLLINS, DAVID et ux Margaret Hatcher	3/8 1846	By John Givens, M.G.
3157 RUKER, JOHN et ux Isabella Gillespie	11/16 1807 issued	"by me" S. George, J.P.
3158 RUCKER, SAML S. et ux Alizabeth Hawk	7/15 1819	By Wm. Griffitts, J.P.
3159 ROOCKER, THOMAS M. et ux Elizabeth Saffel	9/29 1840	By L. S. Marshall, --
3160 ROOP, JOHN et ux Isabel Davis	7/31 1834	By Spencer Henry, J.P.
3161 ROPER, JAMES et ux Peggy McNally	12/23 1819	By Wm. Fagg, M.G. Methodist Church
3162 ROSE, DRURY et ux Susan Juck	3/21 1839	By B. P. Mays, M.G.
3163 ROSE, FRANCIS et ux Nancy Sexton	9/19 1823 issued	No returns
* See 3174		
3164 ROSE, JOHN et ux Sally Halpain	8/25 1831	By John Gould, J.P.
3165 ROSE, JOHN et ux Rebecca Haynes	9/27 1838	By Benj. P. Mays, M.G.
3166 ROSE, ALEXANDER et ux Margaret Best	1/28 1836	By John Maxwell, J.P.
3167 ROSE, DAVID W. et ux Sarah E. Peoples	6/23 1859	By Spencer Henry, M.G.
3168 ROSE, JAMES et ux Sally Cook	1/26 1833	By David McKamy, J.P.
3169 ROSE, J. W. et ux M. E. Saffell	11/28 1854	By Spencer Henry, M.G.

Names	Date Issue Or Celebrated	By Whom/ Security on Bonds
3170 ROSE, LEWIS et ux Fanny Holt	3/15 1817 issued	"Celebrated on 3/15" I. Anderson, --
3171 ROSE, THOMAS et ux Elizabeth McTeer	7/22 1829	By Arch'd Maxwell, J.P.
3172 ROSE, WILLIAM et ux Malenday Ooforth	6/3 1847	By Samuel Tulloch, J.P.
3173 ROSE, WILLIAM et ux Nancy Matthews (Hart widow of Geo. H. M., Rev.)	4/9 1850	By Robert H. Snoddy, M.G.
3174 ROSE, JAMES et ux Meomi Davis	6/8 1834	By John Russom, M.G.
* See 3163		
3175 ROSSIN, WILLIAM et ux Sarah Thomas	3/15 1838	By Geo. Snider, J.P.
3176 ROUSE, JOHN et ux Lydia Remington	7/20 1815	By J. Harris, J.P.
3177 ROUTH, HEZEKIAH et ux Elizabeth Posey	10/3 1818	By John Tedford, J.P.
3178 ROWAN, GEORGE W. et ux Susan Campbell	9/28 1857 issued	(dimly read that may been married, looks like A. Acton, signed)
3179 ROWAN, JAMES H. et ux Margaret Berry	9/19 1832 issued	"by me this day" Darius Hoyt, M.G. (no date)
3180 ROANE, SAMUEL et ux Jean Cowan	8/7 1798 issued	Bond: Samue Gould
3181 ROWAN, SAMUEL E. et ux Katherine Hanley	3/12 1839	By William H. Hodges, M.G.
3182 RUDD, ANDERSON et ux Margaret A. Clark	11/19 1843	By John Morton, J.P.
3183 RUDD, BURLINGTON et ux Mary Ogle	10/4 1849	By John Morton, J.P. Bond: George Rudd
3183 RUDD, GEORGE W. et ux Ellen Teafeteller	9/14 1845	By John Morton, J.P.
3184 RUDD, GEORGE W. et ux Sarah Stallions	1/4 1844 issued	(on back is "Neit solemnized and returned Jan. 1, 1844," then marked through)
3185 RUDD, GEORGE W. et ux Reubecca J. Maxwell	5/19 1842	By Green B. Saffell, J.P.
3186 RUDD, JAMES IRVIN et ux Elizabeth Keeling	8/31 1837	By Joseph Wilson, J.P.
3187 RUDD, SINKLER (or St. Clair) et ux Loucinday Watts	9/22 1859	By John McCully, J.P.

Names	Date Issue Or Celebrated	By Whom/ Security on Bonds
3188 RUDD, STEPHEN et ux Elizabeth Stallions	4/12 1849	By Harvey H. C. Caruthers, J.P.
3189 RUDD, VAUN et ux Martha E. Ragan	11/28 1851	By John Morton, J.P.
3190 RULE, JACOB et ux Caty Hood	10/11 1827	By E. Hitch, Esq.
3191 RULE, PETER et ux Mary McTeer	8/8 1833	By Robt McCamy, J.P.
3192 RULE, SAML et ux Nancy J. Sharp	12/14 1854	By W. M. Burnett, M.G.
3193 RUNIONS, JOSEPH et ux Elizabeth Laurence	10/27 1842	By Joseph A. Hutton, J.P.
3194 RUNNIONS, JOSEPH SR. et ux Jane Parks	2/7 1843	By Joseph A. Hutton, J.P.
3195 RUSH, JOHN et ux Mary Beaty	9/19 1817 issued	"Executed by me" Joseph Walker, J.P.
3196 RUSH, JAMES et ux Mary Caler	12/27 1819 issued	No returns
3197 RUSSELL, GEORGE W. et ux Jane Pasley	12/28 1843	By Thomas J. Russell, M.G.
3198 RUSSELL, HANCE et ux Elizabeth McClannahan	9/21 1795 issued	Bond: James Greenaway
3199 RUSSELL, HENRY et ux Margaret White	6/11 1839	By W. M. Rorex, J.P.
3200 RUSSELL, ISAAC et ux Penelope White	9/30 1839	By W. M. Rorex, J.P.
3201 RUSSELL, ISAAC JR. et ux Jane Gipson	12/20 1853	By C. Long, J.P.
3202 RUSSELL, ISAAC et ux Permelia McDaniel	12/19 1850	By Christian Long, J.P.
3203 RUSSELL, ISAAC et ux Mary A. Russell	7/29 1858	By C. Long, J.P.
3204 RUSSELL, JACOB et ux Patient Long	1/28 1858	By Wm. W. Nuchols, J.P.
3205 RUSSELL, JAMES et ux Mary Hitchcock	8/3 1802 issued	Bond: John Russell
3206 RUSSELL, JAMES et ux Sally McCallie	8/14 1832	By Wm. Billue, M.G.
3207 RUSSELL, JAMES et ux Margaret Martin	4/13 1851	By C. Long, J.P.
3208 RUSSELL, JOHN et ux Jenny McNutt	3/2 1801 issued	Bond: Edward Sharp

Names	Date Issue Or Celebrated	By Whom/ Security on Bonds
3209 RUSSELL, JOHN et ux Rosana Gillespie	6/14 1821 6/14	By Isaac Anderson, P.N.P. Ch.
3210 RUSSEL, JOHN et ux Rebecca Snider	1/27 1832	By Wm. Billue, M.G.
3211 RUSSELL, J. G. et ux Sarah Montgomery	5/3 1853	By D. W. Amos, M.G.
3212 RUSSELL, JONES M. et ux Nancy Clinton	12/31 1818	By Wm. Williamson, J.P.
3213 RUSSELL, JOHN H. et ux Mary S. Thompson	12/19 1848	By A. J. McGee, M.G. of C. P. Church
3214 RUSSELL, JOSEPH et ux Sophina Britt	4/24 1853	By C. Long, J.P.
3215 RUSSELL, LEWIS et ux Mary J. Martin	8/22 1854	By Isaac Anderson, P.N.P. Ch.
3216 RUSSELL, ROBERT P. et ux Nancy Logan	1/24 1850	By A. J. McGee, M.G. of C. P. Ch.
3217 RUSSELL, THOMAS et ux Sydney Ogle	11/4 1837	By W. M. Rorex, J.P.
3218 RUSSELL, THOMAS et ux Sarah E. J. Law	3/9 1846	By Wm. Dever, J.P.
3219 RUSSELL, THOMAS et ux Sophina Cross	1/3 1856	By John Waller, M.G.
3220 RUSSELL, WILLIAM et ux Mary Kirby	2/25 1824 issued	No returns
3221 RUTH, JOSEPH et ux Jane Lea	9/7 1841	By Samuel Tulloch, J.P.
3222 RYEN, FULLER et ux Nancy Brakebill	9/25 1816 issued	No returns
3223 RYLAND, BEDFORD et ux Francis Tucker	11/22 1832	By Isaac Anderson P.N.P. Ch.
3224 SAFFELL, ANDREW J. et ux Elizabeth Lain	12/12 1850	By AnD Ferguson, J.P.
* See 4082		
3225 SAFFELL, GREENBERRY et ux Jane Soroggs	2/22 1827	By Thomas Beveridge, --
3226 SAFFELL, JAMES T. et ux Mary L. Casteel	10/24 1848	By T. M. Rooker J.P.
5227 SAFFELL, JAMES T. et ux Elizabeth A. Johnson	6/29 1858	By James M. Tulloch, J.P.
3228 SAFFELL, SAMUEL H. et ux Malissa A. Cook	2/17 1859	By A. J. Wilson, J.P.
3229 SAFFELL, WILLIAM et ux Mary Hess	4/20 1843	By Wm. Cumming, J.P.

Names	Date Issue Or Celebrated	By Whom/ Security on Bonds
3230 SAMPLES, JOHN et ux Elizabeth Kithcart	10/28 1818 issued	No returns
3231 SAMPLES, MATTHEW et ux Polly Sexton	2/29 1814	By And'w Jackson, J.P.
3232 SAMPLES, MATTHEW et ux Nancy Carson	8/17 1827	By Saml Hamill, J.P.
3233 SAMPLES, WILLIAM JR. et ux Katherine Kerr	2/25 1836	By Thomas S. Kendall, --
* See 3409		
3234 SARTAIN, JAMES et ux Sarah J. Logan	12/19 1849	By A. J. McGee, M.G.
3235 SAWTELL, EPHRAIM et ux Mary Yearout	7/17 1827	By Isaac Anderson, P.N.P. Ch.
3236 SAY, JOHN B. et ux Margaret Hart	10/22 1839	By Fielding Pope, M.G.
3237 SCATES, JOSEPH C. et ux Sarah M. Leeper	12/7 1848	By John Dyke, Pastor Unitia Church
3238 SCATES, ZEBSEDEE et ux Mary Elizabeth Nipper	10/13 1846	By William Colburn, J.P.
3239 SCESSLER, JACOB et ux Virginia Curtis	3/19 1847	By W. Toole, J.P.
* See 3267		
3240 SCOGGINS, JESSE et ux Sarah Owens	9/21 1837	By R. P. Reneau, M.G.
3241 SCOTT, ALEXANDER et ux Lucinda Maxwell	3/18 1838	By James Henry, J.P.
3242 SCOTT, ALFRED et ux Peggy Wines	12/9 1818 issued	No returns
3243 SCOTT, DANIEL et ux Jenny McBryant	9/30 1824	By Saml Davidson, J.P.
3244 SCOTT, JAMES et ux Nancy Hunter	10/1 1818	By Isaac Anderson, --
3245 SCOTT, JAMES et ux Elizabeth Lambert	2/21 1833	By F. Emmett, J.P.
3246 SCOTT, JAMES et ux Parthena Cameron	2/20 1842	By James Matson, J.P.
3247 SCOTT, J. M. et ux L. J. Roddy	10/6 1853	By R. E. Tedford, M.G.
3248 SCOTT, JOHN et ux Marybe Baul (outside is Marybe Ball)	3/6 1810	No returns
3249 SCOTT, JOSEPH et ux Patsy Davis	12/6 1827	By William Eagleton, M.G.

Names	Date Issue Or Celebrated	By Whom/ Security on Bonds
3250 SCOTT, JOSEPH et ux Elizabeth Myers	2/5 1857	By Daniel H. Emmett, J.P.
3251 SCOTT, M. E. et ux Roena Pippins (outside looks like "Pepper") (Groom is Mathew C. Scott)	5/13 1853	By Saml L. Yearout, J.P.
3252 SCOTT, M.D.L. et ux E. J. Barnhill	1/11 1853	By Thos. M. Rocker, J.P.
3253 SCOTT, ROBERT H. et ux Mary Hitch	10/2 1843	By Isaac Anderson, P.N.P. Ch.
3254 SCOTT, RUFUS N. et ux Jane Barnes	10/31 1846	By James Henry, J.P.
3255 SCOTT, T. E. et ux R. R. Crye	7/27 1854	By James M. Tulloch, J.P.
3256 SCOTT, WILLIAM et ux Deidamea Davis	5/18 1824	By Isaac Anderson, P.N.P. Ch.
3257 SCOTT, WILLIAM et ux Sophia Curtis	3/10 1840	By W. Toole, J.P.
3258 SCHRIMSHEER, WILLIAM et ux Rebecka Vann	_____ 1818 issued	No returns (no date in face, above outside)
3259 SCROGGS, DAVID et ux Margaret Delzell	10/6 1819 issued	No returns
3260 SCROGGS, J. C. et ux M. C. Carpenter	10/27 1853	By R. E. Tedford, M.G.
3261 SCRUGGS, MOSES et ux Elizabeth Dunkan	4/23 1830	By Berry Abernathy, L.D.
3262 SEATON, ALFRED et ux Margaret Ann Norton	2/13 1845	By Will Cumming, J.P.
3263 SEATON, ALFRED et ux Mary J. Morton	10/15 1857	By Fielding Pope, M.G.
3264 SECREST, EVAN et ux Mabra Braden	3/20 1823	By Jos' Duncan, J.P.
3265 SEAMANS, JORDAN B. B. et ux Phebe Jane Davis	8/26 1847	By Samuel Tulloch, J.P.
3266 SENTER, WILLIAM et ux Elizabeth Cochran	2/13 1845	By John Morton, J.P.
3267 SERTAIN, JAMES et ux Mary M. Logan	7/23 1851	By B. Abernaty, M.G.
3268 SESLER, THOMAS et ux Sarah M. Pass	3/8 1854	By C. Cowan, J.P.

* See 3239

Names	Date Issue Or Celebrated	By Whom/ Security on Bonds
3289 SEWELL, WILLIAM D. et ux Susannah Brawn	2/21 1822	By Hugh Bogle, J.P.
3270 SEXTON, JAMES R. et ux Polly Paul	6/4 1833	By John Ferguson, J.P.
3271 SHEDDEN, CHARLES K. et ux Ann Wilson	2/26 1822	By Jos' Alexander, J.P.
3272 SHADDEN, JAMES et ux Sarah H. Russell	1/21 1823	By Isaac Anderson, P.N.P. Ch.
3273 SHEDDAN, JAMES C. et ux Lutitia H. Henderson	12/8 1848	By F. Pope, M.G.
3274 SHADDIN, JOHN H. et ux Nancy McMurray	11/21 1820	By Hugh Bogle, J.P.
3275 SHEDDAN, JOSEPH C. et ux Mary C. Malcom	10/21 1856	By Jesse Kerr, Jr., J.P.
3276 SHEDDAN, THOMAS W. et ux Jane McClung	3/28 1850	By A. Vance, M.G.
3277 CHADWICK, BARNET et ux Betsey Nants	8/30 1821	By Wm. Williamson, J.P. Bond: Jacob Chadwick
3278 CHADWICK, MATTHEW et ux Charity King	3/25 1819 issued	No returns
* See 588		
3279 SHAHAN, DANIEL et ux Patsey Hussong	8/10 1820	By Samuel Douthit, --
3280 SHAMBLIN, GEORGE et ux Sarah Hicks	12/29 1819	By George Snider, M.G. of Baptist Order
3281 SHARP, ADDISON et ux Rebecca Hitch	12/26 1821 issued on 12/27 1821	By Billy Holloway, M.G. of Baptist Church
3282 SHARP, ALEXANDER H. et ux Susannah Maxwell	9/10 1816 issued	"Executed--John Waugh, J.P."
3283 SHARP, ARCH'D et ux Parthena Tally	10/10 1846	By B. F. Duncan, J.P.
3284 SHARP, ARCH'D et ux M. A.Hays	12/26 1855	By B. F.Duncan, J.P.
3285 SHARP, EDWARD et ux Malinda Malcum	2/2 1831	By William McTeer, J.P.
3286 SHARP, AJMES C. et ux S. A. Vineyard	11/28 1850	By Wm. M. Burnett, --
3287 SHARP, JOHN et ux Polly Tulloch	5/21 1810 issued	No returns
3288 SHARP, THOMAS et ux Mary A. Vinyard	11/28 1844	By Wm. M. Burnett, --
3289 SHAVER, BARCLY C. et ux Marga N. Harris	4/18 1858	By Elder J. Hamil, M.G.

Names	Date Issue Or Celebrated	By Whom/ Security on Bonds
3290 SHAVER, HOUSTON et ux Harret Hafly	12/30 1856	By James Porter, J.P.
3291 SHAVER, JOHN D. W. et ux Mary Brawner	5/5 1828	By William Toole, J.P.
3292 SHAVER, KERNELEUS et ux Jane Moore	10/16 1832	By Darius Hoyt, M.G.
3293 SHAVER, WM. J. et ux Loucinday Whetsell	1/4 1855	By W. W. Nuchold, J.P.
3294 SHAW, FRANCIS et ux Elizabeth Mosher	2/6 1823	By Samuel Douthit, E.M.E.C.A.D.
3295 SHELTON, AZARIAH et ux Matilda Wright	7/30 1823	By Isaac Anderson, P.N.P. Ch.
3296 SHELTON, JOSEPH et ux Anne Phillips	7/30 1818	By Wm. Williamson, J.P.
3297 SHETTERLY, JOHN et ux Caty Miser	4/10 1823	By R. B. McCully, J.P.
3298 SHEPARD, ROBERT, REV. et ux Elizabeth James (of Robert)	9/15 1853	By Thos' W. Humes, Rector St. Johns Ch., Knoxville. Celb' at Chillhowee in Blount County, Tenn.
* See 2908		
3299 SHERRELL, JOSEPH A. et ux Margaret Breakbill	2/27 1845	By Ben Cunningham, J.P.
3300 SHERRELL, MICHEL et ux Franky Davis	12/5 1847	By Wm. Dever, J.P.
3301 SHERRELL, UTE et ux Jane L. (or S.) Reagan	4/4 1844	By Lewis Jones, J.P.
3302 SHERIL, WILKEY et ux Betty Ann Burch- field	2/23 1841	By Wm. Henry, J.P.
* See 3410		
3303 SHIELDS, BANNER (or Bonner) et ux Peggy Weir	2/5 1800 issued	Bond: Jonathan Trippet
3304 SHIELDS, FREDERICK et ux Mary Oliver	10/25 1838	By William Davis, M.G.
3305 SHIELDS, HENRY et ux Martha Oliver	11/14 1841	By William Henry, J.P.
3306 SHIELDS, JAMES M. et ux Celia Jones	6/1 1837 issued	No returns
3307 SHIELDS, JOSHUA et ux Sarah Johnston	2/6 1834	By Fredrick Emmett, J.P.
3308 SHIELDS, O.C.P. et ux Peggy Greer	7/29 1841	By Lewis Jones, J.P.

Names	Date Issue Or Celebrated	By Whom/ Security on Bonds
3309 SHIELDS, ROBERT et ux Peggy Cayler	9/23 1827	By Saml C. Davidson, J.P.
3310 SHIELDS, ROBT. et ux Margt. Jane Ball	2/15 1852	By S. J. McReynolds,
3311 SHARKLIN, JOHN et ux Lidda Hart	6/14 1796 issued	Bond: Joseph Hart
3312 SHIPLEY, M. M. et ux Ruth A. Jones	3/1 1855	By James Matthews, J.P.
* See SHOOK		
3313 SIMPSON, JAMES et ux Hannah Webster	7/1 1833	By A. Patton, M.G.
* See 3324		
3314 SIMPSON, JOHN H. et ux Nancy Myzell	5/15 1860	By Stephen Matthews, J.P.
3314 SINGLETON, ANDREW et ux Sarah Cox	3/13 1828	By Jesse F. Bunker, M.G.
3315 SINGLETON, JAMES et ux Rebecka Kerbey	2/15 1808 issued	No returns
3316 SINGLETON, JAMES et ux Caroline McBath	1/6 1848	By Robert Porter, J.P.
3317 SINGLETON, JOHN et ux Mary Jones	9/5 1842	By Wesley Earnest, J.P.
3318 SINGLETON, JOHN et ux Elizabeth M. McNutt	6/28 1849	By T. K. Munsey, M.G.
3319 SINGLETON, JOHN et ux Marth Hitch	5/5 1857	By W. A. Lawson, M.G.
3320 SINGLETON, ROBERT et ux Catherine Duncan	4/27 1843	By Leander Wilson, M.G.
3321 SINGLETON, WILLIAM et ux Lucinda Jane Wear	4/17 1838	By D. B. Carter, O.M. M.E. Ch.
3322 SHOOK, JACOB et ux Peggy Harper	3/20 1827	By A. B. Gamble, J.P.
3323 SHOOK, WILLIAM et ux Patsy Pride	7/23 1817	"Executed by John J.P."
3324 SIMPSON, WM. et ux Sarah Beaty	9/21 1802 issued	Bond: John Beaty
* See 3313		
3325 SIMERLY, ABRAHAM et ux Lucinda Long	11/4 1852	By C. Long, J.P.
3326 SIMERLY, HENRY et ux Marg't Teefeteler	12/13 1849	By Christian Long, J.P.
3327 SIMERLY, JACOB et ux Jane Hall	1/31 1853	By J. D. Sewell, --

Names	Date Issue Or Celebrated	By Whom/ Security on Bonds
3328 SIMERLY, JAMES et ux Palina Cupp	5/25 1859	By Wm. H. Anderson, J.P.
3329 SIMERLY, JEREMIAH et ux Ann Averett (See EVERETT)	11/30 1843	By Christian Long, J.P.
3330 SIMERLY, JOHN et ux Lydia McDaniel	5/5 1839	By W. M. Rorex, J.P.
3331 SIMERLY, JOHN et ux Sarah Davis	12/16 1845	By John P. Keney, J.P.
3332 SIMS, JAMES et ux Dortha L. Michel	4/18 1857	By B. F. Duncan, J.P.
3333 SIMMS, JOHN et ux Sally McMurry	7/25 1816	By Hugh Bogle, J.P.
3334 SIMMS, JOSEPH V. et ux Sarah Hooper	8/22 1827	By William McTeer, J.P.
3335 SIMMS, WILLIAM et ux Elizabeth Hubbard	1/12 1864	By Solomon Farmer, J.P.
3335 SIMONS, ARCHEBALD et ux Kitery Moore	3/21 1826	By Saml Hamill, J.P.
3336 SIMONS, JOHN et ux Rutha Carson	5/10 1816	By David McKamy, J.P.
3337 SKINNER, W. H. et ux Martha N. Long	2/28 1859	By W. W. Nuchols, J.P.
3338 SLALTACE, JAMES et ux Sally Whitenberger)	8/28 1804 issued	No returns (May be Wallace of Haltace or Slatace)
3339 SLAUGHTER, GEORGE et ux Martha Chambers	11/27 1859	By Daniel H. Emmert, J.P.
3340 SLEMONS, JOHN et ux Elizabeth Jones	3/10 1825	By Joseph Duncan, J.P.
3341 SLOANE, A. et ux Susan Snider	12/19 1820 issued	No returns (outside Archebald Sloane)
3342 SLONA, MADISON et ux Catherine S. Ross	11/22 1855	By Jesse Kerr, Jr., J.P.
3343 SLOAN, ROBERT et ux Margaret Cook	12/29 1801 issued	Bond: David Book
3344 SLOAN, ROBERT et ux Elizabeth Ross	10/28 1830	By David McKamy, J.P.
3345 SMALLEN, ELKANY et ux Jane Morton	4/28 1840	By John Maxwell, J.P. Bond: David Gardner
3346 SMALLEN, SOLOMON et ux Margaret A. Gardener	11/4 1847	By John S. Craig, M.G.
3347 SMATHERS, DAN'L et ux Nancy Rogers	3/29 1849	By Jesse Kerr, Jr., J.P.

Names	Date Issue Or Celebrated	By Whom/ Security on Bonds
3348 SMELCER, PASCAL et ux Sarah Willis	9/7 1846	By B. F. Duncan, J.P.
3349 SMITH, ALFRED et ux Rebecca Anderson	4/11 1847	By James Henry, J.P.
3350 SMITH, ALEXANDER et ux Sarah Johnson	3/8 1838 issued	Celebrated by me Wm. Billue, M.G.
3351 SMITH, ALLEN et ux Eliza Jane Ragan	5/13 1847	By S. J. McReynolds, J.P.
3352 SMITH, ANDREW J. et ux Mahala Vineyard	4/4 1839	By Fielding Pope, M.G.
3353 SMITH, A. J. et ux Mary Blankinship	7/14 1858	By A. R.James, J.P.
3354 SMITH, BENJAMIN et ux Polly McAlroy	2/1 1817 issued	"Celebrated by me" Charles H. Warren, J.P.
3355 SMITH, BENJAMIN et ux Sarah Campbell	11/16 1837	By John Keys, J.P.
3356 SMITH, BYRD et ux Susan Hume	6/12 1842 issued on 6/23 1842	Executed Jas. Cumming, Elder M.E.C.
3357 SMITH, CALVEN M. et ux Margaret Gibbs	12/26 1842	By Daniel Taylor, J.P.
3358 SMITH, DANIEL et ux Ann Wheeler	8/28 1827	By Wm. Turk, J.P.
3359 SMITH, DANIEL et ux Sarah Harper	5/18 1848	By S. J. McReynolds, J.P.
3360 SMITH, EZEKEL C. et ux Canen (or Caven, Carren) outside is Carew	2/17 1848	By John Key, J.P.
3361 SMITH, GEORGE et ux Peggy Balling (Bolling)	4/3 1825	By Hugh Bogle, J.P.
3362 SMITH, GEORGE et ux Elizabeth Wolf	12/17 1849	By S. J. McReynols, J.P.
3363 SMITH, GEORGE et ux Elizabeth A. Phillips	8/24 1852	By David Spradlin, J.P.
3364 SMITH, GEORGE W. et ux Mahala R. Bledsoe	10/17 1828	By J. Gillespie, J.P.
3365 SMITH, HENRY L. et ux Nancy J. Folkner	11/14 1854	By Geo. Wallace, J.P.
3366 SMITH, HENRY S. et ux Martha J. Pelphrey	10/19 1856	By Wm. M. Brickell, J.P.
3367 SMITH, ISAAC et ux Elizabeth White	10/6 1825	By Wm. Billue, D.D.

Names	Date Issue Or Celebrated	By Whom/ Security on Bonds
3368 SMITH, JACOB et ux Nancy Houk	8/20 1817 issued	"Executed J. Waugh"
3369 SMITH, JACOB et ux Martha Ann Morgan	7/5 1843	By B. F. Duncan, J.P.
3370 SMITH, JACOB et ux Angeline Rowel- lett	9/17 1857	By S. L. Yearout, J.P.
3371 SMITH, JAMES et ux Mary Tedford	3/ 1812 issued	No returns
3372 SMITH, JAMES et ux Jemima Newberry	8/2 1840 issued 8/1 1839	By Eli Richey, J.P.
3373 SMITH, JAMES et ux Nancy Brewer	12/18 1853	By Daniel H. Emmert, J.P.
3374 SMITH, JOHN et ux Sarah Caceper	5/2 1801 issued	Bond: George Townsley
3375 SMITH, JOHN et ux Rebecah McCay Outside Rebe MCaye (looks also as if Meay or Mlay)	4/28 1809 issued	No returns
3376 SMITH, JOHN et ux Issbell Vincent	7/18 1813 issued	No returns
3377 SMITH, JOHN et ux Jane Campbell	3/14 1820 issued	No returns
3378 SMITH, JOHN et ux Rachael Williams	7/6 1834	By James Taylor, M.G.
3379 SMITH, JOHN C. et ux Mary J. Wear	8/29 1848	By Isaac Anderson, P.N.P. Ch.
3380 SMITH, JOHN D. et ux Louisa Jane Bilderback	11/24 1842	By A. A. Mathes, M.G.
3381 SMITH, JOSEPH et ux Martha Tallent	8/30 1840	By William Colburn, J.P.
3382 SMITH, JOSHUA et ux Peggy Keller	6/1 1820	By Jos' Alexander, J.P.
3383 SMITH, PETER et ux Elizabeth Elliott	4/12 1842	By John Morton, J.P.
3384 SMITH, THOMAS et ux Jane M. Paul	7/8 1817	By Wm. Hart, --
3385 SMITH, THOMAS S. et ux Nancy Farmer	1/2 1817	By Alex B. Gamble, J.P.
3386 SMITH, THOMAS H. S. et ux Margaret Gillespie	8/8 1828	By J. Gillespie, J.P.
3387 SMITH, WILLIAM et ux Rebecah Loftis	10/12 1821	By Wm. Williamson, J.P.

Names	Date Issue Or Celebrated	By Whom/ Security on Bonds
3388 SMITH, WILLIAM et ux Christina Fann	9/14 1823	By Saml Davidson, J.P.
3389 SMITH, WILLIAM et ux Salena Law	9/24 1835	By Fredrick Emmett, J.P.
3390 SMITH, WILLIAM et ux Sarah O. ----- (inside is blurred, written over, Farmer-- out is Cameron, was Came ron first)	3/30 1848	By John Chambers, M.G.
3391 SMITH, WM. H. et ux Adaline McBath	1/27 1853	By Isaac Anderson, P.N.P. Ch.
3392 SMITH, WILLIAM M. et ux Ann Greer	6/18 1835	By A. Vance, M.G.
3393 SWISHER, JESSE et ux Rebecca King	3/21 1833	By Jeremiah K. Mosier, M.G. (names as per the Minister of M.E. Church)
3394 SMOOT, CYRUS et ux Fanny J. Gamble	1/3 1828	By Jas. Cumming, Traveling Elder M.E.C.
3395 SNEED, JEREMIAH et ux Sarah Simerley	11/5 1843	By Christian Long, J.P.
3396 SNEED, JOHN et ux Mary Simerley	4/3 1838	By William M. Rorex, J.P.
3397 SNEED, ROBERT et ux Editha Everett	7/24 1845	By S. J. McReynolds, J.P.
3398 SNEED, ROBERT et ux Sarah Russell	9/8 1856	By S. L. Yearout, J.P.
3399 SNIDER, ELIJAH R. et ux Barbary Jane Curtis	7/18 1838	By W. M. Rorex, J.P.
3400 SNIDER, GEORGE et ux Isabell White	10/25 1810 issued	No returns
3401 SNIDER, GEORGE et ux Susan Hanley	2/5 1837	By Spencer Henry, J.P.
3402 SNIDER, GEORGE W. et ux Sarah E. Slaughter	7/3 1851	By Curran Lemons, J.P.
3403 SNIDER, JACOB et ux Susan Elder	1/25 1818 issued	No returns
3404 SNIDER, JOHN W. et ux Anna Neal	11/1 1819 issued	No returns
3405 SNIDER, MORIS (MOSES) et ux Pheobe Roddy	10/16 1826	By George Ekin, M.G. M.E. Ch.
3406 SNIDER, ROBERSON et ux Ritter Staunlor	3/3 1831	By James Taylor, M.G.

Names	Date Issue Or Celebrated	By Whom/ Security on Bonds
3407 SNIDER, WILLIAM et ux Peggy White	11/7 1820	By George Snider, M.G. of the Baptist Order
3408 SNIDER, WILSON et ux Elion Teffeteller	12/1 1842	By Christian Long, J.P.
3409 SAPPINGTON, JAMES M. et ux Jememah Wimberlee	3/7 1820	By Samuel Douthit, M.G.
* See 33233 (3233?)		
3410 SHERILL, WM. W. et ux Sarah M. Steele	2/14 1849	By Adam Haun, J.P.
* See 3302		
3411 SOULTE, ALEXANDER et ux Permeaty Waters	1/14 1839	By William M. Rorex, J.P.
3412 SPARKS, ABSOLOM et ux Sarahann Rose	3/18 1841	By Eli Richey, J.P.
3413 SPARKS, A. L. et ux Nancy J. Lain	6/3 1852	By A. J. McGee, M.G.
3414 SPARKS, JAMES et ux Catherine J. Feezell	11/17 1859	By Curran Lemons, J.P.
3415 SPARKS, JOHN A. et ux Mary E.McClanahan	12/29 1859	By Curran Lemons, J.P.
3416 SPARKS, NATHAN H. et ux Jane Potter	12/23 1852	By Curran Lemons, J.P.
3417 SPARKS, ROBT et ux Martha Blair	12/30 1852	By Curran Lemons, J.P.
3418 SPARKS, S. J. et ux Mary Kennedy	4/5 1850	By Berry Abernathey, M.G. Celebrated the "Thurs- day after date"
3419 SPARKS, WM. et ux Nancy Tate	2/26 1839	By William Henry, J.P.
3420 SPEAR, ANDERSON C. et ux Malinda J. Richards	7/28 1858	By John Gault, J.P.
3421 SPEARS, DRURY et ux Polly Ann Medlock	10/1 1846	By James Henry, J.P.
3422 SPEARES, GEORGE W. et ux Elizabeth Brook	1/5 1843	By William Colburn, J.P.
3423 SPENCE, JAMES H. et ux Caroline Law	9/18 1838	By Isaac Anderso , P.N.P. Ch.
3424 SPENCER, DANIEL et ux Vina Wheeler	10/11 1831 issued	"celebrated by me" George Ewing, --
3425 SPENCER, WILLIAM A. et ux Mary W. Duncan	2/12 1828	By William Eagleton, M.G.

Names	Date Issue Or Celebrated	By Whom/ Security on Bonds
3426 SPILMAN, CHARLES et ux Ferrybe Bell	12/2 1835	By Isaac Anderson, P.N.P. Ch.
3427 SPILMAN, LEWIS L. et ux Ruth McMahan	1/22 1835	By Davia Fleming, M.G. Bond: Clayt. D. Aber- nathy
3428 SPILMAN, THOMAS et ux Chittlen Jones (or-ley)	7/24 1792 issued	Bond: Lewis Jones
3429 SPRADLIN, DAVID et ux Matilda Wimberly	8/13 1828	By Wm. Williamson, J.P.
3430 SPRADLIN, JOHN et ux Zelpha Bryant	3/1 1821 issued	By Wm. Williamson, J.P.
3451 SPRADLIN, LEONIDAS et ux Sarah Everett	9/23 1852	By James M. Tulloch, J.P.
3452 SPRADLIN, NATHEN et ux Betsy Ridg (outside is Ridge)	9/26 1826	By Wm. Williamson, J.P.
3453 SPRADLIN, NATHANIEL et ux Jemima Poland	1/7 1847	By Samuel Tulloch, J.P.
3454 SPRADLIN, PREASENT et ux Rosanah McCool	1/31 1833	By Wm. Williamson, J.P.
3435 SPRADLIN, THOMAS M. et ux Caraline Hawkins	4/23 1857	By James M. Tulloch, J.P.
3436 SPRADLIN, W. B. et ux Mary A. Thompson	1/13 1859	By James M. Tulloch, J.P.
3437 SPRAGAN, ELISHA et ux Sally Boling	1/3 1816	By Hugh Bogle, J.P.
3438 STALLIONS, JOHN et ux Isabella Thomason	11/1 1838	By W. Toole, J.P.
3439 STALLIOS, MANSFIELD et ux Samantha Gibbs	5/24 1861	By John McCully, J.P.
3439 STANBURY, EZEKIEL et ux Matilda Mulvania	12/29 1836	By John Staley, J.P.
3440 STANFIELD, JAMES et ux Elizabeth Bond	3/13 1834	By Leroy Noble, J.P.
3441 STANFIELD, JOHN et ux Elizabeth Griffitts	10/9 1827	By S. Douthit, E.M.E. Ch.
3442 STANFIELD, JOSEPH D. et ux Sarah Mills	5/2 1857	By J. H. Bruner, M.G. Methodist
3443 STANFIELD, THOMAS et ux Esther Rice	9/10 1822	By Charles H. Warren, J.P.
3444 STANFORD, L. L. et ux M. E. Henry	12/12 1854	By John J. Robinson, M.G.
3445 STARR, EZEKIAL et ux Polly Upshaw	2/29 1820	By Andrew S. Morrison, V.D.M.

Names	Date Issue Or Celebrated	By Whom/ Security on Bonds
3446 STARLIEUS, WILLIAM et ux Ruthy Green	9/13 1821	By A. B. Gamble, J.P.
3447 STEED, JAMES et ux Adaline Howard	12/31 1840	By Samuel Tulloch, J.P.
3448 STEELE, BENJAMIN B. et ux Malinda Waters	10/18 1855	By W. W. Nuchols, J.P.
3449 STEELE, DAVID et ux Lucretia Kinneman	2/25 1847	By S. J. McReynolds, J.P.
3450 STEELE, JAMES et ux Naomi Everett	3/11 1852	By C. Long, J.P.
3451 STEELE, JOHN W. et ux Elizabeth C. Hedrick	9/24 1846	By S. J. McReynolds, J.P.
3452 STEELE, JOSEPH et ux Ann Cruse	6/14 1854	By W. W. Nuchols, J.P.
3453 STEELE, SAMUEL et ux Polly M. McClung	7/18 1822	By Isaac Anderson, P.N.P. Ch.
3454 STEELE, W. M. et ux S. E. Warren	8/2 1853	By Wm. Wilis Neal, M.G. of M.E. Ch. So.
STEPHENS, JOSEPH et ux Elizabeth Bland (Knox Reg. of 8/13 1845)	7/29 1845	By Stephen McReynolds, Esq.
3455 STIGALL, BENJAMIN et ux Patsy Denny	8/20 1802 issued	Bond: Joseph Thurman
3456 STEPHENS, C. M. et ux Elizabeth M. Maxwell	3/18 1847	By James Henry, J.P.
3457 STEPHENS, ENOCH et ux Malvina Tipton	11/12 1840	By Robert Porter, J.P.
3458 STEPHENS, JOHN et ux Anny Tipton	11/27 1831	By E. Hitch, Esq.
3459 STEPHENS, JOHN et ux Rebecca Clampet	10/24 1797 issued	Bond: Norton Green
3460 STEPHENS, JOHN et ux Barbara Yountt	12/31 1821	By Wm. Fagg, M.G.
3461 STEPHENS, JOSEPH et ux Elizabeth Poland	7/29 1845	By S. J. McReynolds, J.P. (Knox Reg. of 8/13 says 7/29 1845 also)
3462 STEPHENS, RICHARD et ux Betsy Goddard	6/5 1840	By Robert Porter, J.P.
3463 STEPHENS, WILLIAM et ux Frances Sharp	3/10 1846	By Robert Porter, J.P.
3464 STEPHENSON, JAMES M. et ux Jane Bird	2/1 1844	By John Chambers, M.G.

Names	Date Issue Or Celebrated	By Whom/ Security on Bonds
3465 STEPHENSON, JOSEPH et ux Letitia Payne	3/28 1820	By Andrew S. Morrison, V.D.M.
3466 STERLING, JOHN P. et ux Elizabeth Bell	5/20 1839	By Thomas S. Kendall, M.G.
3467 STERLING, ROBERT A. et ux Nancy L. Brown	1/30 1855	By Wm. Billue, M.G.
3468 STERLING, THOMAS et ux Rebecca J. Endsley	12/11 1845	By Harvey H. C. Caruthers, J.P.
3469 STEWART, ARCHABALD et ux Mary Ann Briant	10/21 1852	By James M. Tulloch, J.P.
3470 STURETT, EDWARD et ux Eliza Hays	3/22 1848	By S. J. McReynolds, J.P.
3471 STUART, JACB et ux Mary Panther	10/25 1819 issued	No returns
3472 STEWART, JAMES et ux Sarah Blair	8/28 1829 issued	"by me" James Taylor, M.G.
3473 STEUART, JOHN A. et ux Elizabeth J. Cochran	1/3 1858	By A. Vance, M.G.
3474 STEWART, JOSEPH et ux Elizabeth Cannon	2/20 1834	By William Colburn, J.P.
3475 STEWART, MARTIN et ux ----ly Blair (over written, blurred)	4/7 1829	By Wm. Hendrix, J.P.
3476 STEWART, ROBERT et ux Elizabeth Hussey	12/22 1800 issued	Bond: Elijah Hereshey
3477 STEWART, THOMAS et ux Sarah Williams	9/21 1826	By Saml Davidson, J.P.
3476 STEWART, THOMAS et ux Mary A. Smith * See 2908	9/3 1857	By David Spradlin, J.P.
3479 STUART, WM. et ux Celia A. Staunton	3/28 1822	By Saml Davidso , J.P.
3480 STINNET, JAMES et ux Patsy Hinton	10/7 1830	By William Toole, J.P.
3481 STINNETT, LEWIS et ux Nancy Forester	3/22 1838	By Robert Porter, J.P.
3482 SAML STINNETT et ux Martha Yearout	2/17 1848	By S. J. McReynolds, J.P.
3483 STINNET, THOMAS et ux Narcissa Howard	3/20 1859	By James Henry, J.P.
3484 STINNOT, WILLIAM et ux Fanny Cowardon	7/27 1848	By John Tipton, J.P.
3485 STINNET, WILLIAM et ux Harriet Yearout	5/17 1849	By Saml Pride, J.P.

Names	Date Issue Or Celebrated	By Whom/ Security on Bonds
3486 STINSON, WILLIAM et ux Franky McCallon	3/12 1823	By James Gillespy, J.P.
3487 STOCKTON, MARSHAL et ux Mary Kendrick	2/4 1801 issued	"February the 5th 1801" David Loveland (on back--no signature)
3488 STONE, CHARLES W. (U.S.A. 1861-65; d. Anderson Prison) et ux Margaret Jane Hamentree (of Phillip)	1/26 1848	By A. Vance, M.G.
3489 STONE, CONWAY et ux Rachel Carter	3/3 1825 (outside Feb. 3)	"Celebrated date above written, Charles H. Warren, --" on out- side
3490 STONE, C. P. et ux Melvina Yearout	8/28 1855	By Jesse Kerr, Jr., J.P.
3491 STONE, JAMES W. et ux Sarah J. Rankin	3/22 1849	By Wm. M. Brickell, J.P.
3492 STONE, JEFFERSON et ux Sophronia White	8/1 1843	By Fielding Pope, M.G.
3493 STONE, JOEL et ux Nancy W. Nipper	3/20 1828	By J. Gillespie, J.P.
3494 STONE, JOHN et ux Jane McCurdy	3/27 1823	By Charles H. Warren, J.P.
3495 STONE, JOHN et ux Isabella E. Bright	2/21 1850	By William Colburn, J.P.
3496 STONE, RICHARD et ux Catharine Snider	9/19 1830	By Robert B. Billue, M.G. of the Baptist Ch.
3497 STONE, WILLIAM et ux Sally Diddle	4/24 1817 issued	No returns
3498 STOUTE, DAVID L. et ux Margaret Ann Lawrance	12/5 1847	By A. J. McGee, M.G.
3499 STOUTE, HENRY et ux Elizabeth Hannah	5/21 1846	By John Morton, J.P.
3500 STOUTE, SAMUEL S. et ux Sarah Hammontree	4/13 1843	By John Morton, J.P.
3501 STOUTE, THOMAS et ux Sarah Hammontree	9/25 1842	By John Morton, J.P.
3502 STOUT, THOMAS et ux Omy (or Amy) Raser	4/26 1849	By Robert Sloan, J.P.
3503 STRAIN, R. B. et ux E. S. Cresham	5/1 1855	By J. S. Craig, M.G.
3504 STRAINGE, F. M. et ux Susan E. Gault	12/4 1857	By J. S. Craig, M.G.

Names	Date Issue Or Celebrated	By Whom/ Security on Bonds
3505 STRANGE, LEWIS A. et ux Isabela J. Biggs	12/9 1840	By William B. Gorsbon, M.G. (surname is not sure)
3506 STRANGE, SAML' L. et ux Myram H. Morton	8/9 1859	By R. E. Tedford, M.G.
3507 STRANAHAN, CHARLES C. et ux Uphama Hale	2/2 1837	By A. Vance, M.G.
3508 STRUTTON, ROBERT et ux Narcessa Nicholds	5/25 1845	By John Rhea, J.P.
3509 STRUTTON, WILLIAM et ux Mahala A. M. Lundy	12/17 1850	By W. M. Brickell, J.P.
3509 STUART, WILLIAM S. et ux Isabella James	5/14 1857	See 290. See Deeds Vol. Z-110
3510 SUIT, GASTON et ux Leah J. Ragan	7/28 1850	By S. J. McReynolds, J.P.
3511 SUIT, JOHNSTON et ux Elizabeth Wilson	10/19 1826	By A. B. Gamble, J.P.
3512 SULLINS, JOHN L. et ux Ann Cook	8/28 1827	By Creed Fulton, M.G.
3513 SUMMY, LEVI et ux Caroline Johnston	7/5 1853 issued	By John Wood, J.P. Bond: Wm. Ellidge
* See 3526		
3514 SUTHERLAND, THOMAS et ux Ann Henry	4/25 1822	By A. B. Gamble, J.P.
3515 SUTTON, CALVIN et ux Clarranday Wood	5/1 1834	By Edmund Wayman, J.P.
3516 SUTTON, COLVIN et ux S. E. Samples	9/9 1851	By James M. Tulloch, J.P.
3517 SUTTON, JAMES et ux Isabella Casteel	2/2 1826	By Leeroy Noble, J.P.
3518 SUTTON, STANFORD et ux Margaret King	2/12 1832	By John Wear, Esq. (written pencil, not sure of name, nor official place)
3519 SWAGGERTY, EDWIN W. et ux Mary Curtis	12/5 1844	By A. B. Gamble, J.P.
3520 SWAN, ISAAC N. et ux Mary R. Green	6/23 1842	By Jas. Cumming, Elder M.E.C.
3521 SWAN, JAMES D. et ux Isabella Hood	11/18 1828	By William Eagleton, M.G.
3522 SWAN, MOSES L. et ux Isabella Gillespie	3/9 1830	By Sam M. Astan, V.D.M.
3523 SWAIN, LEWIS et ux Jane Hackney	11/6 1832	By A. Ish, J.P.
3524 SWANGER, JOHN et ux Peggy Stephens	12/19 1820	By George Snider, M.G. of Baptist Order

Names	Date Issue Or Celebrated	By Whom/ Security on Bonds
3525 SWISHER, HENRY R. et ux Elizabeth King	3/18 1827 issued 12/17 1827, Jack F. Foute, Clk By Dept. D. D. Foute	By John Wood, L.D.
3526 SWISHER, JESSE et ux Rebecca King	3/21 1833	By Jeremiah R. Mosier, M.G. M.E. Ch.
3526 SUMMY, LEVI et ux Caroline Johnston	7/8 1853	By John Wood, J.P.
* See 3513--same bond there		
3526 TALBOTT, ALEXANDER et ux Margaret L. (or S.) James	12/4 1828	By Isaac Anderson, P.N.P. Ch.
3527 TALBERT, JACOB C. et ux Ann Jonson (outside says Ann Jonston)	1/22 1828	By William Eagleton, M.G.
3528 TORBET, HUGH et ux Margaret Eagleton	9/4 1823	By Isaac Anderson, P.N.P. Ch.
3529 TORBET, JAMES et ux Patsy Hall	6/19 1817	By Wm. Lowery, J.P.
3530 TORBETT, JOHN et ux Mary Gault	3/20 1823	By R. H. King--"As per forms of the Presbeterian Church"
3531 TOLBERT (or TALBOT), WM. E. et ux Eugenia H. Anderson	10/22 1856	By R. E. Tedford, M.G.
3532 TALLENT, AARON et ux Bethena Anderson	4/14 1829	By Charles H. Warren, J.P.
3533 TALLENT, BENJAMIN et ux Edy Anderson	1/8 1846	By James Henry, J.P.
3534 TALLENT, ELISHA et ux Sally Moses	12/29 1818 issued	No return
3535 TALLENT, ENOCH et ux Lucinda Wigginton	7/30 1829	By Charles H. Warren, J.P.
3536 TALLENT, JAMES et ux Mary A. Boren	5/11 1848	By Wm. Henderson, J.P.
3537 TALLENT, JONATHAN et ux Polly French	8/1 1833	By J. Gillespie, J.P.
3538 TALLENT, WILLIAM et ux Rebecca Boring	8/29 1843	By William Colburn, J.P.
3539 TALLY, CALVIN et ux Jane Black	12/8 1839	By Leonard Wood, J.P.
3540 TALLA, LANTA et ux Caroline Evens	7/28 1858	By H. I. Hodges, M.G.

Names	Date Issue Or Celebrated	By Whom/ Security on Bonds
3541 TALLEY, WILLIS et ux Isabella Spilman	8/11 1857	By A. J. McGee, M.G.
3542 TATE, ISAAC et ux Jemimah Brickey	4/25 1818 issued	By "James Cameron, J.P." (on back)
3543 TATE, JOHN et ux Elizabeth Farmer	3/21 1824	By James Taylor, M.G.
3544 TATE, JOSEPH et ux Elizabeth S. Waters	1/9 1828	"solomnised in January 1828" Wm. Hendrix, Esq.
3545 TATE, JOSEPH et ux Sarah Tipton	4/30 1835	By Spencer Henry, J.P.
3546 TATE, WILLIAM et ux Vina Sawyers	5/20 1819	By J. Camron, J.P.
3547 TAYLOR, ABRAHAM et ux Jane Barns	10/19 1830	By J. P. Montgomery, J.P.
3548 TAYLOR, BENJAMIN et ux Caroline Smith	1/17 1843	By Green B. Saffell, J.P.
3549 TAYLOR, BENJAMIN et ux Margaret Neal	12/9 1845	By John Morton, J.P.
3550 TAYLOR, DANIEL et ux Kissiah Lotherd	10/3 1849	By A. Vance, M.G.
3551 TAYLOR, DANIEL et ux Elinor Ewing	1/29 1833	By Andrew Vance, M.G.
3552 TAYLOR, DAVID et ux Poly Bigbay	9/9 1817	By William Lowery, J.P.
3553 TAYLOR, GEORGE W. et ux Hannah F. Blair	2/20 1859	By Nicholas Brewer, J.P.
3554 TAYLOR, JAMES et ux Cathorine Gardner	10/22 1846	By John Morton, J.P.
3555 TAYLOR, JAMES et ux Mary A. Duncan	12/21 1848	By William Colburn, J.P.
3556 TAYLOR, JAMES M. et ux Nancy A. Badget	2/25 1852	By C. D. Smith, M.G.
3557 TAYLOR, JAMES A. et ux Mary T. Allen	8/19 1857	By A. Vance, M.G.
3558 TAYLOR, JOHN et ux Susannah Blair	8/6 1823	By Wm. Williamson, J.P.
3559 TAYLOR, JOHN C. et ux Elizabeth Maxwell	11/2 1835	By John D. Wilson, M.G.
3560 TAYLOR, JOHN L. et ux Mary Ann Diddle	4/6 1831	"by me Saml Montgomery, Esq."
3561 TAYLOR, JOSEPH et ux Mary Ann Dixon	2/1 1842	By John Dyke, Pastor Unitia Church
3562 TAYLOR, JOSHUA et ux Mary Brickey	8/24 1825 issued	"Performed by me" James Taylor, M.G.

Names	Date Issue Or Celebrated	By Whom/ Security on Bonds
3563 TAYLOR, PLEASANT et ux Elizabeth Waters	1/7 1830	By Sam Henry, J.P.
3564 TAYLOR, REDDEN S. et ux Nancy W. Warren	9/24 1833	By John Pryor, --
3585 TAYLOR, WILLIAM et ux Elizabeth Snider	1/30 1811 issued	No returns
3566 TAYLOR, WILLIAM et ux Racheal Greer	12/9 1841	By A. Vance, M.G. of Bakers Creek Church
3567 TAYLOR, WILLIAM et ux Susan H. Gilespie	10/1 1857	By J. S. Craig, M.G.
3568 TAYLOR, W. W. et ux E. A. Adams	8/20 1855	"In due time A. Vance, M.G."
3569 TEAGUE, MAGNESS et ux Francis Rogers	1/2 1798 issued	Bond: John Rodgers
3570 TEDFORD, DAVID et ux Sarah Norwood	10/3 1843	By John S. Craig, M.G.
3571 TEDFORD, HENRY C. et ux Elizabeth Ann Cook	11/28 1843	By Green B. Saffell, J.P.
TELFORD, GEORGE et ux Jean Hannah	4/3 1793	Sec. James Telford Wit: David Craig (See Knox Co.)
3572 TEDFORD, HENRY P. et ux Margaret McClung	12/18 1827	By D. Carson, M.G. A.P. Ch.
3573 TEDFORD, JAMES et ux Jane Fergusson (Fergason)	5/2 1839	By Thomas S. -----,M.G. (Kendall)
3574 TEDFORD, JOHN et ux Jean Henderson	12/11 1799 issued	Bond: George Tedford
3575 TEDFORD, JOHN et ux Agnes J. Hender-son	11/16 1826	By Thomas Baveridge, --
3576 TEDFORD, JOHN et ux Elizabeth A. Hamil	1/11 1844	By Green B. Saffell, J.P.
3577 TEDFORD, JOHN M. et ux Martha C. Stuart	7/20 1841	By Robert Delzell, J.P.
3578 TEDFORD, JOSEPH et ux Louisa G. Shaw	12/29 1831	"D. Carson, M. of Ap. Ch."
3579 TEDFORD, RALPH E. et ux Malinda G. Houston	4/12 1836	By Isaac Anderson, P.N.P. Ch.
3580 TEDFORD, ROBERT et ux Jenney White	7/4 1800 issued	Bond: Jno. Craig
3581 TEDFORD, ROBERT et ux Phoebe M. Houston	8/10 1825	By Isaac Anderson,

Names	Date Issue Or Celebrated	By Whom/ Security on Bonds
3582 TEDFORD, ROBERT A. et ux Rebecka McClung (or one is Rebecca McClerg)	2/7 1828	By D. Carson, M.G. C.P. Church
3583 TEDFORD, ROBERT S. et ux Martha Jane Scruggs	2/16 1843	By John Morton, J.P.
3584 TEFERTELLER, DANL' et ux Mary Gains	3/24 1856	By W. W.Nuchols, J.P.
3585 TEDFORD, THOMAS et ux Polly Hannah	10/21 1800	Bond: Robert Hannah
3586 TEEFETELLER, DANIEL et ux Patsy Cortis (outside is Pasy Curtis)	3/14 1817 issued	"Executed--John Waugh, J.P."
3587 TEAFFITELLAR, GEORGE W. et ux Margaret Jane Farre	9/29 1842	By Isaac Anderson, P.N.P. Ch.
3588 TEFFETELLER, MICHAEL et ux Jane Cumming	10/6 1836	By Fielding Pope, M.G.
TEFFETELLER, MICHAEL L. et ux Margaret Z. Gamble of Knox Co.	12/27 1842	By Rev. I. Anderson (says Knox Reg. 1/4 1843)
3589 TEEFATELLER, THOMAS HENRY et ux Tressa (Teressa) Everett	3/5 1839	By W. M. Rorex, J.P.
3590 TEFFETELLER, WILLIAM et ux Sarah McClure	5/28 1845	By S. J. McReynolds, J.P.
3591 TEFFITALLER, WM. et ux Rosannah Vaughn	10/5 1840	By Christian Long, J.P.
3592 TEMPLES, JAMES D. et ux Victoria Heartsell of Hiram	9/18 1858	By Rev'd S. A. Taylor, Louisville, Tenn.
3593 TEMPLE, ROBT. et ux Mary Smith	1/6 1856	By C. Cowan, J.P.
3594 TERRY, SAMUEL et ux Sarah Hail	10/3 1797 issued	Bond: Daniel Hoff
3595 THARP, JOEL et ux Jane Crawley	2/27 1834	By Wm. Billue, M.G.
3596 THARP, JONATHAN et ux Sally Roddy	10/4 1809 issued	No returns
3597 THORNE, EDWARD et ux Melvina Cowden	2/14 1835	By Spencer Henry, J.P.
3598 THOMAS, FREDERICK et ux Patsy McFarland	2/1 1816 issued	"Ex'd J. Turk, Jus."
3599 THOMAS, HENRY et ux Sarah E. McPherson	10/3 1844 issued	"Exc. same day John Russum, M.G."
3600 THOMAS, JOHN et ux Elizabeth Daniels	8/3 1822	By Saml Davidson, J.P.

Names	Date Issue Or Celebrated	By Whom/ Security on Bonds
3601 THOMAS, JOHN et ux Susan M. Mitchell	12/24 1858	By C. Cowan, J.P.
3602 THOMAS, MARION et ux Malinda Rule	5/20 1854 issued celb. 5/22 1854	By Wm. T. Dowell, M.G.
3603 THOMAS, WILLIAM et ux Polly Carver	11/30 1822	By Wm. Williamson, J.P.
3604 THOMAS WM. et ux Nancy Delozier	2/21 1855	By Wm. G. Brooks, J.P.
3605 THOMPSON, ANDREW et ux Katherine Hutsell	1/2 1840	By Henry Hamil, J.P.
3606 THOMPSON, DAVID et ux Lucinday Hutche- son	9/15 1831	By David McKamy, J.P.
3607 THOMPSON, DAVID et ux Mary Karr (outside is Kerr)	1/31 1837	By J. K. Mosier, M.G.
3608 THOMPSON, DAVID et ux Martha A. Chapman	8/28 1844	By John Griffitts, J.P.
3609 THOMPSON, D. C. et ux L. A. Hale (outside is Lucinda A. Hale)	2/9 1854	By A. Vance, M.G.
3610 THOMPSON, GEORGE et ux Polly Neal	11/29 1832	By John Maxwell, J.P.
3611 THOMPSON, G.A.W.B. et ux E. C. Gamble	12/19 1855	"Celebrated" (on back; no other words; no signature)
3612 THOMPSON, HARVEY et ux Peggy Thompson Anderson	11/7 1826	By Alexander McCollum, J.P.
3613 THOMPSON, HARVEY et ux Ann Morrow	10/14 1856	By James Matthews, J.P.
3614 THOMPSON, ISAAC et ux Polly Wheeler	2/6 1828	By George Ewing, J.P.
3615 THOMPSON, ISAAC et ux Ann Roan	8/29 1831 issued	"by me George Ewing, --"
3616 THOMPSON, ISAIAS et ux Hannah Philips	1/13 1819	By George Ewing, J.P.
3617 THOMSON, JAMES et ux Susannah Weir	6/5 1797 issued	Bond: John Weir
3618 THOMPSON, JAMES et ux Polly Brotherton	2/23 1832	By J. P. Montgomery, J.P.
3619 THOMPSON, JAMES et ux Margaret Smith	12/26 1837	By Joseph Wilson, J.P.
3620 THOMPSON, JAMES et ux Polly Carson	12/10 1840	By Eli Richy, J.P.

Names	Date Issue Or Celebrated	By Whom/ Security on Bonds
3621 THOMPSON, JAMES M. et ux Sarah J. Brook	2/27 1849	By W. Earnest, J.P. Bond: James R. Morrow
3622 THOMPSON, JESSE et ux Elizabeth H. Montgomery	5/29 1821	By Isaac Anderson, P.N.P. Ch.
3623 THOMPSON, JESSE et ux Malinda George	10/29 1840	By Isaac Anderson, P.N.P. Ch.
3624 THOMPSON, JOHN et ux Margret M'Conald	5/30 1799 issued	Bond: Samuel Cowan
3625 THOMPSON, JOHN et ux Elender Malcom	9/11 1817	By Hugh Bogle, J.P.
3628 THOMPSON, JOHN et ux Meglothel Stone (Myphael)	2/5 1829	By Wm. Billue, M.G.
3627 THOMPSON, JOHN et ux Marg't McCallan	4/7 1853	By F. Pope, M.G.
3628 THOMPSON, JOHN W. et ux Elizabeth Brown	1/31 1849	By Wm. Brickell, J.P.
3629 THOMPSON, JOSEPH et ux Eliza Cathcart	11/11 1837 issued	No returns
3630 THOMPSON, LARKIN et ux Polly Anderson	7/24 1826	By S. Douthit, E.M.E. E.M.E. Ch.
3631 THOMPSON, LEONIDAS et ux Mary C. Anderson	7/25 1857	By H. Thompson, J.P.
3632 THOMPSON, L. M. et ux Mary J. Cumming	11/1 1858	By George Caldwell, J.P.
3633 THOMPSON, MATTHEW W. et ux Jane Bogle	10/15 1834	By D. Hoyt, M.G.
3634 THOMPSON, NATHAN et ux Ann Eliza Alexan- der	2/5 1839	By Isaac M.Haire, J.P.
3635 THOMPSON, NATHAN et ux Maratha J. Cloud	1/29 1846 issued 1/12	By J. Dyke, Pastor Unitia Church
3636 THOMPSON, ROBERT et ux Elizabeth Berry	9/25 1817	"Celebrated" (no signature)
3637 THOMPSON, ROBERT et ux Nancy Thompson	12/23 1824	By Isaac Anderson,
3638 THOMPSON, RALPH E. et ux Jane Earwood	6/5 1834	By Edward Mitchell, J.P.
3639 THOMPSON, ROBERT et ux Jane Armstrong	6/27 1843	By A. Vance, M.G.
3640 THOMPSON, ROBERT et ux Jane Ball	9/26 1844	By John Morton, J.P.
3641 THOMPSON, SAMUEL et ux Jane Robinson	7/17 1827	By George Ewi g, --

Names	Date Issue Or Celebrated	By Whom Security on Bonds
3642 THOMPSON, SAMUEL et ux Dorcas Brown	5/14 1848	By Lewis J. Neuman, J.P. (or Neiman)
3643 THOMPSON, SPENCER et ux Susannah Montgomery	4/14 1819 issued	No returns
THOMPSON, WILLIAM et ux Sarah Beatty	9/21 1802	
3644 THOMPSON, WILLIAM et ux Rebeckah Wallace	4/24 1811 issued	No returns
3645 THOMPSON, WILLIAM et ux Betsy McTeer	10/7 1829	"Celebrated on 10/8 by (faded) H. B. McAlpin, J.P."
3646 THOMPSON, WILLIAM et ux Katharine Smith	12/27 1832	By John Maxwell, J.P.
3647 THOMPSON, WILLIAM E. et ux M. M. Earnest	5/22 1850 issued	Bond: John R. Lee
3648 THOMPSON, WM. H. et ux Lucinda C. Cook	4/3 1851	By Spencer Henry, M.G.
3649 THURMAN, JOSEPH et ux Elizabeth Tipton	2/4 1841	By Lewis Jones, J.P.
3650 THURMAN, L. A. et ux Nancy C. Smith	2/22 1853	By Daniel H. Emmert, J.P.
3651 THERMON, PRESTON et ux Martha Gibbs	8/16 1846	By James Henry, J.P.
3652 THURMAN, WILLIAM et ux Betsy Snider	5/11 1829	By Wm. Hendrix, J.P.
3653 THURMAN, WILLIAM S. et ux Mary McLenahan	3/1 1846	By Robert Shields, J.P.
TIEGHMAN, N. of Murray Co., Ga. et ux Malinda Russell (of Jno.)--says Knox Reg. of 3/27	3/8 1856	by Rev. S. A. Taylor
3654 TIMBERMAN, ABREHAM et ux Nancy Hakins	1/19 1801 issued	Bond: Christopher Timberman
3655 TIMBERMAN, CHRISTOPHER et ux Mary Forguson	10/14 1800 issued	Bond: Jonathan Timmer- man
3656 TIMMONS, W. B. et ux Nancy J. Brown	12/26 1849	By F. Pope, M.G.
3657 TIMMONS, W. B. et ux Lyda A. Casheon	10/16 1856	By J. S. Craig, M.G.
3658 TIPTON, ABRAHAM et ux Jene Roddy	4/29 1806	(issued or written, no signature of Clerk nor any other)
3659 TIPTON, ABRAM et ux Susan Myers	8/26 1855 issued 8/18	By N. Brewer, J.P.

Names	Date Issue Or Celebrated	By Whom Security on Bonds
3660 TIPTON, BENJAMON et ux Rebeck Cusic "Terretory of U.S. South of Ohio, Blount County" is printed at top on the form-- Attes. Mth'l Couson (or Cowan)	12/19 1795 issued	Bond: Robt. Hook
3661 TIPTON, BENJAMIN et ux Nancy Brooks	10/28 1824	By Hugh Bogle, J.P.
3662 TIPTON, BENJEMIN et ux Mary Maulkem (or Haulkenr) (outside is Mary Halcom)	11/29 1838	By Wm. McTeer, J.P.
3663 TIPTON, CASWELL et ux Lucinda Brooks	2/7 1833	By John Russam, M.G.
3664 TIPTON, DAVID B. et ux Sally Jones	8/17 1823	By Hugh Bogle, J.P.
3665 TIPTON, DAVID B. et ux Rebecca Jones	10/29 1829	By Wm. T. Hendrix, J.P.
3666 TIPTON, DAVID B. et ux Rachel Henry	2/9 1835 issued on 2/12	By "Spencer Henry, J.P."
3667 TIPTON, ELI et ux Peggy Walker	9/16 1814	"Issued by me Joseph Walker, J.P." "Celebrated"
3668 TIPTON, ELBRIDG G. et ux Matilda J. Blankin- ship	12/20 1842	By B. H. Mayo, M.G. C.P.C.
3669 TIPTON, GEORGE W. et ux Nancy Jones	4/20 1831	By A. C. Renfro, J.P.
3670 TIPTON, ISAAC et ux Dama Jones	11/19 1835	By Wm. Dever, J.P.
3671 TIPTON, ISAAC et ux Martha Fulkner	6/15 1858	By C. Cowan, J.P.
TIPTON, JACOB et ux Dorcas Davis	1/27 1837	
3672 TIPTON, JACOB et ux Docia Halcom	3/3 1836 issued 3/3	"executed by me" on 3/3 John Russom, M.G.
3673 TIPTON, JACOB et ux Martha R. Henry	8/8 1837	By Lorenzo Donaldson, J.P.
TIPTON, JAMES et ux Betsy Tipton	11/26 1826	
3674 TIPTON, JAMES et ux Mary Jane Hender- son	12/18 1838	By Isaac Anderson, P.N.P. Ch.
3675 TIPTON, J.W.H. et ux Ann C. Freshour	12/21 1847	By Lowery McBath, J.P.

Names	Date Issue Or Celebrated	By Whom Security on Bonds
3676 TIPTON, JONATHAN et ux Margaret Singleton	10/5 1837	By James Dixon, M.G.
3677 TIPTON, JOHN et ux Mary Helton	4/9 1821 issued	"Executed--S. George, J.P."
3678 TIPTON, JOHN et ux Jane Clark	8/8 1830	By A. C. Renfro, J.P.
3679 TIPTON, JOHN et ux Charlotte M. Hollingsworth	11/16 1834	By Fredrick Emmett, J.P.
3680 TIPTON, JOHN S. et ux Mary Vinyard	1/21 1847	By Ben Cunnin ham, J.P.
3681 TIPTON, JNO. et ux Naomie Abbott	8/4 1854	By Curran Lemons, J.P.
3682 TIPTON, JOSEPH et ux Martha Ingram	1/29 1825	By E. Hitch, Esq.
3683 TIPTON, JOSEPH JR. et ux Polly Mays	6/30 1825	By Hugh Bogle, J.P.
3684 TIPTON, JOSEPH et ux Melvina Davis	9/6 1846	By Wm. Rogers, M.G.
3685 TIPTON, LANDON C. et ux Harriet Dean	3/3 1850	By Wm. McTeer, J.P.
3686 TIPTON, MASHACK et ux Elizabeth McRey- nolds	11/16 1837	By Isaac Anderson, P.N.P. Ch.
3687 TIPTON, M. M. et ux A. M. Rider	1/8 1857	By William Kerr, J.P.
3688 TIPTON, PLEASANT M. et ux Mary Davis	1/18 1832 issued	"Celebrated A. C. Ren- fro, J.P."
3689 TIPTON, THOMAS J. et ux Susana Harris	5/22 1824	By E. Hitch, J.P.
3690 TIPTON, REUBEN et ux Louisa Tipton	3/9 1840	By James Matson, J.P.
3691 TIPTON, REUBEN et ux Elizabeth Teffer- taller	4/3 1844	By Lewis Jones, J.P.
3692 TIPTON, WM. et ux Peggy Tipton	1/22 1802 issued	Bond: John Cunningham Attst.: J. Houston, And'w Thompson
3693 RHEA, JAMES et ux Betsy Tipton (outside was James Tipton to Betsy Tipton)	11/16 1826	By A. B.Gamble, J.P.
* See 3041		
3694 TODD, LOW et ux Polly Simons (J.P. says "Law Todd")	8/14 1821	By Arch'd Maxwell, J.P.

Names	Date Issue Or Celebrated	By Whom/ Security on Bonds
3695 TONEY, GARRET et ux Margaret Francis	5/2 1839	By R. B. Billue, M.G. of Baptist Order
3696 TOOLE, JAMES M. et ux Martha Jane Wallace (daughter of Gen. William W. Wallace, says Knox Reg. of 9/6 1843)	8/22 1843	By Isaac Anderson, P.N.P. Ch.
3697 TOOLE, JOHN E. et ux Jane C. Pope	2/13 1845	By Isaac Anderson, P.N.P. Ch.
3698 TOOLE, WILLIAM et ux Elizabeth Wallace	2/22 1825	By Isaac Anderson, P.N.P. Ch.
3699 TOOLE, WM. JR. et ux M.A.H. Gillespy	2/12 1852	By John J. Robinson, M.G.
TORBETT, JOHN et ux Mary Gantt "says Knox Reg.of 3/28 1823"	3/20 1823	By Rev. R. H. King
3700 TOW, SHADERACK et ux Mary A. Roberts	3/27 1858	By N. Brewer, J.P.
3701 TOWNSEN, JAMES et ux Martha Ellege	9/3 1857	By M. Kounts, J.P.
3702 TOWNSEL, JOHN et ux Nancy Hubbard	11/20 1851	By William McTeer, J.P.
3703 TOWNSAND, THOS. W. et ux Jane B. Graves	12/14 1854	By M. Kounts, J.P.
3704 TRIAS or FRIAR, FRIAS, JOHN et ux Tabitha Ewing	11/11 1799 issued	Bond: Henry Beard
3705 TRICE, JAMES et ux Mary Arnett	2/5 1833	By Wm. Billue, M.G.
3706 TRICE, JAMES et ux Phebe Tipton	10/19 1845	By Robert Porter, J.P.
3707 TRIMBLE, JOHN et ux Elisabeth J. Cargo	5/9 1806 issued	No returns
3708 TROTT, PINCKNEY et ux Margaret Sesler (I think is Sesler)	2/23 1858	By F. Pope, M.G.
3709 TROTTER, AMOS R. et ux Mary Gamble	10/23 1834	By Spencer Henry, J.P.
3710 TROTTER, WILLIAM et ux Elizabeth Hart "Hart Family Book-- daughter of Joseph"	10/4 1821	By James Turk, J.P.
3711 TRUNDLE, DANIEL L. et ux Mary Elizabeth Trundle	1/9 1838	By Isaac Anderson P.N.P. Ch.

Names	Date Issue Or Celebrated	By Whom/ Security on Bonds
3712 TRUNDLE, DAVID L. et ux Mary A. Thompson	3/10 1842	By Leonard Wood, J.P.
3713 TRUNDLE, DANIEL L. et ux Easther Dearmond	2/22 1844	By Saml Pride, J.P.
3714 TRUNDLE, D. L. et ux Martha Dearmond	4/15 1852	By J. S. Craig, M.G.
3715 TUBBS, JOHN et ux Mary More	12/30 1799 issued	Bond: Thos. Rodgers
3716 TUCK, CAREY et ux Anna Thompson	9/22 1819	By Wm. Griffitts, J.P.
3717 TUCK, CAREY et ux Ann McMenas	9/8 1830	By Alexander Ish, J.P.
3718 TUCK, EDWARD et ux Sarah McMenus	4/19 1831	By Leeroy Noble, J.P.
3719 TUCK, HEZEKIAH et ux Margaret Richards	8/21 1852	By Jesse Kerr, Jr., J.P.
3720 TUCK, JOSEPH et ux Elizabeth Bond	1/12 1825	By Samuel Douthit, Elder in M.E. Ch.
3721 TUCK, JOHN et ux Clementine McRoy	8/23 1838	By Benj. P. Mays, M.G.
3722 TUCK, ROBERT et ux Malinda Philips	1/1 1846	By James H. Donaldson, J.P.
3723 TUCK, THOMAS et ux Rebecca Cox	6/25 1840	By William Colburn, J.P.
3724 TUCK, WM. et ux Ann Baun	12/4 1828	By Wm. Griffitts, J.P.
3725 TUCKER, EDMOND et ux Louisa Hunt	12/28 1852	By Andrew Ferguson, J.P.
3726 TUCKER, GEORGE et ux Lebe or Sebe or Sibi or Libi Lackey	11/16 1808 issued	No returns
3727 TUCKER, ISAAC et ux Sarah Keelan	8/22 1849 issued	Bond: Lewis Keelan
3728 TUCKER, JAMES et ux Sally Philips	1/23 1834	By John Maxwell, J.P.
3729 TUCKER, JOHN et ux Sarah Stallions	8/15 1844	By Harvey H. C. Caruthers, J.P.
3730 TUCKER, JOHN et ux Myra Morrow	8/8 1848	By J. Dyke, Pastor Unitia Ch.
3731 TUCKER, WILLIAM et ux Ann James	2/6 1820	By Samuel Douthit, M.G.
3732 TULLOCH, JAMES M. et ux Mary Best	11/17 1836	By J. R. Mosier, M.G.
3733 TULLOCH, SAMUEL et ux Catherine M. Caldwell	10/21 1830	By Saml Hamil, J.P.

Names	Date Issue Or Celebrated	By Whom/ Security on Bonds
3734 TURNBULL, JOHN et ux Nancy (or Mary?) Williams	5/8 1859	By Wm. M. Brickell, J.P.
3735 UNDERWOOD, WESLEY et ux Mary Brown	11/21 1826	By S. Douthit, E.M.E.C.
3736 UNDERWOOD, SAMUEL et ux Sarah E. Sparks	2/9 1858	By W. W.Bayless, J.P.
3737 UTTER, SAMUEL et ux Jane Vance	9/5 1816	By And'w S. Morrison, V.D.M.
3738 UTTER, WILLIAM et ux Sarah Alexander	8/10 1819	By And'w S. Morrison, V.D.M.
* See 3755		
3739 UPTON, JESSE et ux Polly Hackney	2/27 1822 issued	"celebrated by John Lambert, J.P."
3740 UPTON, JOSEPH et ux Susan Yearout	4/19 1831	By Isaac Anderson, P.N.P. Ch.
3741 UPTON, THOMAS et ux Ann E. Yearout	10/15 1822	By Isaac Anderson, P.N.P. Ch.
3742 VANCE, ANDREW et ux Nancy Ann Wilson	3/19 1839	By Sumner Mandeville, V.D.M.
3743 VANN, ISAAC et ux Labinia Scripshir	8/24 1815	By J. Harris, J.P.
3744 VANDERGRIF, GILBERT et ux Mary A. Hunt	10/3 1857	By A. R..James J.P.
3745 VAUGHN, JAMES C. et ux Rebecca McCulley	9/20 1855	By John Davis, M.G.
3746 VAUGHN, WILLIAM et ux Judy Stallions	6/24 1827	By Arch'd Maxwell, J.P.
* See 3754		
3747 VAUGHT, DAVID et ux Nancy Harmon	8/5 1820 issued	No returns
3748 VAUGHT, DAVID et ux Sarah Cotterell	1/20 1830	By Wm. Williamso , J.P.
3749 VAUGHT, HENRY et ux Catheren Whiten- barger	4/24 1805 issued	"on back in different handwriting is April 25, 1804"
3750 VAUGHT, JACOB et ux Polly Colbourn	4/16 1805 issued	No returns
3751 VAUGHT, JOSEPH et ux Eavy Proess (or Eavy P. Ross or Props)	3/16 1816 issued	No returns
3752 VAUGHT, JOHN et ux Rebecca Best	8/19 1841	By Samuel Tulloch, J.P.

Names	Date Issue Or Celebrated	By Whom/ Security on Bonds
3753 VERNOR, W. H. et ux Ellen W. Hannaum	8/2 1854	By Isaac Anderson, P.N.P. Ch.
3754 VAUT, ANDREW et ux Susannah Broils	12/16 1800 issued	Bond: Steph n Boutwell
* See 3746		
3755 UPTON, JAMES et ux Agness Leions of Lyons	4/7 1800 issued	Bond: James Gillespie
* See 3738		
3756 VICKERS, THOMAS et ux Charity Hendrich- son	9/26 1834	By John Ferguson, J.P.
3757 VILES, SAMUEL et ux Eliza Johnson	7/17 1851	By Thos. M. Rooker, J.P.
3758 VINYARD, CHRISTIAN et ux Ann Haddox	7/11 1839	By Robt. Porter, J.P.
3759 VINYARD, FRANKLIN et ux Susan E. Cupp	12/1 1859	By A. Boyd, J.P.
3760 VINEYARD, GREEN et ux Polly Ingram	3/28 1837	By Spencer Henry, J.P.
3761 VINEYARD, LINDSEY et ux Aggrippina Sherrill	12/29 1837	By Jame Ray, J.P.
3762 VINYARD, MUSE et ux Elizabeth Dearmond	12/24 1829	By Isaac Anderson, P.N.P. Ch.
3763 VINYARD, NICHOLS G. et ux Martha A. Chandler	12/5 1844	By Wm. M. Burnett, --
3764 VINYARD, PLEASANT et ux Almirah Lambert	9/6 1860	By John McCully, J.P.
3764 VINYARD, SILAS et ux Jane Roddy	1/1 1846	By Robt. Porter, J.P.
3765 VINYARD, WILLIAM T. et ux Ann Breakbill	8/8 1844	By Ben Cunningjam, J.P.
3766 WAID, DAVID et ux Mary Vaught	12/8 1812 issued	No returns
3767 WADE, WALKER et ux Mary Snider	10/29 1817 issued	No returns
3768 WADDY, GRANVILLE et ux Rachel Tarbet	8/26 1835	By Rev. John Dyke
3769 WADDLE, NOAE et ux Polly Givens	10/4 1824 issued	No returns
3770 WADDLE, THOMAS et ux Eliza Humphries	11/21 1826	By Alex'r McCollum, J.P.
3771 WADDLE, THOMAS et ux Isabella Humphreys	11/24 1859	By M. Jones, J.P.

Names	Date Issue Or Celebrated	By Whom/ Security on Bonds
3772 WALDROP, J. A. et ux H. E. Hammons	8/18 1859	By R. E. Tedford, M.G.
3773 WOLFORD, WILLIAM et ux Mary Cummings	7/31 1851	By Isaac Anderson, P.N.P. Ch.
* See 3847		
3774 WALKER, BENJAMIN et ux Anny Cadwell	10/5 1820	By Hugh Bigle, J.P.
3775 WALKER, DAVID et ux Jane Johnston	12/14 1808 issued	Bond: Josiah Johnston
3776 WALKER, HIRAM et ux Mary McTeer	1/7 1847	By John Morton, J.P.
3777 WALKER, HUGH et ux Nancy Cochran	6/5 1797 issued	Bond: Hugh S. Cochran
3778 WALKER, JAMES et ux Joannah Elliot	4/4 1816	By George Snider, J.P.
3779 WALKER, JAMES et ux Jane Lambert	10/19 1834	By Johnson (his mark, X) Adams, M.G.
3780 WALKER, JAMES et ux Mary Davis	8/8 1847	By W. R.Flinn, J.P.
3781 WALKER, JOHN et ux Esther Henderson	2/6 1834	By D. Carson, M.G. of Presb' Ch.
3782 WALKER, JOHN et ux Polly Mires	1/19 1837	By Johnson Adam, --
3783 WALKER, JOHN et ux Sarah McConnell	10/26 1848	By William R. Flinn, J.P.
3784 WALKER, JOSEPH et ux Polly Boaz	6/21 1816	By William Wilhamson, J.P.
3785 WALKER, JOE et ux Sarah Kaler	1/31 1856	By Frederic Emmet, M.G.
3786 WALKER, JOSEPH et ux Anna Fancier	6/19 1859	By Frederic Emmet, M.G.
3787 WALKER, J. J. et ux Miss Rachel McGhee (of Rev. Alex McGhee) "says T.D. 11/1839 Knox.-McGhee Library"	11/23 1839	By I. Anderson, P.N.P. Ch.
3788 WALKER, JOSEPH N. et ux Elizabeth Brake- bill, Jr.	2/10 8142	By A. B.Gambl , J.P.
3789 WALKER, JOSIAH et ux Martha J. Keelin	5/30 1852	By David Spradlin, J.P.
3790 WALKER, PETER et ux Susannah Dunn	2/6 1851	By Johnson Adams, --
3791 WALKER, PLEASANT et ux Betsy Hedrick	1/18 1826	By Saml Davidson, J.P.

Names	Date Issur Or Celebrated	By Whom/ Security on Bonds
3792 WALKER, PLEASANT et ux F. M. Peery	1/20 1859	By H. J. Henry, J.P.
3793 WALKER, ROBT. F. et ux Margaret E. McConnell	1/13 1858	By A. Vance, M.G.
3794 WALKER, SAML et ux Rebeckah Davidson	3/20 1803 issued	Bond: Jno. Walker Attest: Gideon Black- burn
3795 WALKER, SAML H. et ux Mary Hicks	1/30 1845	By James Taller, Admestreror of the Gosspel
3796 WALKER, SPENCER et ux Orpha McConnell	11/20 1851	By D. R. Lamb, J.P.
3797 WALKER, THOMAS et ux Eliza Myers	3/25 1840	By Johnson Adams, M.G.
3798 WALKER, VANCE et ux Catherine Henry	1/17 1822	By A. B. Gamble, J.P.
3799 WALKER, WILLIAM et ux Barbara Dunn	3/27 1851	By Frederic Emmett, M.G.
3800 WALKER, WILLIAM et ux Nancy C. Brewer	1/1 1852	By A. B. Gamble, J.P.
3801 WALKER, WILLIAM A. et ux Eliza W. Wright	1/17 1850	By I. Anderson, P.N.P. Ch.
3802 WALKER, WM. M. et ux Nancy L. Kaler	2/12 1857	By Daniel H. Emmett, J.P.
3803 WALLACE, ABRAHAM et ux ----- Wallace (given name blank)	9/4 1802 issued	Bond: William Lowery
3804 WALLACE, ABRAHAM M. et ux Mary Ann Hartsell	9/27 1832	By Isaac Anderson, P.N.P. Ch.
3805 WALLACE, A. M. et ux Octavia A. Cox	10/4 1842	By Isaac Anderson, P.N.P. Ch.
3806 WALLACE, A. H. et ux Margaret J. Craston	10/30 1858	By J. S. Craig, M.G.
3807 WALLACE, BENJAMIN et ux Rachel Neil	12/18 1815	By George Snider, --
3808 WALLACE, CAMPBELL G. W. et ux Martha J. Broils	7/19 1852	By S. J. McReynolds, J.P.
3809 WALLACE, DAVID et ux Sarah Justice	4/23 1798 issued	Bond: Moses Justice
3810 WALLACE, JAMES et ux Sarah Runnils	12/31 1801 issued	Bond: William Wallace
3811 WALLACE, JESSE et ux Margret Isom (or Gow, Lraw, or another)	9/7 1801 issued	Bond: Erastus Tippet

Names	Date Issue Or Celebrated	By Whom/ Security on Bonds
3812 WALLACE, JESSE et ux Rosanna M. Gamble	9/15 1838	By Fielding Pope, M.G.
3813 WALLACE, JESSE G. et ux Cynthia E. Pope	10/26 1847	By Isaac Anderson, P.N.P. Ch

WALLACE, JOEL m. Esther Houston (daughter of Jno. Houston,
b. 1726; d. 1798; m. in Ft. Craig; 1st, Sarah Todd,
family history.

3814 WALLACE, JOHN et ux Jean Blackburn	5/22 1798 issued	Bond: John Cowan
3815 WALLACE, JOHN et ux Hannah Hartsell	9/16 1830	By Isaac Anderson, P.N.P. Ch.
3816 WALLACE, SAMUEL et ux Martha Jane Wallace	10/15 1838	By Isaac Anderson, P.N.P. Ch.
3817 WALLACE, SAMUEL et ux Elizabeth Reeder	11/24 1842	By Isaac Anderson, P.N.P. Ch.
3818 WALLACE, WILLIAM et ux Polly Wallace	6/29 1799 issued	Bond: Gideon Blackburn
3819 WALLACE, WILLIAM et ux Polly Chamberlain	6/27 1810 issued	No returns
3820 WALLACE, WILLIAM et ux Margaret (Peggy) Chamberlain	10/17 1816	By Isaac Anderson, --

(I know from the family that these Chamberlain girls were sisters;
the men cousins.)

3821 WALLACE, WILLIAM et ux Mary Briant	2/16 1827	By J. Gillespie, J.P.
3822 WALLACE, WILLIAM et ux Mary Wallace	1/13 1846	By Isaac Anderson, P.N.P. Ch.

(We know she was widow of Matthew Wallace, his uncle; that
she was a Houston, sister to Gen. Sam.)

3823 WALLACE, WILLIAM et ux Mary S. Towne	10/25 1855	By Isaac Anderson, P.N.P. Ch.
3824 WALLACE, ZEBULON B. et ux Catherine L. Foute	5/13 1834	By Isaac Anderson, P.N.P. Ch.
3825 WALLER, HENRY et ux Elizabeth Yates	1/11 1830	By Wm. Fagg, L.D., Methodist Church
3826 WALLER, HENRY et ux Jane Cannon	9/28 1843	By John Morton, J.P.
3827 WALLS, JAMES et ux Betsy Cirkland (See Kirkland)	1/17 1822	By Saml George, J.P.
3828 WALLS, JNO. et ux Malinda O'Neal	7/27 1854	By Wm. M. Brickell, J.P.

Names	Date Issue Or Celebrated	By Whom/ Security on Bonds
3829 WALL, KINCHEN et ux Elizabeth Talent	12/27 1821	By Charles H. Warren, J.P.
3830 WELSH, JOHN et ux Patsy Burk	4/5 1825	By Arch'd Maxwell, J.P. (outside is Walsh)
3831 WARD, DANIEL et ux Sally Melton	12/29 1831	By Jeremiah K. Mosier, -- (He says groom "Word")
3832 WARD, DAVIS et ux Susannah Downey	10/27 1835	By Samuel Tulloch, J.P.
3833 WARD, DAVID N. et ux Elizabeth Lyle	12/28 1858	By Wm. M. Brickell, J.P.
3834 WARD, JOHN et ux Eliza Roach	8/25 1853	By Wm. M. Brickell, J.P.
3835 WAMACK, WM. C. et ux Elizabeth Barnes (outside is Warnack)	11/26 1849	By S. J. McReynolds, J.P.
3836 WARREN, BARTON S. et ux Evaline Singleton	1/16 1827	By Creed Fulton, L.D., M.E. Church
3837 WARREN, JOSHUA et ux Nancy Vanpelt	3/5 1827	By Charles H. Warren, J.P.
3838 WARREN, NOTLEY et ux Polly Vanpelt	3/14 1822	By David Adams, M.G.
3839 WARREN, ROBERT S. et ux Carolina A. Singleton	2/26 1839	By L. S. Marshall, --
3840 WARREN, STEPHEN et ux Ann Eliza Wiseman	9/27 1837	By Henry Hamil, J.P.
3841 WARREN, WILLIAM Y. et ux Mary Tarbet	5/2 1837	By Rev. J.Dyke, --
3842 WASHBURN, SHEROD et ux Mary Hutson	1/26 1800 issued	Bond: And'w Richey
3843 WATERS, ENOCH L. et ux Lizza Matilda Pruet	1/18 1852	By A. B. Gamble, J.P.
3844 WATTERS, JAMES et ux Mary Gamble	2/13 1850	By Christian Long, J.P.
3845 WATERS, WM. P. et ux Isabella Colter	8/14 1856	By S. J. McReynolds, J.P.
3846 WATERS, WILLIAM et ux Safronia Everett	10/28 1858	By W. W. Nuchols, J.P.
3847 WALKER, ANDERSON et ux Jane Ogle	1/9 1845	By W. R. Flinn, J.P.

*   See 3773

Names	Date Issue Or Celebrated	By Whom/ Security on Bonds
3848 WATKINS, JESSE et ux Martah A. Cunning- ham	10/27 1835	By A. Vance, M.G.
3849 WATKINS, WILLIAM et ux Margaret Byerly	3/21 1827	By J. Gillespie, J.P.
3850 WATSON, LEVAN or SEVAR et ux Cethain Nave (outside is Catt Nave) (He may be Lenoir Watson)	10/1 1801 issued	Bond: George Nave
3851 WATSON, WILLIAM et ux Elizabeth Fulker	11/27 1823	By Jame Turk, J.P.
3852 WAUGH, DAVID et ux Catherine Honiger	10/10 1826	"Complied with request within" James Turk, J.P.
3853 WAY, JAMES et ux Susan Danley (or Dauley)	11/6 1830	By A. C. Renfro, J.P.
3854 WAYMAN, CHARLES et ux Elizabeth O'Briant	1/10 1854	By Jas' Matthews, J.P.
3855 WAYMAN, SAMUEL et ux Nancy J. Parker	8/28 1848 issued	"by me on Thursday after the above date, Barry Abernathey, --"
3856 WEAR, DAVID M. et ux Lovicy Poland	10/10 1833	By Jeremiah K. Mosier, --
3857 WEAR, HUGH Jean Wier	1/26 1801 issued	Bond: James Wear
3858 WEAR, HUGH et ux Peggy Chandler	10/7 1825	By George Ekin, Methodist Minister
3859 WEAR, ISAAC D. et ux Miriam A. Blankin- ship	6/7 1849	By A. J. McGee, M.G.
3860 WEAR, JAMES et ux Martha Rankin	7/12 1802	Bond: John Waugh
3861 WEAR, JAMES et ux Winnifred Gardener	7/27 1824	By William Eagleton, M.G., Pastor of Bethel Church
3862 WEIR, JAMES et ux Reubica Perry	5/23 1847	By John P. Keny, J.P.
3863 WEIR, JOHN et ux Jenny Weir	6/3 1797 issued	Bond: Wm. Beard
3864 WEIR, JOHN et ux Polly L. Weir	6/3 1819	By And'w S. Morrison, V.D.M.
3865 WEIR, JOSEPH et ux Sally Martin	11/10 1819	By Jos. Alexander, J.P.
3866 WEAR, ROBERT et ux Margaret Wilkinson	4/14 1831	By Russell Bridwell, M.G.

Names	Date Issue Or Celebrated	By Whom/ Security on Bonds
3867 WEAR, ROBERT A. et ux Barbra R. Anderson	8/25 1858	By W. A. Lawson, M.G.
3868 WEAR, SAML et ux Polly Gellahar	9/30 1799 issued	Bond: Jacb. Johnson
3869 WEAR, SAML D. et ux Sarah Means	8/28 1848	By Isaac Anderson, P.N.P. Ch.
3870 WEAR, WILLIAM et ux Teressa Gardiner	5/18 1824	By Isaac Anderson, P.N.P. Ch.
3871 WEAR, WILLIAM et ux Cinthy McReynolds	1/8 1834	By Isaac Anderson, P.N.P. Ch.
3872 WEAR, WILLIAM T. et ux Rebecca Morgan	2/1 1851	By S. J. McReynolds, J.P.
3873 WEATHERS, GEORGE et ux Reeny Stephens	2/8 1820	By George Snider, M.G. of Baptist Order
3874 WEATHERS, HUGH et ux Maryan Williams	5/22 1821	By Wm. Williamson, J.P.
3875 WETHERS, JOHN et ux Nancy Sutten	12/25 1835	By Edmund Wayman, J.P.
3876 WEAVER, JOSEPH et ux Uny Massy	12/27 1826 issued	"Celebrated by me" Alexander Stewart, J.P.
3877 WEAVER, WILLIAM et ux Ann Adams	4/1 1830	By Wm. Williamson, J.P.
3878 WEBB, HENRY et ux Mary Freshour	12/18 1856	By N. Brewer, Esq.
3879 WEBB, JOHN T. et ux Nancy McCool	1/20 1825	By Charles H. Warren, --
3880 WEBB, MERRY et ux Fanny Couch	4/2 1835	By Samuel Tulloch, J.P.
3881 WEBB, MERRY B. et ux Betsy Yearout	12/7 1843	By Harvey H. C. Caruthers, J.P.
3882 WEBB, THOMAS et ux Nancy Samples	6/6 1821	"Executed"--S. George, J.P.
3883 WEBB, THOMAS et ux Polly Hill	10/27 1821	By Saml George, J.P.
3884 WEBB, WILLIS et ux Anna Vaught	7/16 1817	By Saml George, J.P.
3885 WEBSTER, JOHN B. et ux Margaret L. Foute	3/12 1833	By Darius Hoyt
3886 WEBSTER, WILLIAM et ux Nancy Holcomb	3/5 1835	By John Russom, M.G.
3887 WELBURN, WILLIAM et ux Rebecka Snider	1/14 1819	By George Snider, M.G. of the Baptist Order
3888 WELCH, JESSE et ux Winney Arrwood	12/8 1851	By Wm. M. Brickell, J.P.

Names	Date Issue Or Celebrated	By Whom/ Security on Bonds
3889 WELCKER, B. F. et ux Hester A. Ish	12/28 1852	By D. W. Amos, M.G.
3890 WELLS, GEORGE et ux Catharine Yearout	9/17 1828	By Wm. Turk, J.P.
3891 WELLS, HENRY et ux Elizabeth Greer	4/2 1848	By John Chambers, M.G.
3892 WEST, GILLESPY et ux Etna Thompson	10/21 1858	By A. Vance, M.G.
3893 WEST, ISAAC et ux Elizabeth Cotter	8/28 1855	By David Spradlin, J.P.
3894 WEST, JAMES et ux Mary A. Russell	3/30 1850	By S. J. McReynolds, J.P.
3895 WEST, JAMES et ux Mary Hill	4/4 1852	By Thos' M. Rooker, J.P.
3896 WEST, LEWIS et ux Martha Ragan	8/25 1836	By Andrew Vance, M.G. Bond: John Mcnabb (at top, McNab)
3897 WEST, S. F. et ux Nancy McTeer	8/29 1854	By James M. Tulloch, J.P.
3898 WESTMORELAND, EDWARD et ux Rebecca Hackney	3/17 1822	By Wm. Griffitts, J.P.
3899 WHEELER, ABEL et ux Charlotte Hinson	9/16 1834	By Edward Mitchell, J.P.
3900 WHEELER, GABRIEL et ux Sally Childres	8/28 1823	By E. Hitch, Esq.
3901 WHEELER, JACOB et ux Elizabeth Orman	7/17 1828	By William McTeer, J.P.
3902 WHEELER, JOHN et ux Milly Maze	8/2 1827	By George Ewing, J.P.
3903 WHEELER, JOURDAN et ux Elizabeth Johnson	12/28 1850	By S. J. McReynolds, J.P.
3904 WHEELER, LONGDON et ux Martha Kidd	2/14 1836	By Wm. Billue, M.G.
3905 WHEELER, LANDON et ux Polly Willix(s?)	7/27 1851	By John C. Martin, J.P.
3906 WHEELER, MORGAN et ux Elizabeth Crawley	12/25 1845	By Robt. Porter, J.P.
3907 WHEELER, NEWTON et ux Phebe Tipton	12/24 1843	By James Henry, J.P.
3908 WHEELER, SAMUEL et ux Peggy Cowan	9/3 1816	By John Waugh, J.P.
3909 WHEELER, THOMAS et ux Elizabeth Hitch	11/6 1834 issued	"by me--Wm. Billue, M.G."
3910 WHEELER, WILLIAM et ux Nancy Watson	9/2 1811 issued	"By me" S. George, --

Names	Date Issue Or Celebrated	By Whom/ Security on Bonds
3911 WHEELER, WILLIAM et ux Ann Phillips	10/2 1828	By George Ewing, J.P.
3912 WHITE, JONES et ux Polly Tool	7/20 1802 issued	Bond: John Gillespie Attest: J. Houston
3913 WHITE, AARON et ux Lydia Davis	4/18 1833	By Wm. McTeer, J.P.
3914 WHITE, ALSOP et ux Nancy E. Nuchols	10/9 1851	By C. Long, J.P.
3915 WHITE, JAMES W. et ux E. J. Alexander	12/21 1852	By James Matthews, J.P.
3916 WHITE, JAMES et ux Polly Tool	7/20 1802 issued	Bond: John Gillespie
3917 WHITE, LEWIS et ux Martha Madren (outside is Hadren)	1/8 1829	By Saml Hamill, J.P.
3918 WHITE, WILLIAM et ux Letty Bruner (outside "Lydia Brunier; either, may be Brewer)	7/6 1808 issued	No returns
3919 WHITE, WM. R. et ux Mary W. McGee	10/25 1819 issued	No returns
3920 WHITEHEAD, ALFRED et ux Jincey H. Hollaway	10/15 1840	By John Maxwell, J.P.
3921 WHITEHEAD, ANDREW J. et ux Mary J. Myrrh	12/26 1850	By Christian Long, J.P.
3922 WHITEHEAD, DAVID et ux Elizabeth Martin	3/22 1849	By Christian Long, J.P.
3923 WHITEHEAD, GRANVILLE W. et ux Martha J. Davis	9/13 1857	By Meadison Love, M.G.
3924 WHITEHEAD, SAMUEL et ux Margaret Thompson	8/23 1857	By James D. Sewell, M.G.
3925 WHITTENBERGER, A. C. et ux Orpha Boring	7/14 1847	By William Colburn, J.P.
3926 WHITTENBERGER, CHRISTO- PHER J. et ux Polly Whittenberge	9/22 1831	By Russell Birdwell, M.G., M.E.C.
3927 WHITTENBERGER, DANIEL et ux Salina Heath	6/12 1847	By Robert Porter, J.P.
3928 WHITTENBERGER, JEFFERSON T. et ux Nancy Tallant	9/9 1844	By W. Hendrix, --
3929 WHITTENBERGER, WILLIAM et ux Mary Robbinett	1/30 1796 issued	Bond: Jacob Meek
3930 WIGGINS, JAMES et ux Elizabeth Swearingin	8/14 1819 issued	No returns

Names	Date Issue Or Celebrated	By Whom/ Security on Bonds
3931 WILBURN, JOHN et ux Sarah Davis	8/27 1834	By W. Toole, --
3932 WILBURN, WILLIAM et ux Elender L. Clemons	4/8 1858	By R. E. Tedford, M.G.
3933 WILLOX, MOSES et ux Pariscity Brawner	7/25 1842	By W. Toole, J.P.
3934 WILCOX, WILEY et ux Caroline Delozier	10/15 1846	By John Tipton, J.P.
3935 WILHITE, HIRAM et ux Fanny Dawn (Dacer, Daver, Dacon)	4/24 1828	By Jone Cameron, J.P.
3936 WHILLHITE, JOHN et ux Margaret Rose	10/28 1840 issued	No returns Bond: William Wilson
3937 WILKINSON, JOHN et ux Elizabeth Willis	11/17 1806 issued	No returns
3938 WILKINSON, WM. et ux Elizabeth Cummings	7/17 1849	By Thos. M. Rooker, Bond: M. W. Barnhill
3939 WILLIAMS, ALEX et ux Mary McCampbell	9/5 1855	By J. M. Caldwell, M.G.
3940 WILLIAMS, ELISHA et ux Nancy Williams	3/4 1824	By Wm. Griffitts, J.P.
3941 WILLIAMS, CHARLES et ux Sarah Mitchell	2/14 1857	By Horace Foster, J.P.
3942 WILLIAMS, FREEBORN et ux Levicia Hays	3/28 1841	By Joseph A. Hutton, J.P.
3943 WILLIAMS, GEORGE et ux Nancy Hall	8/5 1822	By Hugh Bogle, J.P.
3944 WILLIAMS, HENRY et ux Bethesheba Janes	7/13 1802 issued	Bond: David Oatts and David Parkhill
3945 WILLIAMS, JAMES et ux Jane Roddy	10/20 1828	By E. Hitch, Esq.
3946 WILLIAMS, JAMES et ux Susannah Blair	11/12 1846	By W. R. Flinn, J.P.
3947 WILLIAMS, JAMES M. et ux Rachel Gamble	1/2 1845	By Wm. Billue, M.G.
3948 WILLIAMS, JOEL et ux Susannah Yearout	7/27 1829	By W. Toole, J.P.
3949 WILLIAMS, JOHN et ux Agness Bogle	9/7 1797 issued	Bond: Saml Bogle
3950 WILLIAMS, JOH(N?) D. et ux Polly Yearout	6/13 1833	By Thos. White, J.P.
3951 WILLIAMS, JOHN R. et ux Nancy Bogle	12/25 1828	By A. McGhee, -- Bond: Joseph Bogle
3952 WILLIAMS, JOSUA et ux Hannah Copeland	6/24 1819	By Wm. Griffitts, J.P.

Names	Date Issue Or Celebrated	By Whom/ Security on Bonds
3953 WILLIAMS, LEMUEL et ux Elizabeth White	2/19 1824	By A. B. Gamble, J.P.
3954 WILLIAMS, L. E. et ux M. J. Yearout	11/23 1854	By Jessee Kerr, Jr., J.P.
3955 WILLIAMS, NATHAN et ux Rachel Bonine (of Daniel)	8/9 1814 issued	"Solomnised by J. Gillespie, J.P."
3956 WILLIAMS, NEWTON et ux Jane W. Coope	8/8 1826	By Etbt' F. Sevier, M.G.
3957 WILLIAMS, NEWTON K. et ux Sarah Jones	6/19 1845	By Wm. Griffitts, J.P.
3958 WILLIAMS, NEIMROD et ux Nancy Nipper	3/17 1854	By W. W. Neal, M.G. M.E.C.So.
3959 WILLIAMS NICHOLAS et ux Olivia Nance	11/7 1819	By S. Douthit, M.G.
3960 WILLIAMS, MARTIN C. et ux Nancy C. Hodges	6/1 1844	By Fielding Pope, M.G.
3961 WILLIAMS, PRESLEY et ux Ann Morse	12/21 1833	By J. K. Mosier, Minister
3962 WILLIAMS, RICHARD et ux Sally Williams	7/25 1800 issued	Bond: Saml Bogle
3963 WILLIAMS, RICHARD et ux Minervy Criswell	1/1 1833	By Wm. McTeer, J.P.
3964 WILLIAMS, SAMUEL F. et ux Martha Maupin	7/24 1835	By Leeroy Noble, J.P.
3965 WILLIAMS, SAMUEL M. et ux Francis J. B. Jackson	12/30 1845	By Hiram Tarter (or Porter) P.M.E. Ch.
3966 WILLIAMS, WESTLEY et ux Eliza A. Wallace	6/27 1830	By Wm. Williamson, J.P.
3967 WILLIAMS, WILLIAM et ux Trophena Milsapps	5/15 1824 issued	"Solominised by me" Wm. Billue, M.G.
3968 WILLIAMS, WILLIAM et ux Sarah M. Steel	10/27 1836	By A. Vance, M.G.
3969 WILLIAMS, WM. et ux Darces Creswell	11/23 1847	By F. Pope, M.G.
1970 WILLIAMS, WM. B. et ux Barbary Ann Luster	6/25 1840	By Isaac Anderson, Pastor New Providence Church Bond: Andrew Bogle
3971 WILLIAMS, WILLIAM B. et ux Mary Ransbarger	11/30 1847	By Wm. Billue, M.G.
3972 WILLIAMS, WM. M. et ux Lucinda C. Bryant	9/1 1858	By H. Thompson, J.P.
3973 WILLIAMSON, ALEX'R et ux Polly Hamill	2/21 1833	By Jeremiah K. Mosier, M.G. of M.E.P. Ch.

Names	Date Issue Or Celebrated	By Whom/ Security on Bonds
3974 WILLIAMSON, JAMES et ux Malenia E. Cry	1/17 1850	By James M. Tulloch, J.P. Bond: John F. Garner
3975 WILLIAMSON, LAFAYETT et ux Sarah B. Hale	11/6 1841	By A. Vance, M.G. Pastor of Bakers Creek Church
3976 WILLIAMSON, LEWIS et ux Nancy A. Allen	8/30 1852	By Jesse Kerr, Jr., J.P.
3977 WILLIAMSON, WILLIAM et ux Rebecca Jones	10/23 1840	By John Dyke, Pastor of Unitia Church
3978 WILLIS, JACOB et ux Margret Majors	8/20 1798 issued	Bond: Armstand Thornhill
3979 WILLS, VANBUREN et ux Elizabeth Dullibanty	11/26 1858	By J. L. Sliermans, Pastor of Cattuelie Ch.
3980 WILSON, ANDREW J. et ux Sarah Kerr	10/21 1841	By Samuel Talloch, J.P.
3981 WILSON, ALEXANDER M. C. et ux Mary Jane Rankin	3/9 1837	By A. Vance, M.G.
3982 WILSON, BARCLEY W. et ux Mariah E. Saffell	10/7 1858	By Wm. H. Anderson, J.P.
3983 WILSON, GEORGE et ux Mary Moore	1/2 1837	By Wm. Hendrix, Esq.
3984 WILSON, GOULD et ux Martha Ann Cook	3/21 1839	By A. Vance, M.G.
3985 WILSON, GOLD et ux Tallitha C. McCasland	10/27 1859	By H. Thompson, J.P.
3986 WILSON, HUGH et ux Susy Shils	2/10 1801 issued	Bond: George Shields Test.: M. Mc. Wallace for James Houston
3987 WILSON, JAMES et ux Elizabeth Wier	11/10 1802 issued	Bond: Josiah Payne
3988 WILSON, JAMES et ux Jane Hutten	10/31 1839	By Andrew Vance, M.G.
3989 WILSON, JOHN et ux Peggy Jackson	10/2 1815 issued	No returns (back is covered with a written form of ceremoney)
3990 WILSON, JOHN et ux Polly McKamy	10/13 1818	By Wm. Gault, J.P.
3991 WILSON, JOHN D. et ux Eleaner Caldwell	11/8 1827	By William Eagleton, M.G.
3992 WILSON, JOHN et ux Caty Freshour	1/4 1819	"I solominsed the within, on date" (no signature)
3993 WILSON, JOHN et ux Mary Elledge	3/18 1840	By Lorenzo Donaldson, J.P.

Names	Date Issue Or Celebrated	By Whom/ Security on Bonds
WILSON, JOHN H. of B. C., Tenn. et ux Betsey Campbell of Grassy Valley--says Knox Reg. of 8/22	8/1 1820	By Rev. R. H. King
3994 WILSON, JOSEPH et ux Jenet Bayless	3/27 1817	By Alex B. Gamble, J.P.
3995 WILSON, JOSEPH et ux Ann Gault	12/9 1824	By Isaac Anderson, P.N.P. Ch.
3996 WILSON, JOSEPH et ux Lucinda Cook	8/10 1830	By Andrew Vance, M.G.
3997 WILSON, LISLE et ux Elizabeth Kerr	1/8 1841	By Andrew Vance, M.G. (outside is Lile Wilson)
3998 WILSON, NEWTON et ux Lavinia Frow	8/16 1832	By Darius Hoyt, M.G.
3999 WILSON, PHILIP et ux Peggy Dawn	6/3 1826 issued on 7/28	By Jas. Cameron, J.P.
4000 WILSON, ROBERT et ux Esther Carrethers	2/22 1814	By And'w Jackson, J.P.
4001 WILSON, WILLIAM et ux Isabella Carson	8/1 1833	By John D. Wilson, M.G.
4002 WILBERLY, MAJOR et ux Mary Sterling	6/29 1825	By Saml Hamill, J.P.
4003 WIMBERLEY, MARK et ux Adaline Hamontree	1/21 1847	By Samuel Tulloch, J.P.
4004 WINDER, NATHANIEL et ux Lucinda Daniels	1/16 1838	By Henry Hamil, J.P.
4005 WINTER, STEPHEN et ux Mary Ann Carter	2/14 1842	By J. Dyke, Pastor of Unitia Church
4006 WINTER, STERLING et ux Dicy Birdwell	1/12 1834	By J.H.R.G. Gardner, M.G.
4007 WINTERS, SAMUEL et ux Polly Jackson	10/5 1832 issued 9/28	By John Ferguson, J.P.
4008 WISEMAN, ABSOLOM et ux Nancy Davis	10/7 1831	By A. C. Renfro, J.P.
4009 WISEMAN, ALBERT et ux Sinah Ormond	11/9 1822	By Samuel Douthit, E.M.E. Ch. A.D.
4010 WISEMAN, WM. G. et ux Polly Kennedy	12/30 1818 issued	No returns
4011 WOLF, CORNELIUS et ux Elizabeth Wheeler	8/16 1849	By Adam Haun, J.P.
4012 WOLF, JAMES et ux Isabella Russell	3/12 1853	By C. Long, J.P.
4013 WOLF, JAMES et ux Margaret Brooks	11/10 1858	By George Caldwell, J.P.

Names	Date Issue Or Celebrated	By Whom/ Security on Bonds
4014 WOLF, MARCUS et ux Catharine Furgason	11/18 1844	By John Clark, J.P.
4015 WOODARD, CHESLEY et ux Elizabeth Boyd	7/18 1846	By Robert Shields, J.P.
4016 WOODARD, JEREMIAH et ux Charlotte Maroon	2/14 1818 issued	No returns
4017 WOODARD, JOHN et ux Jane Williams	11/28 1826 issued	No returns
4018 WOODDY, JAMES et ux Mary Bane	9/24 1817 issued	No returns
4019 WOODY, JOHN et ux Abbe Turner	4/13 1818 issued	No returns
4020 WOODY, JOHN et ux Jane Forister	8/16 1838	By John Russom, M.G.
4021 WOODEN, HENRY et ux Polly Hathway	9/14 1822	By Samuel Douthit, E.M.E. Ch.
4022 WOODEN, JOHN et ux Susannah Forester	7/16 1818	No returns
4023 WOODEN, THOMAS et ux Malinda Ann Rains	10/23 1831	By Leeroy Noble, J.P.
4024 WOODEN, WILLIAM et ux Jane Cartwright	12/12 1829	By S. Douthit, E.M.E. Ch.
4025 WOODS, ALFRED N. et ux Margaret Garons	9/13 1823	By Wm. Gault, J.P.
4026 WOODS, CHRISTOPHER A. (son Samuel Woods of him is Chas. Woods, Chas. Will.) et ux Jane Thompson	10/5 1819	By And'w S. Morrison, --
4027 WOODS, ISAAC et ux Elizabeth Wetherspoon	9/7 1803 issued	No returns
4028 WOODS, JOHN et ux Eliza Young	7/18 1818 issued	"celebrated by me" James Turk, --
4029 WOODS, JOSEPH B. DR. of Morganton et ux Nancy P. Mayo Knox. Reg. of 7/27 1819	7/19 1819	By And'w S. Morrison, V.D.M.
4030 WOODS, LEONARD et ux Jane M. Ewing	11/4 1834	By Phillips Wood, M.G.
4031 WOODS, PATRICK et ux Jenney Hanna	6/12 1799 issued	Bond: Robert Hanna
4032 WOODS, ROBERT et ux Mary King	7/15 1828	By Jas. Cumming, Tra- veling Elder M.E. Ch.
4033 WOODS, ROBERT et ux Louisa Powell	9/24 1854	By Curran Lemons, J.P.

Names	Date Issue Or Celebrated	By Whom/ Security on Bonds
4034 WOODS, SAML T. et ux Margaret Cook	12/29 1853	By Jno. McClain, J.P.
4035 WOODS, WILLIAM et ux Polly Brown	2/25 1821 issued (or 1825)	No returns
4036 WOODS, WILLIAM WOODFORD et ux Patsy Houston	2/16 1826	By Isaac Anderson, P.N.P. Ch.
4037 WOOLSEY, ISREAL et ux Martha E. Taylor	12/25 1851	By F. Pope, M.G.
4038 WOOLSEY, JAMES et ux Frances E. Taylor	3/2 1852	By William Colburn, J.P.
4039 WORMACK, CHARLES et ux Nancy Fields	9/26 1804	By S. George, J.P.
4040 WORSHAM, JEREMIAH et ux Jean King	9/13 1802 issued	Bond: Thos. Simpson
4041 WRIGHT, A. H. et ux Mary Farr	12/21 1854	By John McClain, J.P.
4042 WRIGHT, ALFRED L. et ux Jane Howard	12/31 1835	By Edmund Wayman, J.P.
4043 WRIGHT, DEVAUIX G. et ux Nancy J. Walker	5/13 1852	By Ralph E. Tedford, M.G.
4044 WRIGHT, ISAAC et ux Susan Brown	4/18 1833	By Joseph Vanpelt, M.G.
4045 WRIGHT, JNO. Q. et ux Darcus J. Struton	3/2 1856	By David Spradlin, J.P.
4046 WRIGHT, JONATHAN et ux Sarah King	12/13 1831	"Executed by me" (name undeciphered)
* See 3082		
4047 WRIGHT, SAMUEL M. et ux Elizabeth Sesler	3/12 1862	By J. A. Houston, J.P.
4047 WRIGHT, WILIE B. et ux Elizabeth Henry	9/21 1838	By James Henry, J.P.
4048 WRIGHT, WILLIE B. et ux Sarah L. Singleton	3/15 1842	By T. K. Harmar, M.G.
4049 WRIGHT, WILLIAM E. et ux Elizabeth A. James	2/4 1858	By J. S. Craig, M.G.
4050 WRIGHT, WILLIAM H. et ux Ann Henderson	8/17 1841	By Isaac Anderson, P.N.P. Ch.
4051 WRINKLE, EMERSON 35 ux Sarah McNabb	4/2 1857	By W. A. Lawson, M.G.
4052 WRINKLE, JACOB L. et ux Narcissa B. Henderson	12/23 1858	By W. A. Lawson, M.G.

Names	Date Issue Or Celebrated	By Whom/ Security on Bonds
4053 WYLEY, JAMES et ux Mary Whittenberger	1/15 1828	By Leeroy Noble, J.P.

(It is claimed his 1st wife was a Fuquay; one says issue; another says no issue. See 1260)

Names	Date Issue Or Celebrated	By Whom/ Security on Bonds
4054 WILEY, JNO. C. et ux Mary A. Dawson	9/17 1856	By W. W.Bayless, J.P.
4055 YANDLE, HENRY et ux Cyntha Dyer	3/1 1843	By Larkin Thomson, J.P.
4056 YARBER, WILLIAM et ux Sally Coulson	12/28 1829	By Leeroy Noble, J.P.
4057 YARBER, WILLIAM et ux Sarah Sherrel	5/15 1841	By Lorenzo Donaldson, J.P.
4058 YARNELL, ISAAC A. et ux Rebecca B. Bonham	8/11 1836	By A. McGhee, --
4059 YEAROUT, BENJAMIN et ux Drusilla Early	8/17 1848	By Jno. S. Craig, M.G.
4060 YEAROUT, I. N. et ux Isabella R. Frow	12/28 1852	By J. S. Craig, M.G.
4061 YEAROUT, JOHN et ux Patsy Roulston	10/10 1816	By Jos. Alexander, J.P.
4062 YEAROUT, JOSEPH et ux Joanna Simerly	4/25 1850	By S. J. McReynolds, J.P.
4063 YEAROUT, SAMUEL et ux Rusinah Early	9/12 1837	By Isaac Anderson, P.N.P. Ch.
4064 YEAROUT, WM. R. et ux Myry M. McCully	5/22 1856	By John S. Craig, M.G.
4065 YEATS, CHARLES et ux Mary McMullen	5/22 1855	By John M. Caldwell, M.G.
4066 YATES, SAMUEL et ux Elizabeth Kinneman	4/13 1837	By John Key, J.P.
4067 YOUNG, CLAIBORN et ux Mary Russle	10/2 1827	By Isaac Anderson, P.N.P. Ch.
4068 YOUNG, JAMES et ux Sally Wade	3/14 1816 issued	No returns
4069 YOUNG, JAMES C. et ux Dorothy Jane Yearout	2/19 1841	By A. C. Montgomery, J.P.
4070 YOUNG, JEREMIAH et ux Rutha Boring	3/29 1827	By Charles H. Warren, --
4071 YOUNG, LEWIS R. et ux Sarah Kelly	9/14 1848	By S. J. McReynolds, J.P.
4072 YOUNG, NATHAN M. et ux Mary A. Clemens	1/24 1855	By Saml Pride, J.P.

Names	Date Issue Or Celebrated	By Whom/ Security on Bonds
4073 YOUNG, ROBERT J. et ux Martha J. Young	2/17 1842	By A. C. Montgomery, J.P.
4074 YOUNG, THOMAS J. et ux Rebeccah R. Houston	7/21 1831	By Darius Hoyt, M.G.
4075 YOUNT, ALEXANDER et ux Delary Whaly	4/11 1843	By John Tipton, J.P.
4076 YOUNT, DANIEL et ux Rachel Rogers	1/14 1852	By Saml L. Yearout, J.P.
4077 YOUNT, LARKIN et ux Eliza Austin	6/4 1829	By William Toole, J.P.
4078 YOUNT, PETER et ux Nancy Shook	9/23 1819	By Alex B. Gamble, J.P.
4079 YOUNT, PETER et ux Mary Pain	3/29 1832	By Thos. White, J.P.
4080 DYER, DANIEL et ux Margaret Cope	5/22 1856	By William Kerr, J.P.
* See 1047, 4080		
4081 CAUGHORN, JOHN W. et ux Hanna Johnston (as groom signed: Clerk spelled "Mlaughen")	3/18 1802 issued	Bond: Robert Pearce
* See 644, 2463		
4082 SAFFELL, CHARLES P. et ux Mary E. Mc.(Lain?) Gamble	5/19 1849	Bond: F. A. Dyer (Felix A. Dyer, by Clerk)
* See 3224		
4083 -------, MATTHEW et ux Rebeckah Gawes (She may be Gaeves, Gawer, Gowes, Gower; Groom's name left out)	4/13 1822	By Samuel Douthit, --

MINUTES OF THE FRIENDS (QUAKER'S) MEETING HOUSE

MINUTES FROM 1808 TO 1880

These do not appear in County Records, lost, or never made:

Names	Date Issue Or Celebrated	By Whom/ Security on Bonds
BEALS, JACOB et ux Kezia Lewis	1/1 1848	
BOVINE, DAVID son of Daniel & Mary (Copeland) Bovine et ux Prudence Williams, daughter of William & Rachel Williams	7/7 1808	
ADAMSON, SETH son of John & Mary Adamson et ux Mary, daughter of Thomas and Margaret Jones	3/8 1826	
ELLIS, SOLOMON son of Jacob & Elizabeth Ellis et ux Asenath Jones, daughter of James & Rebecca Jones	3/7 1846	
HACKNEY, THOMAS son of John & Rebecca (Laughlin) Hacaney et ux Elizabeth Jones, daughter of Francis & A-n Jones (Another dec'd. says "Lauthlin")	8/11 1811	
HAMMER, JESSE son of Elisha & Rachel Hammer et ux Lucinda Hackney, daughter of Aaron & Jane Hackney	4/3 1841 near this date	
HAMMER, SETH son of Elisha & Rachel Hammer et ux Elizabeth Hackney, daughter of Aaron & Jane Hackney	11/6 1841	
HINSHAW, DAVID son of Uriah & Mary Hinshaw et ux Elizabeth Lewis, daughter of Henry & Kezia Lewis	10/11 1843	
HINSHAW, URIAH son of William & Margaret Hinshaw et ux Rebecca Allen, daughter of James & Elizabeth Allen	11/3 1838	

Minutes of the Friends (Quaker's) Meeting House Cont'd.

Names	Date Issue Or Celebrated	By Whom/ Security on Bonds
HAMMER, JOHN son of Aaron & Mary Hammer et ux Narcissa Lewis, daughter of Henry & Kezia Lewis	4/4 1846	
JONES, DAVID son of James & Rebecca Jones et ux Rebecca P. Jones, daughter of James & Sarah Jones	6/6 1850	
JONES, FRANCIS son of Francis & Ann Jones et ux Hannah Lee, daughter of Ephriam & Sarah Lee	12/5 1825	
JONES, OBEDIAH son of James & Rebecca Jones et ux Martha Crumley, daughter of Abraham & Elizabeth Crumley	8/6 1842	
JONES, THOMAS son of Thomas & Jane Jones et ux Mary Williams, daughter of Thomas & Arabella Durham	7/10 1811	
JONES, WILLIAM son of Samuel & Joanna (Allen) Jones et ux Ruth Lee, daughter of Ephriam & Sarah Lee (later a Huchall) (Parents of Ignatius)	10/5 1842	
MARSHALL, ELI son of John & Hannah Marshall et ux Rebecca Jones, daughter of Joseph & Elizabeth Jones	12/10 1856	
MORGAN, DAVID son of William & Catherine Morgan et ux Lucinda Lee, daughter of Ephriam & Sarah Lee (D.M. & L.L. uncle & aunt of Ignatius Jones)	2/7 1846	
MORGAN, OBEDIAH son of Thomas & Ruth Morgan et ux Ann Jones, daughter of Thomas & Margaret Jones	11/4 1820	
WILLIAMS, NATHAN son of William & Rachel Williams et ux Charity Williams, daughter of David & Tabitha Williams	8/5 1812	

(Note: In parentheses ( ) added by family telling W.E.P. of the facts.)

From Year 1795 to 1854, inclusive.

I, WILLIAM EDMUND PARHAM, of Maryville, Blount County, Tennessee,
218 Bryan Street, aged past Seventy-Two years! do hereby certify, affirm
and declare that I have carefully hunted for, and copied each and all
the License or Bonds that I could find from the year 1795 to the and
including the year 1859. These were in the old files, I did not com-
pare from 1854 to close of 1859 with the recorded Book of License, as
that is the first Book record we have, but simply the papers as they
could be found. I further certify that I have tried to follow the
spelling of the Clerk or go by the name as the party may have signed on
the Bond or that the Clerk or person who performed the Marriage Ceremony may have changed too when writing the endorcement(sic) on the
License. The Marriage License or bonds in many instances were muti-
lated, stained, faded or in such handwriting as to be hard to be cor-
rectly copied, have done the best I could, and claim to be able to de-
cipher many difficult handwritings. I have been induced to do this
work by the Soceity of the D.A.R. women of Maryville and Blount County,
and because of the Historic Value of these unrecorded papers. Many I
know ere lost in the fires of our Court Houses in 1879 and again in
1906, and no doubt some were lost during the War of 1861-5. In fact
I have seen our License unreturned and in private homes, that should
be in the files. Some that are "Bonds" only, I have seen affidavets
(sic) of record that they "were married," as sworn to by the Party who
performed the Ceremony. I was in hopes that the County would make and
keep a Copy in their care, but so far they have failed to so do.

　　　　Sworn to and signed as on 204 pages (ref. manuscript) and numbered from 1 to 855 on and up to page 42, then #861 to and including
#4083. In the first 42 pages, I found errors in Alphabetical arraing-
ments(sic) and Duplications so rewrote from #25 to 43 over and have
also a page 33½ in so that in fact there are 205 Typewritten Pages,
with 20 couples to the page. This is on page 205 as now numbered.
Finished on Oct. 22, 1932, Begun on Sept. 16, 1932.

　　　　　　　　　　　　　(Signed)　WILL E. PARHAM
　　　　　　　　　　　　　_____

Sworn to before me as correct and as above set out in the Statement
added for the Entire Copies as contained in pages "One to and including
two Hundred and Five."
　　　　This the 29 day of Octo. 1932.

　　　　　　　　　　　　　(Signed)　A. E. CRUZ(?)
　　　　　　　　　　　　　_____
　　　　　　　　　　　　　Notary Public in and for the County
　　　　　　　　　　　　　of Blount, State of Tennessee

My Commission Expires on 4/36 (1933).

BLOUNT COUNTY MARRIAGE LICENSES OR BONDS FOUND OF RECORD
FROM 1795 to 1854-60 SUPPLEMENT

Names	Date Issue Or Celebrated	By Whom/ Security on Bonds
ALEXANDER, J. H. et ux M. F. McCampbell	5/9 1860 issued	No returns Bond: J. F. Anderson
ALLEN, JNO. et ux Ellen Job	2/23 1860	By J. A. Houston, J.P. Bond: Jas. S. Carnes
AMERINE, GEORGE et ux M. J. Rowan	11/7 1861	By L. Wear, J.P. Bond: Elijah Hatcher
AMERINE, JOHN et ux Jane Walker	12/5 1861	By John Gamble, J.P. Bond: J. C. Glass
ANDERSON, M. M. et ux Sarah L. Chapman	2/8 1863	By R. E. Tedford, M.G. Bond: D. G. Wright
ANDERSON, R. H. et ux Malinda Keene	1/24 1861	By Sam Griffitts, J.P. Bond: Lea Thompson
ARMSTRONG, JAMES G. et ux Hannah C. Brown	10/22 1862	By Sam Tullock, J.P. Bond: R. R. Bowerman
BEDGETT, CAMPBELL et ux Emmeline Tipton	3/6 1861	By H. T. Singleton, J.P. Bond: H. T. Singleton
BAILEY, JAMES et ux Nancy Graves	6/23 1864	By Solomon Farmer, J.P. Bond: Wm. H. Keeble
BAKER, JOHN et ux Phebe Smith	5/29 1862	By John Gamble, J.P. Bond: Jacob Smith
BAKER, SAMUEL et ux Arlena Snider	1/24 1862	By E. S. Wilkinson, J.P. Bond: A. C. Long
BARKER, THOMAS et ux Sarah Privett	11/28 1861	By Richard Nuchols, J.P. Bond: W. R. Long
BASS, JOHN et ux Mary Cope	2/7 1862	By Joseph Bruner, J.P. Bond: Edmund Underwood
BATES, JOHN A. et ux Mary T. Branon	2/13 1864 issued	"Celebrated" Bond: T. Sanderson
BEALES, JAMES F. et ux Mary Allen	12/31 1863	By Stephen Matthews, J.P. Bond: S. L. Greer
BELL, ANDREW et ux Polly Ann Hooper	1/18 1864	By Joseph Bruner, J.P. Bond: Street Lain
BELT W. W. et ux D. J. Dyer	8/15 1861	By W. W. Bayless, J.P. Bond: R. C. Belt
BEST, M. C. et ux Letitia Hanay	12/29 1864	By Spencer Henry, M.G. Bond: Wm. Morton
BIRD, JAMES M. et ux Martha Wear	10/24 1863	By James D. Lawson, M.G. Bond: John McCampbell

Names	Date Issue Or Celebrated	By Whom/ Security on Bonds
BLAIR, JAMES et ux Sarah A. Frost	6/14 1860	By A. Templeton, M.G. Bond: A. Ish by J. E. McCoy
BLAIR, THOMAS J. et ux Phibe C. Walker	12/18 1861	By John Gamble, J.P. Bond: W. A. Walker
BLANKINSHIP, GILBERT et ux Eliza Jane Brient	2/3 1864 issued	"Celebrated" Bond: John Moore
BLANKINSHIP, JOHN et ux Sarah A. Edmondson	5/17 1860	By Spencer Henry, M.G. Bond: Isaac Taylor
BLEVENS, CLARK et ux Matitoa W. Land	2/5 1865	By Sam F. Bell, J.P. Bond: James P. Raulston
BOEMAN, CHARLES W. et ux Matilda Keller	12/24 1863	By Solomon Farmer, J.P. Bond: Spen. Donaldson
BOLINGER, WM. F. et ux Nancy C. Headrich	9/26 1861	By A. Boyd, J.P. Bond: Thos. Pickens
BORDEN, WILLIAM et ux Malvina Kite	2/14 1861	By Samuel T. Woods, J.P. Bond: Peter Headrick
BOWERMAN, ISAAC W. et ux Elizabeth Purkeypile	1/15 1865	By G. W. Miser, J.P. Bond: S. W. Colburn
BOYD, J. C. et ux S. J. McCullock	7/26 1860	By R. E. Tedford, M.G. Bond: Wm. H. Lyle
BRANHAM, G. A. et ux Nancy Ann Fagg	5/19 1862	By R. Nuchols, J.P. Bond: Alsup White
BRANNUM, JULIAN et ux Hannah M. Bryant	2/5 1865	By Isaac Stevens, M.G. Bond: S. P. Rowan
BREWER, JAMES C. et ux Sarah Jane Smith	3/23 1861	By H. S. Bright, J.P. Bond: Levi D. Brewer
BRIANT, A. B. et ux Rebecca J. Hays	12/10 1861	By J. F. Woodfin, M.G. Bond: A. P. Wiggs
BRICKELL, WM. M. et ux Jane Ballinger	2/24 1863 issued	No returns Bond: J. B. Brown
BRIGHT, J. E. et ux Mary A. Wayman	12/29 1861	By Joseph Bruner, J.P. Bond: H. Key
BRITT, JACKSON et ux Rebecca Boring	4/11 1863	By R. Nichols, J.P. Bond: Crawford Hall
BROADY, W. C. et ux Nancy J. McReynolds	9/20 1860	By R. E. Tedford, M.G. Bond: McConnell (Torn)
BRYANT, G. H. et ux Amanda Hamill	5/23 1860	By S. T. Woods, J.P. Bond: Best (Torn)
BRYANT, ROBERT et ux Susan Caroline King	8/12 1864	By F. Pope, M.G. Bond: (Torn)
BURCHFIELD, SAMUEL et ux Evaline Davis	1/27 1862 issued	No returns Bond: Curran Lemon

Names	Date Issue Or Celebrated	By Whom/ Security on Bonds
CABE, LUCAS et ux Veny Beathie	2/18 1865	By W. C. Conner, J.P. Bond: R. P. Bowerman
CAGLE, GEORGE et ux Mary G. Simmons	8/17 1862	By Solomon Farmer, J.P. Bond: John Clark
CALDWELL, I. N. et ux R. F. Anderson	6/18 1861 issued	No returns Bond: W. C. McCampbell
CALDWELL, R. R. et ux Ellen C. Moore	3/3 1863	By Samuel Tulloch, J.P. Bond: Sam'l Tulloch
CALOR, BRAXTON et ux Nancy C. Walker	11/28 1862	By Frederick Emmett, J.P. "celebrated" Bond: G. Freshour
CAMPBELL, JOHN S. et ux Elizabeth J. Henry	8/1 1860	"Celebrated in due time by A. Vance" Bond: W. G. Henry
CARNES, JOHN B. et ux Ann C. F. McKenzie	11/29 1864	By A.J. Greer, M.G. Bon : R. P. Bowerman
CARROLL, JAMES E. et ux Arty Jane Fortner	7/25 1864	By George Goodby, M.G. Bond: F. M. Hood
CARRINGER, MARION et ux Pheobe Millsaps	7/25 1860	By H. Heartsell, J.P. Bond: Clayton Farlowe
CATES, C. T. et ux Martha V. Kidd	12/24 1862	By J. F. Woodfin, M.G. Bond: Sam Toole
CATLETT, A. C. et ux Mary E. Hitch	9/29 1861	By W. M. Burnett, M.G. Bond: James Hitch
CAYLOR, GEORGE et ux Elizabeth Brickey	4/22 1864	By Frederick Emmett, J.P. "celebrated" Bond: T. J. Freshour
CAYLOR, WM. et ux R. J. Dunn	3/25 1862 issued	No returns Bond: Jam. Walker
CHAMBERS, JOHN et ux Prudent Mitchell	3/6 1864	By Daniel H. Emmett, J.P. Bond: Elijah Nelson
CHAMBERS, T.D.A. et ux Eliza McClung	1/21 1864	By T. H. Russell, M.G. Bond: H. L. Houk
CHAPMAN, A. P. et ux Sarah Vance	1/12 1865	By A. Vance, M.G. Bond: W. C.Humphries John G. Alexander
CHAPMAN, ROBT. E. et ux Sarah Haire	4/5 1860 issued	No returns Bond: S. A. Humphrey
CHILDRESS, WM. et ux Mary S. Lebow	3/18 1862	By Gransfield Taylor, M.G. Bond: D. E. Lebow
CLARK, P. H. et ux Margaret J. Dearmond	3/22 1860	By Wm. Billue, M.G.

Names	Date Issue Or Celebrated	By Whom/ Security on Bonds
CLEMONS, HENRY et ux Adeline Reid	7/24 1860	By John McCully, J.P. Bond: William Ashley
CLEMONS, S. H. et ux Mary Henry	10/9 1861	By W. T.Dowell, M.G. Bond: J. B. Carnes
CLINE, DAVID et ux Rachael Carr	5/14 1863	By James Taylor, J.P. Bond: Moses Martin
COGGIN, W. M. et ux Isabella Gillespie	3/24 1864	By C. C.Newman Bond: David Lamon
COLLINS, R. A. et ux Mary E. Craig	10/17 1861	By W. W. Bayless, J.P. Bond: D. A. Steele
COLTER, ANDREW et ux Hester Ann Ragan	7/30 1863	By John Gamble, J.P. Bond: Elias Hitch
COOPER, J. D. et ux Araminta Anthony	8/1 1861	By C. Lemons, J.P. Bond: D. D. Foute
COSTON, WM. T. et ux Sarah A. Taylor	7/2 1861	By A. Vance, M.G. Bond: S. Matthews
COX, JOHN P. et ux Margaret Ann	2/9 1865	By Robert H. Culton, Bond: W. R. Henry
COY, J. S. et ux R. C. Mead	3/20 1860	By John S. Craig, M.G. Bond: B. W. Toole
CRAIG, JOHN et ux Nelina Callina Bicknell	8/29 1861	By A. Vance, M.G. Bond: R. A. Collins
CRASS, JOSIAS et ux Celia A. Roddy	3/6 1860 issued	No returns Bond: Isaac Taylor
CROSS, JOSEPH T. et ux Sarah Fultner	3/19 1861	By W. T. Dowell, M.G. Bond: James A. Howard
CUMMINGS, JACOB et ux Josephine Duncan	7/7 1864	By W. C.Conner, J.P. Bond: F. M. Hood
CUMMINGS, JAMES et ux Rebecca Headrick	1/31 1861	By A. Boyd, J.P. Bond: Phillip Cummings
CURTIS, JOHN et ux Eliza Grear	9/14 1862	By Samuel Pride, J.P. Bond: J. W.Hannum
DAILEY, PLEASENT et ux Sarah Hackett	10/15 1864	By Wm. H. Anderson, J.P. Bond: Robert Gibbs
DAVIS, C. B. et ux Margarett Everett	10/24 1863 issued	No returns Bond: J. W. Ogle
DAVID, JOHN et ux Martha E. Linkenfeltner	9/3 1863	By Wm. Brickell, M. Bond: H. B. McClure
DAVIS, JOHN et ux Jane Blair	12/27 1864	By Robert H. Culton, J.P. Bond: James E. Vaughn
DAVIS, MITCHELL et ux Sarah A. Runion	4/17 1862	By J. F. Woodfin, M.G. Bond: J. B. Morris

Names	Date Issue Or Celebrated	By Whom/ Security on Bonds
DAVIS, P. S. et ux Sarah A. Cannon	3/4 1861	By George Caldwell, J.P. Bond: John D. Headrick
DAVIS, SAMUEL C. et ux Sarah H. McMurry	3/2 1863 issued	No returns Bond: Henry Brakebill
DAVIS, THOMAS et ux Sarah J. Bird	9/28 1860 issued	No returns Bond: Davi Davis
DAVIS, WILLIAM et ux Sarah E. Snider	10/12 1862	By Wm. H. McNeeley, J.P. Bond: Lavender Bird
DELOZIER, T. L. et ux Semantha Spillman	1/2 1865	By James Henry, J.P. Bond: J. M. Henry
DEWBERRY, A. S. et ux Jane Hughs	7/20 1861	By S. T. Woods, J.P. Bond: S. K. Belt
DICKSON, J. B. et ux Rachel O. Cummings	1/7 1864	By A. Vance, M.G. Bond: John McConnell
DIXON, DAVID H. et ux Eliza Pryor	8/18 1864	By H. H. Gamble, J.P. Bond: Jeff. Phelps
DIXON, THOMAS et ux Martha Tipton	12/4 1864	By H. H. Gamble, J.P. Bond: George Graham John Murrin
DOAK, S.C.N. et ux Sally A. Warren	2/16 1865	By James Parks, M.V.D. Bond: J. B. Boyd
DONALDSON, SPENCER et ux Elizabeth Kidd	7/23 1860 issued	No returns Bond: James Donaldson
DONALDSON, SPENCER et ux Ann E. Ambrester	1/23 1862	By Solomon Farmer, J.P. Bond: R. J. Davis
DOOPS, GEORGE et ux Nancy Harper	2/20 1862	By A. Boyd, J.P. Bond: A. J. Doops
DUNCAN, R. J. et ux Isabella J. Greer	12/20 1860	By David Strange, M.G. Bond: J. C. McConnell
DUNLAP, SAMUEL P. et ux S. C. Davis	8/11 1861	By A. Boyd, J.P. Bond: D. S. Johnson
DUNN, WILLIAM et ux Martha Kallar	4/9 1864 issued	"celebrated" By Frederic Emmet, J.P. Bond: J. W. Steele
DURHAM, J. et ux T. Burchfield	3/20 1862	By H. S. Bright, J.P. Bond: G. J. Ward
DUVAL, BENJAMIN et ux Nancy Clitheroe	2/26 1865	By Samuel Tullock, J.P. Bond: John Scott
DYER, ALFRED et ux Myra Henry	8/2 1864	By W. C.Conner, J.P. Bond: P. D. Hammontree
DYER, MARTIN S. et ux Harriett A. Howard	8/5 1862	By J. A. Houston, J.P. Bond: Wm. Gourley

Names	Date Issue Or Celebrated	By Whom/ Security on Bonds
EAKIN, H. M. et ux Margaret C. Shadden	10/30 1860	By David V. Strange, D.M.C. Bond: John E. Shadden
EDMONDSON, BENJAMIN et ux M. E. Tallent	3/17 1862	No returns Bond: John D. Jones
ELLEDGE, ANDREW et ux Rebecca Wilson	9/8 1863	By Solomon Farmer, J.P. Bond: Peter Summey
ELLIDGE, JAMES et ux Mary A. Spradlin	12/14 1862	By Samuel Tullock, J.P. Bond: W. A. Walker
ELLIOTT, JAMES et ux Mary Stuart	4/13 1864 issued	"celebrated" Bond: T. N. Ellis
EMMETT, A. W. et ux Elizabeth Kinnaman	10/7 1861	By M. Kounts, J.P. Bond: J. H. Emmett
EMMETT, PINLY J. M. et ux Laura J. Dunn	7/1 1860	By S. Wear, J.P. Bond: J. H. Emmett
ENDSLEY, WM. H. H. et ux Mary J. Brackett	5/14 1862 issued	No returns Bond: John J. Greer
EVERETT, JOHN et ux Elizabeth Robins	2/21 1865	By Mark B. May, Min. Bond: E. W. Sanderson
EVERETT, R. E. et ux Mary A. Davis	8/26 1860	By S. Wear, J.P. Bond: Vincent Everett
EVERETT, SIGNER et ux M. J. Sherrell	12/27 1860	By A. J. Wilson, J.P. Bond: J. A. Davis
EVERETT, WILLIAM et ux Margaret J. Plemons	10/16 1860	By E. S. Wilkinson, J.P. Bond: Andrew J. Smith
FAGG, A. M. et ux R. L. Peterson	12/11 1860	By Dan'l Emmett, J.P. Bond: R. L. Peterson
FAGG, ISAAC et ux S. S. Russell	5/31 1861 issued	No returns Bond: Isaac Russell
FANE, WILLIAM et ux Sarah Bryant	9/15 1864	By Stephen Matthews, J.P. Bond: John Edmondson Gilbert Blankinship
FARMER, JOSEPH et ux Sarah A. Henry	6/20 1861	By P. H. Reed, M.G. Bond: Jas. H. Sherrell
FEAZELL, WM. et ux Mary Shields	11/29 1861	"celebrated by me" (No signature) Bond: James Sparks
FLOYD, ABRAHAM et ux Isabella Snider	8/2 1864	By F. Pope, M.G. Bond: D. N. Broyles
FORRESTER, WM. T. et ux Mary Caldwell	11/29 1860	By A. Boyd, J.P. Bond: J. B. Duncan
FRESHOUR, T. J. et ux Catherine Kalor	3/17 1861	By S. Wear, J.P. Bond: Henry Webb

Names	Date Issue Or Celebrated	By Whom/ Security on Bonds
FROW, JOHN R. et ux Martha Cochran	9/22 1862	By T. J. Lamar, M.G. Bond: F. M. Hood
FROW, ROBT. A. et ux Susan T. Culton	4/5 1860	By John S. Craig, M.G. Bond: Thos. A. Frow
FROW, T. J. et ux M H. Dearmond	9/5 1861	By W. T.Dowell, M.G. Bond: I. N. Yearout
FULKERSON, F. D. et ux E. J. Barnhill	2/25 1862	By A. Vance, M.G. Bond: W. C. Conner
GARDNER, ALEXANDER et ux Susan M. Reeder	10/13 1864	By John M. Caldwell, M.G. Bond: Thos. Sanderson
GARDNER, DAVID et ux Margaret Wheeler	4/30 1860	By H. Heartsell, J.P. Bond: James C. McQuinn
GARNER, AMOX et ux V. J. Davis	3/10 1860	By Michael Kountz, J.P. Bond: John B. Davis
GARNER, JOHN (colored) et ux Eliz. Epps	12/8 1860 issued	No returns Bond: J. D.Headrick
GARNER, M. B. et ux Mary Keeble	5/23 1861	By M. Kounts, J.P. Bond: J. S. Boling
GIBBS, G. W. et ux Martha C. Vaughn	12/5 1860	By John McCully, J.P. Bond: J. C. Dodd
GIBSON, ANDREW et ux Jane Russell	2/5 1861	By Christian Long, J.P. Bond: Thomas Russell
GIBSON, M. J. et ux M. J. Sartin	2/29 1860	By A. Boyd, J.P. Bond: J. F. Flanegan
GIDEON, JOHN B. et ux Jennet Jeffreys	8/9 1860	By John McCully, J.P. Bond: Wm. T. Heartsell
GIDEON, THOMAS P. et ux Martha Goodlink	10/11 1860	By John McCully, J.P. Bond: Robert Kidd
GODDARD, WILLIAM et ux Elizabeth Hutsill	7/31 1862	By R. Nuchols, J.P. Bond: Robert Everett
GOENS, S. A. et ux Nancy Howard	3/17 186-	By J. A. Houston, J.P. Bond: E. E.Carnes
GOODMAN, JAMES H. et ux (copy illegible)	3/10 1864	By Joseph Bruner, J.P. Bond: Wm. C. Humphries
GRAHAM, JAMES et ux Emily Carter	2/1 1863	By Street Lane, J.P. Bond: C. D.Morris
GRAY, LEWIS H. et ux Lavinia Click	1/22 1861	By W. T. Dowell, M.G. Bond: Joseph Hurley
GREEN, S. L. (or Greer) et ux Elizabeth Crowley	3/27 1860	By Wm. M. Brickell, J.P. Bond: T. J. Greer
GRINDSTAFF, WM. et ux Sarah S. Russell	6/2 1861	By E. S. Wilkinson, J.P. Bond: A. Bowman

Names	Date Issue Or Celebrated	By Whom/ Security on Bonds
HALE, JOHN C. et ux Sarah M. Hudgeons	1/16 1861	"celebrated in due time by A. Vance" MG Bond: J. A. McKamy
HALL, SAMUEL et ux Elizabeth Ring	2/15 1862	By R. Nuchols, J.P. Bond: Jeremiah Simmerly
HALL, WILLIAM et ux Eliza Alexander	7/17 1864	By Samuel Tullock, J.P. Bond: Dan'l Delaney
HAMILTON, JOHN et ux Elizabeth Scott	10/26 1860	By John S. Moore, J.P. Bond: P. N. Raulston
HAMMONTREE, JAMES et ux Sinda J. Henry	10/29 1861	By Samuel Tullock, J.P. Bond: John Hammontree
HAMMONTREE, P. D. et ux M. A. Thompson	12/27 1860	"celebrated in due time by me--A. Vance" MG Bond: J. E. Hammontree
HAMPTON, A. R. et ux Matilda J.Hays	1/28 1864	By Robt. McTeer, J.P. Bond: Wm. Conner
HARVEY, CLARKE et ux Lucinda A. Chandler	10/17 1864	By G. W. Miser, J.P. Bond: Edmund Kidd
HARVEY, JOHN R. et ux Harriett K. Jackson	9/27 1860	"in due time" says A. Vance, M.G. Bond: Amos Hart
HATCHER, REUBEN et ux Rebecca Laws	2/28 1860	By Nichlas Brewer, J.P. Bond: E. Hatcher, Sr.
HEADRICK, JOHN W. et ux Isabella Fisher	3/10 1861	By Wm. H. McNeeley, M.G. Bond: John White
HEADRICK, PETER et ux Rutha Nyers	2/17 1861	By S. Wear, J.P. Bond: George Kalor
HENDERSON, JOHN H. et ux Mary Rudd	10/27 1863	By Robert H. Culton, J.P. Bond: Wm. Vaughn
HENDERSON, JOSIAH et ux M. A. McCu-ly	8/31 1860	By Wm. M. Brickell, J.P. Bond: Jones (Torn)
HENRY, G. W. et ux Isabella S. Martin	5/26 1863 issued	No returns Bond: McC---(Torn)
HENRY, P. H. et ux Margaret E. Freshour	7/19 1863	By Daniel H. Emmett, J.P. Bond: (Torn)
HENRY, WM. G. et ux Margaret A. E. Hook	4/10 1862	By T. J. Lamar, M.G. Bond: J. H. Kennedy
HERRIN, WILLIAM et ux Caroline Simerly	10/1 1864	By Samuel F. Bell, J.P. Bond: James Baker
HERRINGTON, SAMUEL et ux Eliza J. Thompson	3/29 1861	By Robert McTeer, J.P. Bond: J. E. True

Names	Date Issue or Celebrated	By Whom/ Security on Bonds
HICKS, THOMAS et ux Martha Gains	12/30 1860	By C. Long, J.P. Bond: Robert Bryant
HICKS, W. H. et ux D. P. Alexander	12/24 1860	By W. W. Bayless, J.P. Bond: John Curtis
HILL, JAMES W. et ux Ellander Scott	3/13 1864	By Abraham Abbott Bond: W. H. Finley
HIPPS, WILLIAM et ux Sarah J. Gibbs	1/1 1864	By R. E.Tedford, M.G. Bond: Elijah Nelson
HODGE, DEMPSEY et ux Rebecca McAfee	6/20 1864	By George Snider, J.P. Bond: J. A.Bowers
HODGE, H. I. et ux Elzena Wrinkle	12/23 1860	By James Dearmond, J.P. Bond: T. J. McCampbell
HODGE, THOMAS et ux Elizabeth Davis	9/11 1864	By Hugh H. Gamble, J.P. Bond: George Graham
HOLLWAY, A. J. et ux Rosanah Henson	3/30 1860 issued	Returned--no endorse-ment Bond: A. M. Pass
HOOD, WILLIAM et ux Eliz. Gibbs	3/21 1860	By H. T. Lincunpelter, J.P. Bond: F. M.Sauter
HOUSER, ALEXANDER et ux Martha Ann Weaver	4/24 1862	By A. Boyd, J.P. Bond: James W. Freuch
HOUSER, PHILLIP et ux Martha Jane Farr	9/11 1864	By Thomas Pickens, J.P. Bond: A. J. Taylor
HOUSER, WM. et ux Nancy J. Rogers	12/1 1861	By Michael Kounts, J.P. Bond: Robert Everett
HUDSON, S. P. et ux M. C. Calloway	2/18 1861 issued	No returns Bond: D. D. Taliferro
HUGHS, JOHN et ux Evelina Carver	9/12 1864	By Samuel Tullock, J.P. Bond: John Hughs W. H. Garner
HUMPHREY, S. A. et ux M. J. Donaldson	1/9 1861	By Wm. M. Brickell, J.P. Bond: J. F. Mooney
HUNT, WM. H. et ux Elizabeth Kidd	5/27 1862	By A. Boyd, J.P. Bond: John Brakebi 1
HUSKEN, W. G. et ux Margaret L. Carson	11/13 1864	By G. W. Miser, J.P. Bond: Wm. Bird R. C. Alfred
HUTSELL, WM. M. et ux Abagail K. Thompson	10/24 1860	By E. S.Wilkinson, J.P. Bond: D. N. Broyles
HUTTON, J. C. et ux Polly Ann Kerr	11/26 1862	By Spencer Henry, M.G. Bond: M. M. Anderson

Names	Date Issue or Celebrated	By Whom/Security on Bonds
INGRAM, ISAAC L. et ux Desdemonia R. Ward	8/6 1863	By H. S. Bright, J.P. Bond: W. Z. Gibbs
IRVIN, M. M. et ux Elizabeth R. Henry	1/1 1863	By John Gamble, J.P. Bond: Moses Gamble
JAMES, ELIJAH et ux Dorcas Clemons	9/6 1860	By W. H. McNeeley, J.P. Bond: S. E.Nelson
JAMES, P. B. et ux Sarah S. Phelps	1/17 1861	By H. Heartsill, J.P. Bond: G. W.Henderson
JENNINGS, JOHN H. et ux Sarah A. Henderson	8/7 1860	By M. G. Callahan, M.G. Bond: W. H. Martin
JOHNSON, WLIJAH et ux Rosanna Peery	10/18 1860	By Wm. M. Burnett, M.G. Bond: M. P. Murphy
JOHNSON, ROBERT et ux Letitia Cameron	1/31 1865	By S. L. Sanford, M.G. Bond: C. Gillespie
JOHNSTON, THOMAS M. et ux S. J. Caldwell	9/4 1862	By Samuel Tullock, J.P. Bond: H.L.W. Johnson
JOHNSON, WM. H. et ux Martha Smith	10/16 1862	By Wm. M. Brickell, J.P. Bond: John Moor
JOHNSTON, EZEKIEL et ux Hetty Colter	9/11 1863 issued	No returns Bond: Alfred Seaton
JONES, E. M. et ux Sarah Hackney	4/11 1861	By W. M. Brickell, J.P. Bond: David Griffitts
JONES, GEORGE et ux Mary Catherine Hill	3/31 1864	By John J. Hudgeons, J.P. Bond: Stephen King
JONES, JOHN W. et ux Theresa A. Caston	1/23 1861	By Stephen Mathews, J.P. Bond: M. M. Shipley
KAIGLEY, JESSE et ux Catherine T. Keeble	3/6 1862	By Michael Kounts, J.P. Bond: Spencer Donald- son
KEEBLE, MARION et ux Martha Jane Clarke	12/21 1864	By T. H. Russell, M.G. Bond: James R. Coulter
KEEN, JOSEPH et ux Rebecca Hoback	3/11 1863	By H. Heartsell, J.P. Bond: Isaac Wright
KENNEY, JOHN P. et ux Margaret Rhea	1/23 1862	By W. T.Dowell, M.G. Bond: J. E. McGinley
KENNEDY, A. C. et ux Margaret M. Thompson	12/15 1861 issued	No returns Bond: Wm. G. Henry
KERR, HENDERSON et ux Mary Smallin	11/16 1862	By James Taylor, J.P. Bond: Elkana Smallin
KEY, JAMES et ux Sarah E. Brown	6/10 1860	By John McCully, J.P. Bond: William Ashley

Names	Date Issue Or Celebrated	By Whom/ Security on Bonds
KEY, MELVIN et ux Caroline Delaney	8/19 1861	By S. J. Griffitts, J.P. Bond: S. N. (D. N.?) Broyles
KINDER, JOHN et ux Catherine W. Shelly	1/24 1864 issued	"celebrated" Bond: Martin Morgan
KING, FRANCIS et ux Keziah D. Perkins	10/9 1860	By Samuel J. Griffitts, J.P. Bond: T. Harle
KING, WILLIAM E. et ux Susan Fuller	8/22 1860	By Samuel J. Griffitts, J.P. Bond: David Turk
KINNAMAN, JOHN et ux E. J. Millsaps	12/5 1861	By M. Kounts, J.P. Bond: James Kinnaman
KINNAMAN, JOHN et ux Margaret J. Pass	1/12 1862	By James Hamil, M.G. Bond: J. L. Wallace
KIRBY, WAYMAN et ux Margaret Murr	1/23 1864	By E. S. Wilkinson, J.P. Bond: Alex. Neiman
KIRBY, RICHARD et ux Sarah Taylor	6/14 1860	By S. C. Delashmidt, M.G. Bond: W.B.W. Heartsill
KIRKPATRICK, B. E. et ux Martha Rainwater	12/11 1864	By John Hudgeons, J.P. Bond: David A. Steele
KITE, HARRISON et ux Margaret Spradlin	6/4 1861	No returns Bond: Alexander Tucker
KOUNTS, SAMUEL et ux Mary D. McTeer	10/28 1860	By Isaac Hines, M.G. Bond: George C. Davis
LAMBERT, GEORGE et ux Nancy Hunt	4/12 1860	By John J. Hudgeons, J.P. Bond: Levi Lambert
LAMBERT, LEVI et ux Omey Howard	3/7 1861	By S. T. Woods, J.P. Bond: Richard Bryant
LANE, SAMUEL J. et ux Louisa C. Hicks	6/10 1860	By S. Wear, J.P. Bond: Sam. Lane
LANE, W. C. et ux R. E. Everett	7/23 1862 issued	"celebrated" Bond: J. W. Ogle
LAIN, JAMES et ux Ana Davis	1/17 1864	By John Gamble, J.P. Bond: John McCampbell
LAWSON, JACOB et ux Jane Webb	4/4 1864	By L. Wear (S.?) Bond: M. H. Tipton
LEA, J. W. et ux Mary B. Prater	11/13 1860	By Fielding Pope, M.G. Bond: John H. Parker
LESTER, J. D. et ux Marcella Henderson	6/18 1862	By M. M. Douglas Bond: John W. Boyd

Names	Date Issue Or Celebrated	By Whom/ Security on Bonds
LOGAN, ALVAN et ux Margaret S. Scott	12/1 1864	By T. J. Lamar, M.G. Bond: F. M. Hood
LOGAN, F. H. et ux Desdemona Pressley	7/4 1860	By W. T. Dowell, M.G. Bond: A. H. Hicks
LONG, A. C. et ux S. E.Headrick	9/29 1861	By E. S. Wilkinson, Bond: James Whetsell
LONG, JAMES et ux Margaret Sparks	1/29 1862 issued	No returns Bond: Edmond Underwood
LONG, R. L. et ux Henrietta Stephens	8/11 1861	By Richard Nuchols, J.P. Bond: Robert Everett
LOVE, W. B. et ux Huldah Graston	8/27 1863	By Fielding Pope, M.G. Bond: Wm. Kidd
LOW, JOHN et ux Mary Ann Gibson	2/15 1865	By John Gamble, J.P. Bond: W. D.McGinley
LOWERY, W. H. et ux Isabella Edmonds	1/17 1865	By John McCully, J.P. Bond: Robert Byerd
McCALL, J. H. et ux Jane McMurrey	2/9 1860	By A. Boyd, J.P. Bond: S. B. Houston
McCAMPBELL, ISAAC et ux Jane Hanley	3/13 1864	By Daniel Emmett Bond: W. H. Lawson
McCANLIE, JAMES et ux Elizabeth Caldwell	2/6 1860	By W. W. Nuchols Bond: Jno. McDanel
McCASLIN, JOHN et ux Sarah Wilson	1/22 1861	By S. J. Griffitts, J.P. Bond: S. A. Humphrey
McCLAIN, JOHN E. et ux Nannie J. Wright	6/9 1863 issued	No returns Bond: J. R. Porter
McCLURE, CHARLES E. et ux Sibby A. Dearmond	11/22 1860	By J. S. Craig, M.G. Bond: D. L. Trundle
McCLURE, CHARLES E. et ux Edith S. Hackney	2/21 1861	By W. M. Brickell, J.P. Bond: A. J.Endsley
McCOLLUM, HARVEY et ux Sarah Penelope Higgins	8/22 1864	By Robt. McTeer, J.P. Bond: Robert W. Thompson John Roberts
McCOLLOM, J. B. et ux Nancy E. Thompson	12/27 1860	"by me in due time" By A. Vance, M.G. Bond: J. E. Hammontree
McCONNELL, M. L. et ux M. L. Clemmons	6/13 1861	By W. T.Dowell, M.G. Bond: J. W. Whetsell
McCULLEY, DAVID et ux Nancy Rudd	2/18 1862	By S. T. Woods, J.P. Bond: Allen Anderson
McCULLOUGH, J. J. et ux Mary C. Jones	10/31 1861	By Wm. M. Brickell, J.P. Bond: W. B. Colburn

Names	Date Issue Or Celebrated	By Whom/ Security on Bonds
McGILL, RICHARD et ux Mary Ann Teague	12/2 1862	By Solomon Farmer Bond: Ann McGill
McGINLEY, W. D. et ux Elizabeth Duncan	5/8 1860	By Fielding Pope, M.G. Bond: John E. Toole
McKENRY, SAMUEL et ux Dorcas Vineyard	4/24 1862	By A. Boyd, J.P. Bond: Wm. B. Parish
McKINLEY, JNO. et ux Angeline Myzell	7/15 1860	By Stephen Mathews, J.P. Bond: John Nunn
McNUTT, H. L. et ux C. J.Ambrister	12/19 1860	By W. T.Dowell, M.G. Bond: R. H. Tedford
McREYNOLDS, FERDENAND et ux Eliza Jane Bell	8/26 1860	By R. E. Tedford, M.G. Bond: W. C. Broady
MAGNIER, JUNIUS et ux Paulien Bovard	4/27 1860 issued	No returns Bond: St. Lanier
MALINEE, H. F. et ux M. J. Scrivener	6/27 1864 issued	"celebrated" J.P. Bond: Jeptha Hinton
MALONEE, JOHN et ux Nancy Privett	4/6 1862	By J. H. Houston, J.P. Bond: Josiah Delaney
MANN, WM. et ux Mary A. Means	3/20 1862	By R. E. Tedford, M.G. Bond: Samuel Wallace
MARSH, MOSLY D. et ux Emily Carter	12/22 1863	By Joseph Bruner, J.P. Bond: James E. Carroll
MILLER, DAVID et ux S. J. Raulston	3/19 1860	By E. S. Wilkinson, J.P. Bond: W. Raulston
MARTIN, DAVID K. et ux Elizabeth A. Best	4/11 1861	By E. S. Wilkinson, J.P. Bond: Samuel Henry
MARTIN, W. H. et ux Victoria Jennings	2/29 1860	By J. M. Caldwell, M.G. Bond: A. L. McCampbell
MATTHEWS, JOSEPH et ux E.S.M. Blair	2/5 1863	By Robt. A. Ferguson, M.G. Bond: Elisha Walker, Jr.
MAUPIN, A. L. et ux H. E. Besla	7/10 1862	By S. Matthews, J.P. Bond: A. R. James
MAYO, JAMES R. P. et ux Miriam A. Mayo	1/24 1862 issued	No returns Bond: Payton Blankinship
MILLER, DAVID et ux S. J. Raulston	3/19 1860	By E. S. Wilkinson, J.P. Bond: W. Raulston
MILLS, HENRY et ux Susan Browner	7/31 1864	By Mark May, B.M. Bond: William Vaughn

Names	Date Issue Or Celebrated	By Whom/ Security on Bonds
MILLS, J. W. et ux M. J. Caldwell	6/24 1860	By James Dearmond, J.P. Bond: H. D. Caldwell
MOON, JOHN et ux C. E. Parks	2/13 1862	By George Caldwell, J.P. Bond: George Caldwell
MOORE, JOHN L. et ux Arty Lukinsey Neale	2/15 1865	By W. B. Bingham, J.P. Bond: Richard Bryant
MORRISON, ENOCH et ux Luce Everett	3/6 1865	By John Gamble, J.P. Bond: Luther Nelson
MORRISON, JESSE et ux Melvina Fortner	1/4 1865	By W. B.Bingham, J.P. Bond: John Byas
MORROW, WM. et ux D. W. Brooks	1/19 1861	By Samuel Griffitts, J.P. Bond: John Alexander
MURPHY, A. B. et ux M. E. Vineyard	6/13 1861	By Isaac Hines, M.G. Bond: W. W. Crews
MURPHY, M. P. et ux M. E. Peery	12/3 1860	By Michael Kountz, J.P. Bond: J. D. French
MURR, ALEXANDER et ux M. J. Thompson	5/4 1861	No returns Bond: I. N. Yearout
MYERS, JOHN et ux Mary J. Myers	5/12 1861	By Daniel H. Emmett, J.P. Bond: F. S. Emmett
MYERS, JOHN et ux Margaret Bird	10/31 1861	By James D. Lawson, M.G.M.E.S. Bond: Wm. Myers
MYERS, PHILLIP et ux Nancy J. Gibbs	10/25 1860	By A. R. James, J.P. Bond: Jethro Hunter
MYERS, SAMUEL et ux Eliza Sawyers	12/15 1864	By George Snider, J.P. Bond: Daniel Myers
NELSON, LUTHER et ux Mary Jane Morrison	3/8 1864 "issued"	"celebrated" Bond: F. M. Hood
NELSON, JAMES et ux S. Culbertson	2/4 1860	By J. C. Wright, J.P. Bond: R. C.Culbertson
NELSON, JAMES W. et ux Mary E. Clemens	10/13 1864	By A. J. Greer, M.G. Bond: John B. Carnes
NELSON, WM. et ux Margaret E. Reed	6/6 1861	By W. T. Dowell, M.G. Bond: J. F. Sharp
NICHOLSON, J. F. et ux Mary E. Alexander	1/24 1861	By S. Matthews, J.P. Bond: Costo--(Torn)
NORRIS, WILLIAM R. et ux Eliza Ann Goddard	9/8 1864	By F. Pope, M.G. Bond: (Torn)
NORWOOD, C.W.C. et ux Mary Strain	1/24 1864	By T. J. Lamar, M.G. Bond: (Torn)

Names	Date Issue Or Celebrated	By Whom/ Security on Bonds
NUCHOLS, ISAAC et ux Mary Jane Grindstaff	11/4 1864	By Samuel F. Bell, J.P. Bond: W. Herron H. M. Hood
NUCHOLS, JAMES W. et ux Elizabeth Williams	12/24 1863	By E. S. Wilkinson, J.P. Bond: Elijah Nelson
O'DENIEL, JOSEPH et ux Sarah E. Holback	3/8 1864	By Joseph Bruner, J.P. Bond: E. S. Wilinson
OGLE, WM. et ux Rebecca Lane	1/20 1864	By Daniel H. Emmett, J.P. Bond: John A. Ellis
OGLE, WM. H. et ux Catherine McGhill	8/27 1861	By John Gamble, J.P. Bond: Wm. Hicks
O'NEAL, JAMES et ux Lucinda Ratledge	12/6 1864	By R. H. Culton, J.P. Bond: George P. Culton
OWENBY, ANDREW et ux Nancy Mathis	1/26 1865	By M. McTeer, J.P. Bond: J. C. Owenby
PARHAM, BAKER A. et ux Angerderina McKenzie	7/19 1860	By John McCully, J.P. Bond: William Ashley
PARKS, JAMES et ux Martha Bell	1/18 1864	By Joseph Bruner, J.P. Bond: Street Lain
PARSLEY, JAMES et ux Eliza Joiner	4/10 1860	By James Dearmond, J.P. Bond: A. L. McCampbell
PARSON, J. C. et ux Galaphray V. Pugh	3/19 1861	By Spencer Henry, M.G. Bond: R. J. Allen
PARSONS, JOHN E. et ux Caroline Ratledge	1/13 1865	By G. W. Miser, J.P. Bond: William Henderson
PASS, WM. et ux Nancy Pass	11/5 1863	By Robert H. Culton, J.P. Bond: John Morgan
PATE, RUFUS et ux Dorothy Hix	6/11 1863	No returns Bond: John Brown
PAYNE, J. W. et ux Mary Ann Whitehead	4/17 1861	By Richard Nuchols, J.P. Bond: Wm. Grindstaff
PEACE, F. P. et ux F. E. Jones	11/10 1864	By T. J. Lamar, M.G. Bond: F. M. Hood
PHELPS, ANDREW et ux Rachel Boatman	1/2 1862	By Wm. M. Bicknell, J.P. Bond: Wm. R. James
PLEMONS, JAMES K. et ux Sarah M. Clemons	9/27 1860	By W. H. McNeeley, J.P. Bond: A. J. Smith
PORTER, ANDREW J. et ux Ann E. Taylor	9/28 1864	By William C. Conner, J.P. Bond: J. C. McCoy

Names	Date Issue Or Celebrated	By Whom/ Security on Bonds
PORTER, JOHN et ux Martha Jane Scott	2/7 1865	By T. J. Lamar, M.G. Bond: E. W. Sanderson
PRATT, ALEXANDER et ux Mary A. Thompson	4/25 1861	By Stephen Matthews, J.P. Bond: W. T. Caston
PUGH, SAMUEL et ux Mary Huffsteller	9/15 1861	By W. T. Dowell, M.G. Bond: John N. Hutton
PUGH, W.J.T. et ux M. J. Griffith	1/18 1865	By A. Vance, M.G. Bond: J. M. Griffith James Tullock
RASOR, J. H. et ux Margaret Chapman	3/25 1862	By James Taylor, J.P. Bond: J. H. Kagley
RAULSTON, WALLACE et ux Sarah Potter	12/6 1860	By John Davis, M.G. Bond: Wm. Herron
REAGAN, WM. et ux Alpha S. Feezell	8/22 1860	By Curran Lemons, J.P. Bond: E. M. McCampbell
REED, JAMES C. et ux Sarah E. Edmonds	11/24 1864	By R. H. Culton, J.P. Bond: J. C. McCoy
REEDER, ISAAC et ux Martha Aikridge	12/28 1863	By A. R.James, J.P. Bond: W. R. Milligan
RIDDLE, JOHN et ux Nancy Jane White	1/22 1865	By J. W. Elliott Bond: Thomas Baker
RIDGE, DAVID et ux Angeline Carver	2/24 1862	By S. T. Woods, J.P. Bond: Lafayette Pugh
ROACH, HARRISON et ux Sarah Catherine Crisp	8/10 1863 issued	No returns Bond: R. H. Anderson
ROBBINS, WM. F. et ux Almyra A. Davis	12/7 1861	By H. S. Bright, J.P. Bond: W. L. Hutton
ROBINSON, ISAAC et ux Rebecca Bly	2/10 1864	By Stephen Matthews, J.P. Bond: F. F. Hackney
ROBINSON, WM. et ux Esther Hall	8/31 1861	By Richard Nuchols, J.P. Bond: C. Hall
RODDY, PRESTON et ux Hester A. Bowen	4/18 1860 issued	No returns Bond: Benjamin Harris
ROE, JOSHUA et ux Sarah E. Phelps	11/7 1861	By Wm. M. Brickell, J.P. Bond: W. R. Jones
ROSS, JOHN et ux Sarah Robbins	3/13 1860	By A. J. Wilson, J.P. Bond: W. F. Robbins
ROSS, W. A. et ux S. M. Saffell	8/15 1861	By W. T. Dowell, M.G. Bond: Wm. Sloan
ROUTLEDGE, ROBERT A. et ux Mary M. Montgomery	7/4 1860 issued	(were married) No re- turns Bond: J. G. Rutledge

Names	Date Issue Or Celebrated	By Whom/ Security on Bonds
ROWAN, SAM. P. et ux M.T.A. Love	8/7 1862	By Wm. H. McNeeley, J.P. Bond: G. W. Winter-bowers
ROWLAND, JAMES W. et ux Nancy J. Smallen	7/3 1864	By Mark May, B.M. Bond: Henry Hamil
ROWLETT, CHARLES W. et ux Hannah A. Stallions	1/30 1861	By John McCully, J.P. Bond: Wm. Ashley
RUMMAGE, WILLIAM et ux Caroline Duncan	2/7 1862	By Joseph Bruner Bond: J. W. Jackson
RUSSELL, JAMES et ux Caroline Delozier	1/26 1865	By Samuel Tullock, J.P. Bond: James M. Greer
RUSSELL, JOHN et ux Nancy Gorf	1/11 1864 issued	"celebrated" Bond: Thomas Whitehead
RUSSELL, RICHARD et ux Jane Russell	11/25 1864	By Moses McConell, J.P. Bond: Alsuf White
RUSSELL, WM. et ux Sarah J. Britt	11/29 1860	By C. Long, J.P. Bond: E. Grindstaff
SANFORD, S. L. et ux Jane Kennedy	3/13 1862	By Wm. Bellue, M.G. Bond: Thomas Sharp
SARTAIN, L. J. et ux Sarah E. Gibson	4/30 1860	By H. T. Lincumpelter, J.P. Bond: David J. Gibson
SCHOFER, FRANKLIN et ux Mary Roddy	5/19 1860	By J. M. Caldwell, J.P. Bond: C. C. Wilder
SCOTT, ISAIAH et ux Winney L. Johnson	7/2 1860	By Stephen Mathews, J.P. Bond: J. Leadbetter
SCRUGGS, R. K. et ux Isabella D. Saffell	1/26 1861	By J. Albert Hyder, M.G. Bond: S. K. Finley
SHANNON, JOHN et ux Emmaline Keeton	10/26 1862	By Fielding Pope, M.G. By Jacob Sesler
SHERRELL, JAMES H. et ux M.J.C.T. Wells	8/21 1862	By W. M. Burnett, M.G. Bond: W. H. Williams
SHOWN, A. B. et ux Dorcas McMillan	5/14 1861	By S. T.Woods, J.P. Bond: Samuel T. Hargus
SIMMERLY, ADAM et ux Mary A. Russell	6/23 1861	By Richard Nuchols, J.P. Bond: H. Simmerly
SIMMERLY, JAMES et ux Jane Teffeteller	6/20 1861	By Richard Nuchols, J.P. Bond: Abr'm Simmerly
SIMMERLY, JOHN et ux Nancy Long	4/9 1863	By R. Nuchols, J.P. Bond: Thomas Russell

Names	Date Issue Or Celebrated	By Whom/ Security on Bonds
SLOAN, WM. et ux M. A. Best	12/25 1861	By James Taylor, J.P. Bond: R. S. Mason
SMITH, JOHN W. et ux Martha E. Henry	10/30 1862 issued	No returns (we know was ok) Bond: J. M. Griffitts
SMITH, SAMUEL et ux Mary M. Rhea	2/25 1864	By A. J. Greer, M.G. Bond: John Keny
SPISER, JAS. S. et ux Nancy Earmond	2/18 1860 issued	No returns Bond: N. B. Williams
SPRADLIN, DAVID et ux Nancy C. Stepp	8/30 1860	By S. T. Woods, J.P. Bond: Lea Logan
SPRADLIN, NATHANIEL et ux Modena McEldry	3/28 1861	By H. Bright, J.P. Bond: Bennet Amburn
STALLIONS, WM. et ux Nancy A. Rudd	7/29 1861 issued	No returns Bond: A. C. Stallions
STEPHENS, WM. B. et ux Arkany McKenzie	3/12 1860	By John McCully, J.P. Bond: C. McKenzie
STERLING, HENRY et ux Eliza Dunlap	10/28 1862	By T. J. Lamar, M.G. Bond: John H. Edmondson
STONE, SAMUEL et ux Elizabeth Parker	12/3 1861	By Wm. M. Brickell, J.P. Bond: Josiah Henderson
STOUPS, SAM'L B. et ux Elizabeth Gibson	6/27 1860	By H. T. Lengenfetner, J.P. Bond: James Gibson
SUTTON, RUSSELL et ux Elizabeth Headrick	7/28 1861	By Daniel H. Emmet, J.P. Bond: J. W. Sutton
TALLENT, J. H. et ux Mary A. Brown	6/19 1860	By John McCully, J.P. Bond: James Key
TALLY, JOHN et ux Louisa West	9/20 1862 issued	No returns Bond: Winston Hafley
TARWATER, HENRY C. et ux Harriett L. Mitchell	9/12 1861	By J. M. Caldwell, M.G. Bond: Michael Rule
TAYLOR, JOHN J. et ux Elizabeth Wilburn	9/2 1860	By Lavator Wear, J.P. Bond: G. W. Waters
TEAGUE, HARRISON et ux Mary Ann Best	1/17 1865	By Mark May, B.M. Bond: Calvin Roddy
TEAGUE, TESSAWAY et ux S. C. Dickson	4/29 1860	By Isaac Hines, M.G. Bond: William Thomas
TEFFETELLER, ANDERSON et ux Elizabeth Dockery	6/9 1861	By James Hamill, M.G. Bond: John Everett
TEFFETELLER, JEFFERSON et ux E. J. Whitehead	7/23 1861	By James Taylor, J.P.

Names	Date Issue Or Celebrated	By Whom/ Security on Bonds
TEFTELLER, WM. R. et ux Sarah E. Christopher	9/25 1863	By Wm. H. Verne(?), M.G. Bond: Thomas Hix
TEMPLE, J. D. et ux S. L. Morton	1/27 1862	By Wm. H. McNeeley, Bond: Alfred Seaton
TEMPLE, WILLIAM M. et ux Sarah C. Nelson	12/27 1864	By S. L. Sanford, M.G. Bond: J. M. Davis
THOMPSON, DAVID et ux Sarah M. Dodson	11/25 1861	By Wm. M. Brickell, J.P. Bond: D. T. Bright
THOMPSON, L. W. et ux Mary McCollom	1/25 1861	"in due tim " says A. Vance, M.G.
THOMPSON, N. H. et ux Miram N. Hughes	5/10 1860	By Harvey Thompson, J.P. Bond: Josiah Powers
THOMPSON, SAMUEL et ux Elizabeth Coulson	11/3 1860	By S. J. Griffitts, J.P. Bond: J. W. Thompson
TIPTON, C. P. et ux Emeline Webb	3/15 1860	By Hugh J. Henry, J.P. Bond: T. J. Freshour
TIPTON, JOHN et ux Jane Blair	10/9 1861 issued	No returns Bond: F. D.Fulkerson
TIPTON, JOHN L. et ux Isabella McMurry	8/11 1861	By A. Boyd, J.P. Bond: Wm. Rogers
TIPTON, PETER H. et ux Mary A. Graves	2/5 1861	By Solomon Farmer, J.P. Bond: John B. Davis
TOMPKINS, WM. et ux Eliza Yarber	8/20 1863 issued	No returns Bond: J. C. McTeer
TUCK, M. H. et ux Elender Richards	1/24 1861	By J. J. Hudgeons, J.P. Bond: F. M. King
TUCK, EDMONDS et ux Elizabeth	1/26 1862	By J. J. Hudgeons, J.P. Bond: J. N. Emmett
TUCKER, ISAAC et ux Jane Hensley	7/27 1861	By S. T. Woods, J.P. Bond: Alexander Tucker
TULLOCK, JOHN M. et ux Sarah Kerr	9/26 1860	By A. J.Wilson, J.P. Bond: David Spradling
TURBEVILLE, FRANKLIN et ux Amanda Jane Houser	1/11 1865	By J. H. Dycke, J.P. Bond: Logan Brown William Hipps
TURNBULL, JOHN et ux Mehala Murray	11/8 1864	By John J. Hudgeons, J.P. Bond: John Blankinship M. M. Anderson

Names	Date Issue Or Celebrated	By Whom/ Security on Bonds
VAUGHN, DAVID L. et ux Almira J. Raulston	6/12 1862	By E. S. Wilkinson, J.P. Bond: David Miller
VINEYARD, JAMES M. et ux Jane Keller	12/24 1863	By Solomon Farmer, J.P. Bond: J. V. Offritt
VINEYARD, JOHN et ux Elizabeth Cupp	12/25 1860	By B. F. Duncan, J.P. Bond: H. Brakebill
WAGGONER, ISAAC et ux Mary E. Sneed	5/28 1861	By James Dearmond, J.P. Bond: Jeff. Kidd
WAITS, WM. et ux Rachel A. Bryant	5/2 1863	By H. Heartsill, J.P. Bond: H. Heartsill
WALKER, ELIJAH JR. et ux Susan A. Henry	4/9 1863	By J. W. Mann, M.G. Bond: Joseph Mathews
WALKER, JAMES et ux Sarah Low	10/28 1862	By John Gamble, J.P. Bond: Josias Gamble
WALKER, JAMES et ux Sarah Rowan	9/22 1864	By John Gamble, J.P. Bond: George Conatser James Walker
WALKER, SPENCER et ux Nancy C. Law	1/1 1861	By John Gamble, J.P. Bond: J. C. Brewer
WALLACE, ABRAHAM et ux Margaret J. Johnson	10/4 1860	By R. E. Tedford, M.G. Bond: John L. Wallace
WATTS, GEO. W. et ux Hester A. Rudd	5/24 1864	By G. W. Miser, J.P. Bond: James Reed
WELLS, JOHN G. et ux Myram E. Rorex	11/7 1861	By Daniel D. Foute, J.P. Bond: J. H. Sherell
WEST, ALFRED et ux Elvira Smith	12/8 1860	By Robert McTeer, J.P. Bond: James West
WEST, GEROGE R. et ux C. D. Bishop	8/8 1861	By Joseph Bruner, J.P. Bond: J. F. Dawson
WEST, J. S. et ux L. E. Jennings	1/18 1860 issued	No returns Bond: W. H. Martin
WHEELER, CASWELL et ux Catherine Skinner	11/10 1864	By Moses Elliott, J.P. Bond: D. C. Eagleton R. C. Alford
WHETSELL, J. W. et ux C. H. Mallinnee	10/20 1861	By R. E. Tedford, M.G. Bond: R. P. Bowerman
WHITE, D. P. et ux Mary Ann McGinley	9/20 1864	By John Gamble, J.P. Bond: John Colter
WHITE, J. A. et ux Demorisa Headrick	4/8 1861	By Wm. H. McNeeley, M.G. Bond: John Headrick
WHITTENBERG, CLEM et ux Sarah Talbut	4/10 1864 "issued"	"celebrated" Bond: James Nipper

Names	Date Issue Or Celebrated	By Whom/ Security on Bonds
WIGGS, A. P. et ux Cathaleen H. Hannum	2/11 1862	By J. F. Woodfin, M.G. Bond: J. F.Woodfin
WILBURN, JOHN et ux Sarah Henson	8/8 1861	By R. E. Tedford, M.G. Bond: Robert Everett
WILDER, C. C. et ux S. F. Headrick	7/24 1860	By B. F. Duncan, J.P. Bond: J. C. Dodd
WILKINSON, E. S. et ux N. J. Carpenter	12/20 1860	By W. T.Dowell, M.G. Bond: W. D. M--inley (McKinley?)
WILLARD, B. F. et ux Lucinda Goddard	10/30 1860	By W. T. Dowell, M.G. Bond: B. F. Goddard
WILLIAMS, WILLIAM et ux Marthy Johnston	8/16 1860	By John McCully, J.P. Bond: C. Williams
WILLIAMSON, SAMUEL L. et ux Elizabeth Anderson	3/7 1861	By Samuel Tullock, J.P. Bond: Samuel Tulloch
WILLOX, ROBERT M. et ux Adaline McNabb	3/10 1861	By James Dearmond, J.P. Bond: T. S. Gibbs
WILSON, A. J. et ux Martha Ann Pugh	7/10 1862	By Jesse Kerr, Jr., J.P. Bond: R. P. Bowerman
WOODFIN, J. W. et ux Juliett A. Montgomery	7/18 1862 issued	(were marrked--ok) No returns Bond: Henry Miller
WOODS, WM. et ux Lydia Underwood	1/8 1864	By Samuel Tulloch, J.P. Bond: Logan Brown
WYLEY, J. R. et ux Mary Hoover	6/5 1861 issued	No returns Bond: B.F.L. Wyley
WYLEY, J. W. et ux J. L. McClain	12/19 1861	By M. Jones, J.P. Bond: J. H. Jackson
ZACHERY, C. C. et ux Nancy E. Bryson	1/14 1864	By F. Pope, M.G. Bond: T. L. Dearing

BLOUNT COUNTY MARRIAGE LICENSES OR BONDS FOUND OF RECOR

SUPPLEMENT TO BOOK "O"

	Names	Date Issue Or Celebrated	By Whom/ Security on Bonds
1	AKENS, ROBERT et ux Lavenia Hawkins	8/2 1858	No returns Bond: Lea Logan
2	ALEXANDER, ALLEN et ux Sarah E. Belt	9/3 1859	No returns Bond: Jno. Montgomery
3	AMBURN, URIAH et ux Elizabeth A. Roach	4/20 1858	No returns Bond: C. H. Chambers
4	ANDERSON, A. L. et ux Eliz. Kirkpatrick	2/2 1858	No returns Bond: A. P. Chapman
5	BARNHILL, J. D. et ux Eliza Rule	12/22 1858	By W. H. Rogers, M.G. Bond: James West
6	BARNHILL, WILLIAM et ux Mary McKethim	5/14 1858	No returns Bond: B. M. Russell
7	BELT, A. R. et ux A. R. Smith	12/27 1855	By Jas. M. Tulloch, J.P. Bond: J. S. Crye
8	BELT, S. K. et ux T. Dewberry	7/30 1856	By James M. Lane, J.P. Bond: J. M. McCall
9	BEST, JOHN et ux M. A. Hencley	10/5 1854	By David Spradlin, J.P. Bond: Lee Logan
10	BLACKBURN, THOMAS et ux L. A. McCasland	7/14 1858 issued	No returns Bond: R. H. Blackburn
11	BOLINGER, JOSEPH et ux Rebecca George	9/3 1854 J.P.	By Wm. M. Brickell, Bond: W. A. Walker
12	BOREN, ABNER et ux Nancy Harrison	5/23 1859 issued	No returns Bond: Sigher Everett
13	BROOKS, SAMUEL H. et ux C. Hoover	8/5 1854 issued	No returns Bond: S. Griffitt
14	BUNGARDNER, C. et ux Rebecca A. Ryne	2/7 1856	By David Spradlin, J.P. Bond: John Earles
15	CAMPBELL, JOHN et ux M. E. Grindstaff	10/21 1856	By S. L. Yearout, J.P. Bond: Jno. Montgomery
16	CARR, SAMUEL (see Kerr) et ux Dorothy C. Hoyle	8/4 1859	By W. W. Bayless, J.P. Bond: J. C. Kerr
17	CARTER, A. J. et ux Catherine Hall	10/6 1857 issued	No returns Bond: Charles W. Hall
18	COLLINS, KIAH et ux Nancy A. Bird	3/6 1855	By Wm. Kerr, J.P. Bond: Lile Wilson
19	COLLINS, ROBERT A. et ux Mary J. Iles	3/19 1858 issued	No returns Bond: James Collins

Names	Date Issue Or Celebrated	By Whom/ Security on Bonds
20 COPELAND, THOMAS et ux Viney Teefeteller	5/8 1858 issued	No returns Bond: George Anderson
21 CUMMINGS, JOHN et ux Rachel Wayman	1/29 1855	No returns Bond: J. B. Cobb
22 CUMPTON, J. C. et ux Sarah Best	5/7 1855	By J. M. Stansberry, J.P. Bond: Jas. C. Hall
23 (Not on copy of manuscript)		
24 DAVIS, JAMES A. et ux Jane DeLozier	8/1 1858	By M. Kounts, J.P. Bond: H. H. Gamble
25 DAVIS, PETER G. et ux S. C. Creswell	10/13 1857 issued	No returns Bond: D. R.McMurray
26 DAVIS, W. N. et ux H. E. Jeffries	10/26 1856	By Michael Kounts, J.P. Bond: J. D. Davis
27 DEARMOND, GEORGE R. et ux M. A. Holland	11/15 1855 issued	No returns Bond: M. F. Garrard
28 DUNN, DANIEL et ux E. J.Adams	11/2 1858	By H. I. Hodge, M.G. Bond: M. V. King
29 ELLIOTT, JOHN et ux Vina Davis	5/10 1858 issued	No returns Bond: G. W. Cline
30 EVANS, DAVIS et ux Mahala Tipton	11/29 1855	By W. A. Lawson, M.G. Bond: S. W. Tipton
31 FANCHER, JOSEPH et ux Ama Fancher	6/19 1859	By Frederic Emmett Bond: John Walker
32 FANVILLE, F. O. et ux L. A. Caulson	7/28 1856	No returns Bond: J. P. Brown
33 FARMER, ADAM et ux Rebecca Wilson	12/2 1859 issued	No returns Bond: Jackson Wilson
34 FINDLEY, WILLIAM H. et ux Dorcas Chandler	9/14 1854	By W. W. Neal, M.G. M.E.C. South Bond: Jno. Rhea
35 GANAWAY, B. Z. et ux M. J. Baldwin	1/1 1857	By S. A. Taylor, M.G. "at Baldwin's" Bond: T. R. Lee
36 GARDNER, WILLIAM et ux Agnes Gardner	1/12 1858 issued	No returns Bond: Joseph Hodgson
37 GARNER, ADAM et ux Talitha Rogers	5/13 1855	By M. Kounts, J.P. Bond: M. Kounts
38 GHORMLEY, HUGH et ux Nancy McEldry	11/7 1856 issued	No returns Bond: John Stuart
40 GHORMLEY, SAMUEL et ux Nelle James	9/11 1854 issued	No returns Bond: J. W. Lenions

Supplement to Book "O" Cont.

Names	Date Issue Or Celebrated	By Whom/ Security on Bonds
41 GIBBS, G. W. et ux Easther Vaughn	12/29 1859 issued	No returns
42 GIBSON, CASWELL et ux Matilda Morrison	3/24 1859	By W. W. Nuchols, J.P. Bond: J. B. Gibson
43 GOING, WILLIAM et ux Susan Shown	10/25 1858 issued	No returns Bond: James Thompson
44 GRIFFIN, JOHN et ux Caroline Griffin	1/22 1858	By J. L. Biemans, Cath. Priest Bond: M. Griffin
45 (Name off of copy) et ux Sarah L. Lee	9/5 1859 issued	Return 11/5 1861 By Stephen A. Aikens, J.P. Bond: F. R. Hackney
46 HEADRICK, WILLIAM et ux Sarah Blount	4/16 1857	By Samuel Pride, J.P. Bond: J. L. Carson
47 HENRY, JAMES H. et ux Amanda C. Owens	3/31 1858 issued	No returns Bond: L. C. Houke
48 HENRY, JOHN et ux R. A. McClannahan	2/22 1857	By N. Brewer, J.P. Bond: George Freshour
49 HENRY, WILLIAM J. et ux Eliza S. Smith	11/29 1854	By Fielding Pope, M.G. Bond: W. McCampbell
50 HITE, JOHN et ux M. A. Ogle	2/1 1855	By David Spradlin, J.P. Bond: C. Cunningham
51 HOOK, H. P. et ux M. A. Dearmond	5/6 1857	By William Billue, M.G. Bond: C. Gillespie
52 HUFFACRE, J. P. et ux E. M. Cunnungham	9/14 1854	By Fielding Pope, M.G. Bond: W. L. Caldwell
53 JAMES, A. M. et ux M. J. Wright	12/26 1855	By R. E. Tedford, M.G.
54 JAMES, BENJAMIN et ux Satiah McClain	12/4 1855 issued	No returns Bond: R. H. Culton
55 JAMES, ISAAC et ux Martha Oady	4/10 1855	By A. M. Goodakountz, J.P. Bond: Thomas Bird
56 JOHNSON, ELIJAH et ux Martha Mays	11/20 1855	By B. F. Duncan, J.P. Bond: J. C. Gillespie
57 JOHNSON, J. H. et ux N. E. Blankinship	11/5 1856 issued	No returns Bond: P. Blankinship
58 JOHNSON, JAMES H. et ux E.W.M.C. Earley	10/10 1857	By J. S. Craig, M.G. Bond: S. L. Yearout
59 JOHNSON, GEORGE C. et ux E. A. McMillan	12/15 1859	By H. Thompson, J.P. Bond: T. A. Ball
60 JONES, A. Y. et ux Eliza Montgomery	5/6 1857	By A. Vance, M.G. Bond: W. P. Wood

Names	Date Issue Or Celebrated	By Whom/ Security on Bonds
61 JENKINS W. H. et ux M. E. Stone	6/17 1856	By A. J. McGhee, M.G. Bond: J. S. Bonham
62 JOHNSON, H.L.W. et ux M.A.W. Caldwell	8/10 1859 issued	No returns Bond: W. L. Caldwell
63 KAGLEY, LOUIS et ux Lucy Carver	8/7 1855	By William Henderson, J.P. Bond: John Montgomery
64 KEENAHAN, MICHAEL et ux Selena Nivens	&/20 1857	No returns Bond: M. M. Anderson
65 KELLY, WILLIAM et ux Julia Ingram	4/30 1857	By S. J.McReynolds, J.P. Bond: G. W. Teefeteller
66 KEY, JAMES R. et ux Mary A. Biddix	2/24 1857	By James Matthews, J.P. Bond: James E. Bright
67 (Name not on copy of manuscript) et ux Phebe A. Hays	2/10 1859	By James M. Tulloch, J.P. Bond: G.C.C. Kerr
68 KIDD, JAMES et ux Nancy Joiner	1/11 1859 issued	No returns Bond: H. I. Hodge
69 KING, WILLIAM A. et ux M. J. Cummings	2/27 1856 issued	No returns Bond: James Arrington
70 LAIN, J. W. et ux P. J. Greenaway	2/21 1856	By James Matthews, J.P. Bond: William Barnes
71 LAWRENCE, J. K. (J.P.L.?) et ux L. H. Bussell	10/28 1854 issued	No returns Bond: Alex' McClain
72 McBATH, ALEXANDER et ux Harriett L. Bogle	10/14 1858 issued	No returns Bond: A. N. McBath
73 McCAMY, SAMUEL H. et ux Harriett Houston	12/4 1855	By F. Pope, M.G. Bond: Robert Pickens
74 McCLURE, C. E. et ux R. C. Dearmond	8/24 1854 issued	No returns Bond: D. L. Trundle
75 McCONNELL, J. H. et ux A. M. Nelson	6/1 1857 issued	No returns Bond: W. M. McConnell
76 McKEEHAN, E. B. et ux Susan Simerly	3/6 1857 issued	No returns Bond: H. P. Clark
77 MAUPIN, T.D.W.C. et ux P. J. Jones	10/16 1856	By Harvey Thompson, J.P. Bond: Wm. Barnes
78 MORTON, H. H. et ux Caroline Best	7/30 1856	By Andrew J. Wilson, J.P. Bond: John Morton
79 NEWMAN, C. C. et ux M. E. Wallace	12/19 1859 issued	No returns Bond: Joel H. Williams

	Names	Date Issue Or Celebrated	By Whom/ Security on Bonds
80	NICKELSE, GEORGE et ux Evaline Howard	6/30 1855 issued	No returns Bond: W. G. Hardin
81	NUN, ELI et ux Nancy Dearmond	10/2 1856	By Fielding Pope, M.G. Bond: R. P. Bowerman
82	OADY, JOHN et ux Lucinda Russell	10/28 1858	By Andrew Ferguson, J.P. Bond: Isaac Jones
83	O'NEAL, HENRY H. et ux Mary A. Proster	6/13 1859 issued	No returns Bond: Leonard Keeling
84	O'NEAL, W. H. et ux A. E. Crisp	3/10 1859 (issued 3/18?)	By Wm. M. Brickell, J.P. Bond: J. E. Davis
85	PARKINS, SAMUEL et ux Nancy J. McCulley	9/7 1854	By W. M. Brickell, J.P. Bond: D. H. Moore
86	PATTERSON, MARION et ux Delila Smith	4/7 1857 issued	No returns Bond: John Kidd
87	PEARSON, N. G. et ux L. C. Shearon	8/22 1854	By L. D. Tipton, M.G. Bond: C. Gillespie
88	PEOPLES, E. et ux S. Grisham	1/19 1858	By Spencer Henry, M.G. Bond: S. L. Strange
89	(Name not on copy of manuscript) et ux C. O. McCronkey(?)	11/15 1855 issued	No returns Bond: P. H. Clark
90	PORTER, S. A. et ux Eliza J. Swan	2/27 1855	No returns Bond: J. A. Houston
91	PRATER, A. L. et ux Sarah Jackson	1/4 1856 issued	No returns Bond: James Prater
92	PRITCHARD, ALFRED et ux N. G. Pass	7/12 1854	By J. S. Craig, M.G. Bond: N. G. Pass
93	ROBERTS, JAMES M. et ux Jane Singleton	8/21 1854 issued	No returns Bond: B. F. Reeder
94	SHAVER, ALEX'R A. et ux Nancy G. S. Malcomb	6/5 1858 issued	No returns Bond: Amos T. Shedden
95	SHAY, MICHAEL et ux Ellen Moon	1/29 1859	By J. L. Biemans, P. Cath. Ch. Bond: Marrice Griffin
96	SIMMERLY, WILLIAM et ux Winney Russell	6/27 1858	By C. Long, J.P. Bond: Thomas Russell
97	SMITH, HENRY et ux Nancy J. Collins	2/7 1855	By J. H. Donaldson, J.P. Bond: John Jones
98	SNIDER, JAMES et ux Ruth Russell	10/1 1857 issued	No returns Bond: N. Simmerly

Names	Date Issue Or Celebrated	By Whom/ Security on Bonds
99 STEWART, JOHN et ux Lucinda Anthoney	2/5 1858 issued	No returns Bond: Thomas Stewart
100 STONE, JEFFERSON et ux Joanna Vineyard	11/27 1858 issued	No returns Bond: James Wolf
101 TEEFETELLER, JOSEPH H. et ux Nancy Hall	11/12 1857 issued	No returns Bond: J. W. Hall
102 THOMPSON, N. et ux N. Morrow	10/14 1856	By James Matthews, J.P. Bond: W. A. Walker
103 UNDERWOOD, EDWARD et ux Sarah C. Sparks	2/29 1858	By W. W.Bayless, J.P. Bond: S. C. Henderson
104 WELLS, S. M. et ux Nancy A. Headrick	10/10 1854 issued	No returns
105 WILKINSON, J. T. et ux Julia A. McClain	12/9 1856 issued	No returns Bond: C. T. Cates
106 WYLEY, J. C. et ux J. A. Blair	2/7 1856	By D. W. Avery, M.G. Bond: R. L. McNutt

I, WILLIAM EDMUND PARHAM, hereby certify as to the above in as full
and correct manner as in the others of this book; copied from the
County Records during the month of August 1937, as additions not on
file in first records, but found in Record Book #1 from in ea ly 1854
to 1860. This is five (ref. manuscript) pages, 204-A, 204-B, 204-C,
204-D, 204-E. This the 31 day August 1937.

W. E. PARHAM, 218 Bryan St., Maryville, Tennessee

(Signed) W. E. PARHAM

Compiled By
Nancy Clarke
Texas City, Texas

NEAL, Polly 180
NEALE, Arty Lukinsey 221
NEIL, Rachel 190
NEIMAN, Esther 100
NELSON, A. M. 232
  Isabella 25
  Nancy J. 91
  Sarah C. 226
NERWOOD, Susanna 48
NEWBERRY, Jemima 168
NEWCUM, Jane 16
NEWMAN, Anne 90
  Susan 45
NEWSOM, Jane 16
NICHELSON, Martha J. 57
NICHOLDS, Narcessa 175
NICHOLS, Rachel 141
NICHOLSON, Nancy 37
  Polly 58
NIGHT, Jane 39
NILES, Alcey 74
NIPPER, Mary Elizabeth 161
  Nancy 198
  Nancy W. 174
NISMAN, Kity 34
NIVENS, Selena 232
NIX, Sarah 19
NOBLE, Bethenia 138
  Betsey 8
NOBLET, Elizabeth 66
  Katherine 57
  Louisa G. 57
  Peggy 66
NOLEN, Mary 124
NORTON, Margaret Ann 162
  Sally 137
NORWOOD, Malvina Jane 107
  Mary Ann 129
  Mavina Jane 107
  Providence 131
  Sarah 178
NUCHOLS, Martha 137
  Nancy E. 196
NYERS, Rutha 215
O'BRIANT, Elizabeth 193
O'DAM, Mary C. 79
O'DEAR, Polly 90
O'DONNELL, Martha 38
O'NEAL, Malinda 191
OADY, Martha 231
OGLE, Jane 192
  Lovenia 43
  M. A. 231
  Margaret A. 102
  Mary 158
  Sydney 160
OLIVER, Betsy 4
  Martha 164
  Mary 164
  Rutha 69
OODY, Martha 95
OOFORTH, Malenday 158
ORMAN, Elizabeth 195
ORMAND, Barby 95
ORMOND, Polly 43
  Sinah 200
ORR, Jane 31
  Nancy 40
  Peggy 64
OWENS, Amanda C. 231
  Jane 146
  Sarah 161
OWING, Matilda 48
PAIN, Mary 204
PALMER, Elizabeth 63

PALMER, Elizabeth 63
  Jean 59
  Margaret 48, 58
  Nancy 157
  Patsy 38
  Sally 7
  Susan 67
PANTHER, Mary 173
PARKE, Emaline 15
PARKER, Elenor 55
  Elizabeth 225
  Ellender 30
  Mary 18
  Nancy J. 193
  Philena A. 45
  Rena 37
PARKINS, Polly 81
PARKS, C. E. 221
  Eliza 89
  Jane 159
  Salina 60
  Susan J. 142
PARMER, Susan 140
PARSINS, Hannah 96
PARSONS, Leva Jane 27
PARTIN, Dorothy 29
PASLEY, Jane 159
PASS, Kesiah 116
  M. T. 101
  Margaret J. 218
  N. G. 233
  Nancy 222
  Rosa H. 85
  Sarah M. 162
PATE, Rebecca 150
  Sarah 8
PATEY, Mary J. 97
PATRICK, Mary 137
  Nancy 90
PATTERICK, Betsy 57
PATTERSON, Susan E. 76
PATTEY, Sarah C. 59
PATTON, Keziah A. 105
PATTY, Emeline 142
  Sarah 7
PAUL, Elizabeth 64
  Jane M. 168
  Nancy 1
  Polly 163
  Rebecka 77
PAYNE, Elizabeth 148
  Letitia 173
PEARCE, Manervia 117
  Rebecca 25
PEARSON, Nancy 66
PEELER, Caroline 101
PEERY, Cathorine 121
  Elizabeth 39
  F. M. 190
  M. E. 221
  Mary A. 141
  Rosanna 217
PELPHREY, Martha J. 167
PEOPLES, Sarah E. 157
PEPPER, Roena 162
PERKEY, Eliza E. 84
PERKINS, Delila 73
  Franky 76
  Isabella 93
  Jane 32
  Keziah 107
  Keziah D. 218
  Mary A. 74
  Phebo 72
  Rachel 110

PERKINS, Reller 133
  Sarah 142, 154
PERKY, Polly C. 58
PERRY, Elizabeth 17
  Reubica 193
PESTERFIELD, Christena 14
  Eleanor J. 4
PETERSON, R. L. 213
  Winny 101
PHELPS, Martha M. 85
  Mary 114
  Sarah E. 223
  Sarah S. 217
  Susan 155
PHILIPS, Elizabeth Ann 152
  Hannah 180
  Malinda 186
  Peggy 108
  Rachel 108
  Sally 186
PHILLIPS, Ann 196
  Anne 164
  Cherry 42
  Elizabeth A. 167
  Nancy 18
  Tabitha 155
PICKENS, Ellen 80
  Margaret 58
  Rebecca 84
PICKERING, Elizabeth 131
  Malanda 72
PICKINS, Polly 128
PIERCE, Mary K. 5
  Orphy 65
PIPPINS, Priscilla 73
  Roena 162
PITMAN, Amey 34
PITNER, Levirea C. 123
  Lovicy C. 123
PITTS, Martha 19
PLEMENS, Sarah Ann 46
PLEMONS, Margaret J. 213
PLUMBLEE, Alley 98
PLUMER, Margaret 144
POINDEXTER, Judah 18
POLAND, Elizabeth 172
  Jemima 171
  Lovicy 193
  Sarah 134
POPE, Catherine 50
  Cynthia E. 191
  Jane C. 185
  M.E.M. 55
  Therresa C. 142
POPLIN, Avey 146
PORTER, Isabella S. 125
  Margaret 114, 136
  Margaret A. 15
  Margaret R. 16
  Margary 48
  Martha 24
  Mary Jane 29
  Paulina A. 8
  Peggy 114, 136
  Polly Ann 38
  Sarah J. 120
POSEY, Elizabeth 158
POSSEY, Betsey 103
POTTER, Jane 170
  Katherine 74
  Sarah 223
POWELL, Louisa 201
PRATER, Mary B. 218
PRESLEY, Martha 107
  Nancy H. 96

BY WHOM
AND
SECURITY BOND
INDEX

Compiled By
Louise Clements Palmer
Texas City, Texas 77590

www.ingramcontent.com/pod-product-compliance
Lightning Source LLC
Chambersburg PA
CBHW021857020426
42334CB00013B/367